E/2005/51/Rev.1
ST/ESA/298

P9-CAL-952

Department of Economic and Social Affairs

World Economic and Social Survey 2005

Financing for Development

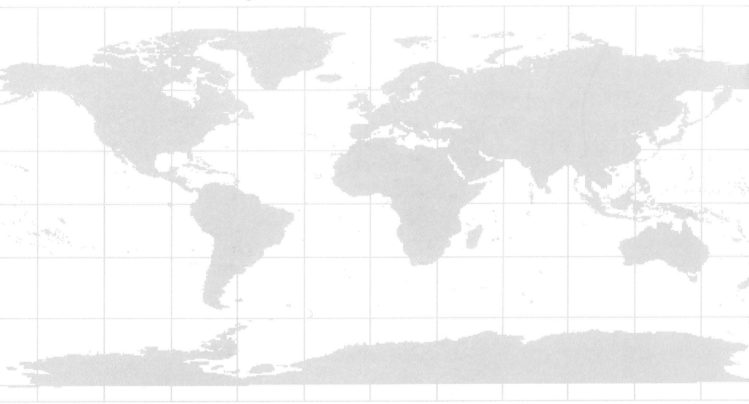

United Nations
New York, 2005

WITHDRAWN

WASH. STATE UNIV.
VANCOUVER LIBRARY

DESA

The Department of Economic and Social Affairs of the United Nations Secretariat is a vital interface between global policies in the economic, social and environmental spheres and national action. The Department works in three main interlinked areas: (i) it compiles, generates and analyses a wide range of economic, social and environmental data and information on which States Members of the United Nations draw to review common problems and to take stock of policy options; (ii) it facilitates the negotiations of Member States in many intergovernmental bodies on joint courses of action to address ongoing or emerging global challenges; and (iii) it advises interested Governments on the ways and means of translating policy frameworks developed in United Nations conferences and summits into programmes at the country level and, through technical assistance, helps build national capacities.

Note

Symbols of United Nations documents are composed of capital letters combined with figures.

E/2005/51/Rev. 1
ST/ESA/298
ISBN 92-1-109149-7

United Nations publication
Sales No. E.05.II.C.1
Copyright © United Nations, 2005
All rights reserved
Printed by the United Nations
Publishing Section
New York

Preface

One of the main tasks facing world leaders at the 2005 World Summit in September will be to examine the implementation of the global vision for development embodied in the United Nations Millennium Declaration, the Monterrey Consensus of the International Conference on Financing for Development and the Plan of Implementation of the World Summit on Sustainable Development (Johannesburg Plan of Implementation).

The *World Economic and Social Survey 2005* provides a comprehensive review of the wide-ranging challenges addressed in the Monterrey Consensus. Its overarching conclusion is that while gains have been made in some areas, an immediate and substantial scaling up of effort is needed, especially in the poorest countries.

Additional resources will be central to this enhanced effort, and will require a sharing of responsibilities and a series of mutual commitments involving not only Governments but also private individuals, firms and civil society organizations. Developing countries are making significant efforts to marshal their domestic resources, and to use them effectively. Especially in the poorest countries, those new domestic resources must be complemented by a quantum increase in international support—additional development assistance, more extensive debt relief and increased trading opportunities. For other developing countries and some economies in transition, improved flows of international private capital will play an important role.

The developed countries have begun to honour the commitments they made in the Monterrey Consensus. But these remain works in progress. Only some trade barriers have been lowered, only some markets have been opened, not all countries are benefiting from these steps, and the overall effort falls far short of what is required.

The same can be said of the international financial system. It has a number of positive features, such as increasing flows of foreign direct investment to developing counties. It has also been strengthened in recent years through improved supervision and regulation. However, the developing world still lacks enough of a voice in decision-making, and the system is not as fully supportive of development as it could be. These limitations are very costly in terms of growth and poverty reduction but could be overcome at very little cost, to the benefit of the international community at large.

In my report to the World Summit, entitled "In larger freedom: towards development, security and human rights for all", I called on Member States to reaffirm their commitment to the global partnership for development. I hope the analysis and suggestions contained in this *Survey* will be useful to all stakeholders as they prepare for the Summit, and in their continuing efforts to contribute to the full and effective implementation of the Monterrey Consensus and other intergovernmental undertakings in the years to come.

KOFI A. ANNAN
Secretary-General

Overview

Having achieved formal status in 2002 through adoption by the Heads of State and Government, the Monterrey Consensus of the International Conference on Financing for Development provides the current framework for international cooperation for development. The Consensus is one of the best-conceived expressions of the contemporary view that such cooperation entails a partnership between developed and developing countries. It covers the full spectrum of issues relating to financing for development, comprising the mobilization of domestic resources for development, trade as an instrument of development financing, private capital flows, official development financing, debt and development, and questions relating to the international financial system as a whole.

The present report looks at the correspondingly broad agenda for action that was set out in the Consensus. It finds that the Consensus was not only a landmark in its approach to development cooperation but also a watershed in drawing attention to the need for implementation, including of actions that had long been recognized as necessary but largely neglected in practice. Much has been achieved by all concerned in the short period since the adoption of the Consensus. At the same time, the Consensus was ambitious and far-sighted hence much more remains to be done, including addressing the new challenges that have arisen since the Consensus was adopted. This report identifies the numerous accomplishments to date but, with a view to maintaining the existing momentum, focuses on the further actions relating to financing for development that need to be undertaken in the years ahead. There remains an imperative need for all to "stay engaged" in financing for development, not only to achieve the Millennium Development Goals but also to fulfil the broader United Nations development agenda.

Mobilizing domestic resources for development

Increases in savings, investment and economic growth and reductions in poverty tend to go together in the developing world. Economic growth appears to be a necessary condition for reducing poverty, but the strength of the link between economic growth and poverty reduction varies depending on income distribution, how the benefits of each country's growth are distributed and on the accompanying economic and social policies. The causal links among savings, investment and growth are less clear. Empirical evidence suggests that, in most developing countries, it is economic growth that lifts domestic savings rather than the contrary, but stable and dynamic growth is always accompanied by a high level of domestic savings. Similarly, it is often growth that leads to increased investment, but a high investment rate is essential to sustaining a dynamic rate of growth. In addressing this matter, investment must be defined in its broadest sense—as including physical and human capital, as well as spending in research and development aimed at spurring innovation.

Those developing countries that have been most successful in moving towards sustained high rates of growth reveal the nature of these links among savings, investment and economic growth. Most of them have experienced a discrete increase in domestic saving and investment rates only some time after they underwent a spurt in growth. In all of them, dynamic growth has been closely linked to increases in the rates of domestic savings and investment. A variety of domestic and external conditions have facilitated such spurts in growth, with government policies playing a role through the creation of an attractive investment climate.

Among the several elements that contribute to a good investment climate, the most crucial are probably credible national development strategies and policies that reduce uncertainty by giving a clear sense of priorities and direction to private and public sector agents and provide a strategy for improving a country's physical infrastructure. Such strategies should aim at broader social progress and, particularly, at achieving the Millennium Development Goals by 2015. Production sector strategies can be critical for sustained expansion of existing sectors and for encouraging private business to enter new areas. Governments, working closely with the private sector, have an important role in identifying and encouraging the development of new activities in which a country, or a region within a country, may possess a potential comparative advantage. There is also a need to look at the development of complementarities and networks, for example, for the diffusion of technological and organizational improvements. The nature of such production sector strategies and policies varies in accordance with an economy's stage of economic development, its size and the state of its institutional development.

Macroeconomic stability is another necessary ingredient for a healthy investment climate. However, macroeconomic stability needs to be understood in a broad sense, so as to include not only price stability and sound fiscal policies, but also smoother business cycles, competitive exchange rates, sound external debt portfolios, a robust domestic financial system and healthy private sector balance sheets. Real instability and financial crises have proved to be even more damaging to investment than moderate rates of inflation.

Well-functioning legal systems and arrangements that ensure an inclusive political system are also essential to a healthy investment climate. There seems to be scope in many countries for reforming certain aspects of the regulatory and legal environment without compromising broader social goals. The degree to which this can be achieved will vary among countries. Nevertheless, improvements in four key areas could have a strong impact on the business environment: facilitating the opening and closing of a business, providing for secure property rights, enforcing contracts and protecting creditor rights.

A balance also needs to be struck between flexibility and stability in the labour market. Flexibility in employment may contribute to economic efficiency but stability of employment encourages productivity growth within firms. Similarly, social protection should be seen as a public investment, since its absence can reduce poor people's investments in education and skills and diminish the current and future stock of human capital.

A sound banking system, well-functioning domestic financial institutions and effective capital markets are central to any successful development strategy. The strength of the banking system has a direct bearing on economic growth; in the extreme cases of the crises of the 1980s and 1990s, the banking system was the weak link in a number of countries. Most developing countries have undertaken reforms to improve the solvency of the banking system, but on many occasions these reforms followed financial crises that themselves had been induced by liberalization and privatization measures undertaken without there being adequate institutional mechanisms in place. It is now generally accepted that financial liberalization should be preceded by the development of strong frameworks for prudential regulation and supervision.

Developing countries are beginning to develop their own domestic capital markets by strengthening the financial market infrastructure, creating benchmark bond issues, expanding the set of "market makers" and other institutional investors, and improving corporate governance and transparency. After the Asian financial crisis of 1997, local bond and equity issuances surged, with bonds becoming the single largest source of funding for the combined public and private sectors in several emerging markets. In addition to mobilizing resources, the continued development of bond markets in developing countries, with bonds denominated in domestic currency, should provide a cushion against the adverse effects of banking crises and reversal of capital flows.

Three aspects of the domestic financial system require particular attention in developing countries: long-term financing, inclusive financing and prudential regulation and supervision. Long-term finance is scarce in developing countries: in inadequately developed financial systems, creditors prefer to offer short-term financing so that they can monitor and control borrowers. Development banks can address some of the unmet demand for long-term financing but, if public ownership is involved, provisions must be in place to ensure the efficient administration of the institutions concerned. In order that some of the previous pitfalls of public ownership may be avoided, public-private partnerships have become increasingly common and successful in some areas, particularly in financing infrastructure.

The poor also have large unmet needs for access to the financial system. Microfinance has grown rapidly, but still reaches only a small percentage of potential beneficiaries. Efforts are being made to offer services to the poor by bridging formal and informal finance networks, and technology is also opening up possibilities for extending banking to the poor. Nevertheless, this remains an area where considerable further effort is required to enhance the social benefits of domestic financial development.

Prudential regulation and supervision are aimed at reducing systemic risk. Over time, the tendency has been to move away from direct towards indirect control of financial intermediaries, whereby only the minimum standards of prudent conduct are set. Such standards are increasingly set globally, mostly in more advanced markets, and their adoption in less developed settings is encouraged by peer pressure and market forces.

With the advent of liberalization, the financial sector has become more pro-cyclical, that is to say capital is abundant in good times but scarce in bad times. Counter-cyclical policy should be conducted mainly through macroeconomic policy, but prudential regulations that avoid overly pro-cyclical credit patterns can also play an important role. One possibility is provisioning on a forward-looking basis, taking the full business cycle into account, so that there is an accumulation of provisions against loan losses during cyclical upswings that provide increased protection during downturns.

Trade

The Monterrey Consensus characterized "international trade as an engine for development" and affirmed that a "universal, rule-based, open, non-discriminatory and equitable multilateral trading system, as well as meaningful trade liberalization, can substantially stimulate development worldwide, benefiting countries at all stages of development". Since the early 1990s, the exports of developing countries as a whole have grown robustly, outpacing the growth of world exports: 12.2 versus 8.7 per cent annually for 1991-1995; 7.7 versus 4.8 per cent annually for 1996-2000; and 7.4 versus 5.8 per cent annually in 2001-2003.

However, many developing countries have not participated fully in this trade boom. A country's pattern of specialization affects its ability to reap the rewards of an increasingly open trading system and the poorest countries have generally not fared as well because of their continued reliance on agricultural exports and labour-intensive manufactures. Over the period 1985-2002, the most dynamic categories of exports in world trade were electronic and electrical goods, chemicals and miscellaneous manufactures. Only a few developing economies, particularly from East Asia, were able to benefit from these trade flows. At the other end of the spectrum, a number of developing countries experienced a decline in their merchandise exports over the past two decades because of combinations of excessive dependence on one or two primary products, civil conflict, and politically motivated trade embargoes.

An additional consequence of the reliance of many of the poorest countries on exports of primary commodities is that these products have been subject to a long-term decline in prices relative to those of manufactures, and exporting countries have been subject to volatility in export earnings. Only diversification into manufactures and services can help to address the first of these problems, but a number of instruments have been used over the years in attempts to mitigate price instability in commodity markets. Current schemes emphasize the use of market-based financial instruments and techniques to manage commodity price risk (for example, forward contracts and derivatives). However, there are numerous limitations that prevent many developing countries from benefiting from such risk management strategies. Attention should be focused on the development of mechanisms that address these limitations.

The broader agenda set to address the problems and vulnerabilities of commodity-dependent countries should give the highest priority to measures to improve the access of primary commodity exports to developed-country markets, including through the elimination of market-distorting subsidies (such as those for cotton). Other necessary actions are a reduction of excess supply in some commodity markets and increased use of more flexible compensatory financing schemes to mitigate the adverse impact of cyclical shortfalls in export earnings. For countries that will continue to derive a large proportion of their export earnings from extractive industries in the hydrocarbons and mining sectors, the adoption of policies to promote the effective and transparent management of fiscal revenues will be an important element of the development strategy.

Several rounds of multilateral trade liberalization have taken place since the signing of the General Agreement on Tariffs and Trade (GATT) in 1948 and contributed to the sustained growth of international trade during the intervening period. The Uruguay Round (1986-1993) created the World Trade Organization and brought renewed order to the multilateral trading system by applying multilateral disciplines to sectors—agriculture, textiles and services—that had not been subject to them under GATT and by introducing a new dispute settlement mechanism. It also presented developing countries with additional obligations but left room for further liberalization in areas of particular export interest to them.

A new round of multilateral trade negotiations was launched in Doha in 2001, pledging to place developing countries' "needs and interests at the heart of the work programme". Negotiations, however, have been advancing slowly despite the adoption of a framework agreement in August 2004 (the "July package") which established modalities for negotiations and a series of mini-Ministerial meetings that have provided the Round with additional momentum. An equitable, developmentally oriented and prompt conclusion to the Round is of particular importance to the achievement of the Millennium Development Goals. Estimates of the gains in global welfare that the Round could potentially generate vary widely, with many results in the range of $250 billion-$400 billion per year. While these benefits are not equally or equitably distributed, such estimates nonetheless highlight the importance of a successful multilateral trade agreement.

Among the potential areas of benefit, agriculture is of particular importance for poverty reduction, as some 75 per cent of the world's poor live in rural areas and work in agriculture or agriculture-related activities. From the point of view of developing countries, improvements in the trade regime in this area require additional market access, the elimination of export subsidies, and a substantial reduction of trade-distorting domestic subsidies. In the area of non-agricultural market access, the question of manufactures subject to tariff peaks and tariff escalation according to the level of processing of the raw materials is of great significance to developing countries. In both agriculture and manufacturing, concrete steps are also required to deal with such barriers to market entry as product standards and regulations, and sanitary and phytosanitary measures. The development potential of trade in services also needs to be improved by liberalizing the temporary supply of labour services (Mode 4) and the cross-border supply of services (Mode 1) used in outsourcing and offshoring.

While there will be large long-term benefits from a new global trade agreement, there will also be short- and medium-term adjustment costs, in particular higher import bills for net food importing countries, the adverse impact of the erosion of preferences on countries highly dependent on preferential access to markets, the displacement of some local producers in the face of increased competition, lower fiscal revenues from tariffs and reduced "policy space". Built-in flexibilities and a sufficiently long implementation period may help developing countries to deal with such challenges and should form part of the negotiations. Policy interventions may also mitigate some of these negative effects, although resource-constrained developing countries may not be able to afford them. This suggests the need for trade adjustment and aid-for-trade funds to ease the transitions of developing countries into the new trading environment and to build up production and technological capacities that will support diversification and reduce dependence on preferential markets. Such measures will contribute to ensuring that all countries benefit from the increased trading opportunities that completion of the negotiations will provide.

Despite the acknowledged benefits of multilateralism, many countries have been pursuing preferential trade agreements. Since 1990, the number of free trade agreements has risen from 50 to almost 230, with some 60 more in various stages of formation. Some of these schemes reflect a "new geography" of trade, with blocs being formed among developing countries that have become trading partners. Other arrangements involve both developing and developed countries. These trends may also reflect the search for greater bargaining leverage and for alternatives to slow-moving multilateral trade negotiations.

The current spate of preferential trade agreements is considered a novel phenomenon by some, who regard them as reflecting what they term "open regionalism", and differentiate the current schemes from those of the 1960s and 1970s. They argue that the current schemes are more trade-creating and more consistent with multilateralism than the more inward-looking arrangements of the past. Moreover, they involve reciprocity among members. These arrangements may therefore have a beneficial role to play, but their compatibility with multilateralism cannot be presumed and vigilance is needed to ensure their consistency with the goals, objectives and tenets of the multilateral trading system. Preferential agreements may be a useful addition to multilateralism, but they are not a substitute for it.

International private capital flows

Private capital flows can make a major contribution to development to the extent that they flow from capital-abundant, usually developed countries to capital-scarce developing countries and help to smooth spending throughout the business cycle in the recipient countries. However, capital, and particularly financial, flows have been highly volatile and reversible in recent decades, generating high costs for developing countries. In addition, such flows have largely bypassed the poorest countries. These features are by no means inevitable: national and international policies can be adopted to generate increased and more stable private financial flows that will be of benefit to a larger number of developing countries.

During recent decades, there have been two external financial cycles that left strong imprints in the developing world: a boom in the 1970s, followed by a debt crisis in a large part of the developing world in the 1980s; and a new boom in the 1990s, followed by a sharp reduction in net financial flows after the eruption of the Asian crisis in 1997. Improved economic conditions in developing countries, as well as higher global growth and low interest rates, had driven a recovery of private capital flows to developing countries in 2003 and 2004, perhaps signalling the beginning of a new cycle. However, the vulnerability of developing countries was reflected in periods of increased volatility in yield spreads in 2004 and early 2005, in response to uncertainty in the pace of interest rate increases in developed countries (particularly the United States of America).

More importantly, net transfers of financial resources from developing countries have not experienced a positive turnaround and, on the contrary, continued to deteriorate in 2004 for the seventh consecutive year, reaching an estimated $350 billion. Such negative transfers were initially the result of capital outflows from the developing world, but the latest data increasingly reflect the large foreign-exchange reserve accumulation taking place in many developing countries, particularly in Asia. This accumulation of reserves initially had a large component of "self-insurance" (a "war chest") against financial crises and involved a rational decision of individual countries in the face of the limited "collective insurance" provided by the international financial system against such crises. However, reserve accumulation in several countries in Asia now exceeds the need for self-insurance, raising increasing questions about the balance of costs and benefits of additional accumulation, especially if such reserves are invested in low-yielding assets and in a currency that has experienced substantial depreciation, the United States dollar.

Different types of capital flows are subject to different degrees of volatility. Foreign direct investment (FDI) is less volatile than other forms of financial flows and this is considered a source of strength. FDI can also support development through technology transfer and providing market access. However, even if adjusted by the economic size of recipient countries, FDI is concentrated in middle-income countries.

Developing countries have historically adopted investment policies to maximize the benefits from FDI. In the current environment, the development impact of FDI can be bolstered through policies that promote linkages between foreign firms and the host economy, in particular to encourage exports with higher value-added and the transfer of skills, knowledge and technology. Backward production linkages between foreign and domestic firms can be promoted through better information flows. Incentives can also be provided for foreign firms to invest in employee training. Successful clusters attract foreign investment; their success depends on the existence of an enabling investment climate, skilled labour and infrastructure. To increase the contribution of FDI in extractive industries to the development of the host country, initiatives on transparency-related codes of conduct (for example, the Extractive Industries Transparency Initiative) should be supported and the feasibility of their application to other sectors examined.

The different forms of financial flows have different implications for development. Trade financing is essential to facilitating international trade and is particularly important for poorer countries, given their limited access to other forms of financial flows. In this regard, the role of export credit agencies and multilateral development banks could be enhanced if they acted in a more counter-cyclical manner by providing guarantees and trade credit loans to countries after crises in order to avert a trade credit "squeeze" and to facilitate export-led recoveries.

Bank lending and portfolio flows tend to be volatile and pro-cyclical. There were negative net flows of both to developing countries during the Asian crisis but flows have recovered since 2003. International banks have retrenched from cross-border lending since 1997 and have shifted towards lending through their domestic subsidiaries. Portfolio debt flows, though volatile, can be a valuable source of external financing to both the public sector and large private firms in the developing world.

There has been a global explosion in the development of financial derivatives since 1990. Derivatives can be very efficient in pricing and adequately distributing risks among market agents, but they can also facilitate speculation and increase macroeconomic volatility. Short-term instruments are particularly destabilizing but derivatives tied to longer-term instruments seem less risky. Even in developed countries, regulators find it difficult to monitor and regulate derivatives and it is even more difficult to do so in offshore markets. Well-designed regulations can nonetheless minimize risk.

To counter boom-bust cycles, market institutions and instruments can be designed to encourage more stable flows. Introducing explicit counter-cyclical elements in the risk evaluations of the multilateral development banks and export credit agencies for guarantees for lending to developing countries would be valuable. This could help catalyse long-term private credit, especially for infrastructure, during periods of declining capital flows. Multilateral development banks could also play a bigger role in guaranteeing developing-country bonds in periods of capital drought.

Commodity-linked bonds and gross domestic product (GDP)-linked bonds can reduce the likelihood of debt crises and defaults, by smoothing debt-service payments through the business cycle. Industrialized countries should establish the example of issuing such bonds in order to help establish precedents for their issuance by developing countries. Similarly, local currency bonds help reduce currency mismatches. Foreign investment funds that invest in a diversified portfolio of such emerging market local currency debt could provide, because of diversification, risk-adjusted rates of return that are attractive to foreign investors.

Capital-account regulations can provide room for counter-cyclical macroeconomic policies and improve external debt profiles of developing countries. When these regulations are well implemented, such benefits outweigh any costs. Both price-based and quantity-based regulations can be useful. Permanent regulatory regimes that are tightened or loosened during the cycle are superior to ad hoc interventions. Capital-account regulations facilitate sensible counter-cyclical macroeconomic policies, but they are not a substitute for them.

The right regulatory regime for banks is essential for financial stability. The New Basel Capital Accord (Basel II) has positive features but there is a risk that it will increase the pro-cyclicality of bank lending, both domestically and internationally. Furthermore, it is likely to reduce international lending to developing countries and increase its cost. It would measure risk more precisely, and would therefore be technically correct, if the benefits of the diversification of lending by international banks to developing countries were explicitly incorporated into the Accord; this would also be economically desirable, as it would avoid an excessive reduction of bank lending to developing countries and reduce its pro-cyclicality.

Low-income countries are at a disadvantage in attracting capital flows and so special national and international efforts are needed to increase private flows to these countries. Improved information flows for potential investors are essential in this regard. Programmes are also required to support the development of market instruments to mitigate risks (for example, markets in exchange-rate futures) and the broader use by low-income countries of bilateral and multilateral instruments to deal with risk mitigation for private investments (insurance and guarantee schemes). Donors should also consider providing targeted funding with additional resources to multilateral agencies (such as the Multilateral Investment Guarantee Agency (MIGA) and the political risk insurance facilities being opened up in regional banks) and bilateral agencies to cover political and other non-commercial risk at a lower cost in these countries. New facilities could also be set up in the form of separate funds owned by international financial institutions to address both the entry cost and the post-entry risk barriers for investors.

Migrant remittances differ from capital flows and have become an increasing and stable source of foreign exchange for many developing countries. While most remittances are savings from migrants' earnings that provide financial support for families in home countries, many initiatives can be adopted to increase their developmental impact. These include channelling remittances to finance investment projects in the local communities of origin of migrants and organizing remittance-backed housing purchases and other investments by migrants in their countries of origin. Financial intermediaries in host and home countries should be encouraged to continue to reduce the transaction costs of remittances and to diversify their services by offering savings accounts, microcredit and various types of insurance to migrants' families; more generally, they should be used as a bridge in providing banking services to both migrants and recipient families. Because of the multiplicity of policy initiatives, there is a role for internationally agreed guidelines on such measures; these guidelines could be formulated and coordinated within the United Nations.

Official development financing

Official assistance continues to play a crucial role in supplementing the resources of developing countries, particularly the poorest among them. However, from a peak of over 0.5 per cent of developed-country gross national income (GNI) in the 1960s, official development assistance (ODA) had declined until it reached a historic low of 0.21 per cent as Heads of State and Government were approving the United Nations Millennium Declaration. To counter this tendency, the Monterrey Consensus sought to reaffirm the 0.7 per cent target. This motivated many developed countries to announce increased ODA contributions and many pledged to meet fixed target dates for reaching the 0.7 per cent goal. As a result, the decline in the share of ODA in developed-country GNI was reversed and it rose to 0.25 per cent in 2003 and 2004. Despite this positive trend, the current and projected levels of ODA for the period from 2006 to 2010 still fall far short of the various estimates of the support deemed necessary for the developing countries to attain the Millennium Development Goals by 2015. Furthermore, when corrected for price and exchange-rate changes, the recent reversal of the decline in aid flows has barely brought assistance back to its real levels in 1990.

In order to secure the increased ODA required, the Secretary-General of the United Nations has urged all developed countries to establish fixed timetables for reaching the 0.7 per cent target by 2015 at the latest, with an intermediate target of roughly doubling aid to 0.5 per cent of the GNI of the developed countries in 2009. Currently only Denmark, Luxembourg, the Netherlands, Norway and Sweden meet or exceed the 0.7 per cent target. The 15 pre-enlargement member States of the European Union (EU) have recently set a target date of 2015 for reaching the 0.7 per cent goal, with an intermediate target of 0.51 per cent of GNI by 2010. Those countries that joined EU after 2002 have agreed to strive to achieve a ratio of 0.17 per cent of their GNI by 2010 and 0.33 per cent by 2015.

Not only has ODA to increase substantially in order for the developing countries to achieve the Millennium Development Goals, it is also essential that more ODA be directed to the poorest developing countries. With the adoption of the Programme of Action for the Least Developed Countries for the 1990s, developed countries agreed that, within their 0.7 per cent overall ODA target, they would provide at least 0.15-0.20 per cent of their GNI to assist these countries. Nevertheless, aggregate ODA flows to the least developed countries declined to about half that ratio during the 1990s. There has been a reversal in trend, however, since Monterrey: ODA to the least developed countries has increased sharply and eight countries met the target in 2002 and 2003.

While the decline in total ODA has been reversed, at the same time its recent composition appears to make its contribution to meeting the Millennium Development Goals less efficient. Over the 1990s, the shares of debt relief, emergency aid and technical assistance in total aid flows increased. While these flows have important objectives, emergency aid is not designed to assist long-term development and debt relief does not generally provide additional resources to debtor countries. Technical cooperation, in turn, can provide a variety of benefits for development, but its financial impact is small. Consequently, despite the recent recovery in recorded donor contributions, ODA has been a declining source of budgetary resources for the developing countries. The call to increase ODA must translate into real increases in financial resources to support the Millennium Development Goals that are channelled through the budgets of recipient countries.

Donors have been increasingly concerned with the effectiveness of their aid in meeting the international development objectives. The Rome High-level Forum on Harmonization focusing on joint progress towards enhanced aid effectiveness held in 2003 elaborated a plan of action to harmonize aid policies, procedures and practices of donors with those of their developing-country partners. Participants at the second High-level Forum held in 2005 committed to a practical blueprint through which to provide aid in more streamlined ways and to improve accountability by monitoring the blueprint's implementation. They defined five major principles of aid effectiveness: (a) ownership of development strategies by partner countries; (b) alignment of donor support to those strategies; (c) harmonization of donor actions; (d) managing for results; and (e) mutual accountability of donors and partners. Full implementation of these principles, based on a clear set of targets (some of which have already been agreed), is essential to increasing the quality of aid flows.

In addition to official government financing, developing countries receive loans from the World Bank and regional and subregional development banks. The multilateral development banks will continue to play a fundamental role in several areas. First, they need to channel funds to low-income countries, where their role is central. With regard to middle-income countries, they will continue to play a particularly important role, not only as lenders under better financial conditions than those offered by the private markets, but as a counter-cyclical balance to fluctuations in private capital markets, giving developing countries access to long-term borrowing during times of crisis. As crises hurt the poor, the counter-cyclical character of multilateral development banks financing is consistent with their role in poverty reduction.

The multilateral development banks also perform a vast array of financial tasks, encompassing, inter alia, the traditional "value added" of multilateral financing, and lending-related technical assistance; knowledge generation and brokering; and the provision of global and regional public goods, including, in the case of most regional and subregional development banks, support to regional integration processes. In addition, new functions of multilateral development banks have grown in recent years, for example, the provision of guarantees issued for the support to public-private partnerships in infrastructure. They could also be used more actively to guarantee bond issues by countries that have experienced financial crises, as well as initial bond issues by developing (especially poor) countries entering private capital markets. They could also play a more prominent role in trade financing during crises, and in the promotion of local currency bond markets in developing countries, and as "market makers" for commodity- and GDP-linked bonds. Recent discussions have also emphasized the need for multilateral development banks to embrace intellectual diversity and to avoid the hegemony of a single view of economic development. There have also been calls to reduce the financial and non-financial costs of doing business with the multilateral development banks by clarifying policies, simplifying procedures, streamlining internal processes and reducing conditionality in lending operations.

The revealed success of several regional and subregional development banks clearly indicates that this is a promising area of cooperation among developing countries. These are successful financial institutions that have earned good credit ratings without capital from industrialized countries. Furthermore, a different approach to conditionality makes them attractive to borrowing countries. This should become a priority for South-South cooperation.

A number of countries have followed up on the call in the Monterrey Consensus to investigate alternative mechanisms to supplement official assistance, as attested by, for example, the group of independent experts formed at the request of the President of France; the initiative to combat hunger and poverty launched in January 2004 by the presidents of Brazil, Chile and France, with the support of the Secretary-General, and later endorsed also by the Governments of Spain, Germany and Algeria; and the meeting of more than 100 world leaders convened by the President of Brazil and held at the United Nations in September 2004. The conclusions of a special study led by the United Nations University/World Institute for Development Economics Research had also been presented to the General Assembly in September 2004. In April 2005, the Development Committee and the International Monetary and Financial Committee reviewed proposals to complement increased aid flows with innovative mechanisms.

An International Finance Facility (IFF) was initially proposed by the United Kingdom of Great Britain and Northern Ireland in 2003 and the Secretary General has called upon the international community to launch it in 2005. Since the Facility builds on commitments to reach the 0.7 per cent ODA target no later than 2015, it constitutes a complement to traditional commitments. Its particular function is to enable the front-loading of aid flows through issues of bonds guaranteed by participating Governments, allowing aid commitments to be spent before they are budgeted. A pilot IFF is being created whose resources will be used for immunization.

Among other additional sources of innovative financing for development mechanisms studied in the various reports were: several nationally applied but internationally coordinated taxes (environmental, on international financial transactions, on aviation fuel or ticket prices, and on arms sales); allocation of special drawing rights (SDRs) for development purposes; mobilizing emigrant remittances for development; and private donations. Most of the technical reports concluded that financial transactions taxes and environmental taxes might provide the largest amounts of additional resources in the long term. However, realizing the potential of such sources would normally require the full agreement of, and compliance by, most countries and this might not be easy—or possible—to achieve. Therefore, it might be necessary to concentrate first on the sources that can be mobilized on a regional or other non-universal basis, while consensus is developed on the others. European Finance Ministers are considering a proposal for a pilot voluntary tax on airline tickets to increase aid to fight HIV/AIDS. All reports stressed that the proposals should be seen as strictly additional and complementary to existing ODA commitments and targets.

External debt

External finance is meant to supplement and support developing counties' domestic resource mobilization. However, since the nineteenth century, developing countries have repeatedly experienced periodic increases in debt-service burdens that led to slower growth or recession, resulting, in many cases, in rescheduling and renegotiations. As debt service currently absorbs a large proportion of external official aid and private lending, the Monterrey Consensus recognized that the elimination of excessive debt burdens would make available a major source of additional finance for development. Debt reduction may thus support the introduction of policies that promote mobilization of domestic resources as well as free domestic resources from debt service so that they can be used to achieve the Millennium Development Goals; but alleviating debt overhang is only part of the solution for, as emphasized in the Consensus, debt must be maintained at sustainable levels if it is going to be effective in complementing domestic mobilization of resources for development.

While progress has been made in reducing the impediment of unsustainable debt burdens for developing countries, much more needs to be done. In contrast to the debt burdens of developing countries in general, those of the poorest developing countries had continued to increase through the first half of the 1990s. To respond to this problem, the Heavily Indebted Poor Countries (HIPC) Initiative was launched in 1996, enhanced in 1999 and recently extended by two years to allow those countries that are eligible to fulfil the criteria so as to actually benefit from debt relief under the Initiative. To date, 27 HIPCs have received debt relief, with 18 countries having reached completion point and 9 countries at decision point. Although the Initiative has already reached its initial expiry date, it is still not fully funded. Full funding is essential if the Initiative's objectives are to be met.

Despite the extension of the HIPC Initiative and its success in increasing social spending for some countries, the commitments on social spending by some countries have exceeded the savings on debt service, leading to accumulation of additional indebtedness. It is now realized that several of the assumptions on which HIPC programmes had been based were over-optimistic, in terms of the evolution of GDP, the level of exports and the evolution of commodity prices, among other variables. Also, most of the debt reduction that took place in the HIPC countries took the form of writing off bilateral debts already in arrears, thus freeing up a smaller amount of real resources for poverty reduction spending than had been originally foreseen.

Even though the evidence is persuasive that the HIPC process has unlocked resources that are critical for the achievement of the Millennium Development Goals, it still falls far short of what is needed. To move forward, the 2005 report of the Secretary-General entitled "In larger freedom: towards development, security and human rights for all" proposes that debt sustainability be redefined as the level of debt that allows a country to achieve the Millennium Development Goals and reach 2015 without an increase in its debt ratios. This implies placing development objectives at the centre of debt sustainability; in particular, the capacity to repay debt must take into account national priorities of human development and poverty reduction, as well as determine a level of debt that does not hinder future growth. For most HIPC countries, this will require exclusively grant-based finance and 100 per cent debt cancellation.

A number of proposals have been under discussion for additional reduction in stocks or in debt service. At a meeting of the G-8 Finance Ministers in early June 2005, a compromise proposal for debt reduction was agreed, for approval by Heads of State and Government at the G-8 Summit in July and by the shareholders of the lending institutions in September. Donors agreed to provide additional development resources to provide full debt relief for the heavily indebted poor countries on outstanding obligations to the International Monetary Fund (IMF), the World Bank and the African Development Bank, and to the International Development Association (IDA) and the African Development Fund, according to a performance-based allocation system. Donors also agreed to a formula to ensure that the measures would not reduce the resources available to other developing countries, or jeopardize the long-term financial viability of international financial institutions.

For many heavily indebted non-HIPC and middle-income countries, debt sustainability will require significantly more debt reduction than has yet been proposed. Although these countries have not yet been included in the discussion on additional debt relief, new mechanisms have been proposed, such as the Paris Club "Evian approach", that seek to give more latitude in dealing with debt overhang in these countries.

Even after agreement on fuller debt relief, long-term sustainability of debt depends very much on the growth and export prospects of debtor countries. Debt sustainability should be part of the overall development strategy of a country, which treats debt, trade and finance in a coherent framework. Development partners could also contribute to finding durable solutions to developing countries' debt problems if debtor countries were adequately supported in enhancing their export capacity. It is also important to strengthen developing countries' capacity on debt management, which should be an integral part of the institutional and policy framework, and should be consistent with the broad macroeconomic and sectoral policies of a country.

Finally, it is important to recognize the contribution that efficient and equitable burden-sharing between debtors and creditors can bring to alleviating unsustainable debt burdens. Given the large number of financial crises in the 1990s, a debate began on the creation of a mechanism to provide an orderly international debt resolution based on existing private sector bankruptcy legislation applied at the national level. It is important that the explorations of debt workout mechanisms, including voluntary codes and international mediation or arbitration mechanisms, continue with the full support of all stakeholders. The adoption in recent years of collective action clauses (CACs) by a number of debtors represents a highly positive step, particularly as it has not led to increases in the cost of the bonds issued; however, CACs will resolve collective action problems only once all outstanding bonds with CACs are retired.

Systemic issues

The systemic agenda addressed by the Monterrey Consensus covers two broad groups of issues. The first relates to the structural features of the international monetary and financial system, and the possible vulnerabilities that they generate for the world economy or for developing countries in particular. The second relates to the institutional design of the current international financial system. It is urgent that the international community address these issues, and take measures to help overcome the challenges they present.

The importance of the first of these issues has been highlighted by growing concerns about global macroeconomic imbalances. Currently the global economy is characterized by large and increasing imbalances across regions. These imbalances have become larger and lasted longer than in the 1980s. The risks associated with various ways in which the imbalances might be adjusted will have direct implications for world economic growth. Problems would be accentuated if sharp adjustment in exchange rates was accompanied by falls in the prices of bonds and stocks. There is growing agreement that the measures that need to be taken include restraining of aggregate demand in deficit countries and more expansionary policies in the surplus countries to stimulate their aggregate demand. However, progress in their implementation is very limited, at a time when urgent and decisive action is required.

Even if the imbalances were sustainable, or could be adjusted in a smooth manner, their large magnitude and skewed distribution suggest a less than efficient and less than equitable allocation of global resources between developed and developing countries. This also counters basic economic logic which suggests that, in the longer term, the industrialized countries should be running current-account surpluses and lending to, and investing in, the developing world, not the reverse.

There is a clear need for greater international cooperation and coordination to ensure a smooth global rebalancing that does not lead to a slowdown of global growth, nor to problems in financial markets. IMF should play a far more central role in ensuring consistency and coherence of macroeconomic policies of major economies. Indeed, IMF is the only international forum where developing countries can express their views on the macroeconomic imbalances of the industrialized economies. Multilateral surveillance should focus not only on crisis-prone countries, but increasingly on the system as a whole; this implies a more central role for IMF in the management of the world economy.

The global financial system has undergone profound changes over the past several decades. Though they have important positive effects, these changes may pose new and often yet unknown potential increases in systemic risk. Factors such as increased concentration in the financial industry, which has led to the formation of a small number of large financial conglomerates, and expansion of loosely regulated or unregulated activities (such as derivatives) and institutions (such as hedge funds) have transformed and possibly increased risk. Opaqueness of risk transfer is also problematic. Consequently, there are fears that increased opportunities for risk transfer may imply that risk ends up in parts of the financial system where supervision and disclosure are weakest.

The transformation of the financial system and its greater emphasis on market-based risk evaluation seem to have increased the likelihood and frequency of boom-bust cycles. It is therefore increasingly important that macroprudential elements be incorporated into financial regulation, both in developed and in developing countries. This would complement the more traditional microprudential focus of regulation. More specifically, as noted previously, it implies introducing counter-cyclicality into financial regulation, for example, by forward-looking provisions against future loan losses, to compensate for the tendency of banks to be pro-cyclical in their lending.

Many developing countries have made significant domestic progress in reducing their vulnerability to crisis, including improvements in financial regulation, use of more flexible exchange rates and higher levels of reserves. However, they continue to be vulnerable to external shocks, caused by changes in commodity prices, rises in developed countries' interest rates, and capital flow volatility, as well as natural disasters.

There is therefore a need to further enhance IMF facilities to help ensure that external shocks do not impose excessive costs on developing-country and global growth, and to facilitate counter-cyclical national macroeconomic management. To deal with capital flows, volatility and contagion, it would be desirable to put in place a new IMF facility that could be disbursed automatically to countries with good fundamentals, according to pre-established criteria, or to countries favourably evaluated by IMF in Article IV consultations.

For both middle-income and low-income countries, there is also an important need for IMF facilities to more fully compensate for temporary terms-of-trade shocks, and to do so with lower conditionality than at present. For low-income countries, the most appropriate mechanism seems to be an enhanced Poverty Reduction and Growth Facility, requiring continued sufficient funding of the Facility. Expanded IMF facilities for low-income countries, to ameliorate external shocks, could reduce the negative impact of "silent crises", which can have such a devastating effect on low-income countries' growth and poverty levels. This would thus help to meet the Millennium Development Goals.

In the 1990s, IMF conditionality had expanded to include structural reforms, which resulted in increases in the number of performance criteria. The adoption by the IMF Executive Board of guidelines for streamlining conditionality was therefore a welcome development; however, progress in their implementation has been slow and uneven. Furthermore, IMF has agreed that domestic ownership of macroeconomic policies is the main obstacle to effective programme implementation. In broader terms, the conditionality attached to all forms of international financial cooperation should be streamlined and made consistent with the principle of ownership of macroeconomic and development policies by recipient countries. Ownership would also be promoted by an effective discussion of the virtues of alternative policies.

The more active use of SDRs would also improve the functioning of the international monetary system. Recent proposals in this regard follow two different models. The first calls for SDRs to be issued temporarily during episodes of financial stress, and destroyed once financial conditions normalize. This would develop a counter-cyclical element in world liquidity management, helping to finance additional IMF programmes during crises, without generating permanent increases in global liquidity. The second would use permanent allocations to generate a more even distribution of seigniorage powers at the global level. Allocations to industrialized countries could be used to finance international development cooperation. The additional global liquidity created would, in any case, be small. For example, the most recent allocation of SDRs approved in 1997, but not yet ratified, of SDR 21 billion, represents less than 0.5 per cent of the money supply (M2) of the United States and an even smaller proportion of the world's total money supply.

A valuable complement to the role that IMF plays at the global level can be provided by regional reserve funds. Such funds can offer a first line of defence, particularly as large currency crises have been regional in nature, and provide a framework for macroeconomic policy dialogue and coordination. Positive experiences in this regard include the Latin American Reserve Fund, active for some time in the Andean region, and the more recent Chiang Mai Initiative of the Association of Southeast Asian Nations (ASEAN), China, Japan and the Republic of Korea. The latter has recently agreed a significant increase in its $39 billion bilateral swap programme. Looking into the future, an organizational structure might be conceived where a dense network of complementary multilateral and regional institutions could be established in the international monetary field, to provide complementary financing, as well as possible macroeconomic surveillance. This system would be akin to that of the multilateral development banks or, in the monetary area, to the European Central Bank and the federal structure of the United States Federal Reserve System.

Democracy is becoming an increasingly important aim of nations and of the international community. Developing countries have significantly increased their share in the world economy. As a consequence, a clear mandate was given in the Monterrey Consensus to improve the voice of developing countries in international economic decision-making and norm-setting institutions. This would not just increase these institutions' legitimacy, but also make them more effective. Unfortunately, progress on increasing voice and participation of developing countries has been slow. Discussions on ways to improve voice and participation of developing countries in the Bretton Woods institutions have already started, and it is important that the political will be present to take and implement decisions in this regard. However, the Consensus goes beyond the Bretton Woods institutions and highlights the need to extend the discussion of voice and participation to other policymaking and standard-setting bodies, including informal and ad hoc groups. These include the Bank for International Settlements, the Financial Stability Forum and financial standard-setting bodies, such as the Basel Committee on Banking Supervision, the International Association of Insurance Supervisors, the International Accounting Standards Board, the International Organization for Standardization and the International Federation of Stock Exchanges. In several of these institutions, no formal participation of developing countries exists today. It is therefore time to initiate discussions regarding these institutions.

José Antonio Ocampo
Under-Secretary-General
*   for Economic and Social Affairs*
June 2005

Contents

Financing for Development

Boxes

Figures

Tables

Explanatory Notes

The following symbols have been used in the tables throughout the report:

.. **Two dots** indicate that data are not available or are not separately reported.

– **A dash** indicates that the amount is nil or negligible.

- **A hyphen (-)** indicates that the item is not applicable.

- **A minus sign (-)** indicates deficit or decrease, except as indicated.

. **A full stop (.)** is used to indicate decimals.

/ **A slash (/)** between years indicates a crop year or financial year, for example, 1990/91.

- **Use of a hyphen (-)** between years, for example, 1990-1991, signifies the full period involved, including the beginning and end years.

Reference to "dollars" ($) indicates United States dollars, unless otherwise stated.

Reference to "tons" indicates metric tons, unless otherwise stated.

Annual rates of growth or change, unless otherwise stated, refer to annual compound rates.

In most cases, the growth rate forecasts for 2004 and 2005 are rounded to the nearest quarter of a percentage point.

Details and percentages in tables do not necessarily add to totals, because of rounding.

The following abbreviations have been used:

ADR	American Depository Receipt
APEC	Asia-Pacific Economic Cooperation
ASEAN	Association of Southeast Asian Nations
BIS	Bank for International Settlements
CAC	collective action clause
CACM	Central American Common Market
CARICOM	Caribbean Community and Common Market
CCL	Contingent Credit Line (IMF)
CFF	Compensatory Financing Facility (CFF)
CGE	computable general equilibrium (model)
c.i.f.	cost, insurance and freight
CIS	Commonwealth of Independent States
CMI	Chiang Mai Initiative
COMESA	Common Market for Eastern and Southern Africa
COMTRADE	United Nations Commodity Trade Statistics Database
CPIA	Country Policy and Institutional Assessment (World Bank)
CPSS	Committee on Payment and Settlement Systems
DAC	Development Assistance Committee (OECD)
EAEC	East Asian Economic Caucus
EBRD	European Bank for Reconstruction and Development
ECA	Economic Commission for Africa
ECE	Economic Commission for Europe
ECLAC	Economic Commission for Latin America and the Caribbean
ECOWAS	Economic Community of West African States
EIB	European Investment Bank
ESCAP	Economic and Social Commission for Asia and the Pacific
EU	European Union
FATF	Financial Action Task Force on Money Laundering
FDI	foreign direct investment
FLAR	Latin American Reserve Fund
FSF	Financial Stability Forum
FTAA	Free Trade Area of the Americas
GAVI	Global Alliance for Vaccines and Immunization
GDDS	General Data Dissemination System (IMF)

GDP	gross domestic product	**OECD**	Organization for Economic Cooperation and Development
GNI	gross national income	**PPP**	purchasing power parity
GSP	Generalized System of Preferences	**PRGF**	Poverty Reduction and Growth Facility (IMF)
HIPC	heavily indebted poor countries	**PRSP**	Poverty Reduction Strategy Paper (IMF and World Bank)
IAIS	International Association of Insurance Supervisors	**R&D**	research and development
IASB	International Accounting Standards Board	**ROSC**	Report on the Observance of Standards and Codes (IMF)
IBRD	International Bank for Reconstruction and Development	**ROSCA**	rotating savings and credit association
ICT	information and communication technologies	**SADC**	Southern African Development Community
IDA	International Development Association	**SDA**	Special Disbursement Account (IMF)
IFAC	International Federation of Accountants	**SDDS**	Special Data Dissemination Standard (IMF)
IFC	International Finance Cooperation	**SDR**	Special Drawing Right
IFF	International Finance Facility	**SDT**	special and differential treatment
IIF	Institute of International Finance	**SEC**	United States Securities and Exchange Commission
ILO	International Labour Organization	**SITC**	Standard International Trade Classification
IMF	International Monetary Fund	**SRF**	Supplemental Reserve Facility (IMF)
IOSCO	International Organization of Securities Commissions	**TIM**	Trade Integration Mechanism (IMF)
IRB	internal ratings-based	**TNC**	transnational corporation
LAIA	Latin American Integration Association	**UDEAC**	Central African Customs and Economic Union
LIBOR	London Interbank Offered Rate	**UNCTAD**	United Nations Conference on Trade and Development
M&A	mergers and acquisitions	**UN/DESA**	Department of Economic and Social Affairs of the United Nations Secretariat
MERCOSUR	Southern Common Market	**UNDP**	United Nations Development Programme
MFN	most favoured nation	**UNFPA**	United Nations Population Fund
MIGA	Multilateral Investment Guarantee Agency	**UNU**	United Nations University
NAFTA	North American Free Trade Agreement	**URR**	unremunerated reserve requirement
NBER	National Bureau of Economic Research (Cambridge, Massachsetts)	**WIDER**	World Institute for Development Economics Research (WIDER)
NDF	non-deliverable forwards	**WIPO**	World Intellectual Poverty Organization
NPL	non-performing loan		
NPV	net present value		
ODA	official development assistance		

The designations employed and the presentation of the material in this publication do not imply the expression of any opinion whatsoever on the part of the United Nations Secretariat concerning the legal status of any country, territory, city or area or of its authorities, or concerning the delimitation of its frontiers or boundaries.

The term "country" as used in the text of this report also refers, as appropriate, to territories or areas.

For analytical purposes, the following country groupings and sub-groupings have been used:

Developed economies (developed market economies):
Europe, excluding the European transition economies
Canada and the United States of America
Japan, Australia and New Zealand.

Major developed economies (the Group of Seven):
Canada, France, Germany, Italy, Japan, United Kingdom of Great Britain and Northern Ireland, United States of America.

European Union:
Austria, Belgium, Cyprus, Czech Republic, Denmark, Estonia, Finland, France, Germany, Greece, Hungary, Ireland, Italy, Latvia, Lithuania, Luxembourg, Malta, Netherlands, Poland, Portugal, Slovakia, Slovenia, Spain, Sweden, United Kingdom of Great Britain and Northern Ireland.

Economies in transition:

Southern and Eastern Europe
Albania, Bulgaria, Croatia, Romania, Serbia and Montenegro, The former Yugoslav Republic of Macedonia.

Commonwealth of Independent States (CIS)
Armenia, Azerbaijan, Belarus, Georgia, Kazakhstan, Kyrgyzstan, Republic of Moldova, Russian Federation, Tajikistan, Turkmenistan, Ukraine, Uzbekistan.

Developing economies:
Africa
Asia and the Pacific (excluding Japan, Australia, New Zealand and the member States of CIS in Asia).
Latin America and the Caribbean.

Subgroupings of Asia and the Pacific:

Western Asia:
Bahrain, Iraq, Israel, Jordan, Kuwait, Lebanon, Oman, Qatar, Saudi Arabia, Syrian Arab Republic, Turkey, United Arab Emirates, Yemen.

East and South Asia:
All other developing economies in Asia and the Pacific (including China, unless listed separately). This group has in some cases been subdivided into:

China

South Asia: Bangladesh, India, Iran (Islamic Republic of), Nepal, Pakistan, Sri Lanka.

East Asia: all other developing economies in Asia and the Pacific.

Subgrouping of Africa:

Sub-Saharan Africa, excluding Nigeria and South Africa (commonly contracted to "sub-Saharan Africa"):
All of Africa except Algeria, Egypt, Libyan Arab Jamahiriya, Morocco, Nigeria, South Africa, Tunisia.

For particular analyses, developing countries have been subdivided into the following groups:

Oil-exporting countries:
Algeria, Angola, Bahrain, Bolivia, Brunei Darussalam, Cameroon, Colombia, Congo, Ecuador, Egypt, Gabon, Indonesia, Iran (Islamic Republic of), Iraq, Kuwait, Libyan Arab Jamahiriya, Mexico, Nigeria, Oman, Qatar, Saudi Arabia, Syrian Arab Republic, Trinidad and Tobago, United Arab Emirates, Venezuela, Viet Nam.

Oil-importing countries:
All other developing countries.

Least developed countries:
Afghanistan, Angola, Bangladesh, Benin, Bhutan, Burkina Faso, Burundi, Cambodia, Cape Verde, Central African Republic, Chad, Comoros, Democratic Republic of the Congo, Djibouti, Equatorial Guinea, Eritrea, Ethiopia, Gambia, Guinea, Guinea-Bissau, Haiti, Kiribati, Lao People's Democratic Republic, Lesotho, Liberia, Madagascar, Malawi, Maldives, Mali, Mauritania, Mozambique, Myanmar, Nepal, Niger, Rwanda, Samoa, Sao Tome and Principe, Senegal, Sierra Leone, Solomon Islands, Somalia, Sudan, Timor-Leste, Togo, Tuvalu, Uganda, United Republic of Tanzania, Vanuatu, Yemen, Zambia.

Landlocked developing countries:
Afghanistan, Armenia, Azerbaijan, Bhutan, Bolivia, Botswana, Burkina Faso, Burundi, Central African Republic, Chad, Ethiopia, Kazakhstan, Kyrgyzstan, Lao People's Democratic Republic, Lesotho, Malawi, Mali, Mongolia, Nepal, Niger, Paraguay, Rwanda, Swaziland, Tajikistan, The former Yugoslav Republic of Macedonia, Turkmenistan, Uganda, Uzbekistan, Zambia, Zimbabwe.

Small island developing States:
Antigua and Barbuda, Bahamas, Bahrain, Barbados, Belize, Cape Verde, Comoros, Cook Islands, Cuba, Cyprus, Dominica, Dominican Republic, Fiji, Grenada, Guinea-Bissau, Guyana, Haiti, Jamaica, Kiribati, Maldives, Malta, Marshall Islands, Mauritius, Micronesia (Federated States of), Nauru, Niue, Palau, Papua New Guinea, Saint Kitts and Nevis, Saint Lucia, Samoa, Sao Tome and Principe, Seychelles, Singapore, Solomon Islands, Saint Vincent and the Grenadines, Suriname, Tonga, Trinidad and Tobago, Tuvalu, Vanuatu.

Heavily Indebted Poor Countries:
Angola, Benin, Bolivia, Burkina Faso, Burundi, Cameroon, Central African Republic, Chad, Comoros, Congo, Côte d'Ivoire, Democratic Republic of the Congo, Ethiopia, Gambia, Ghana, Guinea, Guinea-Bissau, Guyana, Honduras, Kenya, Lao People's Democratic Republic, Liberia, Madagascar, Malawi, Mali, Mauritania, Mozambique, Myanmar, Nicaragua, Niger, Rwanda, Sao Tome and Principe, Senegal, Sierra Leone, Somalia, Sudan, Togo, Uganda, United Republic of Tanzania, Viet Nam, Zambia.

The designation of country groups in the text and the tables is intended solely for statistical or analytical convenience and does not necessarily express a judgement about the stage reached by a particular country or area in the development process.

Chapter I
Mobilizing domestic resources for development

The Monterrey Consensus of the International Conference on Financing for Development (United Nations, 2002a) places the mobilization of domestic financial resources for development at the centre of the pursuit of economic growth, poverty eradication and sustainable development. It points to the need for "the necessary internal conditions for mobilizing domestic savings (and) sustaining adequate levels of productive investment" and stresses the importance of fostering a "dynamic and well-functioning business sector". At the same time, it recognizes that the "appropriate role of government in market-oriented economies will vary from country to country" and calls for an effective system for mobilizing public resources and for investments in basic economic and social infrastructure, as well as active labour-market policies.

The present chapter analyses these concerns. The first section examines the historical relationships among savings, investment and economic growth in the developing countries over the past three decades. The subsequent section addresses "investment climate" and focuses on some key economic, legal and labour-market requirements. The third section examines the role of the financial sector and the institutions that are required to guarantee the adequate provision of financial services for investment, access by the poor and small enterprises to such services, and the prudential regulation and supervision required to guarantee the stability of the financial system.

Savings, investment and growth

A long-standing view of the macroeconomic dynamics of the development process was that a poor country had to raise its savings rate (that is to say, to change from a "12 per cent saver" to a "20 per cent saver") and transform the increased savings into productive investment in order to achieve an economic "take-off" (see, for example, Lewis, 1954). Emphasis was usually placed on increasing investment in industrial sectors, but public investment in such physical infrastructure as power, transportation systems and health and education facilities was also seen as critical.

Subsequently, technological progress was introduced as a determinant of long-term growth, with some analysts arguing that its role was dominant, or even exclusive (Easterly and Levine, 2001). With the advent of so-called endogeneous growth models, however, investment was again recognized as a critical factor for long-term growth. Overall, theories of economic growth have been refined, modified and expanded over the years and now encompass a wide range of factors, ranging from the purely economic to social and cultural considerations. Nevertheless, most explanations include, to varying degrees and in various combinations, three underlying economic factors, namely, investment, innovation and improvements in productivity, with the three being interrelated in a variety of ways.

The relationships among savings, investment and growth have been found to be more complex than initially imagined, but it remains generally accepted that increasing savings and ensuring that they are directed to productive investment are central to accelerating economic growth. These objectives should therefore be central concerns of national policymakers.

Raising the savings rate was formerly seen as necessary to achieve economic "take-off"

More recent analysis emphasized investment, innovations and productivity improvements

Yet raising savings and directing them to productive investment are still crucial

Overall trends in developing regions, 1970-2002

There was a strong correlation among savings, investment, economic growth and the reduction of poverty over the period 1970-2002, especially in Asia ...

In all developing regions, savings, investment, economic growth and the reduction of poverty have been positively correlated over the past three decades (see figure I.1). In most of Asia, savings and investment rates have increased, the region has grown increasingly rapidly and the incidence of poverty has declined considerably. Although there have been improvements in all these dimensions in all the major subregions of Asia, there remain considerable differences in the absolute levels: rates of savings, investment and growth in South Asia in 1990-2002, for example, were less than those in China in the 1970s, with China having improved further in the meantime. East Asia falls between these two positions.

... while in sub-Saharan Africa declining rates of saving, investment and growth increased poverty. In the Middle East and Northern Africa, boosts to savings from surges in oil prices did not improve long-run growth

Sub-Saharan Africa' situation is opposite to that of Asia. For the region as a whole, the rates of savings, investment and growth had declined between the 1970s and the 1980s and declined further in the period 1990-2002. The Middle East and Northern Africa constitute a unique case in that domestic savings had exceeded 35 per cent of gross domestic product (GDP) as a result of the two surges in oil prices in the 1970s, but fell towards 20 per cent after 1980. The boost to savings in the 1970s did not translate into either investment or improved growth: investment has remained between 20 and 25 per cent of GDP throughout the three decades and growth of per capita GDP has been volatile but generally low, and was even negative in the 1980s

In Latin America, rates of saving and investment were lower than in Asia. Overall growth was volatile and the incidence of poverty hardly changed over 30 years

In Latin America, savings and investment rates have been lower than those in Asia, with little apparent regional trend over time. The 1970s had been characterized by domestic savings and investment rates of about 20 per cent of GDP and growth of 4-5 per cent. Thereafter, savings and investment rates fell to 17 and 19 per cent of GDP, respectively, and average growth fell to 1 per cent. More recently, savings have dropped further but investment and growth have recovered somewhat. Overall, growth has been volatile and the incidence of poverty has remained relatively unchanged for 30 years.

Savings and investment have recovered in the transition economies after the initial transformational recession

The economies in transition represent a unique case in that savings and investment rates had been artificially high under their centrally planned system, but then fell precipitously, reviving in Eastern Europe and the Baltic States in the early 1990s and in the Russian Federation and the other members of the Commonwealth of Independent States (CIS) after the Russian financial crisis of 1998. Since that time, savings and investment rates in the region, together with growth, have recovered.

Savings and growth

The Asian countries saw the sharpest rise in their savings rates— and the fastest growth rates

In the 1970s, the highest regional rate of savings had been in the Middle East and Northern Africa (see figure I.1). Revenues associated with the first oil shock accounted for a large part of savings at that time and the savings rate subsequently declined as oil prices fell. Among the remaining regions, the savings rate in the 1970s was low in East Asia and the Pacific but rose subsequently. The savings rate in South Asia had been the lowest of any region in 1970 but increased continuously thereafter while sub-Saharan Africa moved in the opposite situation: from over 20 per cent in the 1970s, its savings rate fell towards 15 per cent in the 1990s. Latin America is an intermediate case: it had maintained, and even marginally increased, its domestic savings rate of over 20 per cent from the 1970s to the 1980s, but the rate fell below 20 per cent in the 1990s.

Figure I.1.
Savings, investment, growth and poverty reduction, 1970-2003

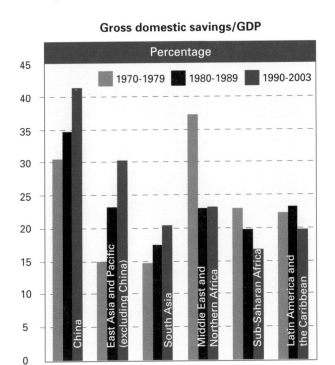

Gross domestic savings/GDP

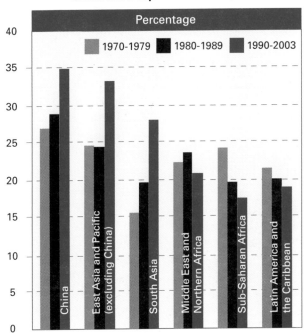

Gross fixed capital formation/GDP

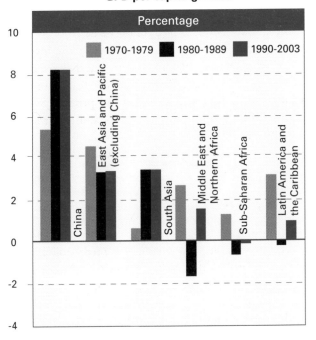

GPD per capita growth

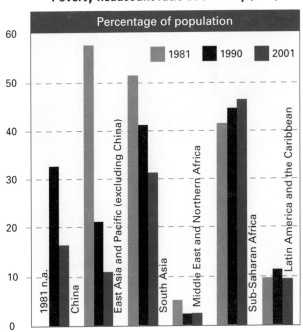

Poverty headcount ratio at $1 a day (PPP)

Source: World Bank, *World Development Indicators.* Washington, D.C.: World Bank.

In China and other take-off countries, savings rates increases from 20 per cent to 34 per cent between 1970 and 1992-1994. They had lower initial incomes per head than many less successful countries

Domestic saving and growth were positively correlated, particularly in Asia

In China and nine other developing countries identified as achieving an economic take-off, savings rates are estimated to have risen from 20 per cent in 1970-1972 to 34 per cent in 1992-1994 (Loayza and others, 1998).[1] In 1970, the take-off countries had lower incomes per head than many less successful countries but they were able to embark on a virtuous circle of higher savings, higher investment and faster growth. It was also found that savings in low-saving countries exhibited higher volatility than in countries with higher rates of saving. Savings and investment rates were lowest among the least developed countries and the heavily indebted poor countries (HIPC) for much of the period.

Domestic saving and growth in output per head were positively correlated in all developing regions over the period 1970-2003, although the strength of the correlation varied across regions and time periods (see figure I.2). African countries have had varied experiences, eliminating the possibility of regional generalizations. The few countries with higher savings rates grew faster, while low savings rates were associated with low or negative growth. For Asian countries, however, there has been a consistently strong positive correlation between the two variables over time. For Latin American countries, there had been almost no correlation between savings and growth in the 1970s, but a positive relationship (that is to say, an upward slope) increasingly developed in the 1980s and 1990s. Moreover, by the 1990s, the correlation was approaching that in Asia although, in absolute terms, savings rates and growth rates were less. Within Latin America, such countries as Chile and Costa Rica, with consistently good growth rates, were able to achieve higher savings rates.

The direction of causality is as follows: growth causes savings, rather than the reverse

It is frequently assumed that increases in savings rates are necessary to achieve higher growth but empirical evidence suggests that the causality runs in the opposite direction. Empirical studies—typically based on cross-country analyses—find in general that savings usually lag growth and that it is therefore economic growth that gives rise to increased national saving, rather than the reverse (Carrol and Weil, 1993; Attanasio, Picci and Scorcu, 1997; and Gavin, Hausman and Talvi, 1997). That growth causes saving can also be seen from the fact that, while episodes of economic boom positively affect saving

Box I.1

Raising household savings in China

The increase in savings in China was accompanied by a shift in its composition. The share of public and corporate saving in total savings fell from 59.1 per cent in 1978 to 19.6 per cent in 1995, while the share of household saving increased from 12.8 to 51.2 per cent over the same period of time. However, the latter may have been caused at least partially by an increase in private sector activity and, in particular, by the growing role of small firms, whose savings are often recorded as those of households in official statistics.

Financial deepening in China was an important factor in promoting private savings because it increased private households' propensity to keep a part of their income as savings in the financial system. A further determinant has been the monetization of income as employees of State-owned enterprises increasingly received their salary in monetary terms rather than in the form of goods, allowing them to keep greater amounts of money as savings. This positive effect on savings was further increased by policies in support of household income, in some cases combined with mandatory saving.

Finally, during the reform period, policies aimed at limiting population growth led to a reduction in the ratio of people under 15 years of age to the working population from 0.96 shortly before the start of the reform period to 0.41 at the end of the 1990s. This expanded the proportion of potential savers (those of working age) in the population, while the accompanying decline in the role of the family increased individuals' propensity to save. It has been argued that this demographic factor was a major determinant of the increase in savings in China (Modigliani and Cao, 2004).

Figure I.2.
Savings and growth, 1970-1979, 1980-1989, 1990-2003 and 1970-2003

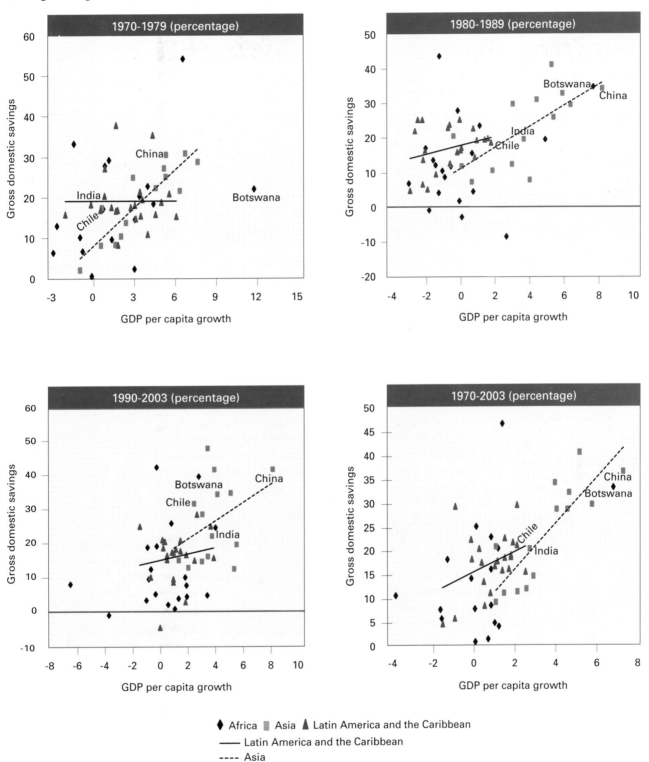

Source: World Bank, *World Development Indicators.* Washington, D.C.: World Bank.

rates and such an impact persists over time, saving booms do not translate into sustained growth (Rodrik, 2000a). Such countries or areas as Chile, Hong Kong Special Administrative Region (SAR) of China, the Republic of Korea and Singapore improved their investment climate and succeeded, often through government interventions, in boosting investment and raising overall growth before experiencing a boom in the savings rate (Rodrik, 2000a).

Policy should therefore concentrate on the broad determinants of growth

The finding that growth normally precedes an increase in savings suggests that government policies and measures to improve growth should not be limited to boosting the savings rate and ensuring that the financial sector facilitates the productive use of saving. Governments also have to consider a larger number of determinants of growth, including improving infrastructure, enhancing human capital through education and training, facilitating and contributing to innovative production processes through research and development, and ensuring macroeconomic stability and a healthy investment climate.

Saving and investment

Most investment in developing countries is financed by domestic sources

The bulk of capital formation in most countries in all developing regions is financed by domestic savings so that, in most cases, gross fixed capital formation is roughly equal to gross domestic savings (see figure I.3). Not surprisingly, therefore, gross fixed capital formation as a share of GDP exhibits regional trends that are broadly similar to those of savings, with the ratio in East Asia and the Pacific having risen over time to over 33 per cent of GDP and in South Asia to 28 per cent, while that in other regions converged in a range of between 17 and 22 per cent (see figure I.1). The most marked difference between savings and investment occurred, as noted above, in the Middle East and Northern African region in the 1970s, when the region's surge in oil revenues had enabled it to become an exporter of capital.

Some countries, however, such as Singapore in Asia, and African and Latin American countries, tried to use foreign savings to boost investment, but the success of this strategy varied across regions

In the 1970s, Asian countries—possibly with the exception of Singapore and a few others that opted for attracting foreign capital—had relied mostly on internal resources. Several African and Latin American countries, on the other hand, relied more extensively on foreign sources. Some African countries had low savings rates during the period and were able to achieve higher rates of gross fixed capital formation only because of inflows of foreign capital, often in the form of aid. During the 1980s, flows of foreign capital to Latin America and Africa dried up and these regions had to rely more heavily on domestic resources. In the meantime, Asian countries had started to attract significant amounts of foreign resources. The process continued and strengthened in the 1990s, up to the Asian crisis of 1997.

The different sectoral compositions of investment in India and China can explain some of the differences in their investment rates

In the two largest developing countries, India and China, the smaller share of investment in output in the former compared with the latter was partly a reflection of the different sectoral sources of growth: India concentrated on services while China concentrated on manufacturing, which is more capital-intensive. In India, the sectoral incremental capital output ratio declined in all service subsectors over time, while the ratios for the manufacturing sector increased and surpassed those in the service sector (Virmani, 2004a, 2004b). This means that additional investment in the services sector was more efficient in stimulating additional output than it would have been in the manufacturing sector.

Figure I.3.
Savings and investment, 1970-1979, 1980-1989, 1990-2003 and 1970-2003

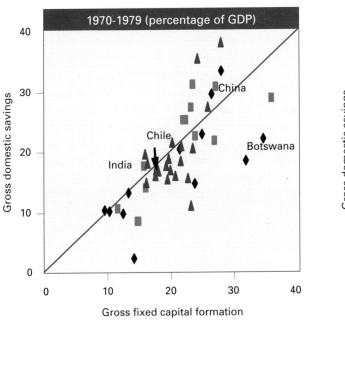

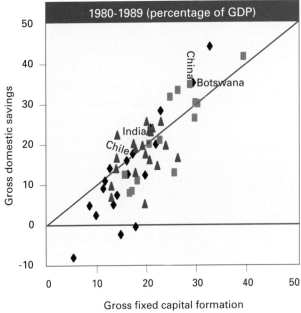

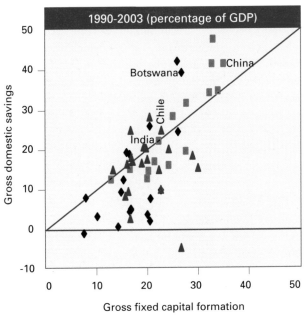

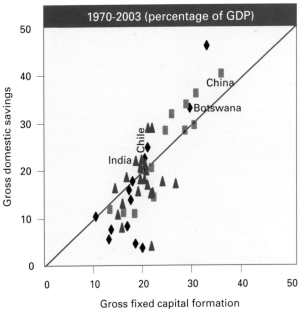

♦ Africa ▉ Asia ▲ Latin America and the Caribbean

Source: World Bank, *World Development Indicators.* Washington, D.C.: World Bank.

The role of foreign savings

It is not just the volume of foreign savings that matters, but often the new technology and skills that it introduces

Foreign savings, even in economies where they are relatively large, are almost always less than domestic savings (as can be deduced from figure I.1), but they may make a disproportionately greater contribution to economic growth. In large economies, such as China and India, foreign savings are likely to be small in relation to domestic savings but they can have broader benefits. In the case of foreign direct investment (FDI), for example, they may be accompanied by the introduction of new technology and skills and can make a critical contribution to growth (see chap. III). In many smaller economies, especially those caught in a low-income savings trap, foreign savings can be the spur needed to set them on a course of sustained growth.

Foreign savings can help a country move out of a low-income savings trap, as the experience of Botswana illustrates

Botswana represents a success story in Africa that reveals how foreign savings can be attracted so as to make possible long-term national development. As Botswana was one of the poorest countries in Africa in the 1960s, its leaders had decided to attract investment from high-class companies operating in Africa to search and develop its mineral wealth. Foreign capital brought together by mining companies financed the exploration and the initial development of the mining sector (see figure I.3). These companies had been attracted by the secure investment climate and, in the case of diamonds, spent 12 years exploring before the rich deposits were revealed. The profitable diamond business then became self-financing. Botswana subsequently enjoyed high investment rates, sustained by strong savings rates, over an extended period (see figures I.3). More recently, high HIV/AIDS prevalence has depressed economic growth despite relatively strong investment rates.

There is no clear evidence that foreign capital flows "crowd out" domestic savings: their impact varies across regions and over time

In circumstances where capital is mobile and countries have access to foreign savings, there is the question whether the level of domestic savings is affected by foreign capital flows. Some empirical studies find a degree of "crowding out" of domestic savings by foreign savings (see Schmidt-Hebbel, Servén and Solimano, 1996)—which also means that a part of foreign savings is consumed rather than invested—but the impact of foreign saving on domestic saving varies greatly across regions and over time. In Latin America, the evidence suggests that temporary (particularly short-term) capital flows are consumed, while more permanent foreign capital flows are invested (Titelman and Uthoff, 1998). In Asia, foreign savings have complemented domestic savings, contributing to the overall increase in investment. Similarly, in Eastern Europe and the Baltic States, there has not been a crowding out: rather, both foreign and domestic savings have been used to increase investment in many sectors.

In Latin America, foreign capital inflows during the 1980s had been low, but they recovered in the 1990s. However, the fact that domestic savings did not rise commensurately raises questions about the sustainability of growth

In Latin America, the picture has changed over time. In the 1970s, domestic savings had remained at relatively high levels on average, without much visible substitution. In the 1980s, the region experienced both low domestic savings and a low inflow of foreign savings. However, in the 1990s, the inflow of foreign capital increased, but domestic savings did not do so commensurately. The result has been a greater dependence on external savings as a source of investment, with any slackening of capital inflows having a damaging effect on investment and growth. In general, it had been thought that a recovery of investment in the region that was financed by external savings rates in excess of 3 per cent of GDP was not sustainable because of the vulnerability of such a pattern of accumulation to shifts in the international economic environment. This experience suggests that achieving high and stable economic growth rates requires domestic savings and investment to be raised at the same time (Economic Commission for Latin America and the Caribbean, 2002, pp. 51-52).

One view is that much of the difference between Latin American and Asia can be explained by the composition of their respective foreign capital inflows: FDI formed a higher proportion of foreign inflows in Asia than in Latin America. This view is supported by the fact that, among the Latin American countries, Chile has received proportionally more FDI and there has not been the crowding out of domestic saving that occurred in the other countries in the region. Others have argued that the differences in behaviour are more the result of secular patterns and that such patterns do not depend on the composition of foreign savings but rather on other longer-term variables.

Foreign direct investment was a much higher proportion of foreign inflows into Asia than into Latin America

Investment and growth

The evidence suggests that there is a virtuous circle between higher investment and higher growth. In the case of Asian countries, there was a strong relationship between gross fixed capital formation and per capita growth in all decades from the 1970s to the present (see figure I.4). In Latin America, investment levels also followed growth patterns: high investment levels during the 1970s, a sharp decline during the "lost decade" of the 1980s and some recovery in the 1990s. In Africa, economic performance had been poor but there was a return to positive growth in the 1990s, even though rates of investment were low.

There is a virtuous circle between higher investment and higher growth

Regarding causality, a distinction should be made between the short and the long term. In the short term, investment depends on the expected rate of growth, capacity utilization and the liquidity constraints faced by firms. For these reasons, growth may lead investment over the business cycle (although a recession may have long-term effects if it causes a major decline in investment). In the long run, it is generally believed that capital investment is an important source of growth. Particularly, it is unlikely that a higher rate of growth will be sustainable without an increase in investment. This suggests a virtuous circle between growth and investment.

Growth may lead investment over the business cycle, but in the long term investment is essential to sustaining growth although ...

Nevertheless, the evidence also suggests that investment rates alone do not fully account for economic progress: other factors, in particular the quality of human capital and technology, are involved in achieving sustained growth and some analysts argue that technological progress is the main source of growth. One view is that increased growth raises the utilization of existing resources and thereby raises productivity, giving rise to another virtuous circle (Kaldor, 1978; Ocampo, 2005).

... investment rates alone do not fully account for growth

For example, among the regions, the South-East Asian "miracle" appears to have been more a result of capital accumulation than of productivity growth (see table I.1).[2] For China, the data suggest a break between the 1970s and 1980s which probably reflects the movement towards a more market-based system undertaken by the country in 1978. China illustrates how investment can lead to growth and the more efficient use of capital equipment, resulting in higher rates of growth of productivity.

The contribution to growth not accounted for by capital and human inputs varies across regions

Low investment rates explain Africa's overall poor growth record, but poor investment productivity was also a factor. In Latin America, productivity had been a major factor affecting growth during the 1960s and 1970s but, as the investment rate declined in the 1980s, productivity fell sharply and had a negative impact on growth. In the 1990s, productivity growth again became positive (though lower than in the 1960s and 1970s). As in other cases, the causality is not clear: as indicated above, productivity growth might have been a consequence of improved economic growth (and the negative productivity performance of the 1980s the result of low growth during the debt crisis) rather than a cause of it.

Low productivity often accompanies low investment rates

Figure I.4.
Investment and growth, 1970-1979, 1980-1989, 1990-2003 and 1970-2003

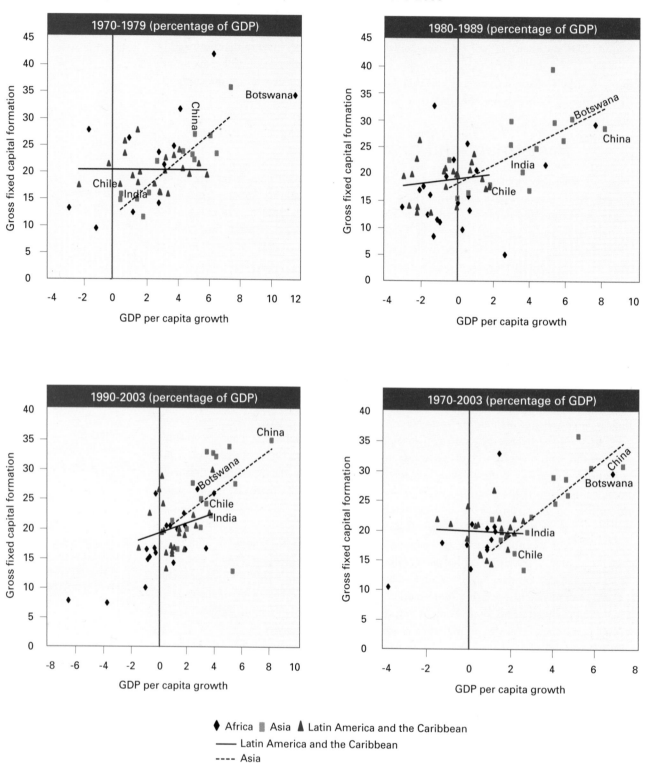

Source: World Bank, *World Development Indicators*. Washington, D.C.: World Bank.

Table I.1.
Contribution of physical capital, human capital and productivity to the
growth of output per worker, world and developing regions, 1961-2000

Region and number of countries	Growth of output per worker	Contribution of		
		Physical capital	Eduction	Factor productivity
World (84)				
1961-2000	2.3	1.0	0.3	0.9
China (1)				
1961-1970	0.9	0.0	0.3	0.5
1971-1980	2.8	1.6	1.4	0.7
1981-1990	6.8	2.1	1.4	4.2
1991-2000	8.8	3.2	0.3	5.1
1961-2000	4.8	1.7	0.4	2.6
East Asia less China (7)				
1961-1970	3.7	1.7	0.4	1.5
1971-1980	4.3	2.7	0.6	0.9
1981-1990	4.4	2.4	0.6	1.3
1991-2000	3.4	2.3	0.5	0.5
1961-2000	3.9	2.3	0.5	1.0
South Asia (4)				
1961-1970	2.2	1.2	0.3	0.7
1971-1980	0.7	0.6	0.3	-0.2
1981-1990	3.7	1.0	0.4	2.2
1991-2000	2.8	1.2	0.4	1.2
1961-2000	2.3	1.0	0.3	1.0
Africa (19)				
1961-1970	2.8	0.7	0.2	1.9
1971-1980	1.0	1.3	0.1	-0.3
1981-1990	-1.1	-0.1	0.4	-1.4
1991-2000	-0.2	-0.1	0.4	-0.5
1961-2000	0.6	0.5	0.3	-0.1
Latin America (22)				
1961-1970	2.8	0.8	0.3	1.6
1971-1980	2.7	1.2	0.3	1.1
1981-1990	-1.8	0.0	0.5	-2.3
1991-2000	0.9	0.2	0.3	0.4
1961-2000	1.1	0.6	0.4	0.2

Source: Barry Bosworth and Susan M. Collins, *The Empirics of Growth: An Update*
(Washington, D.C., The Brookings Institution, 2003).

It is difficult to separate the effects on growth of physical and human capital and technological progress

Overall, there are numerous interactions between physical and human capital and technological progress; growth is the result of the joint accumulation of all three, with the specific linkages varying from case to case and over time. Moreover, the separation of physical capital accumulation, human capital accumulation and technological progress is artificial since there are strong interrelationships and complementarities among them. Physical capital and innovation are inseparable, as most technological innovation is embodied in new machines and equipment. Moreover, if all firms benefit from technological progress and the latter is driven by capital accumulation, the social return on capital is much higher than its private return.[3] At the same time, physical capital and skill formation are complementary, as new technologically advanced equipment requires a labour force with adequate skills and education. Furthermore, the reallocation of labour among industries as investment takes place may also raise productivity, making it difficult to separate the contributions of labour productivity and physical capital.

Fostering a favourable investment climate

A favourable investment climate will encourage domestic savings and investment and also attract foreign inflows

Encouraging private investment requires both a favourable environment for such investment and financial institutions that can mobilize and direct financial resources to the persons and entities that can be expected to earn the greatest return commensurate with the risk. Many of the factors that create a favourable investment climate also inspire confidence in savers, so that investment and savings should both increase with an improvement in investment conditions. Similarly, the factors that encourage domestic investment are also likely to be conducive to foreign investment. At the same time, however, efforts to improve the investment climate should take into account their impact on overall development and related national goals, such as ensuring adequate economic and social protection for all members of society, including those in the labour force.

The Monterrey Consensus outlines some of the essential components of an enabling domestic environment

The Monterrey Consensus (para. 10) stresses that an "enabling domestic environment is vital for mobilizing domestic resources, increasing productivity, reducing capital flight, encouraging the private sector, and attracting and making effective use of international investment and assistance". It outlines the essential components of this enabling environment, including good governance, appropriate policy and regulatory frameworks, sound macroeconomic policies, transparency, adequate infrastructure and a developed financial sector. Certain institutions are crucial, especially effective legal systems, sound political institutions and well-functioning State bureaucracies.

It is difficult, though, to quantify a "favourable investment climate"

The importance now attached to developing a favourable investment climate is reflected in the numerous efforts to quantify its major components. There are, however, limits to the usefulness of measures of the quality of institutions and governance. In the first instance, as the experience of both developed and developing countries shows, there is no unique set of effective institutions for successful development; even in the recent past, there have been countries that achieved sound economic growth and a sustained reduction in poverty without conforming to the currently widely prescribed norms for governance, and institutional development and their links to national competitiveness. Second, there are methodological weaknesses in many such indicators (Herman, 2004). Finally, these indicators are likely to be subject to the bias of the organization undertaking the measurement (Lall, 2001).

National development strategies

Surveys by the World Bank (2005a) of more than 26,000 firms in 53 developing countries found that overall policy uncertainty was perceived as the most important negative aspect of a country's investment climate. A national development strategy in which a country's main objectives—including its response to the Millennium Development Goals and other internationally agreed targets—and policy orientations are made explicit can reduce uncertainty and thereby contribute to the creation of a favourable investment climate. The formulation of such a strategy assists in setting priorities and deciding on an appropriate sequence for government actions. The process of formulating a strategy itself provides an opportunity for consultations with business, labour and consumers, enhancing the chances of convergence regarding socio-economic objectives, production sector strategies and policy measures.

> A national development strategy can reduce uncertainty and help create a favourable investment climate

A central element of a national development strategy should be the identification of proposed government actions to improve the country's physical infrastructure. Infrastructure is an important determinant of firms' profitability, since it affects their costs of production. Limitations in physical infrastructure—especially power, telecommunications and transport—are a major obstacle for the activities of enterprises in developing countries. Concretely addressing such bottlenecks is the ultimate solution but identifying such proposed government actions beforehand should reduce the uncertainty about intentions, facilitating private sector planning and thereby stimulating investment.

> An essential part of this strategy should be the actions to improve the country's physical infrastructure

Production sector strategies, including those addressing agricultural and agro-industrial development, can provide similar support to the sustained expansion of existing businesses and to the willingness to enter new lines of business. Market-led growth or business activities may surge spontaneously in a particular branch of industry, agriculture or services. It is partly the task of the government to create conditions for the widening of such impulses and to bring about a sustained economic expansion. Policymakers, in interaction with the private sector, have an important role in identifying and encouraging the development of new sectors and activities in which a country, or a region within a country, may possess a potential comparative advantage. This requires the provision of quality infrastructure, education and training and policies to strengthen technological research and development and encourage innovation and learning in areas that have proved promising. In successful countries, export promotion has also played a key role in underpinning economic growth (see chap. II).

> Production sector strategies can help the expansion of existing businesses or the development of new businesses

There is also a need to look closely at the development of complementarities and networks, such as production sector clusters, that enhance the diffusion and impact of technical and organizational change (Ocampo, 2005). All these should aim to strengthen entrepreneurship and develop competitive firms in dynamic sectors that would generate economy-wide benefits and provide an impetus to growth and development. However, there is no single configuration of such production sector strategies for developing countries: the requisite policies need to vary in accordance with, inter alia, the economy's size and stage of economic development.

> Production sector networks can enhance the diffusion and impact of technical and organizational change, and so should be encouraged and strengthened

Macroeconomic stability

Macroeconomic
instability is a major
deterrent to
investment

Macroeconomic
stability comprises not
only nominal or
financial stability but
also real stability in
output and
employment

The surveys by the World Bank referred to above found that macroeconomic instability is the second most important negative aspect of a country's investment climate. Macroeconomic stability comprises not only nominal or financial stability but also real stability in output and employment.

Macroeconomic stability refers, first of all, to an economic environment characterized by sustainable fiscal accounts, moderate inflation, low interest rates and, importantly, low volatility of interest rates, of the exchange rate and, increasingly, of asset prices (stocks, real estate, etc.). The inefficiencies resulting from distortions and excessive volatility in these prices are likely to reduce the rate of sustainable growth and therefore have a dampening effect on investment; but macroeconomic stability also refers to a low volatility of growth and employment and its determinants, such as low interest rates and competitive exchange rates. In fact, *real* macroeconomic instability may have a larger negative influence on private investment than that exerted by a moderate rate of inflation. The importance of real macroeconomic stability has been demonstrated in Latin America, where volatility in macroeconomic variables has adversely affected private investment over the years (Economic Commission for Latin America and the Caribbean, 2004b).

Policymakers should
now pay attention to
"new fundamentals"
such as the strength of
the banking system

Improving the investment climate also requires that attention be given to an array of "new fundamentals", such as the strength of the banking system; the quality of bank supervision; the emergence of asset price bubbles; the exchange-rate exposure of the financial sector, the non-financial business sector and the government; distortions in the economy that cause inefficiency; the adequacy of the legal and financial infrastructure; and the use to which financial inflows have been put (Wachtel, 1999, pp. 315-316). In sum, the overall conduct of economic policy that provides the confidence necessary to raise savings and investment requires not only price stability and sound fiscal policies, but also policies that smooth the business cycle, maintain competitive exchange rates and ensure that external and internal sovereign debt portfolios, domestic financial systems and private sector balance sheets are all sound.

The legal and regulatory environment

Laws and regulations
evolve over time to
serve the public
interest and so there is
no ideal set

The purpose of laws and regulations is to safeguard the public interest. Laws and regulations in the industrialized countries have evolved with changing social, political and cultural conditions. As a result, they tend to vary among countries; for example, certain aspects of the legal and regulatory environment relating to businesses in European countries differ from those in Japan and the United States of America. There is no single or simple configuration of laws and regulations that can be termed ideal.

They can be inimical to
business by imposing
unnecessary costs,
increasing uncertainty
and risks and erecting
barriers to entry

Laws and regulations sometimes fail to meet their intended social objectives and, at the same time, harm the business environment by imposing unnecessary costs, increasing uncertainty and risks and erecting barriers to competition. There is therefore scope in many countries to improve the investment climate by reforming certain aspects of the regulatory and legal environment without compromising broader social goals. The ease with which such reforms can be implemented will vary among countries in line with their historical experience, their culture and their political institutions. In identifying priorities, there are three key areas where the legal and regulatory framework can have a strong impact on the business environment.

A first area relates to opening and closing a business. The World Bank suggests that the bureaucratic requirements with respect to starting a business in many countries are excessive and time-consuming. Latin America and sub-Saharan Africa are the regions in which it takes the most time to start a business. Nevertheless, improvements are being made in developing countries in all regions, as well as in many transition economies; notable examples are Argentina, Jordan, Morocco, Nepal and Sri Lanka (World Bank, 2005a).

The ability to close a business can be as important as opening a business because it may avert freezing usable assets in unproductive activities. At present, laws and regulations in a number of developing countries restrict the ability of enterprises to restructure or shut down. As part of their reforms in this area, a number of countries have improved their bankruptcy laws, an important aspect of which is the need to safeguard productive assets in the event of bankruptcy.

A second critical aspect of the legal and regulatory environment relates to property rights. In many developing countries, a large part of land property is not formally registered. Property titling can improve land values and access to credit (since land and capital may be used as collateral to obtain bank loans), especially for small enterprises and the informal sector. It also provides security for owners by reducing the risk of the laying of a claim to their land by someone else. However, property titling programmes need to be accompanied by a number of complementary measures if they are to be effective in achieving these objectives. Most importantly, there need to be accompanying improvements in the cost and efficiency of property registry so that property does not continue to be bought and sold informally. Among developing countries, some East Asian countries have developed an efficient property registration system. Complementary improvements are also required in collateral laws (so that it is not too expensive to mortgage property) and in the legal system (so that banks can seize collateral, if warranted, when a debtor defaults).

Third, the effective enforcement of contracts and the protection of creditor rights are of key importance to a well-functioning financial system (see below) and for an enabling business environment. These, in turn, require a well-functioning court system. The judicial procedure for resolving commercial disputes tends to be more bureaucratic in developing countries than in developed countries, although a number of developing countries have been making improvements in this area (World Bank, 2005a). Improved transparency and information can also facilitate the enforcement of contracts by enabling firms to know their potential partners' business history and credit standing in advance (see also below). Collateral law reform, mentioned above, should also help to enhance creditor rights.

Laws and regulations on such matters should be as simple as possible (compatible with achieving their objective), consistent with one another and simple to understand and apply. Moreover, they need to be backed by effective enforcement. This often calls for a strengthening of the administrative infrastructure and of the courts and ensuring that both operate in a fair and transparent manner.

Labour-market regulation, social protection and labour rights

The nature of the competitive market economy is such that enterprises will look for ways to cut costs. The government should set the boundaries of acceptable behaviour in this regard, so that cost-cutting represents efficiency gains and not exploitation of workers, of consumers or of any other subset of society. Labour standards are meant and designed to

The time required to open a new business is declining in many developing countries

Bankruptcy laws are also being revised to safeguard the productive assets in the event of bankruptcy

Property needs to be registered efficiently and improvement made so that mortgaging a property is easier and collateral can be seized in the event of default

A well-functioning court system is essential for the effective enforcement of contracts and the protection of creditor rights

Laws and regulations should be as simple as possible but backed by effective enforcement

Labour standards are needed to protect workers, but should not stifle the growth of private businesses

protect workers from actions of employers that are deemed to be socially undesirable. However, such standards can sometimes become overly stringent—for instance, in some countries, employers may be hindered by unnecessary reporting and detailed rules that do not achieve their intended effect but instead stifle the growth of private businesses and, by association, new job-creation. They may also contribute to the expansion of the informal sector where workers usually have no protection.

While flexibility in labour standards is advisable, stability of employment can increase the gains from "learning by doing" and encourage firms to invest in training

While moving towards greater flexibility in labour standards, countries should ensure that employment stability is not overly affected. There is evidence that stability of employment (tenure) is positively related to productivity gains; it can increase the gains from "learning by doing", as well as provide incentives for firms to invest in training (International Labour Organization, 2005). The objective should thus be to strike an adequate balance between flexibility and stability in employment.

Social protection should accompany any reform of labour standards

The reform of labour standards should include measures to ensure that workers receive the necessary social protection. Societies differ in how they define and provide social protection depending on their culture, values, traditions and institutional and political structures. Social protection is defined by the International Labour Organization as the set of public measures that a society provides to protect its members against the economic and social distress that may be caused by the absence, or a substantial reduction, of income from work as a result of various contingencies (sickness, maternity, employment injury, unemployment, invalidity, old age, or the death of a breadwinner). It also includes the provision of health care and the provision of benefits for families with children. By this definition, it is estimated that there is no formal social protection for some 80 per cent of the world's population, exposing them to enormous risk and vulnerability (García and Gruat, 2003).

Globalization has increased the need for social protection

The need for social protection has become greater as a result of globalization which, along with its benefits, has increased the vulnerability of workers to job insecurity and unemployment. Such risks can arise from competing imports, reversals in FDI or other capital flows, and cost-cutting by firms, including the introduction of labour-saving technologies. The pressures of global competition can lead to the use of non-standard and less secure forms of employment, such as part-time or temporary work. There is also a danger that the labour standards referred to above may not always be adhered to under such arrangements. Finally, there is evidence that the pressures of globalization are giving rise to increased "informalization" of the labour market, with the majority of the world's labour force working in the informal sector where conditions are often hazardous and there is little or no security of employment or income.

Social protection can be viewed as a sound investment ...

Social protection should be considered an investment. While its economic and financial affordability may sometimes be problematic in the short term, the longer-term economic and social costs of neglecting it can be immense. These costs include decreasing life expectancy, health and productivity, and rising poverty, none of which are propitious for investment. The absence of social support can also reduce poor people's investments in education and skills and thereby diminish the current and future stock of a country's human capital. Finally, there may be a loss of social capital: social trust and cohesion are essential for the functioning of democratic societies and their loss could adversely affect political stability.

... as it promotes human and social potentials and opportunities

Given concerns about the inadequacy of coverage provided by orthodox social protection, it has been argued that its focus should be extended beyond the provision of minimum well-being and the protection from risk, to the promotion of human and social potentials and opportunities (García and Gruat, 2003). Such an approach calls for measures that guarantee access to essential goods and services, promote active socio-economic security and advance individual and social potential for poverty reduction and sustainable development.

Overall, a critical challenge is to find an appropriate balance between the social protection of the world's population and the provision of an enabling investment climate for business. In the longer term, the two go hand in hand since, in its broadest sense, adequate social protection not only serves to reduce poverty (and thereby raise demand) but also facilitates the development of a healthy, skilled and confident workforce and helps control the social and political risks that businesses face.

Social protection and a healthier investment climate go hand in hand

Domestic financial institutions and development

A well-functioning financial system enhances investment and growth. Developing countries diverge significantly in their level of financial development. While many countries continue to have significant limitations in this regard, others have experienced substantial financial deepening in recent years. This process is a continuing one, as financial markets and institutions have evolved with both the national economy and the international financial system. The major challenges for economic policy lie in three areas: guaranteeing an adequate supply of long-term financing in the domestic currency; making financial services available to all groups of society; and developing an adequate system of prudential regulation and supervision that guarantees the stability of the financial system. Through either direct or indirect interventions, economic policy plays an essential role in all of these areas.

A well-functioning financial system enhances investment and growth

Development of the banking sector

The advent of commercial banks reflects an early phase of the development of the financial sector in almost all countries and commercial banks usually continue to serve as the cornerstone of the financial system even as other financial institutions emerge with the evolution of the financial sector. In many developing countries, however, the development of the financial sector has not advanced far beyond commercial banks. Moreover, these institutions are usually limited in the range of financial services that they provide, often as a matter of choice but sometimes in response to government directives. As a result, many needs for financial services remain unmet, compromising development possibilities. Compounding this difficulty, banking systems have failed in several developing and transition economies in recent decades, wreaking havoc on development in the countries concerned, frequently with adverse spillover effects on other countries.

In many developing countries, financial services are provided only by commercial banks, which in turn supply only a limited range of services

Weaknesses in the banking system contributed to the severity of the Mexican peso crisis of 1994 and the Asian crisis of 1997-1998, among others. The costs of resolving these failures can be large and their economic impact severe: the fiscal cost of the banking crisis in Chile in 1981-1985 is estimated to have been 41 per cent of GDP while the equivalent costs of the Asian crisis for Thailand and Indonesia were 32 and 29 per cent of GDP, respectively. The recovery of the banking sector in crisis countries is usually a lengthy process, often conditioned by slow progress in corporate restructuring. Improving the institutional framework of the sector is widely seen as the best approach to preventing or resolving these crises.

Failures of banking systems have generated severe costs

Recent reforms, and
an improving global
economy, have
strengthened banking
systems in developing
countries

Recent reforms of the banking sector in many developing countries and economies in transition are already showing in the performance of banks (see table I.2). The improved global economic situation since 2003 has supported the recovery of banks in these countries. Financial soundness indicators on average point to solid rates of return on assets and sustained improvements in capital and asset quality. Especially in Central and Eastern Europe and Asia, banks are performing well; but, despite economic recovery, other regions still have underlying weaknesses in the banking sector.

Asian banking systems
have shown
considerable
improvement, but
some problems remain

In Asia, banks' earnings, asset quality and capital adequacy have steadily improved since 2003. In key countries, banks' performance has been bolstered by Government-supported disposals of impaired assets. However, the region's ratio of non-performing loans (NPLs) to total assets, while declining, remains high; problem loans are especially prevalent at State-owned banks. Corporate restructuring is also lagging behind other regulatory reforms in some countries. Authorities in the region are moving towards addressing these structural issues in their banking systems. In China, for instance, the Government is making efforts to redress weaknesses at State-owned banks, some of which have been recapitalized.

European transition
economies have seen
heavy involvement of
foreign banks, but
currency mismatches
could cause future
problems

European transition countries have achieved a faster improvement in their banking sectors, with a declining likelihood of default, higher profitability and better prospects for growth. This improvement has been reflected in strong bank ratings. Expansion by foreign banks in a number of countries is driving the improved results. However, rapid credit growth, especially in the retail sector and intermediated mostly by foreign banks, poses a risk in some countries. The risks are greater in countries where a high degree of dollar/euroization, including of loans, exposes banks to direct exchange-rate and related credit risk. In some countries, mortgage credit has been a major component of new lending and banks have become correspondingly more exposed to the real estate market.

Improvement was also
marked in Latin
America while ...

Banking systems in Latin America generally appear sound, with the exception of those in countries emerging from financial crises. Even the countries most affected by major financial crises have seen some rebound in financial intermediation and an increase in bank soundness. Both stock indicators, such as capitalization and NPL ratios, and flow indicators, such as profitability, are stable or improving and so is investor confidence. The

Table I.2.

Indicators of bank financial soundness in developing regions and European emerging markets, 2002-2004

Percentage									
	Return on assets			Non-performing loans to total loans			Regulatory capital to risk-weighted assets		
	2002	2003	2004	2002	2003	2004	2002	2003	2004
Asia	0.8	1.0	1.5	12.7	11.2	10.1	14.5	15.2	14.8
Latin America	-2.6	1.0	1.4	12.5	10.1	8.6	13.2	14.3	16.2
Western Asia	1.1	1.3	..	15.4	15.2	..	15.6	15.0	..
Sub-Saharan Africa	2.7	3.0	..	19.9	17.3	..	17.7	15.7	..
Emerging Europe	1.5	1.6	1.7	9.3	8.0	7.8	17.5	17.1	16.0

Source: IMF, *Global Financial Stability Report: Market Developments and Issues: April 2005* (Washington, D.C., IMF, 2005), p. 35.

depreciation of the United States dollar may have contributed to financial strengthening in countries with currencies tied to the dollar. In general, banking systems in the region look well placed to handle an increase in international interest rates (which is relevant where banks are funded by net foreign borrowing) and the direct credit risk from rapidly growing consumer and mortgage lending.

Performance in banking systems in Western and Central Asia and Africa has been more mixed. Generally, banks in the oil-exporting countries remain highly liquid and profitable, but financial soundness indicators point to a marginal weakening in banks' performance in Western Asia. There have been improvements in the banking sector in South Africa, a regional financial centre, but banking systems in a number of other African countries continue to have serious weaknesses and reforms are progressing slowly. A large exposure to sovereign debt and a high degree of dollarization remain the main risks in most countries.

... performance of banking systems in Western and Central Asia and Africa has been more mixed

Despite the current relatively benign state of affairs and most banks' improved resilience, banking systems in developing countries continue to face risks. In countries in which banks have funded themselves on the international market, low global interest rates have contributed to a strengthening of balance sheets because of increased profits resulting from the wider margins earned on domestic loans. To the extent that these gains have been distributed and on-lent rather than added to capital or reserves, banks will need to adjust to the opposite effects on their balance sheets if, as widely expected, international interest rates rise.

Banking systems in developing countries still face important risks

Development of domestic capital markets

Driven both by domestic economic development itself and by the innovation and globalization of financial markets, domestic capital markets in developing countries and the economies in transition have expanded rapidly since the early 1990s. In several cases, they now provide a viable alternative to domestic bank lending and international capital flows as a source of funding for private sector investment. In particular, there has been a surge in local bond issuance in a number of developing countries (see table I.3); in some cases, bonds have become the single largest source of domestic funding for the public and private sectors.

Domestic capital markets in developing countries and economies in transition have expanded rapidly since the early 1990s

The use of financial markets by public and private sectors differs across regions. For the public sector, bonds have become the largest source of local financing in certain developing countries. In Latin America, domestic bonds have also become the dominant source of funding for the corporate sector. There has also been a sharp increase in corporate bond issuance in a number of Asian countries. In Central and Eastern Europe, domestic bank lending is also the largest source of corporate finance but privatization has helped make domestic equity issuance the second largest.

Different regions rely on different domestic sources of finance: bonds, bank loans and equity

There are many reasons for the development of local capital markets, especially bond markets, in developing countries over recent years. One has been the competitive urge to improve the intermediation of domestic savings by offering new financial instruments that broaden the set of savings options available. This has become more important as a number of developing countries have privatized their pension systems. In Chile, for example, private pension and insurance funds have generated demand for corporate bonds, reflecting a desire to obtain longer-term assets that better match their obligations and, at the same time, earn a higher rate of return than can be obtained on bank deposits

Many factors, including the development of private pension schemes, are contributing to the development of local capital markets

Table I.3.

Capital raised in domestic financial markets of developing countries and economies in transition, by region, 1997-2002

	Billions of dollars						
	1997	1998	1999	2000	2001	2002	1997-2002
Total[a]	675	869	514	695	685	879	4 317
Equities	37	33	43	25	19	17	174
Bonds	399	639	394	456	510	522	2 920
Bank loans	239	198	77	214	155	340	1 223
Asiab[b]	160	243	268	326	339	662	1 998
Equities	28	17	36	21	11	15	127
Bonds	7	43	47	98	148	235	577
Bank loans	125	184	186	206	181	411	1 294
Latin America[c]	478	556	191	315	258	153	1 952
Equities	8	9	5	4	7	1	34
Bonds	349	548	287	300	297	245	2 027
Bank loans	122	-2	-100	11	-47	-93	-109
Central Europe[d]	37	70	54	54	87	64	367
Equities	1	7	3	1	1	0	14
Bonds	43	48	60	57	65	42	315
Bank loans	-8	16	-9	-4	21	22	38

Sources: Dealogic; IMF, *International Financial Statistics;* Standard & Poor's, *Emerging Market Database;* Hong Kong Monetary Authorities; and Tesouro Nacional, Brazil.

a   Including sovereign issuances.
b   Comprising China, Hong Kong SAR, Malaysia, Republic of Korea, Singapore and Thailand.
c   Comprising Argentina, Brazil, Chile and Mexico.
d   Comprising Czech Republic, Hungary and Poland.

(International Monetary Fund, 2003b). A parallel reason for the development of local capital markets has been the effort to attract foreign savings, including those of foreign institutional investors.

Local capital markets also contribute to domestic financial stability

Local capital markets can also contribute to domestic financial stability. Deeper local currency bond and equity markets reduce reliance on the foreign currency debt that has made the corporate sector in several developing countries vulnerable to currency movements and to the volatility and pro-cyclicality of international capital flows. Local currency corporate bonds also reduce the maturity mismatches that occur as a result of firms' financing long-term projects with short-term loans from the banking system. Finally, local capital markets reduce the concentration of risks within the banking sector and thereby ensure greater dispersion of risk across the economy as a whole.

A range of measures have been taken to develop local capital markets ...

Measures adopted to develop local capital markets have typically encompassed efforts to strengthen market infrastructure, create benchmark bond issues, expand the set of institutional investors and improve corporate governance and transparency. With respect to market infrastructure, the priority has often been the establishment of a liquid government security benchmark in order to facilitate the pricing of corporate bonds, followed by the development of trading, clearing and settlement systems and the establishment of independent rating agencies. However, these measures are unlikely to be sufficient unless key underlying constraints on the issuance and purchase of corporate securities are also addressed (Sharma, 2001).

Measures to expand the set of institutional investors are of key importance in developing a strong issuer and investor base. Local pension funds have played an important role in the development of local securities markets in Latin America and Central Europe and are also beginning to have an impact in some Asian countries. At the same time, many countries control the allocation of pension funds' assets in order to prevent excessive risk-taking and this has slowed the growth of the investor base in some cases. For its part, the growth of an investor base can, in turn, be an important stimulant to developing the requisite infrastructure for capital markets.

... including expanding the range of institutional investors

The growth of an investor base is also related to corporate governance and transparency. Corporate governance can be strengthened in a number of ways, including through laws to protect investors, better enforcement of these laws and contracts, and improved regulation, disclosure and supervision. Other measures to strengthen corporate governance and transparency include changes to laws governing capital markets and approving best practice codes in order to, among other things, improve disclosure and protect minority shareholder rights. Studies show that better protection of minority shareholders is correlated with the development of equity markets, although overregulation can impose large costs on issuers and thereby restrict the development of local capital markets. For example, rigid laws protecting minority shareholders could deter larger investors, including foreign investors. Reflecting such concerns, minority shareholder rights were reduced in Brazil in 1997 in order to speed up the privatization process (International Monetary Fund, 2003b).

Improving corporate governance and transparency helps expand the investor base

The base of issuers and investors can also depend on institutional arrangements and concentration in the corporate sector. In a number of South-East Asian countries, there is evidence that the interlocking relationships among corporations, banks and Governments have dissuaded companies from issuing bonds (Sharma, 2001). At the same time, there may be a negative relationship between concentration of control in the corporate sector by a few business families and indicators of judicial efficiency and enforcement (Claessens, Djankov and Lang, 1999; La Porta, Lopez-de-Silanes and Vishney, 1996). In such cases, policy measures to develop corporate bond markets could include making the banking sector more arm's-length in its dealings with companies and reducing the concentration of wealth and strengthening competition in the corporate sector.

Institutional factors and the degree of concentration in the corporate sector can also affect the development of the bond market

There is also the question how to sequence these measures and, more broadly, the growth of local securities markets as compared with other financial institutions, such as banks. There is no simple optimal sequencing strategy. Local capital markets provide an alternative source of financing to the banking system (especially debt markets), but a healthy banking sector is essential to the development of these complementary markets. Especially in the case of bond markets, banks can play an important role in providing liquidity to market operators, as well as in settling transactions. They also provide custodial services and undertake investment banking functions, such as underwriting and serving as market-makers. A healthy banking sector is an important precondition for the development of securities markets.

While the sequencing of measures to develop different financial institutions is important, a healthy banking sector is a precondition for the development of securities markets

Long-term financing

Developing countries
need fixed capital
investment and
infrastructure, and
therefore long-
term finance

As argued above, fixed capital investment is essential for long-term growth. Adequate physical infrastructure is, in turn, a necessary component of a favourable investment climate. Developing countries' needs for infrastructure are growing rapidly. The World Bank (2004f) estimates that the financing needs for new infrastructure investment and maintenance expenditures are about 7 per cent of GDP for all developing countries and as much as 9 per cent of GDP for low-income countries. Both fixed capital and infrastructure are long-term investments and, ideally, require corresponding long-term financing.

Yet long-term finance
is insufficient in
developing countries

Private financial markets in developing countries, left to themselves, usually fail to provide enough long-term finance to undertake the investments necessary for economic and social development. Firms in developing countries often hold a smaller portion of their total debt in long-term instruments than do firms in developed countries (Demirgüç-Kunt and Maksimovic, 1996).[4]

Market imperfections
can explain some of
the shortage of long-
term finance

There are three main reasons for the insufficient provision of long-term finance: market imperfections in the financial sector; the characteristics of borrowers in the country; and macroeconomic factors that may inhibit the provision of long-term credit. First, market imperfections, or institutional factors, in financial markets contribute to the insufficiency of long-term finance. Credit providers—typically commercial banks in developing countries—typically have short-term liabilities and thus prefer the use of short-term lending as a way of reducing the risks associated to a mismatch in their portfolio. They also use short-term credit as a means to monitor and control borrowers and they are more likely to use this approach if the financial infrastructure, including accounting, auditing and contract enforcement systems, is inadequately developed. In these circumstances, it is costly, if not impossible, to enforce loan covenants and to monitor the balance-sheet positions of the borrower over a long period of time. Lenders prefer short-term lending because it allows them to check the borrower's position frequently and, if necessary, change the terms of the financing before the borrower is forced to declare default.

Different firms have
different needs for
long-term finance

Second, the term structure of finance in an economy also depends on the characteristics of firms. Firms are likely to try to match the maturity of their assets and liabilities; firms with mostly fixed assets, such as land, buildings and heavy equipment, are likely to seek and to be able to obtain a longer debt maturity structure. A "new" industry, which is likely to experience a long gestation period before producing any profits, needs long-term finance to match these characteristics. Small retailers, restaurants and similar businesses, on the other hand, do not require, nor would they likely receive, substantial long-term debt.

Larger firms find it
easier to raise long-
term finance

Firm size is another characteristic that affects the term structure of a country's finance, even in the most developed financial system. It is generally more expensive to acquire information about small firms because they are less likely to be publicly traded, and because the disclosure requirements for smaller firms are more lenient than for larger ones. This information deficiency is likely to encourage creditors to offer a series of short-term credits instead of one long-term credit.[5] Even in developed countries, small and medium-sized enterprises receive a smaller portion of their external financing in the form of long-term debt. Developing countries, where small firms are more dominant, are therefore likely to have less overall long-term debt.

High and
unpredictable inflation
can deter investment
in long-term
instruments

Third, high inflation or unpredictable inflation discourages savings in financial instruments, particularly those with a long maturity, unless they are designed to compensate for such instability, for example, through indexing (and even this is generally an imperfect form of compensation). On the other hand, policies to curb inflation usually involve high real interest rates and these reduce the effective demand for credit: firms claim that they would like more credit, but not at the prevailing market interest rate.

A typical answer to the underprovision of long-term financing by the private sector is provided by public sector financial institutions. Development banks have been created not only in developing countries, but also in developed countries. These institutions have often provided industry with long-term finance for industrial development or for national reconstruction, as was the case after the First and Second World Wars. Some of them are recognized as having played a critical role in the rapid industrialization of some countries (de Aghion, 1999).

Development banks have been a means to provide finance for longer-term development and reconstruction

Although there is a clear trend towards increasing private sector participation in banking services around the world, public sector banks continue to play a central role in many countries. By the 1970s, the State had owned 40 per cent of the assets of the largest commercial and development banks in industrialized countries and 65 per cent of assets of the largest banks in developing countries (Levy Yeyati, Micco and Panizza, 2005). By the mid-1990s, a wave of privatizations had reduced these shares to about one quarter and one half of the assets of the largest banks in the industrialized and developing countries, respectively. There were, however, large differences across regions: the State owned nearly 90 per cent of the assets of the largest banks in South Asia, whereas the corresponding ratios in Latin America and East Asia were about 40 per cent and in sub-Saharan Africa 30 per cent (Micco and Panizza, 2005).

Not all the development banks established in developing countries to provide long-term credit for development purposes have been able to replicate earlier successes. Inadequate cost-benefit evaluation of projects, mismanagement and high arrears have often brought national and regional public development banks to the brink of collapse. The critical question is what distinguishes success from failure.

The record of development banks has been a mixed one in developing countries

Some development banks succeeded because they fostered the acquisition and dissemination of expertise in long-term industrial financing: success was less dependent on the quantity of credit they supplied. The corollary is that commercial banks in developing countries are unable to provide long-term finance because they are unwilling to bear the large risks that they associate with financing such projects and this is related, in turn, to the lack of the specialized skills to examine and monitor risky long-term investment, suggesting that it may be desirable to design institutional arrangements in which development banks play an essential role in the creation of new markets, including different mechanisms for long-term lending, but with a clear view to allowing the private sector to play the leading role as the new market mechanisms spread out. This means, in turn, that there could be several possible public-private partnerships, co-financing arrangements or even co-ownership.

Where they succeeded was through acquiring and disseminating expertise in long-term financing

Another common feature of successful development banks is their clearly set time limit on the advantages that they provide to borrowers. Successful development banks tend to keep interest rate subsidies minimal in the case of directed credit programmes or to extend subsidized loans only to small firms. After the expiry of the loan period, borrowers are often expected to "graduate" from development financing and raise funds in the market. In contrast, some development banks in many developing countries have subsidized interest rates heavily, sometimes making them negative in real terms, and have directed loans to monopolistic enterprises, many of them established by the government. In such circumstances, development banks do not put enough effort into collecting information on borrowers and monitoring their activities. Especially when the projects are politically selected, the development bank tends to view the government as the ultimate and only risk-holder.

Successful development banks have tended to set a time limit to their involvement

The role of
development banks
should be viewed as
complementary to,
rather than as
substituting for, private
sector financial
development.

This means that national development banks can play a role both in the creation of markets for long-term financing and in guaranteeing access to financial services by the poor (see below). However, the institutional design should avoid excessive public sector risks and badly targeted interest rate subsidies, and should incorporate a view of the activities of development banks as complementary to those of the private sector and, indeed, a view of the banks themselves as agents of innovation that should in the long-run encourage rather than limit private sector financial development.

The changing roles of the public and private sectors in financing infrastructure

The public sector plays
a central role in the
provision and
financing of
infrastructure but its
shortcomings have led
to the direction of
attention to private
sector involvement

It has long been recognized that capital markets are likely to underfinance such socially desirable investments as infrastructure and that the public sector has a potential role in overcoming this market failure (Atkinson and Stiglitz, 1980; Stiglitz, 1994). A first option, which applies particularly to investments in infrastructure, is for the public sector to undertake the investment itself and then to own and operate said infrastructure as a public utility. However, the perceived shortcomings of public ownership have resulted in partial or complete privatization of public utilities over recent years. At the same time, fiscal constraints have increasingly placed limits on public infrastructure spending in many developing countries.

Private investment in
infrastructure had
peaked in the late
1990s but then fell

These factors had prompted many countries to try to attract private investors into infrastructure in the 1990s. Initially, private participation in infrastructure in developing countries expanded rapidly, reaching a peak of close to US$ 130 billion in 1997. However, it subsequently collapsed and was only a little above US$ 40 billion in 2004.

A new balance
between public and
private funding is
being sought

In parallel with this decline in the quantity of private funding, a new balance between public and private sector roles for infrastructure financing and service provision has emerged. In particular, it is increasingly recognized that the viability of private participation in infrastructure may vary widely across sectors, countries and even regions within countries. Private funding has been successful in the telecommunications sector and can also have an important role in financing and participating in the power sector. However, private considerations do not always adequately capture the broader externalities, in particular the longer-term economic and social benefits, in such areas as transportation, water and sanitation. Therefore, the public sector continues to play an essential role in the financing and provision of such public goods. It may also be appropriate for multilateral development banks to become more active in financing projects in these areas (see chap. IV).

Public/private
partnerships have both
advantages and
disadvantages ...

Public/private partnerships offer an intermediate between full State control and complete private ownership. Public/private partnerships have been successfully undertaken in a number of sectors, such as telecommunications, highways and airports, where user fees can be established and investors are able to earn adequate returns (World Bank, 2004f). However, these partnerships often have high transaction costs, are difficult to establish and sustain, and may require significant public sector guarantees that involve uncertain future public sector liabilities. Many of them have failed to meet expectations.

... so each Government
must decide on the
optimal public/
private mix

Each Government must decide on the optimal public/private mix. In areas where private participation is desired, one objective should be to maximize the amount of private capital per unit of available public resources. One means of doing so would be to strengthen the ability of multilateral development banks to engage with sub-sovereign infrastructure-related entities and to develop instruments for risk mitigation at that level.

There has been considerable discussion of the welfare effects of private provision of essential utilities and services—such as water, health and transport—by local or foreign investors. The general concern about the underprovision of services that may not necessarily be the most profitable but that have social value is particularly pronounced in such areas. In addition, privatization requires the introduction of user fees and, without accompanying subsidies, the poor may not be able to afford essential services (Kessler and Alexander, 2004).

To some degree, the welfare outcomes of private provision depend upon the accompanying policy and regulatory frameworks (Kikeri and Nellis, 2004). These could include, for example, subsidy mechanisms to ensure that the poor have access to affordable essential services, better tailoring of privatization to local conditions and a regulatory system that promotes competition yet also takes into account each country's unique political, legal and institutional context. In practice, however, achieving these conditions may be difficult for developing countries that have weak regulatory capacity. Moreover, there is no evidence that subsidy systems under private provision are any more effective than those under public provision (Kessler and Alexander, 2004).

Therefore, the private provision of essential services by foreign and local investors is more likely to have positive welfare impacts in those countries that have compatible regulatory, policy and institutional frameworks. However, many developing countries fall short in this respect and building capacity in these areas is usually a long-term and evolutionary process. In such countries, at least in the short term, there may be options for successfully reforming existing public infrastructure services without changing ownership.

The development of inclusive financial sectors

Financial services in the form of savings accounts, loans, insurance and payments facilities, including international remittances, are available only to a small proportion of the world's population. Countries in sub-Saharan Africa are far behind most other regions in expanding the reach of financial access (except South Africa, where about half the population has access). In Brazil and Colombia, only about 40 per cent of the population has a bank account (Peachey and Roe, 2004). However, Asian and Central European countries have made greater progress in facilitating financial access (Imboden, 2005).

Typically, it is the poor who have no or very limited access to the financial system. This lack of access to finance has become a matter of wider development-related concern because deeper and more inclusive financial systems are linked to economic development and poverty alleviation.

Limited access to financial services by the poor has various causes: physical distance from retail facilities, lack of financial literacy and business skills, high transaction costs for financial institutions (which are passed on as high fees), deficiencies in understanding and managing risk in lending to the poor, and biases against certain segments of the economically active population. An additional factor in some countries is the mistrust of potential clients towards formal financial institutions. In some Latin American countries, for example, poor people lost confidence in the banking system after they had lost their life savings during financial crises or when Governments froze the funds of financial institutions to restore financial order. In some cases, financial institutions collapsed owing to the theft or fraudulent use of the people's funds.

Special issues are raised when essential services, such as water, health and transport, are provided by private sources ...

... highlighting the need for appropriate policy and regulatory frameworks

However, capacity-building in these areas is a lengthy process

The reach of financial services is limited in developing countries ...

... with the poor having little or no access

This limited access has many causes

A large proportion of the poor would like to have access to the financial system for saving purposes. Savings may cover consumption needs, assist in special or emergency family situations, or be used as "seed" money for microentrepreneurial activities. At the same time, starting micro- and small enterprises often requires access to lending, because spending on working capital and technology usually exceeds the limited amounts saved. Given the limited access to the financial system by the poor, the need for financial services has been either unmet or covered by informal institutions or moneylenders.

There is a need for the poor and micro- and small enterprises to have access to financial services

The absence of complementary institutions also restricts access to financial services by the poor. In some countries, parts of the financial infrastructure—sources of information on borrowers (for example, credit bureaux), effective and independent courts and bankruptcy legislation—are missing or inadequate. For example, a study of Kenya found that limited information-sharing on borrowers, uncertainties regarding the effectiveness of the legal and judicial system, the limited number of reputable banks and non-transparency and uncertainty in banking markets were the major factors restricting access to the financial system.

Complementary institutions such as credit bureaux and effective courts and bankruptcy legislation are missing

Millions of the poor who do not have access to financial institutions nevertheless save and lend in small quantities through informal institutions. Among the best-known informal institutions are the rotating savings and credit associations (ROSCAs) which take "deposits" from a group of individuals and lend the total receipts to each member sequentially. They require smaller amounts of money for the initial deposit than formal institutions do, and are more flexible in the services offered, terms of lending, payback period and form of repayment, which might be, for example, in currency, in service, or in kind. In general, loans offered by rotating savings and credit associations have lower transaction costs and lower risk of default than formal loans. Most of these institutions are part of the community they lend to and are able to use their knowledge about borrowers to screen loan participants. Peer pressure and social sanctions can be important in reducing monitoring and enforcement costs.

In the absence of formal institutions, the poor often have recourse to informal institutions such as rotating savings and credit associations

Informal finance often accounts for two thirds of the finance in rural areas of Africa, but the proportion is lower elsewhere. Surveys in Madagascar and Pakistan indicate informal institutions accounted for about one third of informal credit in the early 1990s. While providing an essential service, informal lending institutions may hinder the advancement of the poor and the development of micro- and small businesses. Informal loans are usually small and short-term and the geographical area serviced is often limited.

Some informal credit sources and moneylenders demand high interest rates (from 5 to 30 per cent per month) and are able to do so because of their monopolistic power and the risks involved in this type of transaction. People pay the high interest rates to moneylenders because they have no alternative. A variety of financial institutions have been established to create an alternative for extending small-scale loans and offering savings services to the poor, but their charges are typically also high because of the high cost of such small transactions. These lenders include small non-governmental organizations, and savings and credit cooperatives, some of which, such as the Grameen Bank of Bangladesh, have become large institutions.

The fact that informal credit sources and moneylenders can demand high interest rates has led to the creation of alternative sources of financing for the poor

Microfinance has improved the prospects for many small enterprises around the world. Microfinance activities involve small loans, typically for working capital, employ substitutes for collateral and streamlined procedures, and offer swift and frequent access. Microfinance clients are often self-employed low-income entrepreneurs and households in both urban and rural areas. Loan amounts vary according to the country and regional settings. The Grameen Bank in Bangladesh, imitated with varying degrees of suc-

Microfinance has grown rapidly, but still reaches only a small percentage of potential beneficiaries

cess in more than 45 countries, has provided credit to over 2 million poor people. Today, about 60 million people benefit from microcredit around the world. Yet, however large it is in absolute numbers, the reach of microcredit is small in terms of the potential beneficiaries. In Western Africa, for example, 5 million people benefit from microcredit, but this represents only 7 per cent of the total population and only 15 per cent of the economically active population.

Several initiatives, coming from both Governments and the private sector, have attempted to extend the access of formal financial institutions that offer services to the poor by bridging formal and informal finance networks. By 1995, a federation of 155 credit unions in Togo with 50,000 members had linked its member unions to financial institutions, so that each union was able to increase funds for lending, place liquid funds in low-risk financial instruments and diversify risk. The Badan Kredit Kecamatan in Indonesia and the Bank for Agriculture and Agricultural Cooperatives in Thailand are other examples of institutions that reach the poor and still make a profit. Other formal institutions have lent directly to group-based financial arrangements (for example, ROSCAs), non-governmental organizations and credit unions or created ROSCAs themselves, for example, in India and the Republic of Korea. In Senegal, a reform of the agricultural credit programme entailed forming village groups that elected a president who, acting as an intermediary, screened, allocated and enforced credit terms (United Nations, 1999).

In many countries, access to financial services has been limited by the absence of a bank in poor neighbourhoods. Today, telecommunications and information technologies are opening up new possibilities for the poor. Satellite connections and hand-held devices, including cellular phones, are reducing the barrier of geographical distance, thereby making it feasible for financial institutions to serve the poor. In Mali, for example, agents of savings and credit cooperatives are able to offer and update banking services to dispersed clients by using a hand-held electronic device, while in India, the ICICI Bank has put ATMs on trucks so that clients in distant villages can carry out transactions and have easier access to their accounts.

Remittance flows have become an increasingly important source of financial resources for the families of emigrants and a potential component of an inclusive financial sector. A large proportion of these flows, however, are transmitted through informal channels, lessening the potential positive impact on the migrants' families and their communities. Informal channels are used because of insufficient interest on the part of the financial system in small money transactions (which often average between 100 and 300 United States dollars) and because of the socio-economic situation of many migrant families, with recipients living in distant areas and low levels of schooling.

There is a potential for using remittances to introduce the poor to financial institutions specialized in their needs, such as microfinance institutions, savings and credit cooperatives and postal savings banks. Tapping this potential could have multiplicative effects on the local and regional economies. Some private and multilateral initiatives to decrease the transmission cost of remittances and support microfinance projects, for instance, through the Multilateral Investment Fund of the Inter-American Development Bank, have had positive results. Remittances could serve as the basis for financial institutions' opening and expanding their services, to include, for example, savings accounts and microcredits to the families and local communities of emigrants.

Efforts are being made to offer services to the poor by bridging formal and informal finance networks

Telecommunications and information technologies are opening up possibilities of extending financial services to the poor

Remittances are often sent through informal channels ...

... whereas they could serve as a basis for an expansion of financial services

The "missing middle"—larger than a microenterprise but too small to be serviced by a commercial bank—also needs financial services

While such improvements in access of the poor to savings, credit and transfer payment services, as well as micro-insurance, are important, there is a limit to the gains that can be made at the "micro" level, in particular as regards support of enterprises. Greater needs for management skills, working capital, technology and access to markets have been among the main obstacles faced by small enterprises as they try to expand. Microbusinesses must gain economies of scale if they are to contribute more substantially to employment-generation and economic growth. This points to the need for expanded financial services for the "missing middle" of enterprises that are too big to be adequately serviced by microfinance institutions but not large enough to be an attractive customer for a commercial bank.

The future direction of microcredit is a subject for debate

Microcredit itself has followed a small business enterprise model in many countries while it has expanded into large institutions of national scope in a few countries. A major topic for debate in the microfinance industry globally is whether, and then how, to become more like a bank, without succumbing to the risk incurred by these institutions of losing their focus on servicing the poor.

Towards sounder national financial systems

There has been an extensive liberalization of the financial sector in the last few decades

Over the past few decades, there has been extensive liberalization of the financial sector in many countries, including the decontrol of interest rates, the reduction of direct government allocation of credit, the removal of barriers to entry of competing financial institutions and the elimination or reduction of restrictions on financial activities. Such measures have, in many cases, been accompanied by varying degrees of privatization and liberalization of controls on capital flows in and out of countries.

In many developing countries, the fact that financial liberalization had often been attempted without having in place adequate regulatory capacity led to banking crises

In many developing countries, particularly in Asia, financial liberalization has increased the size and depth of the financial sector. In many instances, however, financial market liberalization preceded the development of an adequate regulatory capacity. While direct controls had been largely dismantled, new, indirect mechanisms of regulation were not put fully in place. This resulted in credit booms, maturity mismatches (lending long-term on the basis of short-term deposits), currency mismatches (that is to say, lending in local currency but borrowing in foreign currency) and, eventually, banking crises.

The resulting crises prompted regulatory reform ...

Such experiences themselves prompted regulatory reform. Indeed, many regulatory reforms in developing countries have come about as a reaction to crises or problems in the financial system rather than as pre-emptive undertakings (Stallings and Studart, 2002). There is now widespread recognition that reforms of the financial system require parallel reforms, and frequently strengthening, of the relevant legal, regulatory and administrative structures and that these should be phased in gradually as the financial sector develops.

... aimed at guaranteeing the stability of the financial system and that of the economy at large

Financial regulation aims primarily at reducing the risks that some form of miscalculation or other error by a financial institution might pose for the financial sector more generally and thus for the economy at large. This is achieved by imposing restrictions both on the way banks and similar institutions finance their operations and on how they allocate their portfolios. The aim is to ensure that financial institutions engage in adequate assessment of the risks implied in their activities, make provisions for expected losses and maintain sufficient capital to absorb unexpected losses.

These reforms have followed, with a lag, reforms of financial regulation in the industrialized countries which, since the late 1970s, have entailed just such a move from a "top-down" approach to an indirect approach involving a framework of rules and guidelines that set minimum standards of prudent conduct within which financial institutions are free, or at least more free, to take commercial decisions. This may be interpreted as a move away from regulation and towards supervision, that is to say, a move away from compliance with portfolio constraints towards an assessment of the overall management of a financial firm's business and the multiple sources of risk that it is likely to confront (Crockett, 2001a).

Financial regulation and supervision do not exist in a vacuum. For financial regulation to be effective, there should be a solid infrastructure that allows the economy to function properly. In addition to sound and sustainable macroeconomic policies, this includes a legal and judicial framework, particularly workable bankruptcy arrangements, reliable accounting practices used to value financial assets, the availability of relevant statistics, procedures for the efficient resolution of problems in financial institutions, an appropriate safety net, an effective payment and settlement system and sound principles of corporate governance (see, on some of these issues, the discussion on the enabling business environment). These preconditions for effective financial supervision are not firmly in place in all developed nor in many developing countries (International Monetary Fund, 2004). Weaknesses in the underpinning infrastructure can render useless the most careful supervisory oversight.

As regards necessary regulatory preconditions, unsatisfactory creditor protection and dubious accounting practices are considered to be the major problems in many countries. In respect of the latter, for instance, capital ratios, as well as disclosure and transparency, are meaningless if flawed accounting masks the true state of balance sheets. In this regard, it has been suggested that, if the information supplied by banking organizations is poor and the auditing profession is underdeveloped, then the examination of financial statements is not sufficient. Rather, regulators should focus on validating accounts and records, valuing risk assets and verifying the accuracy of financial statements. In the developed countries, supervisors played this role at an earlier stage in the evolution of their banking systems (Bies, 2002).

Even in an era of financial liberalization, there remain needs for some direct regulatory controls, for example, where there are market imperfections or a need to cope with sudden emergencies, such as a sharp reversal in capital flows. By the same token, policymakers might not wish to forgo completely the ability to allocate credit to priority sectors or to certain geographical areas through government-sponsored banks (see above). However, government ownership may itself create additional regulatory problems, including weak corporate governance, political interference with decision-making, conflicts of interest, difficulties in implementing and enforcing remedial measures, and the absence of market discipline (International Monetary Fund, 2004k). In short, State-owned financial firms have the same need for adequate supervision as privately owned entities.

With the advent of liberalization, the financial sector, both at the national and at the international level, has become more pro-cyclical. Market agents tend to underestimate risk during booms, making loans to borrowers with lower credit quality (Ocampo, 2003e). The rapid increase of asset prices during booms further stimulates credit growth. The tendency for provisions to be related to the current rate of loan delinquency further increases this pro-cyclical bias. During booms, delinquencies are few and provisioning for loan losses is limited; this reduces the apparent costs of lending and thus increases credit

Such reforms have followed (with a lag) the indirect approach to regulation adopted in the industrialized world

For financial regulation to be effective, there should be a solid infrastructure that allows the economy to function properly

Unsatisfactory credit protection and dubious accounting practices are major problems in many countries

The need for direct regulation remains, and government ownership of financial institutions creates special regulatory problems

The financial sector has become more pro-cyclical with liberalization

growth. On the contrary, during downturns delinquencies increase, provisioning has to increase and lending tends to be curtailed, and may even lead to a "credit squeeze" that amplifies the economic downswing. Concern about weaknesses in the financial system during a downturn may prompt the introduction of stronger regulatory requirements, further aggravating in the short term the problem of the availability of credit.

Forward-looking provisions can be a useful counter-cyclical tool

Counter-cyclical policy has a clear role to play in this context. It should be conducted first and foremost through macroeconomic policy, but the effectiveness of such measures should not be compromised by a pro-cyclical bias in the financial system and in the mechanisms of financial regulation. One possible means of removing this bias is forward-looking provisioning that is estimated on the basis of expected or latent losses (rather than on prevailing losses) when loans are disbursed, taking into account the full business cycle. This would help smooth out the cycle by increasing provisions or reserves during boom periods and thereby help to reduce the credit crunch during downturns.

Forward-looking provisions should be based on an entire business cycle ...

Most countries do not allow for such forward-looking provisions that would cover the business cycle, but rather use a one-year horizon to measure risk. However, in December 1999, Spain issued regulations requiring counter-cyclical provisions calculated by statistical methods that estimated the "latent risk" based on past experience over at least one entire business cycle. Along with this, and in parallel with it, regulators should encourage the adoption of risk management practices and models that would allow lending strategies that are less sensitive to short-term factors (see, for instance, Griffith-Jones, Spratt and Segoviano, 2003).

... and can be complemented by discrete counter-cyclical provisions

It has been suggested that if financial regulators are sceptical about their ability to measure changes in risk and to evaluate the probability of systemic stress, such provisions could be usefully supplemented by more discrete counter-cyclical provisions to be applied by the regulatory authority to the financial system as a whole, or by the supervisory authority for special financial institutions, on the basis of objective criteria—such as the growth rate of credit, the growth of credit for specific risky activities or assets (Goodhart and Danielsson, 2001; Ocampo, 2003e).

Additional discretionary action can also help

Regulators could also dampen the credit boom through additional discretionary action. Cash reserve ratios and secondary liquidity requirements could be increased. Loan-to-value ratios might be tightened, collateral requirements strengthened and margin requirements for speculative trading increased. Such measures were very commonly used in industrialized countries in the 1960s and 1970s. They have been or are currently used effectively in several jurisdictions, including Hong Kong Special Administrative Region of China and Singapore (White, 2004).

Financial regulations could shift risks from financial to non-financial institutions ...

There is a danger that some financial regulations may have the effect of shifting risks from financial to non-financial institutions rather than of truly reducing excessively risky behaviour. For example, standards that either involve lower risk-ratings for short-term credit or attempt to avoid maturity mismatches between borrowing and lending will reinforce the financial institutions' bias towards short-term lending. Borrowers then may either finance their long-term credit needs with short-term domestic borrowing (with the result that they incur a maturity mismatch) or secure long-term financing from abroad (in which case they incur a currency mismatch). Although the direct risk may have migrated to the non-financial institution in both cases, domestic financial institutions continue to face the indirect risks associated with the possible delinquency of non-financial firms.

Consequently, counter-cyclical regulations and supervision could be complemented by regulations in other areas. In particular, prudential regulation should establish strict rules to prevent currency mismatches, especially those incurred by firms operating in non-tradable sectors that borrow in foreign currencies, liquidity requirements and limits on loan-to-collateral-value ratios or rules on the valuation of collateral designed to reflect long-term market trends in asset prices.

... requiring complementary regulations

The globalization of finance and the growing internationalization of financial crises in recent years have resulted in increased efforts to adopt similar regulatory arrangements across countries (Knight, 2004a). There is no formal power to set and enforce regulations worldwide and, according to many, the creation of such centralized power would be neither feasible nor desirable (Crockett, 2001a). Instead, supervisors from most developed countries have been drawing up a set of standards and codes whose broader adoption is encouraged by virtue of peer pressure and market forces. Indeed, the quality of individual countries' regulatory and supervisory systems is increasingly judged by reference to these international standards: it is ever more important to be seen to be adhering to these standards as a means of attracting and retaining international capital flows.

Supervisors from most developed countries have been drawing up standards and codes whose broader adoption is encouraged by peer pressure and market forces

The East Asian crisis of 1997 was instrumental in raising the importance given to globally coordinated financial regulation and to ensuring that the multiplicity of such regulations were considered together. The Financial Stability Forum (FSF), established by the Finance Ministers and Central Bank Governors of the Group of Seven (G7) in February 1999,[6] was given responsibility for defining this required set of standards and codes. This was the first attempt to develop a single set of international rules and principles for domestic policy in the financial and monetary spheres that all countries would adhere to. However, the implementation of standards and codes was announced to be voluntary and implementation was to vary according to the circumstances of different countries and firms.

The Financial Stability Forum was given responsibility for defining standards and codes whose implementation would be voluntary and vary according to the particular circumstances

Standards and codes are seen to play a central role in promoting global financial stability. One of the principles underlying their preparation encompasses the view that the transparency of the institutional and regulatory structures and the public availability of the associated information will reduce financial vulnerabilities. However, identifying standards is a complex task. Moreover, the dynamic nature of financial markets and their increasing sophistication mean that these standards have to be flexible enough to respond to continuous change.

The standards being set must be flexible enough to respond to continuous change

The Financial Stability Forum has identified 70 standards. From among these, the G7 countries and the multilateral financial institutions have identified a subset of standards that are deemed necessary to ensure financial stability. These fall into three areas: macroeconomic policy and data transparency; institutional market infrastructure; and financial regulation and supervision (see table I.4).

The standards are divided into three groups

Mechanisms have also been established to assess compliance. The key instrument is the Report on the Observance of Standards and Codes (ROSC), prepared by IMF as a part of Article IV consultations or through Financial Sector Assessment Programmes (FSAPs) conducted jointly by IMF and the World Bank. As of early 2005, there were over 500 Reports covering almost 100 countries.

The key instrument with which to assess compliance is the Report on the Observance of Standards and Codes

Despite the proliferation of ROSCs, they are not yet living up to their full potential for providing transparency about the situation in financial markets. They are not standardized, often provide very limited information, are frequently dated and are difficult for the non-specialist to understand; moreover, there is no continuous stream of information, nor an announced schedule of coverage. There are also problems in priority-setting

Yet these Reports are still not living up to their full potential

Table I.4.
Key standards for financial systems

Subject area	Key standard	Issuing body
Macroeconomic policy and data transparency		
Monetary and financial policy transparency	Code of Good Practices on Transparency in Monetary and Financial policies	IMF
Fiscal policy transparency	Code of Good Practices in Fiscal Transparency	IMF
Data dissemination	Special Data Dissemination Standard (SDDS)/ General Data Dissemination System (GDDS)	IMF
Institutional and market infrastructure		
Insolvency	Principles and Guidelines on Effective Insolvency and Creditor Rights Systems	World Bank
Corporate governance	Principles of Corporate Governance	OECD
Accounting	International Accounting Standards (IAS)	International Accounting Standards Board (IASB)
Auditing	International Standards on Auditing (ISA)	International Federation of Accountants (IFAC)
Payment and settlement	Core Principles for Systematically Important Payment Systems	Committee on Payment and Settlement Systems (CPSS)
	Recommendations for Securities Settlement Systems	CPSS and International Organization of Securities Commissions (IOSCO)
Money laundering	The Forty Recommendations/ Nine Special Recommendations on Terrorist Financing	Financial Action Task Force on Money Laundering
Financial regulation and supervision		
Banking Supervision	Core Principles for Effective Banking Supervision	Basel Committee on Banking Supervision (BCBS)
Securities regulation	Objectives and Principles of Securities Regulation	International Organization of Securities Commissions (IOSCO)
Insurance supervision	Insurance Core Principles	International Association of Insurance Supervisions (IAIS)

Source: Financial Stability Forum.

and in sequencing follow-up action. In particular, if they are to contribute to a reduction in financial vulnerability, the Reports should focus on the critical weaknesses and players in financial markets (Schneider, 2005).

Standards and codes represent "best practices". Their adoption by individual countries, adapted as necessary to local circumstances, can make an important contribution to the mobilization of domestic resources for development by strengthening overall trust and confidence in the financial system. From an international perspective, however, and for a variety of reasons explored in subsequent chapters, standards and codes alone are unlikely to provide complete protection from the vagaries of international capital markets. For this, a more far-reaching and comprehensive array of national and international, macroeconomic and firm-level policy measures are required. In all these areas, ongoing work needs to be continued and refined as part of the effort to build national financial systems that contribute to development and are sufficiently robust to adjust to the rapid evolution of financial markets.

Notes

1   In addition to China, which was considered separately, the nine take-off countries or areas were Chile, Hong Kong Special Administrative Region of China, Indonesia, Malaysia, Mauritius, the Republic of Korea, Singapore, Taiwan Province of China and Thailand. Botswana was excluded because of the lack of acceptable data.

2   It is argued, however, that this would make growth in the region subject to an upper bound (Krugman, 1994).

3   Romer (1987) estimates the social return of capital to be twice its private return.

4   The average ratios of long-term debt to total debt exceeded 40 per cent in 15 out of the 19 developed countries examined in this study, while only 1 country among the 11 developing countries studied—South Africa—was the ratio to 40 per cent. Small firms had smaller long-term debt ratios than larger firms.

5   Another way for commercial banks to overcome information problems is to build long-term relationships with smaller firms (see Aoki, 2001, chap. 12).

6   Its membership comprises representatives of the national authorities responsible for financial stability in selected Organization for Economic Cooperation and Development (OECD) member countries, Hong Kong Special Administrative Region of China and Singapore, and of major international financial institutions, international supervisory and regulatory bodies and central bank expert groupings.

Chapter II
Trade

Since the early 1990s, growth of exports of developing countries as a whole has been robust. In both the first and second halves of the last decade, the average annual growth of developing-country exports surpassed the growth rate of world exports (12.2 versus 8.7 per cent for 1991-1995 and 7.7 versus 4.8 per cent for 1996-2000). Moreover, this trend continues—with global exports having expanded at an annual rate of 5.8 per cent per year in 2001-2003, compared with a comparable rate of 7.4 per cent for developing countries. A number of developing countries have focused explicitly on encouraging exports and have been remarkably successful with their strategies. In some instances, this vigorous trade growth has led to what has been termed a "new geography" of trade, with developing countries finding new markets for their commodities in other developing countries.

Progressive multilateral trade liberalization has supported this robust trade performance. Further multilateral trade liberalization, with a view to generating an equitable outcome to all participants, can contribute to growth and development in developing countries. In fact, the Monterrey Consensus of the International Conference on Financing for Development (United Nations, 2002, annex) acknowledged that "(a) universal, rule-based, open, non-discriminatory and equitable multilateral trading system, as well as meaningful trade liberalization, can substantially stimulate development worldwide, bene-fiting countries at all stages of development" (para. 26).

The present chapter begins by examining the relationship between trade and growth. It shows that the composition of its trade may affect a country's ability to reap trade gains. In particular, dependence on primary commodity exports adversely influences a country's capacity to benefit from trade and globalization. The second section of the chapter turns to the discussion of trade "vulnerabilities". Dependence on primary commodity exports constitutes one such vulnerability. However, there are also geographical vulnerabilities, particularly those that affect small island developing States and landlocked developing countries.

The Doha Development Round of the World Trade Organization, discussed in the third part of this chapter, is taking place at a unique juncture. It has the opportunity to increase market access for products and services of interest to developing countries in agriculture and highly protected manufactures and to foster the increased provision of services through cross-border supply and the temporary movement of people for work-related purposes. The Round thus has the potential to be a major contributor to making the multilateral trading system more responsive to the needs of developing countries. Many developing countries, in an attempt to boost exports, are participating in the formation of preferential trading agreements. There are currently 230 such agreements (including bilateral ones), with about 60 more in formation. An important question raised in the last section of the chapter is whether such arrangements are consistent with the multilateral trading system.

Since the early 1990s, developing-country exports have expanded at a robust pace, supported by multilateral trade liberalization

Export composition may affect the potential gains from trade

The Doha Development Round has a role to play in making the multilateral trading system more responsive to the needs of developing countries

Trade, growth and specialization

Over the past two
decades, developing
countries have
increased their share
of world exports and
diversified their
exports

Between 1981 and 2003, developing countries increased their share of world exports from 27 to 33 per cent. A concomitant of this expansion was increasing diversification. The export concentration index for developing countries as a whole declined strongly between 1980 and 2003—from nearly 0.6 to about 0.2 (United Nations Conference on Trade and Development, 2004g). Hence, over the past two decades, developing countries have not only increased their share of global trade but, as a group, managed to move beyond their traditional specialization in agricultural and resource-based exports into manufactures.

The overall share of manufactures in developing-country exports, which had stood at 20 per cent in 1980, reached 65 per cent in 2001 and 75 per cent in 2003. Further, the share of high-value-added exports, which consist of manufactures with medium- to high-level skill and technology inputs, increased from 20 to nearly 50 per cent in the period from 1980 to 2003. Both low- and middle-income countries shared in this trend. Moreover, China and India were not the only countries driving these increases. When these two countries are excluded, the share of manufactures increased from 10 to more than 60 per cent of total exports of low-income developing countries in the period from 1980 to 2003.

While the share of manufactures rose in most geographical regions, there have been significant regional differences (see figure II.1). In the East Asian economies, almost 70 per cent of goods exports were manufactures in 2001 and over 80 per cent in 2003. Moreover, the relevant exports were often at the higher end of the value-added chain and many were also globally dynamic goods and services. At the other extreme, the share of manufactures in the exports of goods was only 47 per cent in Africa in 2003, still up from 31 per cent in 2001, and mostly in the area of processed primary commodities—which included exports of food products and preparations, as well as processed chemicals and materials. Latin America and the Caribbean was in an intermediate position, with manufactures accounting for 57 per cent of goods exports in 2001.

The shift away from
commodities since
1980 has
counterbalanced
the long-term decline
in commodity prices

This shift away from commodities was important to counterbalance the long-term decline in commodity prices that was experienced during this period. In 2002, the price index of agricultural commodities deflated by the price index of manufactured exports of industrialized economies in United States dollars was half its 1980 value (74 as against 145). Still, half of all developing countries—mostly least developed countries and small island developing States—continued to be dependent on primary non-fuel commodities for over half their export earnings (United Nations Conference on Trade and Development, 2004h).

However, not all
developing countries
shared in this
"trade boom"

Not all developing countries participated in this "trade boom". Forty-nine countries experienced negative real growth rates of their merchandise exports over the period in question. Poor performance was attributable to combinations of excessive dependence on one or two primary products (Cameroon on oil, Nauru on phosphates and Zambia on copper), civil conflict (including the Comoros, Rwanda and Timor-Leste) and politically motivated trade embargoes (including the Libyan Arab Jamahiriya and the Sudan).

A closer look at the dynamics of manufactures in world trade, classified according to their skill contents, reveals also the variable capacity of different developing countries to benefit from them. Whereas export growth of raw primary products has been relatively low—about 2 per cent per year since 1981—export growth rates for processed agricultural products (such as meats, processed foods, alcoholic beverages, tobacco products

Figure II.1.
Distribution of exports by commodity groups, 1960-2001
(Billions of dollars)

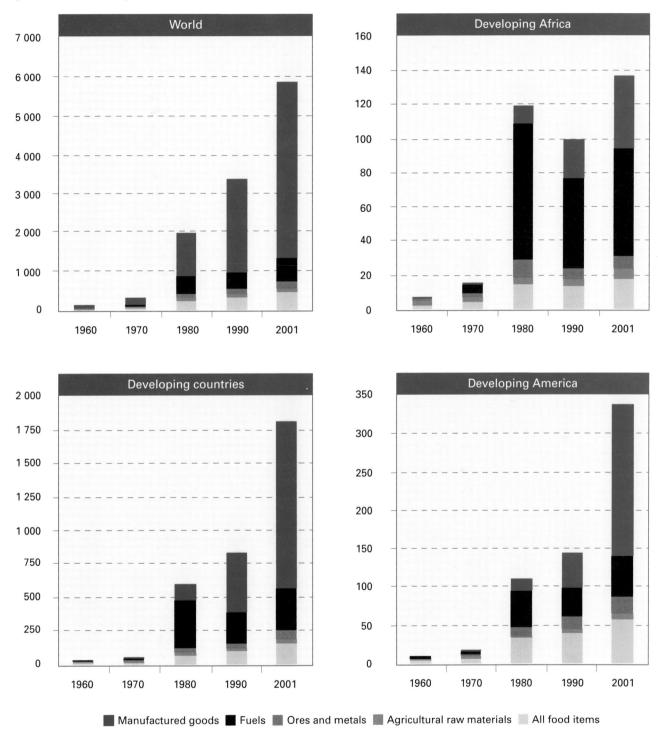

Figure II.1 (cont'd)
Distribution of exports by commodity groups, 1960-2001
(Billions of dollars)

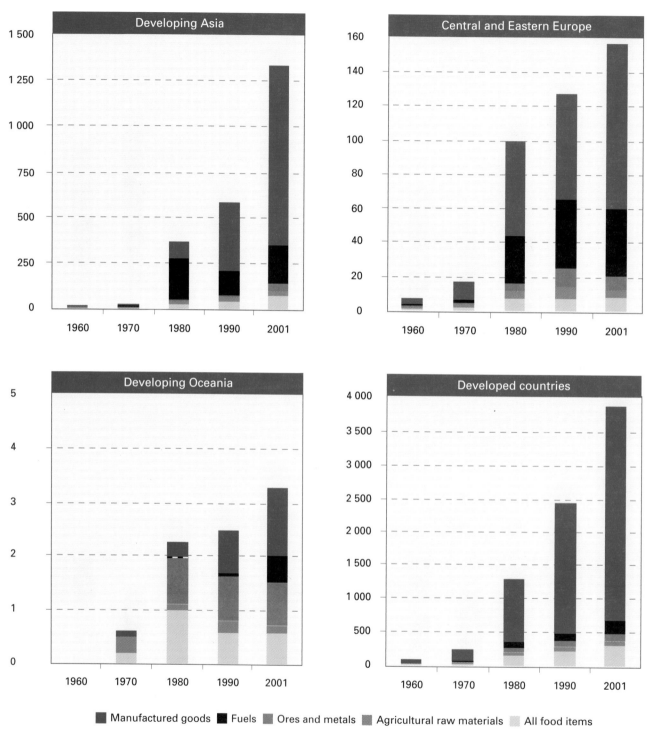

Source: DESA, based on UNCTAD GLOBSTAT website and UNCTAD, Handbook of Statistics, online.

and processed woods) have been significantly higher, 6 per cent globally. Meanwhile, trade in low-technology manufactures (such as textiles and clothing), simple manufactures (such as toys and sporting goods) and iron and steel products grew at rates that were well above the world average and highest of all for low-income developing countries. Similarly, in medium-technology manufactures (such as automobiles and components), growth rates of exports from low- and middle-income developing countries far outstripped comparable growth rates of exports from high-income countries. Meanwhile, exports of high-technology goods (for example, electronic goods, such as computers, televisions and components) grew more than twice as fast as overall world trade; and exports of these products from low- and middle-income countries grew more rapidly still.[1]

Over the period 1985-2002, the most "dynamic" exports in world trade fell into three groups: electronic and electrical goods (Standard International Trade Classification (SITC) divisions 75-77); chemicals (SITC section 5) and miscellaneous manufactures (SITC section 8). "Dynamism" can be described in two ways—in terms of either the absolute increase in market share or average annual export value growth. Following the first criterion, four product categories stood out between 1985 and 2002 as belonging to the 40 most dynamic product groups: electronic and electrical goods; chemicals; engines and parts; and textiles and clothing. Following the second benchmark, a number of agricultural and processed foods and beverage items cropped up in the "top 40" (United Nations Conference on Trade and Development, 2004g).

Despite the dynamic growth of manufacturing exports from developing countries, developed countries generally accounted for the lion's share of the total export value of products requiring high research and development (R&D) expenditures and characterized by high technological complexity (SITC section 5 and division 87), the exception being optical instruments. It was only a limited number of East Asian economies—for example, Malaysia, the Republic of Korea, Singapore and Taiwan Province of China—that made significant inroads as suppliers of higher-skill, higher-tech products to world markets.

Most developing countries are thus involved in the low-skill assembly phases of production. Because they have often increased their participation in the labour-intensive segments of production of high-tech goods, the question which arises is whether being engaged in the low-skill assembly stages of the production chain carries the same benefits as the export of more high-skill, high-tech products or whether, to the contrary, a form of "commoditization" is occurring. As an increasing number of developing countries export standardized, labour-intensive commodities, prices are likely to decline, necessitating ever-increasing export volumes.

The importance of these questions lies in the possible ramifications of trade and export expansion for growth. Orthodox economic analysis has argued that trade liberalization has a positive effect on resource allocation and economic growth.[2] The assumptions underlying orthodox theories are perfect competition, full employment of resources, and constant returns to scale in production. However, the real world is more complex—with market imperfections, high levels of unemployment and underemployment and economies of scale in many branches of industrial production worldwide. As notable an economist as Paul Samuelson has questioned the assumption that liberalization always has a benign outcome. As he pointed out recently (Samuelson, 2004), "it is dead wrong about the *necessary* surplus of winnings over losings". In reality, unfettered trade liberalization has, at times, imposed heavy adjustment costs including output contraction, higher unem-

Some developing countries have benefited by being the source of dynamic exports

However, developed countries generally accounted for the bulk of the total export value of products with high R&D content, while most developing countries were involved in the low-skill assembly phases of production

Short-run costs of liberalization may infringe on expected long-term gains

Table II.1.

The 40 most dynamic products in world non-fuel exports ranked by annual average exports value growth, 1985-2002, and share of developing countries, 2002

		Percentage	
SITC 2 code	Product	Average annual growth rate of world exports (1985-2002)	Share of developing countries (2002)
7524	Computer storage units	39	22
7643	Radiotelegraphic and radiotelephonic transmitters	23	22
7528	Off-line computers	22	28
2239	Flours or meals/oil seeds	20	25
2634	Cotton, carded or combed	18	53
6552	Knitted/crocheted fabrics	18	22
7764	Electronic microcircuits	18	15
6416	Building board	17	21
6880	Depleted uranium	17	1
5416	Glycosides; glands or other organs and their extracts	17	4
8462	Cotton undergarments	17	57
5417	Medicaments	17	4
7439	Parts of pumps, compressors, fans and centrifuges	17	9
8743	Non-electrical instruments for measuring, checking flow	16	17
8996	Orthopaedic appliances	16	3
6352	Casks, barrels, vats, tubs and buckets	16	7
6642	Optical glass and elements of optical glass	16	15
2223	Cotton seeds	15	12
5148	Nitrogen-function compounds	15	6
8710	Optical instruments and apparatus	15	12
8741	Surveying and hydrographic equipment	15	10
0488	Malt extract	15	9
5332	Printing ink	15	8
7923	Aircraft	15	23
2225	Sesame seeds	14	91
8732	Revolution counters, taximeters	14	11
5839	Polymerization and copolymerization products	14	7
5155	Organo-inorganic compounds	14	8
8742	Drawing, marking-out, disc calculators	14	7
7924	Aircraft	14	2
7832	Road tractors and semi-trailers	14	10
0546	Vegetables, frozen or in temporary preservative	14	24
5530	Perfumery, cosmetics and toiletries	14	11
8931	Packing materials	14	24
7712	Electric power machinery	14	32
8211	Chairs and other seats and parts	14	39
6589	Other articles of textile materials	14	60
1110	Non-alcoholic beverages	14	20
7144	Reaction engines	13	5
1122	Fermented beverages	13	17
	All 40 products	19	15

Source: United Nations Commodity Trade Statistics Database (COMTRADE).

Note: Average annual growth rates are computed using current values of exports. Lower average annual growth rates would be obtained if constant values were used, although the ranking would remain unchanged.

ployment and deeper trade deficits (Ocampo and Taylor, 1998). These short-term costs may reverberate and impair the realization of promised long-term gains.

From the viewpoint of growth and development, what is important is the ultimate impact of trade liberalization on domestic variables, such as output, employment, wages and investment; but evidence of the influence of trade on the domestic economy is hard to come by. Empirical studies are marred by data problems, by issues of causality and by the difficulties inherent in attempting to quantify social variables. Therefore, there is an ongoing debate as to the nature of the correlation between openness and growth.

Since the 1970s, several investigations have found evidence that outward-oriented economies grow faster (among the earlier studies, see Michaely, 1977). The widely known study by Sachs and Warner (1995), which examined the experience of over 100 developed and developing economies from the post-Second World War period to the mid-1990s, found a strong association between openness and growth. Within the group of developing countries, per capita GDP in the open economies grew at 4.49 per cent per annum, whereas in the closed economies, it grew at 0.69 per cent per annum.[3] Using comparative data for 93 advanced and developing countries over the period 1980-1990, and nine different estimates of "openness", Edwards (1997) also concluded that, regardless of how openness was defined, "more open countries have indeed experienced faster ... growth. More recently, an analysis of 73 developing countries indicated that "per capita growth rates have increased among the globalizing economies in the 1990s relative to the 1980s" (Dollar and Kraay, 2001). Recognizing that most of these countries had been engaged in wide-ranging economic reforms, the authors did not attribute all of the improvement in growth to greater openness. They nevertheless give a pivotal role to the fact that the faster growers were "globalizing" that is to say, they maintained that changes in trade volumes had had a strong positive relationship with changes in growth rates.

However, a growing number of studies have critiqued these conclusions from a variety of perspectives. In an extensive review of several of the aforementioned studies, Rodriguez and Rodrik (1999) argued that the indicators of openness used by researchers were generally measures of trade performance rather than of trade barriers (and thus of the extent of trade liberalization) or, alternatively, in effect measured other sources of bad economic performance (such as macroeconomic instability) rather than, again, trade liberalization. Indeed, an equally copious literature has shown that there is no association between growth and direct measures of protection (tariffs and non-tariff barriers) and thus that dynamic export performance has taken place under different trade regimes (United Nations Conference on Trade and Development, 1992, part two, chap. I; Rodriguez and Rodrik, 1999; Rodrik, 2001; Ocampo and Martin, 2003). Furthermore, the industrial upgrading necessary to spur the export of higher-value-added manufacturing exports does not occur automatically. Rather, it requires other policies, such as the development strategies undertaken in several East Asian economies "to incubate high-tech firms, and to attract high-tech investments by multinational corporations" (Woo, 2004). Another examination of these associations noted that trade liberalization often occurred at the same time as many other reforms, so that identification problems plagued the inference that differences in growth rates were due to differences in trade policy (Nye, Reddy and Watkins, 2002).

Thus, while there is growing acceptance of the positive association between export performance and GDP growth, the more specific association between trade *liberalization* and growth remains largely unproved. In several instances, export success has been associated with industrial and other supply-side policies, and even with the coexistence of protectionist and export promotion policies. Indeed, as Chenery, Robinson and Syrquin

There is an ongoing debate as to the precise nature of the correlation between openness and growth

While acceptance of a positive association between export performance and GDP growth has increased, the more specific association between trade *liberalization* and growth continues largely unproved

(1986) pointed out some time ago, the import substitution policies pursued by several countries in the past—even if less relevant today as a strategy—might have been essential in building the supply capacities that were reflected in their later export success. Equally, there appears to be no definitive evidence as to the effects of trade liberalization on employment and wages (Hoekman and Winters, 2005; Lee, 2005). The consensus at this point seems to be that trade liberalization "will create some losers (some even in the long run)" (Winters, 2000). Hence, government intervention may be warranted (Baldwin, 2003).

As some of the data cited earlier implies, the actual strength of the relationship between trade and growth also depends on the pattern of trade specialization of a country. Lowering trade barriers and increasing trade may be the consequence of the pattern of specialization, rather than the cause. According to Birdsall and Hamoudi (2002): "Countries with high natural resources and primary commodities in their exports are not necessarily 'closed' nor have they necessarily chosen to 'participate' more in the global trading system. For them, reducing tariffs and eliminating non-tariff barriers to trade may not lead to growth. In this context, terms like openness, liberalization and globalization are red herrings". In other words, most commodity-dependent countries were not able to raise their trade-to-GDP ratio, whether they cut tariffs steeply or not. Similarly, the majority of the least commodity-dependent countries saw increases in their trade-to-GDP ratio irrespective of any tariff cuts.

Trade vulnerabilities

Commodities

There has been a long-run trend decline in the terms of trade of most non-oil commodity prices when measured against the prices of manufactured goods since the 1950s, coupled with volatile swings around the long-term trend

A variety of domestic interventions and international agreements have been developed since the early twentieth century

International commodity policy focuses on the impact on developing countries of heavy dependence on exports of one or a few commodities for the bulk of their foreign-exchange earnings. Two features of commodity price trends are important in this regard. The first is the long-run trend decline in the terms of trade of most non-oil commodity prices when measured against the prices of manufactured goods. This long-term trend had raised the alarm in the 1950s and was the basis of what came to be known as the Prebisch-Singer thesis. Numerous empirical studies have confirmed this thesis in recent decades and analysed the consequences for developing countries that specialize in commodity exports.[4] The second feature of commodity price trends is reflected in the observation over the years that these price changes can be subject to volatile swings around the long-term trend for a variety of reasons related to unpredictable supply shocks and other market disturbances.

These concerns have led to the development of different domestic interventions and international agreements since the early years of the twentieth century. Since the 1950s, under the new umbrella of development cooperation, they gave rise to international commodity agreements (ICAs) and compensatory financing schemes. International commodity agreements were legally binding intergovernmental agreements between major commodity producers and consumers. Several of them were negotiated and implemented within the framework of the United Nations Conference on Trade and Development (UNCTAD) Integrated Programme for Commodities. These agreements contained economic clauses and specific instruments aimed at balancing supply and demand, and at reducing price volatility in international markets for the benefit of both producers and consumers. International commodity agreements for sugar, tin, coffee, cocoa and natural rubber operated with stabilization mechanisms at one time or another from the 1970s to the late 1990s. Agreements without economic clauses, which were often established after attempts at price stabilization schemes had failed, served as trade associations aimed at protecting the interests of producing and consuming countries.

Price stabilization instruments were either buffer stocks or export quotas. A buffer stock scheme removed excess supply from the market during periods of low prices—where low prices were understood to be prices falling below some notional assessment of a long-run equilibrium price—by buying and warehousing the commodity until prices increased. An international commodity agreement based on exports quotas controlled the supply-demand balance in global markets much in the same way—though the responsibility for withdrawing the excess supplies to keep within their quota lay with individual surplus countries—and tried to limit price fluctuations to specific price bands within which the commodity was bought and sold.

Most international commodity agreements gradually ceased to function as price stabilization mechanisms during the 1980s and early 1990s.[5] All were assessed as having achieved only limited success in securing stable, remunerative prices in international markets (Gilbert, 1987; International Task Force on Commodity Risk Management in Developing Countries (ITF), 1999). International commodity agreements with economic clauses came under additional and persistent criticism by major consuming countries to the effect that such stabilization schemes were "non-market" mechanisms that artificially manipulated prices and interfered with efficient allocation of global commodity resources (Maizels, 1994, p. 57).

Compensating financing schemes are financial mechanisms that have been and can be used to provide counter-cyclical financing to compensate developing countries for temporary shortfalls in earnings from commodity exports. The financing mechanisms were designed to provide loans and grants to qualified recipients so as to partially offset the collapse in export earnings. The most well-known compensatory financing schemes are the Compensatory Financing Facility (CFF) of the International Monetary Fund (IMF)—which was also known as the Compensatory and Contingency Financing Facility (CCFF) for a brief period until the contingency financing element was dropped—and the STABEX, SYSMIN and FLEX facilities of the European Union (EU).[6]

The STABEX and SYSMIN facilities provided compensatory financing to beneficiary African, Caribbean and Pacific (ACP) countries in order to offset losses in earnings from commodity exports to EU. Both facilities were judged as having achieved only limited success in their original objectives by the time they were abandoned at the conclusion of the Lomé IV Convention in 2000. The FLEX facility in the Cotonou Partnership Agreement (the successor agreement to the Lomé Convention) provides support to beneficiary ACP countries to compensate Governments for the impact on their budgets of export earnings instability from exports of agricultural and mineral commodities. The facility also provides financial support under conditions that extend beyond previous facilities—and is linked less to earnings shortfalls from commodity exports—in cases where losses in export revenues have caused increased public deficits that threatened social and economic reform programmes that were being implemented at the same time. The FLEX scheme is expected to put more emphasis on rewarding commitments to economic reforms and sound economic management and possibly provide financing for price risk-management arrangements (Page and Hewitt, 2001).

Even before the collapse of the major price stabilization and compensatory schemes, developing countries had been encouraged to use market-based financial instruments and techniques to manage commodity price risk. This strategy involved the use of basic forwards, futures and options contracts and a wide range of commodity-backed deriv-

Even before the breakdown of the major price stabilization and compensatory schemes, developing countries were encouraged to use a variety of market-based financial instruments and techniques to manage commodity price risk

ative financial instruments. These tools were either tailor-made for specific transactions or traded publicly on international commodity exchanges.

Forward contracts, which are used extensively by commodity producers in developing countries (usually through brokers and other intermediaries), provide some (usually short-term) hedge against price risk. However, because of these risks of default, and several other reasons discussed in more detail in the specialized literature, forward contracts and similar instruments are generally not considered ideal hedging instruments through which to offset commodity price risk (United Nations Conference on Trade and Development, 1994).

Futures and options contracts, on the other hand, are considered better hedging instruments mainly because they are traded on organized international commodity exchanges such as the Chicago Board of Trade, the London Metals Exchange, the New York Mercantile Exchange, the Tokyo Commodity Exchange and commodity exchanges based in developing countries such as Argentina, Brazil, China, India, Malaysia, Singapore, South Africa and Thailand (in contract volume, the world's largest commodity exchange is now in the city of Dalian, China). Commodity exchanges operate with strict rules governing the financial solvency of traders, trading practices, contract settlement terms and other terms and conditions designed to guarantee and preserve the integrity of market operations. Commodity futures also offer institutional investors and hedge funds additional opportunities for portfolio diversification and hedges against inflation and interest rate changes.[7]

Commodity exporters in developing countries were encouraged to use relatively standard non-speculative risk management techniques such as options and swaps (financial contracts that resemble futures, but are easier to handle in terms of cash flow requirements) to trade away price risk and hedge future export earnings from volatile and unexpected price changes. Non-speculative hedging techniques offset losses from sales of the physical commodity with corresponding gains in futures, options and swap market transactions, and vice versa. In this way, the exporter would be guaranteed a known and predictable return from future sale of the commodity.

Several developing countries have independently used commodity derivatives over the years with some degree of success. The majority of commodity exporters, however, especially poor least developed countries in Africa, lack the institutional capacity or face considerable obstacles with respect to trading in commodity derivatives. UNCTAD studies have reported on successful and extensive use of futures markets and other commodity derivatives by countries such as Brazil, Chile, Colombia, Costa Rica, Indonesia, Malaysia, Mexico, Papua New Guinea and Venezuela (Bolivarian Republic of) to manage commodity price risk and hedge export revenues, import costs and government budget revenues.[8]

In Africa, the use of commodity derivatives is less widespread. Côte d'Ivoire and Ghana have in the past used forward contracts extensively in their cocoa export trade, and other West African countries for cotton exports (Commission for Africa, 2005, p. 266). Maize is traded in regional markets through the Johannesburg Stock Exchange (which has absorbed the South African Futures Exchange) but Africa so far lacks a major international commodity exchange that caters to regional or global commodity trade.[9]

Commodity risk management techniques started receiving much greater attention in international development assistance policies after the release of a report in 1999 by the International Task Force on Commodity Risk Management in Developing Countries that had been convened by the World Bank.[10] The Task Force, which comprised representatives and experts in commodity markets and financial institutions drawn from a wide cross-section of international organizations, the private sector, the academic community and

Following a 1999 report, commodity risk management techniques began to garner much greater attention in international development assistance policies

independent experts, recommended the adoption of specially designed risk management instruments and trading techniques, which were cautiously presented as user-friendly financial instruments that would provide insurance cover for commodity exporters.[11]

The Task Force compiled a large list of bottlenecks, obstacles and unanticipated difficulties of implementing its 1999 proposals after a series of pilot projects in several developing countries.[12] Severe limiting factors on both the demand and supply sides pointed to the weak financial institutional structures in most countries, and lack of knowledge and skills in trading sophisticated financial instruments. Moreover, despite the known benefits of transactional hedging techniques, many countries viewed trade in commodity derivatives as risky and speculative because of highly publicized accounts of massive fraud and mismanagement of derivatives trade on commodity exchanges in the 1980s and 1990s (United Nations Conference on Trade and Development, 2003d).

There was also a strong need for simple derivative instruments that would be easily understood by both buyers and sellers, which was a requirement that proved difficult to implement because simpler instruments could not provide the required protection from all price risk. A "simple" forward or futures contract, for example, might have to be hedged further with offsetting options contracts that could significantly increase the complexity of the entire transaction. From the point of view of the large international commodity risk management intermediaries, the regulatory framework and reporting requirements would make it costly and cumbersome to work with large numbers of developing countries.

Some commodity producers/exporters were more concerned about volume and revenue risk than price risk. Output volumes could fluctuate widely depending on vagaries of the weather, civil and political strife, armed conflict and a wide range of other unanticipated events in the domestic and global economies that could severely affect agricultural and mining output and sales. The concept of commodity risk, along with the development of appropriate market-based instruments to cope with such risks, has been broadened correspondingly to include weather-related risks as well as risks of volatile price swings in import prices for food and crude oil.

While acknowledging the usefulness of market-based risk management strategies in setting price floors for commodity producers, a group of eminent persons on commodity issues meeting under UNCTAD auspices in 2003 outlined a broader and more comprehensive agenda to address the problems and vulnerabilities of commodity-dependent exporters stemming from severe price erosion and adverse terms-of-trade developments (United Nations Conference on Trade and Development, 2003f). The recommendations of the group contained specific proposals for short- and medium-term actions in the international community that would improve the development prospects of commodity-dependent countries.

The highest priority among the group's recommendations was given to measures to improve market access of primary commodity exports in developed-country markets, including through the elimination of market-distorting subsidies for cotton and other commodities; reduction of excess supply in some commodity markets and increased use of more flexible compensatory financing schemes to mitigate the adverse impact of export earnings shortfalls owing to the erosion of commodity prices. The recommendations called for closer considerations of export earnings potential in debt sustainability analyses and debt relief and longer-term measures to promote economic diversification in commodity-dependent countries. Further elaboration of current international commodity policy was contained in the São Paulo Consensus, adopted by UNCTAD at its eleventh session on 18 June 2004, which resolved to establish the International Task Force on Commodities

While the usefulness of market-based risk management strategies in setting price floors is acknowledged, a broader and more comprehensive agenda to deal with the problems and vulnerabilities of commodity-dependent exporters has been proposed

The highest priority has been given to measures to improve market access of primary commodity exports in developed-country markets involving all stakeholders dealing in the production and trade of commodities to conduct a comprehensive review of commodity issues and solutions to existing problems (United Nations Conference on Trade and Development, 2004f, annex, sect. B).

For countries that will continue to derive a large proportion of export earnings from extractive industries in the hydrocarbons and mining sectors, an important element of international commodity policy will be the adoption of appropriate policies to promote effective and transparent management of fiscal revenues. IMF publishes fiscal transparency reports containing assessments of country practices for nearly 70 countries which were drawn up according to a Code of Good Practices on Fiscal Transparency that was first adopted in April 1998.[13] The need for fiscal transparency was further underscored following the introduction of the Extractive Industries Transparency Initiative (EITI) which had been launched at the World Summit on Sustainable Development held in Johannesburg, South Africa, from 26 August to 4 September 2002.[14]

Geographically disadvantaged countries

Landlocked developing countries and small island developing States face exceptional difficulties in their trade relations—in the case of landlocked developing countries, owing to their lack of direct access to sea transport and their isolation and remoteness from major world markets and in the case of small island developing States, owing to the difficulties associated with both transportation and the disadvantages of "smallness"

Two sets of developing economies have been internationally identified as being "geographically disadvantaged"—the landlocked developing countries; and small island developing States, which were termed island developing countries before 1994. Sixteen of the 30 designated landlocked developing countries are least developed countries as well. While the "small island developing States" categorization is more loosely defined, a number of the economies that fall under this designation are also members of the least developed country category.

This overlap is not a coincidence. Both landlocked countries and small island developing States face exceptional difficulties in their trade relations, difficulties that undoubtedly impact their growth and development prospects. In the case of the former, the problems emanate from their lack of direct access to sea transport and their isolation and remoteness from major world markets. This may make their ability to respond quickly to export-demand shocks problematic and they may face obstacles when it comes to delivering goods on time, thus undermining their competitiveness. In the case of small island developing States, difficulties are associated not only with transportation but also with the disadvantages of "smallness".

The majority of landlocked countries specialize in agriculture and mineral products for export. Only a small number, namely, the Lao People's Democratic Republic, Lesotho, Nepal, the former Yugoslav Republic of Macedonia and Zimbabwe, specialize in manufactures. Commodities are of great importance to many of these economies for external revenue, income and employment. Moreover, this dependence on commodities is exacerbated by the extreme concentration of their exports on fewer than five of them. For example, in Africa, 7 of 11 landlocked developing countries depend on only two or so commodities for more than half of their export revenue. Landlocked developing countries also have a lower level of trade openness (export-to-GDP ratio) compared with non-landlocked economies. Additionally, regional trade is often important for these countries, given that a large proportion of such trade incurs lower average transport cost in light of the shorter distances involved.

Landlocked developing countries face high transport and transit costs

The most specific disadvantage experienced by landlocked developing countries are high transport and transit costs. Indeed, ad valorem transport costs, which include freight and insurance, are higher for landlocked countries than for either developed or developing countries (see table II.2), though such costs vary considerably from under 5 per

Table II.2.
Transport costs, including freight and insurance costs of various groups, 1995

Percentage	
Country group	Total export value
Landlocked countries	14.1
Least developed countries	17.2
Developing countries	8.6
Developed market economies	4.5

Source:
UNCTAD (2003e).

cent for Nepal and Swaziland to over 50 per cent for Chad and Mali. The significance of this lies in the fact that there is evidence of a negative correlation between transport costs and exports, as high transport costs may significantly reduce the potential for export-led economic growth (United Nations Conference on Trade and Development, 2003e).

High transport and transit costs also imply that the costs of importing are higher for landlocked developing countries. In 1995, freight costs as a share of the landed cost of imports were roughly 3.5 per cent of cost, insurance and freight (c.i.f.) import values for developed economies, about 7.4 per cent for developing countries as a whole and about 10.7 for landlocked developing countries (United Nations Conference on Trade and Development, 2003e). Such high transport costs inflate import costs of consumer goods, as well as of capital goods and intermediate inputs, thus increasing the cost of any domestic production that relies on imports.

Given these statistics, it is not surprising that one analysis comparing transport costs in landlocked developing countries with those in coastal countries found that that the median landlocked country faces transport costs that are some 50 per cent higher than those of a median coastal county and that the former have trade volumes that are 60 per cent lower (Limão and Venables, 1999).

Landlocked developing countries generally border other developing countries. Thus, their transit neighbours are typically in no position to offer a transport system of high technical and administrative standards. Landlocked countries may often therefore find themselves competing with their transit neighbours for scarce, and not exceptionally efficient, transport facilities. This is probably less of a problem, however, for the landlocked countries of Latin America—Bolivia and Paraguay (which, in any case, relies a great deal on river transport)—and of Southern Africa—Botswana, Lesotho and Swaziland—whose immediate neighbours have relatively developed transport infrastructures.

Second, insofar as frontiers and the need to transfer from one national transport system to another constitute institutional impediments to the flow of goods and persons, landlocked countries face greater impediments to trade than do their coastal neighbours. This added burden may be termed the "frontier transiting cost" and may be reckoned in terms of both expenditures incurred and time lost. Furthermore, dependence on transit through another country gives rise to foreign-exchange outlays that would not arise if the country had access to the sea. Fourth, and most important, is the fact that a landlocked country finds itself dependent on another country's transport policy, transport enterprises and transport facilities. This can be a special problem since, in many instances, landlocked countries are in potentially competitive situations vis-à-vis their transit neighbours, which makes compatible harmonization of transit facilities a more elusive and hence difficult undertaking.[15]

Landlocked countries may find themselves competing with their transit neighbours for scarce, and not exceptionally efficient, transport facilities

While the recent attention in relation to both landlocked developing countries and small island developing States has been on geographical disadvantages, the focus on "smallness" actually goes back to 1957, at which time the implications of small size were discussed at a meeting of the International Economics Association.[16] Since that time, the Commonwealth Secretariat has been among the main bodies that have taken up the concerns of this category of economies in recent decades. In 1997, the problems of small States were discussed at a meeting of the Commonwealth Heads of State and Government and thereafter the Commonwealth Secretariat together with the World Bank established a Joint Task Force on Small States. Consideration of small economies has been undertaken in the World Trade Organization as well, including in the 2001 Doha Ministerial Declaration (see document A/C.2/56/7, annex; of 26 November 2001).

There has been an increasing emphasis on the vulnerabilities of small island developing States—not only to climate change and potential natural disasters, such as hurricanes, but also to exogenous shocks, such as commodity price and other trade shocks, as well as the loss of trade preferences

In turn, since 1992, the United Nations has phased out its designation of "island developing countries" in favour of the more focused small island developing States category. The 1992 United Nations Conference on Environment and Development adopted Agenda 21 (United Nations, 1992, resolution 1, annex II), which contained a special section devoted to the sustainable development of small island developing States. The United Nations Conference on Environment and Development was followed by two major global conferences dedicated to this group of countries (one held in Barbados in 1994 and the other in Mauritius in 2005). Through this process, there has been an increasing emphasis on the vulnerabilities of small island developing States—not only to climate change and potential natural disasters, such as hurricanes, but also to exogenous shocks, such as commodity price and other trade shocks, and the loss of trade preferences. Such setbacks are more difficult for small island developing States to overcome, since small States frequently lack natural resources, and have a limited domestic market, and a heavy dependence on imports and a few exports, generally coupled with trade-inhibiting distances from other markets (in other words, remoteness), with archipelagos subject to specific challenges even in relation to domestic communications. All of these factors potentially reduce competitiveness and make it more difficult for small States to successfully diversify into dynamic products (Ocampo, 2002b).

While some small island developing States have seen increased private financial flows since the 1990s, particularly foreign direct investment (FDI) (for example, the Bahamas, Jamaica, Saint Kitts and Nevis and Trinidad and Tobago), others have experienced declines as FDI was attracted to larger markets (for instance, Bahrain, Guyana, Papua New Guinea and Vanuatu) (United Nations, 2002, chap. I, resolution 1, annex). Much of FDI was attracted to the tourism industry. Growth in tourism and in other service sectors has fared well in several small island developing States over recent decades. Similarly, growth in the financial services sector and other business sectors, including insurance, has advanced in some small island developing States. In Mauritius, for example, the contribution of this sector to GDP increased from about 10 per cent in 1992 to almost 17 per cent in 2001. However, those States still heavily dependent on non-oil commodity exports have not done as well, because of both declines in commodity process and the loss of preferential market arrangements.

Because exports of small economies are sometimes highly concentrated in a few sectors, such States are characterized by higher income volatility than their larger counterparts

Because exports of small economies are sometimes highly concentrated in a few sectors, such States are characterized by higher income volatility than their larger counterparts. Whether this is due to export concentration or openness is a subject of debate (Jansen, 2004). However, while some small island States are characterized by commodity export concentration (including Cape Verde with its dependency on mining and Jamaica and Trinidad and Tobago with their dependency on bauxite and petrochemicals, respectively), some small island States belong to an "export-diversified cluster".[17] Included therein are many Caribbean countries, as well as Cyprus (Liou and Ding, 2002). Indeed, the actual heterogeneity of small island developing States has led to a debate in the literature. The dominant assumption is that smallness creates diseconomies of scale. Conversely, some analysts have cited the benefits of smallness—such as the possibility of higher levels of social cohesion. Indeed, "a number of small island countries have somehow succeeded in achieving relatively high standards of living, as evidenced by relatively high average per capita incomes, sustained levels of economic growth and a high ranking on the human development index" (Prasad, 2003).

The fact remains, however, that smallness may exacerbate the effects of any global volatility. From this perspective, these States need support for their efforts to reduce their exposure to both external and internal shocks.

Multilateral trade liberalization

The signing of the General Agreement on Tariffs and Trade (GATT) in 1948 provided a clear set of rules governing international trade in a non-discriminatory and reciprocal fashion, thus reversing the break-up that the multilateral trade order had experienced during the interwar period. Subsequently, several rounds of trade liberalization took place, lowering industrial tariffs from an average of 40 per cent in 1947 to some 5-6 per cent in most developed countries in the early 1980s (World Bank, 1987). Admittedly, developing countries' exports gained relatively less from tariff reductions, and a significant number of their export products remained outside GATT disciplines (for example, agriculture and textiles). Developing countries, however, were not asked to make major commitments on tariffs and were extended preferential market access. Moreover, they were allowed considerable latitude in the use of quantitative restrictions for balance-of-payments and infant industry purposes.

Fast economic growth during the "golden years" of the post-Second World War facilitated liberalization. With lower growth since the mid-1970s, protectionism intensified. Non-trade barriers were increasingly resorted to, including numerous anti-dumping measures and voluntary export restraints—which came to be called the "grey area" of international trade—thus reducing effective market access despite the relatively low tariff environment. Threats of unilateral action to promote national policy objectives further eroded the multilateral system.

The Uruguay Round of multilateral trade negotiations (1986-1993), which created the World Trade Organization, brought renewed discipline to the multilateral trading system. Among other provisions, agriculture and textiles were included in GATT rules, a flexible framework for the liberalization of services through "positive lists" was created (the General Agreement on Trade in Services (GATS)),[18] and multiple forms of protectionism were prohibited. An effective dispute settlement mechanism was installed, thus reinforcing members' rights and obligations. Developing countries were asked to accept greater commitments in all areas, though "special and differential treatment" was maintained, particularly for low-income countries. The Uruguay Round adopted a "single undertaking" approach, with transitional measures envisaged to bring developing countries to the same level of obligations as that of developed countries (United Nations Conference on Trade and Development, 2002). On the other hand, in view of their considerable technological capability differences, the upward harmonization of intellectual property standards of developing countries with those of industrialized countries entailed additional

Several rounds of trade liberalization had lowered industrial tariffs from an average of 40 per cent in 1947 to some 5-6 per cent in most developed countries in the early 1980s

costs and loss of policy space by the former. Developing countries also accepted multilateral discipline in relation to production and export subsidies, and the prohibition of measures that had been widely used to promote domestic content of assembly activities, through trade-related investment measures (Ocampo, 1992).

The Uruguay Round therefore brought benefits, but also challenges to developing countries. Further, it left considerable scope for further liberalization, particularly in the areas of export interest to developing countries: agriculture, labour-intensive manufactures and the supply of services through the temporary movement of natural persons. In the case of agriculture, for instance, the Uruguay Round brought limited liberalization to the sector as the levels of protection and export and domestic subsidies were kept relatively high (see box II.1 below).

The new round of trade negotiations launched in Doha in November 2001 pledged to place developing countries' "needs and interests at the heart of the work programme adopted". Over three years later, limited progress has been made

After a failed attempt in Seattle, Washington, in 1999, a new round of trade negotiations was launched in Doha in November 2001. Ministers pledged to place developing countries' "needs and interests at the heart of the work programme adopted", thus taking into account the major concerns these countries had expressed at Seattle. Over three years later, limited progress has been made. Negotiations suffered a setback in Cancún, Mexico, in 2003, and the agreed date for the conclusion of the round (1 January 2005) was postponed. In July 2004, a framework for negotiations on modalities represented a first breakthrough. In all, developing countries have encountered resistance in steering negotiations to their benefit. Yet, they have been able to form successful coalitions that have succeeded in bringing into the negotiating agenda issues of interest to them, such as cotton and property rights of medicines, as well as forcing others to be dropped out of the agenda, such as government procurement, competition and investment rules. The sections below provide a brief summary of some of major issues at stake and the state of multilateral negotiations as of mid-2005.

Assessing the potential benefits of multilateral trade liberalization

Extensive research is available quantifying the possible gains that the Doha Round could generate. Most of this research uses computable general equilibrium (CGE) models, which take into account interactions across different sectors of the economy and allow researchers to observe the effects of liberalization and other policy scenarios on volumes, prices and income. These models therefore estimate the impact of trade on national income through changes in allocative efficiency, as market distortions are removed and resources are reallocated to more productive uses, and through changes in a country's import and export prices. Besides the usual caveats related to data availability and quality, these models are often a simplified representation of the economy and rely on crude assumptions. Therefore, results produced are only a reference in respect of possible outcomes and not accurate assessments of costs and benefits (Stiglitz and Charlton, 2004).

Estimates of potential global welfare gains from the Doha Round vary widely, with several results within the range of $250 billion-$400 billion per year

The estimates of annual global welfare gains range widely, with several results within the range of $250 billion-$400 billion, depending on the type of gains assessed (static or dynamic), the modalities and depth of liberalization, the number of sectors and countries considered, whether existing preferences are incorporated into the models or not, and so on (see table II.3). Models often assume that the Uruguay Round was fully executed and that implementation of Doha commitments would start in 2005. The implementation schedule, however, varies across models. Results, therefore, are not comparable across mod-

Box II.1

A snapshot perspective on tariffs and domestic support

Despite progress brought about by the Uruguay Round of multilateral trade negotiations, agricultural markets remain highly distorted. Liberalization has been modest. In both developed and developing countries, average tariffs on agricultural products are two to four times higher than those on manufactures (see table 1). Tariff dispersion is marked, and tariff peaks are pronounced, indicating "sensitive" products.

Table 1.
Average tariffs applied to agriculture and manufactures by selected countries, 1999-2001

	Percentage				
	Mamufactures	Agriculture			
Country or country group	Average tariff	Average tariff	Maximum tariff	Standard deviation	Binding proportion of lines covered
Quad	4.0	10.7	..	..	86.7
Canada	3.6	3.8	238.0	12.9	76.0
EU	4.2	19.0	506.3	27.3	85.9
Japan	3.7	10.3	50.0	10.0	85.5
United States	4.6	9.5	350.0	26.2	99.3
Middle-income countries	12.9	26.2	..	..	96.3

Source: World Bank (2004b). Tariff estimates comprise MFN, applied, ad valorem, out-of-quota duties.

Developed countries often impose lower tariffs than developing countries—not only on agricultural but also on industrial products—and tariffs applied on traditional agricultural exports by developing countries are either zero or minimal. However, the fact that tariffs usually increase with the level of processing helps to discourage higher-value-added activities in developing countries, or on those products (for example, fruits and cut flowers) that have faster growth potential.

Products sheltered by high tariffs often receive domestic support and require export subsidies to be placed in international markets (Laird, Cernat and Turrini, 2003). Producer support reached some $257 billion on 32 per cent of total farm receipts in Organization for Economic Cooperation and Development (OECD) member countries in 2003, having declined from 38 per cent in 1986-1988. While distorting forms of support have decreased (market price support, output and input payments), they still constitute the most widely used form of support granted to farmers (about 75 per cent). Moreover, as indicated by the producer subsidies equivalent, the concept used prior to 1999 to measure producer support in OECD economies, support had increased between 1979-1981 (29.5 per cent) and 1986-1988 (47 per cent), which was used as the benchmark for the reduction in support (OECD, 1988 and 1992). The use of peak years as the benchmark for the reduction of agricultural support thus limited the extent of the commitments effectively made by developed countries during the Uruguay Round. Total support for agriculture (producer, consumer and general services support) was about $350 billion in 2003 (Organization for Economic Cooperation and Development, 2004).

Producer support is a complex and controversial issue. It may contribute to improving a country's food security. Yet, producer support may contribute to widening income inequality in the subsidizing country, as a considerable share of these transfers goes to the larger farms. Furthermore, by maintaining

Box II.1 (cont'd)

domestic prices artificially high, domestic support can also be detrimental to consumers, particularly the poor. In the international sphere, domestic support, by encouraging additional production that would not have taken place in the absence of such subsidies, has contributed to lower international prices. The latter are beneficial for foreign consumers but hurt producers abroad, as they erode producers' competitiveness and discourage production in non-subsidizing countries.

The trade of least developed countries is particularly affected by OECD agricultural subsidies: over 18 per cent of their exports, on average, are products receiving domestic support by at least one of their World Trade Organization partners. The average for other developed countries, which have more diversified exports, is below 4 per cent. On the other hand, a larger share of least developed countries imports (9 per cent) involves subsidized products, most of it food, compared with the corresponding share of other developing countries (3-4 per cent) (Hoekman, Ng and Olarreaga, 2003).

Tariffs on industrial goods are on average low, but this hides the existence of tariff peaks, which are frequent both in developed and in developing countries. In developed countries, tariff peaks exist on low-skill, low-technology products, while products requiring high skills and sophisticated technology that are exported by the more advanced developing economies and by developed countries face considerably less protection (Baccheta and Bora, 2004). Most protected sectors, therefore, are precisely those that are of interest for developing countries (textiles and clothing, leather and footwear, fish and fish products) (see table 2). Tariff escalation is also present in non-agricultural goods, as evidenced by the fact that tariffs on semi-processed and processed raw materials are relatively high, thus discouraging diversification by commodity exporters.

In turn, many developing countries have bound their industrial tariffs at a very high level (that is to say, they have committed not to increase tariffs beyond that level) but apply much lower tariffs (see table 3). The difference between bound and applied tariffs leaves these countries with some policy flexibility for meeting industrial development objectives or facing temporary difficulties (for example, a balance-of-payments crisis). Other developing countries, least developed countries in particular, have not yet bound a significant share of their tariff lines.

Table 2.
Tariff escalation in selected countries, 2001-2003

	Percentage							
	Process	United States 2002	EU-15 2002	Japan 2002-2003	Canada 2002	China 2002	India 2001-2002	Brazil 2003	South Africa 2002
Total	First stage of processing	4.4	8.1	14.5	5.0	11.3	28.6	7.9	5.5
	Semi-processed	4.8	4.9	4.9	3.9	9.7	32.3	9.6	12.9
	Fully processed	5.5	7.0	7.8	8.9	14.0	33.0	13.4	11.5
of which									
Food, beverages and tobacco	First stage of processing	3.6	13.2	23.6	10.2	15.3	36.3	9.4	10.7
	Semi-processed	8.8	19.1	20.3	6.8	28.1	36.6	12.6	10.3
	Fullyprocessed	12.5	18.7	22.6	34.1	21.5	48.2	15.0	15.4
Textiles, clothing and leather	First stage of processing	3.8	1.0	10.2	1.1	13.0	25.9	9.1	5.0
	Semi-processed	9.3	6.7	6.8	6.9	15.1	28.4	15.8	22.1
	Fullyprocessed	10.1	9.8	12.0	13.5	20.4	34.2	19.3	32.4

Source: Acharya and Daly (2004).

Box II.1 (cont'd)

Table 3.
Most Favoured Nation (MFN) tariff binding by developing countries

	All	Latin America and the Caribbean	Western Asia	East Asia	South Asia	Africa	Least developed countries
Average binding (percentage of total product lines)	66.9	93.2	85.4	75.5	34.5	47.4	43.4
	Number of countries						
Proportion of tariff lines bound (B) (percentage)							
B = 100	36	19	5	3	0	9	7
90 ≤ B < 100	14	4	0	3	0	7	2
50 ≤ B < 89.9	10	1	2	4	1	2	2
35 ≤ B < 49.9	3	0	1	1	1	0	0
10 ≤ B < 34.9	10	1	0	0	1	8	7
0 ≤ B < 10	17	0	0	1	1	15	11

Source: World Trade Organization (2004a).

els. Yet, they provide a general idea of who the major beneficiaries are and in which areas trade liberalization can bring the most benefits. Some assumptions are very optimistic, often above what can be realistically achieved. Additionally, models do not incorporate any policy measure that the simulated liberalization may trigger. For instance, not all sectors of a given economy may gain from liberalization. This may trigger protectionist measures, which can reduce benefits for countries that are expected to profit from liberalization. Additionally, CGE models do not address issues of adjustment costs. Thus, net gains may be less than those estimated here. On the other hand, the vast majority of models capture only static gains and do not take into account the long-term effects on the growth rate.

As a minimum, models assess gains from increased market access via tariff cuts, both in agriculture and in manufacturing, in view of the existing scope for continued liberalization in these areas (see box II.1). Other models also incorporate a reduction or elimination of agricultural export subsidies and domestic support, liberalization of services and trade facilitation. Research indicates that the gains are roughly equally shared between developed and developing countries, with some advantage to developed countries in certain models largely owing to agricultural liberalization. Among developing countries, Asian economies reap relatively bigger gains than Latin American and African countries owing to their competitive advantage in labour-intensive manufactures. Across regions and groups, however, a major source of gains is countries' unilateral liberalization. However, perhaps more important than assessing relative gains across countries is evaluating the potential gains that the liberalization of specific sectors can bring to developing countries in particular.

Table II.3.
Selected estimates of annual welfare effects from multilateral trade liberalization

Source	Region	Unit	Total annual welfare gains	Gains from developed countries' liberalization	Gains from developing countries' liberalization	Agriculture and food and other primary	Manufactures
Anderson and others (2001) Full merchandise trade liberalization	Global	$ 1995 billion	254.3	139.6	114.7	167.5	86.8
	Developed		146.2	96.6	49.6	121.8	24.4
	Economies in transition		6.4	4.5	1.9	3.5	2.9
	Sub-Saharan Africa		4.6	2.6	2.0	4.0	0.6
	Norththern Africa and Middle East		0.3	-1.0	1.2	-3.1	3.4
	Latin America		35.7	17.9	17.8	23.0	12.7
	Asian NIEs[a] and China		22.3	5.1	17.2	1.6	20.7
	South Asia		15.4	9.0	6.4	5.7	9.7
	Rest of the world		23.4	4.9	18.5	11.0	12.4

Source	Region	Unit	Total annual welfare gains	Agriculture	Manufactures	Services	
Brown, Deardorff and Stern (2002) 33 per cent tariff reduction on goods; 33 per cent reduction on service barriers	Global	$ 1995 billion	686.4	-8.1	267.3	427.2	
	Developed countries		544.4	-1.8	190.9	355.4	
	Asia		103.0	5.2	58.4	39.3	
	Latin America		24.9	-6.7	8.0	23.6	
	Northern Africa and Middle East		14.1	-4.8	10.1	8.9	

Source	Region	Unit	Total annual welfare gains	Agriculture and food	Textile and clothing	All other sectors (goods only)	
World Bank (2002a) Elimination of all import tariffs, export and domestic production subsidies (goods only)	Static gains Global	$ 1997 billion	355.0	248.0	41.0	70.0	
	High-income		171.0	106.0	17.0	50.0	
	Low- and middle-income		184.0	142.0	24.0	20.0	
	Dynamic gains Global	$ 1997 billion	832.0	587.0	189.0	62.0	
	High-income		539.0	196.0	66.0	35.0	
	Low- and middle-income		293.0	390.0	123.0	27.0	

Source	Region	Unit	Total annual welfare gains				
Laird, Cenart and Turrini (2003) Worldwide 50 per cent reduction of all merchandise tariffs	Global	$ 1997 billion	39.6				
	Developed		20.1				
	Economies in transition		0.6				
	Sub-Saharan Africa		--				
	Norththern Africa and Middle East		3.7				
	Latin America		1.4				
	Asian NIEs[a] and China		11.6				
	South Asia		1.4				
	Rest of the world		0.8				

Table II.3 (cont'd)							
Source	Region	Unit	Total annual welfare gains	Trade facilitation	Services	Manufactures	Agriculture
François, van Meigl and van Tongeren (2003) Full liberalization on border measures and subsidies and trade facilitation (3 per cent of value trade)	Global OECD countries Developing countries	$ 1997 billion	367.3 205.2 162.1	150.9 95.7 55.2	53.1 38.0 15.0	54.2 17.4 36.9 0.5	109.1 54.1 55.0

a   Newly industrializing economies.

Most models indicate significant gains due to liberalization in agriculture, benefiting largely consumers in developed countries.[19] A closer look at these estimates points to different outcomes depending on whether tariff reduction, or cuts in domestic support and/or export subsidies—the three pillars of agriculture negotiations under Doha—are pursued.

Net food importers would be negatively affected by the removal/reduction of (food) subsidies in Organization for Economic Cooperation and Development (OECD) countries as their food bill would increase, at least initially. In fact, research seems to indicate welfare losses for most developing regions when domestic support is cut in OECD economies, owing to deterioration in their terms of trade (see table II.4).[20] In some countries, these losses are manageable, but other countries may face sizeable difficulties. Of particular concern are the potential welfare losses incurred by sub-Saharan Africa, which is already facing severe constraints in dealing with existing challenges. Countries will require additional assistance in dealing with these costs.

Tariff cuts on agricultural products can generate relatively higher global benefits, including for the majority of developing countries. Additionally, they can mitigate most of the negative impact of a larger food bill. Net food importers will also benefit from increased market access for their exports, which may offset losses coming from higher food prices.

All regions will benefit from liberalization of manufactures trade, although some will gain more than others. Sub-Saharan Africa's gains (excluding South Africa), for instance, are negligible in most models owing to its reduced supply capacity, its limited competitiveness and surging imports from Asia (Laird, Cernat and Turrini, 2003).

Considerable potential gains could accrue from liberalization of trade in services, owing to the large share of services in the consumption of many countries and to the fact that services are also a major input to other productive activities. Yet, caution is called for, as there are severe data and modelling deficiencies related to trade in services, particularly in developing countries. Additionally, liberalization per se will not be sufficient to bring benefits for this group of countries. Developing countries have already identified several factors that need to be taken into account and acted upon for them to fully benefit from service liberalization. These include supply constraints; the existence of certain preconditions, policy measures and technical assistance to ensure capacity-building and competitiveness by

Significant gains from agricultural liberalization, largely benefiting consumers in developed countries, are projected

Net food importers are expected to be negatively affected by the removal/reduction of (food) subsidies in OECD countries

All regions will benefit from liberalization of trade in manufactures and estimates suggest that considerable potential gains might accrue from liberalization of trade in services as well

Table II.4.
Selected estimates of annual welfare effects from multilateral trade liberalization

Source	Unit	50 per cent tariff cut	50 per cent domestic support cut	Elimination of export subsidies
Hoekman, Ng and Olarreaga (2003)	$ 1995 billion			
World		16.8	0.2	..
Industrialized countries		14.5	0.5	..
Developing countries		2.3	-0.3	..
Least developed countries		0.0	0.0	..
François, van Meigl and van Tongeren (2003)	$ 1997 billion			
World		57.0	8.7	..
EU-15		9.8	8.4	..
Northern America		2.7	2.2	..
High-income Asia		16.1	-0.5	..
Middle- and low-income Asia		7.5	-0.3	..
Central and Eastern Europe		1.7	0.0	..
Mediterranean		15.0	-0.6	..
South America		2.0	-0.2	..
Sub-Saharan Africa		2.7	-0.1	..
Others		-0.5	-0.2	..
Laird, Cenart and Turrini (2003)	$ 1995 billion			
World		30.3	..	-4.7
Developed countries		11.1	..	1.9
Transition economies		0.2	..	-0.9
Developing countries		9.5	..	-2.9
NIEs[a] and China		4.4	..	-0.2
South Asia		0.3	..	0.0
Sub-Saharan Africa		0.2	..	-0.4
Northern Africa and Middle East		3	..	-2.2
Latin America		1.3	..	0.1
Others		0.3	..	-0.2
Dimaranan, Hertel and Keeney (2004)	$ 1997 billion			
Developing countries		..	-0.4	..
Asia		..	-0.1	..
Latin America		..	0.1	..
Northern Africa and Middle East		..	-0.3	..
Sub Saharan Africa		..	-0.1	..
Others		..	0.0	..

a Newly industrializing economies.

their domestic sector; the need for proper sequencing of liberalization and policy flexibility; and ensuring universal access to certain essential services (Manduna, 2004). On the other hand, further liberalization of Mode 4 of service provision—liberalization of temporary movement of workers—could bring more immediate benefits.[21] According to Winters (2002), a 3 per cent increase in industrialized countries' quota of temporary workers (both skilled and unskilled) would increase global welfare by $156 billion per year, with $70 billion accruing to developing countries. Potential benefits would also accrue from a more liberal Mode 1 provision (cross-border supply (outsourcing)).

Notwithstanding the above, the benefits of multilateral liberalization are often of a long-term nature, while implementation costs frequently occur in the short term. The latter include tariff revenue losses, lower output and employment losses in import competing sectors, implementation costs of agreed commitments and reduced policy flexibility (Laird, Fernandez de Cordoba and Vanzetti, 2003). Additionally, the Round will also imply some long-term adjustment costs. For instance, some developing countries have been concerned with the erosion of preferences that further most favoured nation (MFN) tariff reduction may entail for these countries' competitiveness in preferential markets (see box II.2).

Built-in flexibilities and a sufficiently long implementation period may help developing countries to deal with the challenges mentioned above and should be provided for in the negotiations. Policy interventions may mitigate some of these negative effects. Yet, developing countries, already resource-constrained, may not afford these measures and thus have fewer policy instruments available to them. In this regard, the IMF proposal of a Trade Integration Mechanism (TIM) is a welcome development. TIM, however, addresses only one aspect of the adjustment costs—those leading to balance-of-payments difficulties, which are often of a temporary nature. The fiscal implications of World Trade Organization induced reforms, besides lower tariff revenue, need to be tackled as well.

More importantly, some countries—particularly preferences-dependent economies—will require support beyond assistance with short-term adjustment costs. They will need to build production and technological capacities aimed at diversifying their economies and allowing them to fully benefit from their integration into the world economy on a sustainable basis. In fact, the inadequacy of existing support mechanisms has been recognized and several proposals have been put forward. Among others, Mr. Peter Mandelson (2004), the European Commissioner for Trade, has recently called for the establishment of a special trade adjustment fund for investment in trade capacities in poor countries and assistance with mitigating the costs of liberalization. Similarly, the United Nations Millennium Project Task Force on Trade urged the creation of a temporary "aid for trade fund", in addition to current aid flows, to support countries in dealing with costs resulting from the implementation of Doha (UN Millennium Project, Task Force on Trade, 2005).

The Doha Round: where does it stand?

After the setback in Cancún, negotiations drifted for a while. The adoption of the framework agreement of 1 August 2004, the "July package", provided the Round with a renewed momentum, particularly in view of the need to produce tangible results for consideration by the Sixth Ministerial Conference of the World Trade Organization in Hong Kong, Special Administrative Region (SAR) of China in December 2005 and the evolving consensus among World Trade Organization members to conclude the negotiations no later than the end of 2006. Additional political momentum has been provided through a series

The benefits of multilateral liberalization are often of a long-term nature while implementation costs tend to occur in the short run

Built-in flexibilities and a sufficiently long implementation period may help developing countries to deal with such challenges and should be provided for

Preference-dependent economies will require support beyond assistance with short-term adjustment costs

The adoption of the framework agreement of 1 August 2004, the "July package", provided the Round with a renewed momentum

Box II.2

Multilateralism or preferential access?

Developed countries extend non-reciprocal preferential market access treatment to developing countries under the Generalized System of Preferences (GSP) and through special schemes such as those available to least developed countries. While the former often excludes products of export interest to developing countries, but are applied to a large number of qualifying developing countries, the latter is more restrictive in terms of beneficiaries but, in many instances, provides virtually quota- and duty-free treatment, thus giving beneficiaries significant preference margins in relation to tariff peak products. Differences between MFN and GSP treatments, however, can be small (see table below).

Most Favoured Nation and Generalized System of Preferences
tariffs and least developed country preferential treatment in
Canada, European Union, Japan and the United States, 2002-2003

Percentage		
	MFN	GSP	Least developed countries
United States (2002)	5.2	4.2	2.8
World Trade Organization agricultural products	10.4	9.3	6.5
Textiles and clothing	9.7	9.4	9.4
EU (2002)	6.4	4.5	1.7
World Trade Organization agricultural products	16.1	14.5	9.0
Textiles and clothing	8.4	7.2	0.0
Japan (2002-2003)	6.9	5.7	3.6
World Trade Organization agricultural products	20.0	19.3	18.3
Textiles and clothing	7.0	5.4	0.1
Canada (2002)	6.8	5.4	4.1
World Trade Organization agricultural products	21.7	20.8	18.2
Textiles and clothing	9.9	8.9	7.1

Source: Acharya and Daly (2004).

Despite advantages, the utilization rates (defined as the ratio of imports actually receiving preference to covered imports) of such programmes are not as high as expected and are often concentrated in a few countries and few products. For instance, UNCTAD (2003a) found that, on average, the least developed countries utilization rate had been about 67 per cent in 2001.

Low utilization rates are in part due to supply constraints in most beneficiary countries. This indicates, as recognized by the Monterrey Consensus of the International Conference on Financing for Development, that increased trade opportunities are not enough to put a country on a faster growth path and that necessary conditions need to be created and implemented in order for countries to benefit from increased liberalization. Low utilization rates are also due to stringent rules of origin, complex standards and other requirements (United Nations Conference on Trade and Development, 2003g). Moreover, most preference schemes carry some degree of uncertainty, as the benefits either are timed and renewed at the judgement of the offering country or can be withdrawn if performance requirements (often policy-related) are not fulfilled by the beneficiary. There is therefore a great deal of discretion that beneficiaries are not able to influence.

The impact of preference erosion on beneficiaries may be on average less than feared. Assuming a 40 per cent reduction in each beneficiary's aggregate preference margin, full utilization of pref-

Box II.2 (cont'd)

erences and no gains from lower MFN tariffs in third markets, export revenue losses for the group of middle-income countries have been estimated to be small, ranging from 0.5 to 1.2 per cent of total exports. Vulnerability, however, is much higher in those countries whose exports are concentrated in preferential markets or dependent on sugar and bananas (in particular a large number of small island economies) and to a lesser extent, on textiles (Alexandraki and Lankes, 2004).

In the case of least developed countries, Subramanian (2003) estimates losses from preference erosion at 1.7 per cent of the group's total exports, reflecting the fact that only a few least developed countries actually enjoy relatively large preference margins. Only five countries (Cape Verde, Haiti, Malawi, Mauritania and Sao Tome and Principe) are to suffer losses above 5 per cent of their export revenue. In value terms, the group as a whole is estimated to lose $530 million in export revenue, 75 per cent of which is concentrated in five countries (Bangladesh, Cambodia, Malawi, Mauritania and the United Republic of Tanzania).

It has been argued that these losses would be gradual as liberalization occured over a number of years and that because the losses were anticipated, it could be easier for countries to adjust (Subramanian, 2003). This, however, does not imply that preference-dependent economies may not need financial and technical assistance to facilitate their adjustment, particularly taking into account their limited resources and the multiple handicaps they confront.

It thus seems more advantageous for developing countries, on average, to obtain more secure MFN reductions, particularly on export products of interest to them, as mandated by the Doha Declaration, rather than for existing preferences to be maintained. Multilateralism offers a more predictable and stable trading environment. There is also some evidence that the granting of preferences (non-reciprocal and otherwise) has implied higher MFN tariffs for non-beneficiaries than would otherwise have been the case (Limão, 2003).

This is not to say that preferences do not have a role to play. Preferences offer developing countries an opportunity to develop new sectors or to overcome certain disadvantages in promoting existing sectors. The challenge for beneficiaries is thus the transformation of an enhanced competitiveness brought about by preferential treatment into one based on increased productivity and product upgrading, which can create lasting benefits for the economy once preferences are removed. Independently of the final outcome of the Doha Round, some preferences are bound to be reduced anyway owing to reforms in preferential markets or past agreements at the multilateral level. The reforms in the EU sugar regime—including those triggered by the recent World Trade Organization ruling on export subsidies—and its banana regime are cases in point. The recent expiration of the Agreement on Textiles and Clothing is another.

---

of mini-Ministerial meetings (Davos, Kenya and Paris). The road to Hong Kong SAR, however, has proved to be as difficult as the road to Cancún. Negotiations have not advanced and there is urgent need to expedite the process in time for Doha to contribute to the achievement of the Millennium Development Goals.

The July framework envisages, in the case of **agriculture**, the complete elimination of export subsidies, and substantial reductions in trade-distorting measures and in overall tariffs according to a tiered formula, which imply that members with higher levels of trade-distorting measures and/or tariffs will make deeper cuts.

The World Trade Organization Agreement on Agriculture[22] classifies domestic support policies according to their level of trade distortion (amber, blue and green boxes).[23] The July framework maintains this distinction, placing a cap on blue box support while criteria for green box inclusion will be reviewed and clarified. Developed countries, however, can maintain high tariff protection on "sensitive products" provided that other products receive deeper cuts. Developing countries can designate "special products" that would be eligible for a "special safeguard mechanism". Special and differential treatment (SDT) is accorded to developing countries in terms of reduced commitments (or no commitments by least developed countries) and longer implementation periods (World Trade

The July framework envisages the complete elimination of agricultural export subsidies

Organization, 2004b). A subcommittee was created to look at cotton as a "special issue" within the agriculture negotiations.[24] The framework, however, only pointed to the general direction of negotiations (United Nations Conference on Trade and Development, 2004e). The amount and schedule of liberalization as well as base periods, modalities and other relevant details have remained open, subject to further negotiations.

The major issues in
non-agricultural
market access are tariff
reduction and
tariff binding

The major issues in **non-agricultural market access** are tariff reduction and tariff binding. A non-linear formula approach will be applied on a line-by-line basis and on the bound rates. For unbound tariff lines, twice the level of the MFN applied tariff was suggested. This implies that higher tariffs would receive relatively deeper cuts. All proposals submitted up to early May 2005 were based on a "Swiss" harmonizing formula, which narrows the gap between high and low tariffs and produces a maximum final rate. Developing countries, therefore, would undergo relatively larger liberalization owing to the relatively higher tariffs. Besides developing countries' concerns over deindustrialization and reduced policy instruments for industrial development, this could bring negative implications for countries dependent on tariffs for government revenue. Technical discussions have been difficult regarding how to convert specific tariffs into ad valorem tariffs or how to deal with unbound tariffs.

The framework also has provisions on autonomous liberalization provided that these resulted in tariffs lines being bound on an MFN basis at the World Trade Organization. Countries having binding coverage of less than a given percentage (35 per cent was suggested) are not required to participate in the formula approach but are expected to bind their tariffs. This, however, may leave these countries with relatively higher levels of obligation in future rounds. Developing countries will also have longer implementation periods (not specified) for tariff reduction. They may also apply less than formula cuts (within some specified parameters) to some tariff lines or may keep tariff lines unbound.

The framework also envisages a sectoral tariff component aiming at the harmonization or elimination of tariffs on products of export interest of developing countries. Product coverage is still to be identified.

The General
Agreement on Trade in
Services contains a
built-in agenda,
committing members
to "progressive and
higher levels of
liberalization"

Like agriculture, **services** were incorporated into the multilateral trading rules with the Uruguay Round. The General Agreement on Trade in Services contains a built-in agenda as members committed to "progressive and higher levels of liberalization". Negotiations had been to start in 2000 on the basis of national policy objectives and the level of development of individual members (both overall and in individual sectors), with flexibilities for developing countries to liberalize fewer sectors and types of transaction. Negotiating guidelines were adopted in March 2001 and established a "request-offer" approach as the modality of negotiations (World Trade Organization, 2001b).

The Doha Declaration reaffirms the 2001 guidelines "as the basis for continuing the negotiations" and sets deadlines for the submission of request and offers, which were subsequently extended by the July package to May 2005. By early 2005, some 90 initial requests and 50 offers had been received, the latter mostly from developed countries. The offers often bypass sensitive sectors such as health, audiovisual and labour-intensive lower-skill services, particularly those rendered through Mode 4, that is to say, areas and modes where developing countries have most competitive advantage and interest. Recently, some developing countries have also increased participation of Mode 1 of services supply —India is the most prominent example of such trend— although from a small base.

Currently, General Agreement on Trade in Services commitments in Mode 4 are more restrictive than in the other modes of delivery. Yet, limited liberalization has been offered in this area so far, and most Mode 4 offers often refer to highly skilled labour and require commercial presence in the country (Mode 3). Additionally, offers seem not to advance previous commitments made and, in some cases, imply reciprocity (United Nations Conference on Trade and Development, 2005b). In all, the process is proceeding behind schedule and the extent of liberalization offered has been limited.

The Agreement on Trade-related Aspects of **Intellectual Property Rights**[25] (TRIPS) establishes minimum levels of protection that World Trade Organization members have to extend to one another. Compliance with TRIPS, however, has proved costly and difficult to implement for developing countries. Moreover, the Agreement does not necessarily pay due attention to these countries' needs.[26] For instance, it places restrictions on practices to promote industrial development, and does not provide enough protection to traditional knowledge and folklore. It also implies potentially higher prices and reduced access to some goods. A particularly important issue in this regard has been that of medicines, where the Agreement can be a source of significant difficulties if countries confront acute health crises.

At Doha, Ministers addressed some of these concerns as well as implementation and built-in issues of the Agreement. The following issues were to be tackled: (a) public health; (b) geographical indications; (c) biodiversity issues, including the relationship between TRIPS and the Convention on Biological Diversity[27], and the protection of traditional knowledge and folklore; (d) non-violation disputes; and (e) technology transfer to least developed countries.

As in other areas, negotiations have been contentious. On the eve of the Cancún meeting, the General Council adopted a decision that allowed countries to export pharmaceuticals produced under compulsory licensing to countries lacking such manufacturing capacity, provided that both importing and exporting countries met specific conditions (World Trade Organization, 2003). The Decision is a temporary waiver to particular TRIPS obligations, which are to be permanently amended. As of early May 2005, however, no importing or exporting country had notified the World Trade Organization about its intention to make use of the decision. This is due in part to the difficulties faced in fulfilling the stringent requirements specified in the decision and in part to the fact that large pharmaceutical companies have been providing the required medicines at reduced cost. More worryingly, no agreement on how to modify the Trade-related Aspects of Intellectual Property Rights was reached by the established deadline of end of March 2005. While the decision remains binding until the Agreement is amended, the system has not been tested and its usefulness cannot be properly assessed (Page and Conway, 2004).

Turning to the other TRIPS-related issues, a decision has been adopted on the establishment of a mechanism to ensure monitoring and implementation of commitments that developed countries made to provide incentives to the private sector and institutions for the transfer of technology to least developed countries. Nonetheless, no agreement has yet been reached on the other mandated areas of negotiation mentioned above.

The July framework also includes modalities on negotiations on **trade facilitation**. They represent a new approach in respect of special and differential treatment, as both the extent and timing of commitments are to be related to developing countries' implementation capacity. There is concern, however, over implementation costs despite the potential benefits of trade facilitation measures.

At Doha, Ministers agreed that "all **special and differential treatment** provisions shall be reviewed with a view to strengthening them and making them more precise, effective and operational" (para. 44). They also instructed the Committee on Trade and Development to identify which of those special and differential treatment provisions were

While the Agreement on Trade-related Aspects of Intellectual Property Rights establishes minimum levels of protection, compliance with the Agreement has proved costly and difficult to implement for developing countries

mandatory, and to consider the implications of making mandatory those that were currently non-binding (World Trade Organization, 2001c). The July framework reiterates that the needs of developing countries and least developed countries are at the centre of the Doha round and that SDT is an integral part of the World Trade Organization agreements, but it does not advance additional guidelines for negotiations.

The revision of SDT provisions has not advanced smoothly. Deadlines were postponed. One of the difficulties is related to different interpretations of the Doha mandate. Developing countries argue that strengthening existing SDT provisions requires making past negotiations effective. They thus call for changes in the language of World Trade Organization agreements. However, some analysts caution about the legal difficulties in making some of the "best endeavour" into mandatory provisions (Keck and Low, 2004). Developed countries, on the other hand, argue that changes in existing agreements are subject to new negotiations and are unwilling to adopt changes that would alter the "balance of Member's rights and obligations". Moreover, they maintain that proposals should be assessed in relation to the objectives SDT aims to achieve (International Centre for Trade and Sustainable Development (ICTSD), 2003). The latter position opens up an entire range of questions. In the developing countries' perception, these issues extend beyond the Doha mandate, which is agreement specific.

Another contentious issue—and one that is perhaps more difficult to deal with—is that of the segmentation and/or graduation of developing countries. Developed countries argue that the different levels of development across the developing world call for different types of treatment across countries. Moreover, they claim that they would be able to offer deeper preferences if these applied to a more restricted number of poorer countries.

Differences between developed and developing countries remain significant, however, even when those considered to be "more advanced" are taken into account. Additionally, there is overall concern that several World Trade Organization obligations were drafted on the basis of policy practices in developed countries, which may not be compatible with the reality and the developmental path of developing countries, thus justifying the need for increased flexibility in the implementation of agreed commitments. Moreover, it is not obvious why measures to facilitate development should discriminate among countries, nor whether preferential treatment extended to developing countries would imply significant additional costs for developed countries.

The revision of special and differential treatment provisions has not advanced smoothly

Regional trade arrangements

The number of regional trade arrangements has increased sixfold in the past two decades and fourfold since 1990, and totalled roughly 230 as of early 2005

When a World Trade Organization member enters into a regional integration agreement[28], it grants more favourable terms to its trade with other parties to that arrangement than to its trade with other World Trade Organization members. It is thus departing from the guiding principle of non-discrimination as defined, for example, in article I of the General Agreement on Tariffs and Trade (GATT) and article II of the General Agreement on Trade in Services. Nevertheless, World Trade Organization members are permitted to enter into such arrangements under specific conditions.[29] Meanwhile, other preferential schemes—such as non-reciprocal preferential agreements involving developing and developed countries—require World Trade Organization members to seek a waiver from its rules.

Despite the need for waivers and exemptions, a variety of arrangements, encompassing various forms of preferential agreements including bilateral, regional and multilateral accords, have proliferated. The number of such agreements has increased sixfold in the past two decades and fourfold since 1990, and totalled roughly 230 as of early 2005 (Crawford and Fiorentino, 2005).

These types of accords, allowing members to grant preferences to other members that are denied to outsiders, have the potential to reconfigure trade flows as well as the workings of the global trading system. This raises two concerns. The first is whether the trade that an agreement generates is welfare-enhancing, both for members and for the global system. This is the traditional "trade-creation" versus "trade diversion" concern first analysed by Jacob Viner (1950) more than half a century ago.[30] The second concern is whether the creation of such preferential agreements distracts from the workings of the multilateral trading system or, conversely, aids in the process of global trade liberalization. The present section looks at the validity of these concerns. It argues that, while multilateralism is the best means to achieve a better integration of developing countries into the global economy, preferential agreements may aid in this process.

Such accords, allowing members to grant preferences to other members that are denied to outsiders, have the potential to reconfigure trade flows as well as the workings of the global trading system

The proliferation of trading blocs and free trade agreements

While the formation of preferential trading agreements has flourished in recent years, the movement towards such trade agreements goes back to the 1950s and 1960s. Both the European Economic Community (established by the 1957 Treaty of Rome) and the European Free Trade Association (established 1960), had their origins in that period, as did the Central American Common Market (established 1960), the Andean Pact (established 1969), now the Andean Community, the Latin American Integration Association (LAIA) (formed in 1960) and the Southern African Customs Union (established 1969).

The trend towards such trade agreements goes back to the 1950s and 1960s

By the time the European Community (EC) had segued into EC-92 in July 1987—envisaging further enlargement, as well as the free movement of goods, services and factors by 1992—similar efforts were under way elsewhere, resulting for example, in the United States of America-Canada Free Trade Agreement of 1988. In turn, many developing countries initiated their own schemes, for example, the Southern Common Market (MERCOSUR), which was formed in 1991. In Asia, the Association of Southeast Asian Nations (ASEAN), whose orientation had been a relatively political one when it was founded in 1967, established the ASEAN Free Trade Area in 1992.

The new integration agreements differed from the older ones both qualitatively and quantitatively. To begin with, the focus is now far broader and extends beyond trade in goods to encompass trade in services as well as investment protection, intellectual property rights and, in some cases, labour standards, environmental issues and some domestic regulations that may affect international trade. Further, trade facilitation measures are often an important element in these schemes. In addition, the newer schemes tend to be more outward-looking, thus following a policy of "open regionalism" (Economic Commission for Latin America and the Caribbean, 1994). Finally, schemes are emerging that link developed and developing countries, such as the North American Free Trade Agreement (NAFTA), the EU-Turkey Customs Union (1 January 1996) and the proposed Euro-Mediterranean economic area, to be formed by 2010.

Newer integration agreements differ from the older ones qualitatively as well as quantitatively

This process has been interwoven with the proliferation of free trade agreements. Since 1990, the number of free trade agreements has risen from 50 to almost 230 as of 2004. According to the World Trade Organization, another 60 are in various stages of formation. Only 12 countries or territories are currently not a party to at least one such agreement.[31] Moreover, many countries belong to several such schemes. On average, a country belongs to six arrangements, though there is a great deal of variation depending on the region and the level of development. For example, for the 25 countries constituting OECD, plus Lichtenstein, there are, on average, 11 arrangement per country and as many as 29, in some instances. In Latin America and the Caribbean, there are 8 schemes, on average, per country, and as many as 19 in some cases; for East Asia and the Pacific, the comparable numbers are 2 and 7.

> As a single country becomes a member of several schemes, a "spaghetti bowl" of overlapping arrangements evolves

The result, as a single country becomes a member of several schemes, is what has been termed a "spaghetti bowl" of overlapping arrangements. Such arrangements generally have different provisions—different tariff schedules, different rules of origin and different periods for implementation—all of which strain trade policy and trade administration and complicate customs procedures.

Impact of preferential agreements and policy implications

> Trade agreements, which have the potential to deviate trade flows, have not necessarily done so

Trade agreements have the potential to deviate trade flows. Nonetheless, it is not valid to generalize that they have necessarily done so (see table II.5). Rather, looking back as far as 1970, three patterns appear to predominate. First, there are schemes where intra-trade clearly increased. Asia-Pacific Economic Cooperation (APEC)[32] (though it actually did not

Table II.5.
Trade within selected regional trade blocs, 1970-2002

	Percentage of total bloc exports					Percentage of world exports	
	1970	1980	1990	1998	2002	1970	2002
High-income and low- and middle-income economies							
APEC[a]	57.8	57.9	68.3	69.7	73.3	36.0	46.0
EU	59.5	60.8	65.9	56.8	60.6	45.6	37.9
NAFTA	36.0	33.6	41.4	51.7	56.7	21.7	17.2
Latin America and the Caribbean							
Andean Group	1.8	3.8	4.1	12.8	9.5	1.9	0.8
CACM	26.1	24.4	15.3	15.8	11.1	0.4	0.4
CARICOM	4.2	5.3	8.1	17.3	12.5	0.4	0.2
LAIA	9.9	13.7	10.8	16.7	11.1	4.5	5.0
MERCOSUR	9.4	11.6	8.9	25.0	11.6	1.7	1.4
Africa							
COMESA	8.7	6.0	6.3	7.7	6.4	1.6	0.4
ECOWAS	2.9	10.1	7.9	10.7	10.6	1.1	0.4
UDEAC	4.9	1.6	2.3	2.3	1.5	0.2	0.1
Asia							
Arab Common Market	2.2	2.4	2.7	4.8	4.8	1.6	0.6
ASEAN	22.9	18.7	19.8	21.9	23.7	2.0	6.3
Bangkok Agreement	2.7	3.7	3.7	5.0	5.6	1.6	5.1
EAEC	28.9	35.6	39.7	42.0	48.2	11.3	25.2

Source: DESA, based on World Bank, *World Development Indicators, 2004.*

a   No preferential trade agreement.

have an operational preferential trade agreement over the period 1970-2002), NAFTA, the Bangkok Agreement[33] and the East Asian Economic Caucus (EAEC)[34] are included in this set. A second group of arrangements experienced an increase in intra-bloc exports as a share of total bloc exports, but the "peak" had been in fact achieved in the second half of the 1990s and declined thereafter. This has been the case for the Andean Community,[35] the Caribbean Community and Common Market (CARICOM),[36] LAIA, formerly the Latin American Free Trade Area, [37] MERCOSUR, the Economic Community of West African States (ECOWAS)[38] and the Arab Common Market.[39] A final observed trend was for intra-bloc trade as a share of total exports to either not increase, or actually decline, over the period in question. In the case of EU, for example, intra-trade had been already substantial and therefore did not grow significantly over the period. However, intra-trade declined within the Central American Common Market (CACM),[40] the Common Market for Eastern and Southern Africa (COMESA)[41] and the Central African Customs and Economic Union (UDEAC).[42]

These trends indicate, in short, that it cannot simply be presumed that, following the formation of a trading bloc, trade flows will deviate from outside to inside the bloc. In part, this may be due to the fact that many recent schemes overlap with already existing agreements, so that possible further shifts in the direction of trade are likely to be marginal. Moreover, especially in OECD countries, the importance of such preferences is less than it might be because of already reduced tariff barriers among members.

The situation for many developing countries is different, however, because the number of low-duty tariff lines is small. South-South blocs are, therefore, potentially far more important as regards the preferences gained. Nevertheless, many developing countries have endeavoured to reduce tariff levels over the past two decades—though most of these reductions can be attributed to autonomous liberalization and not to trade agreements. According to an estimate by Martin and Ng (2005), only 10 per cent of total tariff reductions between 1983 and 2003 could be attributed to regional agreements, compared with 25 per cent to multilateral agreements and 66 per cent to autonomous liberalization. A recent analysis of the South Asian Preferential Trading Agreement—initiated in 1995 and comprising Bangladesh, Bhutan, India, Maldives, Nepal, Pakistan and Sri Lanka—makes precisely this point, maintaining that it was not regionalization but "previous unilateral liberalization efforts" that " had a positive impact in boosting both intra- and extraregional trade" in the South Asia region (Pitigala, 2005).

For trade agreements to have a positive impact on their member economies in terms of integration into the global economy, it is necessary for such schemes to stimulate overall trade flows, not just intra-trade. The evidence in this regard is difficult to measure and appraise. Part of the difficulty emanates from the fact that such agreements generally encompass far more than trade and even far more than economic objectives, thus including broader socio-political and regional concerns. Then, too, global developments may swamp regional trends, making it difficult to disentangle the two. Moreover, trade between countries and regions may grow spontaneously, without preferential schemes, as box II.3 suggests in relation to the growing trade of China with Latin America and Africa. Figures in table II.5 do make clear, however, that it was only in the Asian region that bloc exports as a share of world exports expanded dramatically between 1970 and 2002. In Africa, the opposite was the case.

Two basic methods that are used to examine the effects of trade agreements are ex ante general equilibrium simulation studies, which look forward to potential gains, and ex post econometric analyses via a gravity model, which look back at actual performance.[43]

South-South blocs are potentially very important as regards the preferences gained by members

Analyses examining the effects of trade agreements produce widely disparate results

Box II.3

Current trends in trade relations between China and Latin America and China and Africa: potential and challenges

With real GDP growth of 9.5 per cent and an increase in its trade volume by approximately 30 per cent in 2004, the continued strong performance of the Chinese economy is often seen as a major determinant of recent developments in international trade conditions and, in particular, the rise of global commodity prices. However, in addition to this price effect, China's economic growth also appears to be accelerating the emergence of a "new geography" of trade, describing the dynamic rise of new South-South trade flows.

In this context, besides the increasing role of intraregional trade in Asia, the rising importance of trade relations between China and Latin America and between China and Africa appears particularly noticeable. Combined with a potentially positive effect on FDI inflows, the improvements in trade conditions create an opportunity to achieve significant progress in economic and social development in the exporting countries concerned.

Data show that there has been a uniform increase in the relative importance of trade relations between China and Latin America as well as between China and Africa. China's exports to Latin America as a share of its total exports increased from 1.9 per cent in 1993 to 2.6 per cent in 2003, while the share of exports to China in total exports of Latin American economies more than tripled in the same period, from 1.2 per cent to 3.8 per cent (see table). Similarly, the share of China's exports to Africa in total exports increased from 1.6 to 2.3 per cent whereas the share of Africa's exports to China in its total exports increased from 1.0 to 4.8 per cent over the same period.

With respect to the composition of trade, evidence suggests that trade flows from Latin America to China consisted mainly of raw materials, while in the case of Africa, fuel products played a dominant role (see figure). In the reverse direction, Chinese exports to both Latin America and Africa consisted especially of manufactured goods as well as machines and transportation equipment.

An interesting implication of these developments is the significant benefit that China is generating for other developing countries with respect to their increasing their earnings from commodity exports, a major change with respect to patterns observed in previous decades. Furthermore, the benefits may be extended to other areas, particularly with respect to FDI. Indeed, the increasingly significant trade relations

Significance of China's trade with Latin America and Africa: percentage share of imports from/exports to partner region in total imports/exports of reference region, 1993-2003

| Reference region: | China | | China | | Latin America | | Africa | |
| Partner (from/to): | Latin America | | Africa | | China | | China | |
Year	Imports	Exports	Imports	Exports	Imports	Exports	Imports	Exports
1993	1.9	1.9	0.8	1.6	0.9	1.2	1.4	1.0
1994	1.9	2.0	0.7	1.4	1.1	1.2	1.6	0.9
1995	2.2	2.1	1.1	1.7	1.3	1.3	2.0	1.4
1996	2.6	2.0	1.1	1.7	1.1	1.4	2.0	1.3
1997	2.6	2.4	1.7	1.7	1.4	1.3	2.5	2.1
1998	2.1	2.8	1.1	2.2	1.5	1.1	3.1	1.5
1999	1.8	2.6	1.4	2.1	1.5	1.0	3.2	2.2
2000	2.1	2.8	2.1	2.0	1.8	1.3	3.8	3.3
2001	2.7	3.0	1.9	2.2	2.1	1.9	4.6	3.6
2002	2.8	2.8	1.8	2.1	2.5	2.4	4.8	3.8
2003	3.6	2.6	2.0	2.3	2.9	3.8	5.6	4.8

Sources: IMF/DOT database; and United Nations calculations.

Box II.3 (cont'd)

Composition of trade between China and Latin America, and China and Africa, 2003

Imports by China from Latin America, 2003

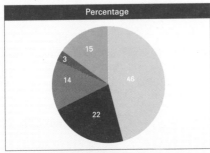

Exports from China to Latin America, 2003

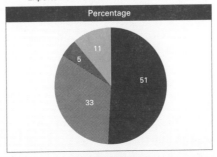

Imports by China from Africa, 2003

Exports from China to Africa, 2003

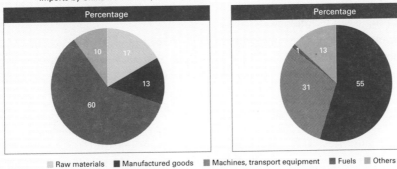

☐ Raw materials   ■ Manufactured goods   ■ Machines, transport equipment   ■ Fuels   ☐ Others

Sources: COMTRADE database; and United Nations calculations.

of China with Latin America and with Africa are likely to be accompanied by increasing flows of FDI from China to those two regions. Thus, according to some forecasts, China's investments in Latin America will amount to US$ 100 billion over the next decade.[a] In parallel to this, China's investment in Africa is also expected to rise, particularly in the oil sector. This is likely to at least partially offset the effects of China's role as a competitor for FDI, which is often seen as one of the difficulties that other developing countries face in attracting international investment funds.

Such FDI flows are likely to be channelled particularly into the primary sector of the recipient countries, given the prominent role of primary goods and commodities in Latin American and African exports to China. One reason for this is that Latin America and Africa are rich in natural resource endowments. A further reason lies in China's demand for raw materials, which is based on its need to sustain an economic growth that is driven especially by the raw material-intensive and energy-dependent industry sector as well as construction. In addition, rising per capita incomes and urbanization in China have given rise to lifestyle changes as well as a change in the composition of the demand for food products, including an increase in imports by China of non-traditional products such as coffee and cocoa. The latter effect can help to not only increase the magnitude of the benefits of China's economic expansion for Latin American and African economies, but also spread these positive effects over a larger number of developing countries.

Especially in the area of agricultural products, an important international determinant of the extent to which Latin American and African economies will be able to reap the benefits of increasing demand from China is the design of the world trade system and, in particular, the support from developed countries for the further liberalization of international trade. Only a further reduction in subsidies and the phasing out of measures that support domestic producers in the developed economies will help to avert a situation where a disproportionate share of the benefits of the improved conditions in the world market for agricultural products accrues to firms and producers in the developed world.

The challenge for policy makers in countries in Latin America and Africa will be to maximize the actual social welfare effects of both higher export revenues and an increase in investment flows into their primary sectors stemming from the positive developments in trade relations with China.

a   BBC News, 17 November 2004, available from http://news.bbc.co.uk/1/hi/ world/americas/4018219.stm (accessed 13 June 2005).

Such analyses can produce widely disparate results. For example, one assessment of the recent spate of preferential trade agreements that emerged in the 1990s, "found no indication that the 'new wave' of regionalism boosted intra-bloc trade significantly" (Soloaga and Winters, 1999). However, an investigation of the effects of NAFTA—10 years after its inception—found that it played an important role in boosting trade and financial flows in the region (Kose, Meredith and Towe, 2004). Likewise, estimates of the potential effects of the Free Trade Agreement of the Americas and of a trade agreement between MERCOSUR and EU suggests that these schemes will be net trade-creating ((Harrison, Rutherford and Tarr, 2001; Harrison and others, 2003). Finally, an investigation that distinguished between various degrees of integration and implementation of trading schemes found that "more integrated arrangements"[44] generated greater total trade-creation (Ghosh and Yamarik, 2004).

> While concern with the welfare effects of trade-creation and trade diversion has been associated with static analyses, in recent years, dynamic considerations have become progressively more important

Concern with the welfare effects of trade creation and trade diversion has been associated with static analyses. However, in recent years, because of vastly increased flows of capital, people and technology, dynamic considerations have become progressively more important. One of the benefits of a preferential agreement, for example, may be its impact on technology diffusion, which will be greater from partner than from non-partner countries. Thus, one examination of Mexico in the context of NAFTA found that Mexico had benefited from the R&D content of its trade with its Northern neighbours, as well as from direct contact and close exchanges of information, especially in the case of subcontracting firms that were more closely integrated with the United States and Canada than with the more distant countries of the rest of OECD (Schiff and Wang, 2003).

> While the evidence is generally favourable as regards the benefits to member countries of participation in a preferential scheme, according to several empirical analyses, the ramifications for non-member countries are negative

If the evidence is generally favourable as regards the benefits to member countries of participation in a preferential scheme, several empirical analyses indicate that the ramifications for non-member countries are negative. For instance, an assessment of the welfare gains associated with nine of the new proposals for regional trade arrangements in the Asia-Pacific region—using both the gravity model and CGE approaches—suggests that there may be significant welfare gains associated with some of these proposals. The gains appear largest when the group considered is large and diverse. However, it also appears that these schemes "often impose substantial costs on non-members" (Gilbert, Scollay and Bora, 2001). Similarly, the examination of the Free Trade Area of the Americas (FTAA) found that excluded countries lose, in the case not only of that scheme, but of other regional agreements as well (Harrison, Rutherford and Tarr, 2001).

> There is a concern as to the impact of the current wave of regionalism on the multilateral trading system

The fact that membership in multiple agreements creates a so-called spaghetti bowl of overlapping arrangements has already been noted. However, the most important aspect of this is its impact on the multilateral trading system. One analysis (Andriamananjara, 1999) has argued that "there is a real possibility that, left on its own, the current wave of regionalism will not lead to global free trade". Another study (Karacaovali and Limão, 2005) was equally sceptical. Preferential trade agreements, it is maintained, slowed down multilateral trade liberalization. It has further been pointed out that the effects of preferential agreements may be detrimental for multilateral bargaining. The reason is that countries in such an arrangement may want less broad-based liberalization through World Trade Organization channels because their preferential access to each other's main export markets would thereby be eroded (Mattoo and Subramanian, 2005).

In summary, the current spate of preferential trade agreements is seen as a novel phenomenon by some, who regard them as reflecting what they term "open regionalism", and who differentiate such schemes from those of the 1960s and 1970s. The older schemes generally involved countries at more or less similar levels of development, usually in close geographical proximity and focused on the liberalization of trade in goods, primarily as a means of overcoming small market size-related limitations faced by import-substituting industries (Majluf, 2004). Today, in contrast, integration agreements and free trade agreements have a broader perspective, intended to promote competitiveness and aid in integrating members into the world economy. From this standpoint, current schemes may be more trade-creating and more consistent with multilateralism than were some of the more inward-looking arrangements of the past. Moreover, they involve reciprocity among members. Furthermore, such schemes allow countries to maintain some level of trade protection—an important consideration since total elimination of protection is not always optimal for a country. Thus, these arrangements may have a beneficial role to play. However, their compatibility with multilateralism cannot be presumed and policy vigilance is needed to ensure their consistency with the goals, objectives and tenets of the global trading system. Preferential agreements may be a useful addition to multilateralism, but they are not a substitute for it.

While current schemes may be more trade-creating and more consistent with multilateralism than were some of the more inward-looking arrangements of the past and may have a beneficial role to play, their compatibility with multilateralism cannot be presumed

Notes

1   Data from World Bank (2004b), table 2.1.

2   According to these analyses, estimates of the efficiency gains from trade reform associated with a reallocation of resources to more productive uses range from 1-2 per cent of gross domestic product (GDP) per annum up to 10 per cent of GDP per annum if production is characterized by increasing returns to scale. Moreover, elimination of incentives to smuggle, lobby or evade tariffs (all termed "directly unproductive profit-seeking activities") can add additional indirect benefits that have been estimated to be as high as 6 per cent of GDP in countries such as India and Turkey. See Thomas and others (1991).

3   The authors classified the developing economies into one of three sets: those that had always been open; those that had opened by 1994 after initial closure; and those that had been closed as of the end of 1994.

4   See a summary of alternative explanations in United Kingdom Department for International Development (DFID) (2004). While the view that there is persistent long-term decline has been subject to a heated debate, the recent literature has shown that there are recurrent adverse shocks that become permanent, giving rise to such long-term decline. See, for example, Ocampo and Parra (2003). UNCTAD (2003b) describes the situation in Africa where most commodity-dependent countries are located.

5   Price stabilization schemes on tin ended in 1985, on cocoa in 1988 and on coffee in 1989. Buffer stock activities of the International Sugar Agreement were suspended in 1985 and abandoned in 1992. The most durable and last surviving price stabilization scheme, the International Natural Rubber Agreement, collapsed in 1999 under the weight of the Asian financial crisis after Malaysia and Thailand, two of the world's largest suppliers, had withdrawn from the Agreement.

6   United Nations Conference on Trade and Development (1992), pp. 267-268, contains an account of the shortcomings of the IMF Compensatory Financing Facility and the STABEX facilities. On the CFF, see also chap. VI.

7   A considerable literature has been devoted to explaining the investment properties of commodity-linked derivatives. For example, Gorton and Rouwenhorst (2005, p. 28) found that commodity futures were an "attractive asset class to diversify traditional portfolios of stocks and bonds".

8   See United Nations Conference on Trade and Development (1998). One of the most comprehensive and successful risk management schemes is Mexico's Agricultural Products Options Programme established by the Support Services for Agricultural Marketing Agency (ASERCA) in 1994. The programme successfully uses futures and options contracts on the Chicago, Kansas City and New York Boards of Trade and the Chicago Mercantile Exchange to guarantee price floors for cotton, corn, wheat, sorghum, soybeans and other agricultural commodities; see International Task Force (ITF) (1999), pp. 46-48; and http://www.infoaserca.gob.mx/coberturas/sublistacoberturas.html.

9   It may be interesting to note that in the agreement establishing the African Economic Community (the predecessor of the African Union), such a regional exchange is mentioned as one of the key "instruments of integration" for Africa. See chap. VIII, article 46 (1) (d), of the Treaty establishing the African Economic Community (AEC) (Abuja Treaty), which was signed by the African Heads of State and Government of member States of the Organization of African Union at Abuja, Nigeria, on 3 June 1991. The text of the Treaty is contained in the annex to document A/46/651 of 15 November 1991 and is also available from the Afirican Union website at: http://www.au2002.gov.za/docs/key_oau/aectreat1.htm (accessed 10 June 2005).

10   International Task Force (ITF) (1999). It should be noted, however, that UNCTAD had started receiving donor support for training activities in this area 10 years earlier, in 1989, and that the World Bank had a series of country projects in risk management in the first half of the 1990s.

11   The 1999 recommendations of the Task Force contained much more comprehensive operational and institutional details pertaining to the functions of an intermediary institution that would assist developing countries in managing their price risks. See International Task Force (ITF) (1999) for a detailed account of the 1999 proposals.

12   Descriptions of results of the pilot projects can be found in several documents and annual reports of the International Task Force at the World Bank's Commodity Risk Management Group website, http://www.itf-commrisk.org (accessed 10 June 2005).

13   The IMF Revised Code of Good Practices on Fiscal Transparency is available from http://www.imf.org/external/np/fad/trans/code.htm (accessed 10 June 2005).

14   The Statement of Principles and Agreed Actions of the Extractive Industries Transparency Initiative (EITI) can be found at http://www2.dfid.gov.uk/pubs/files/eitidraftreportstatement.pdf (accessed 10 June 2005) and the EITI official website at www.eitransparency.org (accessed 10 June 2005).

15   The 2003 Almaty Programme of Action: Addressing the Special Needs of Landlocked Developing Countries within a New Global Framework for Transit Transport Cooperation for Landlocked and Transit Developing Countries (United Nations, 2003), which covers the core areas necessary for the progressive integration of landlocked developing countries into the international trading system through the establishment of efficient transit transport systems, constitutes one attempt to overcome the inherent problems of landlocked developing countries.

16   For a more detailed exposition of the history and problems of small island developing States, see UNCTAD (2004a).

17   Cluster analysis, a statistical method, was used by Liou and Ding (2002) to subgroup small States based on their socio-economic characteristics. One such characteristic, or factor, is the degree of export diversification. The designation "export-diversified" reflects a situation of having "moderately diversified commodity exports" (ibid., p. 1295).

18   The full text of the Agreement is available from http://www.wto.org/english/docs_e/legal_e/26-gats.pdf (accessed 9 June 2005).

19   In the model of Anderson and others (2001), developed countries' welfare is increased by $110 billion owing to their own liberalization in agriculture, while the World Bank (2002a) put that estimate at about $73 billion. Most of these gains will go to consumers who have access to cheaper products. Producers would lose unless lower domestic protection was replaced by some other type of income support. In any case, as mentioned in note 20 below, domestic support in OECD countries is expected to decline owing to fiscal considerations.

20   Budgetary constraints in developed economies will build up pressures for lower support for agriculture in these countries—despite resistance from farmers—and developing countries need to prepare themselves for these changes. In the case of EU, for instance, the recent enlargement contributed to the revision of the Common Agricultural Policy. Similarly, in its budget proposal for fiscal 2006, the United States Government lowered the support that is to be extended to farmers.

21   The General Agreement on Trade in Services recognizes four modes of supply: cross border supply (Mode 1), consumption abroad (Mode 2), commercial presence (Mode 3) and temporary movement of natural persons (Mode 4).

22   The full text of the Agreement is available from http://www.wto.org/english/docs_e/legal_e/14-ag.pdf (accessed 13 June 2005).

23   Measures that are considered to distort production and trade (with some exceptions) belong to the amber box. These include support price measures and subsidies directly linked to production quantities. Amber box support is currently subject to certain limits. Support measures that require some kind of reduction of production (acreage, number of animals, etc.) fall into the blue box. There are currently no established limits to blue box subsidies. The green box support consists of no trade distorting measures or at least minimally trade distorting measures, often not targeted at a particular product and not linked to price support or production. These subsidies do not face any limit either.

24   Benin, Burkina Faso, Chad and Mali had called for a speedy elimination of cotton subsidies as well as compensation to cover for economic losses caused by these subsidies.

25   The full text of the Agreement in available from http://www.wto.org/english/docs_e/legal_e/27-trips.pdf (accessed 13 June 2005).

26   A group of developing countries is proposing changes to the mandate and functioning of the World Intellectual Property Organization (WIPO) in order to incorporate a development dimension in the activities of the Organization. See proposal by Argentina and Brazil for the establishment of a development agenda for WIPO: document prepared by the WIPO secretariat (WO/GA/31/12, 24 September 2004). Another 12 developing countries co-sponsored the proposal. WIPO was to organize a series of meeting on intellectual property and development to consider this proposal and additional ones submitted by other members.

27   United Nations, Treaty Series, vol. 1760, No. 30619.

28   Following the World Trade Organization convention, the term "regional trade agreement" will be taken as synonymous with "preferential trade agreement". It includes reciprocal free trade or customs areas, as well as bilateral and multicountry agreements. These are all to be distinguished, however, from non-reciprocal voluntary arrangements, such as the Generalized System of Preferences.

29   These are spelled out in three sets of rules: first, paras. 4-10 of article XXIV of GATT, which provide for the formation and operation of customs unions and free trade areas covering trade in goods; second, the so-called Enabling Clause (decision of 28 November 1979 on differential and more favourable treatment, reciprocity and fuller participation of developing countries), which deals with preferential trade arrangements in trade in goods between developing-country members; and third, article V of the General Agreement on Trade in Services, which governs preferential arrangements in the area of trade in services, for both developed and developing countries.

30   Trade-creation involves substituting for domestic production imports from a lower-cost and more efficient producer and is therefore welfare-enhancing. Trade diversion, meanwhile, suggests that imports from a lower-cost supplier from outside the arrangement are replaced by imports from a higher-cost supplier from within, and is welfare-reducing.

31   American Samoa, Bermuda, Channel Islands, Guam, Isle of Man, Monaco, Mongolia, Northern Mariana Islands, Palau, Puerto Rico, Timor-Leste and the Virgin Islands.

32   Australia, Brunei Darussalam, Canada, Chile, China, Hong Kong Special Administrative Region of China, Indonesia, Japan, the Republic of Korea, Malaysia, Mexico, New Zealand, Papua New Guinea, Peru, the Philippines, the Russian Federation, Singapore, Taiwan Province of China, Thailand, the United States and Viet Nam.

33   Bangladesh, India, the Lao People's Democratic Republic, the Philippines, the Republic of Korea, Sri Lanka and Thailand.

34   Brunei Darussalam, China, Hong Kong Special Administrative Region of China, Indonesia, Japan, the Republic of Korea, Malaysia, the Philippines, Singapore, Taiwan Province of China and Thailand.

35   Bolivia, Colombia, Ecuador, Peru and Venezuela (Bolivarian Republic of).

36   Antigua and Barbuda, the Bahamas (member of the Caribbean Community but not of the Common Market), Barbados, Belize, Dominica, Grenada, Guyana, Jamaica, Montserrat, Saint Kitts and Nevis, Saint Lucia, Saint Vincent and the Grenadines, Suriname and Trinidad and Tobago.

37   Argentina, Bolivia, Brazil, Chile, Colombia, Ecuador, Mexico, Paraguay, Peru, Uruguay and Venezuela (Bolivarian Republic of).

38   Benin, Burkina Faso, Cape Verde, Côte d'Ivoire, the Gambia, Ghana, Guinea, Guinea-Bissau, Liberia, Mali, Mauritania, the Niger, Nigeria, Senegal, Sierra Leone and Togo.

39   Egypt, Iraq, Jordan, the Libyan Arab Jamahiriya, Mauritania, the Syrian Arab Republic and Yemen.

40   Costa Rica, El Salvador, Guatemala, Honduras and Nicaragua.

41   Angola, Burundi, the Comoros, the Congo, Djibouti, Egypt, Eritrea, Ethiopia, Kenya, Madagascar, Malawi, Mauritius, Namibia, Rwanda, Seychelles, the Sudan, Swaziland, Uganda, the United Republic of Tanzania, Zambia and Zimbabwe.

42   Cameroon, the Central African Republic, Chad, the Congo, Equatorial Guinea and Gabon.

43   For more on these assessment methods, see World Bank (2004).

44   "Degrees of integration" in that investigation followed the conventional definitions of "preferential tariff agreement", "free trade area", "customs union", "common market" and "monetary union", with the level of integration increasing with each type (see Ghosh and Yamarik, 2004, p. 3).

Chapter III
International private capital flows

Standard economic theory argues that international private capital flows will make a major contribution to development to the extent that they will flow from capital-abundant industrialized countries to capital-scarce developing countries, and help to smooth spending throughout the business cycle in capital-recipient countries.

In recent years, reality has contradicted both aspects of this standard theory. For the last seven years, developing countries have transferred large amount of resources to developed countries. In addition to this, private capital flows to developing countries are highly concentrated in a group of large middle-income countries and are particularly insufficient for low-income and small countries. Secondly, private capital flows to developing countries have been highly volatile and reversible; as a consequence, they have been a major factor in causing developmentally costly currency and financial crises. Rather than smooth domestic expenditure, private capital flows seem to have contributed to making it more volatile.

These features are by no means inevitable. An appropriate domestic and international environment can improve the capacity of developing countries to benefit from private capital flows. The present chapter analyses both characteristics of private capital flows to developing countries and the policy options that would improve their development impact. It looks first at the main features of those flows, then follows with a deeper analysis of different categories of private flows (foreign direct investment (FDI), and financial flows, including bank credit and portfolio flows) and of the impact of derivatives. It then considers policy options to counter pro-cyclicality of private flows, the expected effects of the new framework for banking regulation (Basel II) on developing countries, and measures to encourage private flows to poorer and smaller developing economies. The chapter ends with some considerations regarding workers' remittances, which, although they do not constitute a capital flow, do represent one of the most dynamic private flows to developing countries.

> In theory, private capital should flow to capital-scarce developing countries and help smooth spending

> In practice, there have been large net transfers from developing countries to developed ones and private flows have been very volatile.

Main features of private flows to developing countries

The volatility and reversibility of capital flows to emerging countries and the marginalization of many of the poorer and smaller developing economies with respect to financial markets are rooted in the combination of financial market failures and basic asymmetries in the world economy (Ocampo, 2001).

Instability is inherent in the functioning of financial markets (Keynes, 1936; Minsky, 1982). Indeed, boom-bust patterns in financial markets have occurred for centuries (Kindleberger, 1978). The basic reason for existence of these patterns is that finance deals with future information that, by its very nature, is not known in advance; therefore, opinions and expectations about the future rather than factual information dominate financial market decisions. This is compounded by asymmetries of information that characterize financial markets (Stiglitz, 2000). Owing to the non-existence or the large asym-

> Boom-bust patterns in capital flows have occurred for centuries ...

metries of information, financial agents rely to a large extent on the "information" provided by the actions of other market agents, leading to interdependence in their behaviour, that is to say, contagion and herding. At the macroeconomic level, the contagion of opinions and expectations about future macroeconomic conditions tends to generate alternating phases of euphoria and panic. At a microeconomic level, it can result in either permanent or cyclical rationing of lending to market agents that are perceived by the market as risky borrowers.

... but their depth and frequency seem to have increased

Herding and volatility are accentuated by some features of the functioning of markets. The increasing use of similar market-sensitive risk management techniques (Persaud, 2000) and the dominance of investment managers aiming for very short term profits, and evaluated and paid at very short term intervals (Griffith-Jones, 1998; Williamson, 2003), seem to have increased the frequency and depth of boom-bust cycles. The downgrade by a rating agency or any other new information available to investors may lead them to sell bonds and stop banks from lending to specific markets; simultaneously, reduced liquidity—owing, for example, to margin calls associated with derivative contracts in these markets—or contagion of opinions about the behaviour of different market segments that are believed to be correlated with a market facing a sell-off, will lead market agents to sell other assets or to stop lending to other markets. Through these and other mechanisms, contagion spreads both across countries and across different flows.

Different types of capital flows are subject, however, to different volatility patterns. In particular, the higher volatility of short-term capital indicates that reliance on such financing is highly risky (Rodrik and Velasco, 1999), whereas the smaller volatility of FDI vis-à-vis all forms of financial flows is considered a source of strength. The instability of different types of capital flows vis-à-vis developing countries will be explored in detail in the following sections of this chapter.

In turn, the basic asymmetries that characterize the world economy are largely (though not exclusively) of an industrialized country versus developing country character (Ocampo and Martin, 2003). In the financial area, such asymmetries underlie three basic facts: (a) the incapacity of most developing countries to issue liabilities in their own currencies, a phenomenon that has come to be referred to as the "original sin" (Eichengreen, Hausman and Panizza, 2003; Hausman and Panizza, 2003);[1] (b) differences in the degrees of domestic financial and capital market development, which lead to an undersupply of long-term financial instruments in developing countries; and (c) the small size of developing countries' domestic financial markets vis-à-vis the magnitude of the speculative pressures they may face (Mead and Schwenninger, 2000).

Financial markets in the developing world are more "incomplete" than in the industrialized world

Taking the first two phenomena together, they imply that domestic financial markets in the developing world are significantly more "incomplete" than those in the industrialized world and therefore that some financial intermediation must necessarily be conducted through international markets. As a result, developing countries are plagued by variable mixes of currency and maturity mismatches in the balance sheets of economic agents. Naturally, such risks tend to become less important as financial development deepens.

Boom-bust cycles of capital flows are very damaging for developing economies

Owing to these asymmetries, boom-bust cycles of capital flows have been particularly damaging for developing countries, where they both directly increase macroeconomic instability and reduce the room for manoeuvre to adopt counter-cyclical macroeconomic policies, and indeed generate strong biases towards adopting pro-cyclical macroeconomic policies (Kaminsky and others, 2004; Stiglitz and others, 2005). Furthermore, there is now overwhelming evidence that pro-cyclical financial markets and pro-cyclical macroeconomic policies have not encouraged growth and, on the contrary, have increased growth volatility in those developing countries that have integrated to a larger extent into international financial markets (Prasad and others, 2003).

The costs of financial volatility for economic growth are high, as it can generate cumulative effects on capital accumulation (Easterly, 2001). Indeed, major reversals of private flows have led to many developmentally and financially costly crises, which lowered output and consumption well below what they would have been if those crises had not occurred. Eichengreen (2004) estimated that income of developing countries had been 25 per cent lower during the last quarter-century than it would have been had such crises not occurred, with the average annual cost of the crises being just over $100 billion. Griffith-Jones and Gottshalk (2006) have estimated similar though somewhat higher annual average cost of crises in the period 1995-2002, of $150 billion in terms of lost gross domestic product (GDP).

Reversals of private financial flows can lead to developmentally costly crises ...

Capital-account cycles involve short-term fluctuations, such as the very intense movements of spreads and interruption (rationing) of financing. These phenomena were observed during the Asian and, particularly, during the Russian crisis. However and perhaps more importantly, they also involve *medium-term* fluctuations, as the experience of the past three decades indicates. During those decades, the developing world experienced two such medium-term cycles that left strong imprints on the growth rates of many countries: a boom of external financing (mostly in the form of syndicated bank loans) in the 1970s, followed by a debt crisis in a large part of the developing world in the 1980s, and a new boom in the 1990s (now mostly portfolio flows), followed by a sharp reduction in net flows since the Asian crisis. The withdrawal of funds since the Asian crisis had initially reflected investors' perception of increasing risk of investing in developing countries, as a result of financial turmoil and crises. With the bursting of the bubble in technology and telecommunication stock prices in 2000 and the subsequent global economic slowdown, risk aversion on the part of investors also rose.

... and medium-term fluctuations are also very problematic

Improved economic conditions in developing countries, as well as the higher global growth and low interest rates, drove a recovery of private capital flows to developing countries in 2003 and 2004, perhaps signalling the beginning of a new cycle (table III.1). However, periods of increased volatility in yield spreads on emerging market bonds in 2004 and 2005, in response to uncertainty in the pace of interest rate increase in developed countries (particularly the United States of America), underscored the vulnerability of financial flows to acceleration in increases in interest rates.

There has been a recovery of private flows to developing countries ...

More importantly, net *transfers* of financial resources[2] from developing countries have not experienced a positive turnaround and, on the contrary, continued to deteriorate in 2004 for the seventh year in a row, reaching an estimated $350 billion in 2004 (see table III.2). Periods of negative net transfers of financial resources from developing countries (especially from Latin America) have been frequent throughout history; indeed, Kregel (2004) provides evidence that these negative net transfers have been the rule rather than the exception.

... but net transfers remain negative and large

Recently, these large and increasing net transfers of financial resources are explained by the combination of relatively low net financial flows and accumulation of very large foreign-exchange reserves. Indeed, the most significant aspect of the net outflows from developing countries in recent years has been the growth in official reserves, particularly in Asia (table III.1). Accumulation of reserves had initially a large component of "self-insurance" against financial instability (or, as it is also called today, a "war chest" developed against financial crises), a rational decision of individual countries in the face of the limited "collective insurance" provided by the international financial system (see chap. VI).

These transfers from developing countries are now largely a reflection of the accumulation of reserves

Table III.1.

Net financial flows to developing countries and economies in transition, 1993-2004

Billions of dollars				
	Average 1993-1997	Average 1998-2002	2003	2004
Developing countries				
Net private capital flows	151.5	48.3	92.1	152.3
Net direct investment	87.7	141.1	132.8	158.3
Net portfolio investment[a]	65.0	-8.5	-9.7	13.1
Other net investment[b]	-1.2	-84.3	-31.0	-19.1
Net official flows	12.3	9.3	-51.4	-55.9
Total net flows	163.8	57.6	40.7	96.4
Change in reserves	-79.3	-97.9	-328.2	-454.9
Africa				
Net private capital flows	6.0	8.9	12.7	9.0
Net direct investment	3.9	13.0	15.3	15.5
Net portfolio investment[a]	4.0	0.2	-0.6	2.9
Other net investment[b]	-1.9	-4.3	-2.0	-9.4
Net official flows	1.2	0.7	1.8	-1.2
Total net flows	7.2	9.6	14.5	7.8
Change in reserves	-7.2	-7.2	-22.9	-38.7
Eastern and Southern Asia				
Net private capital flows	73.4	-1.4	60.0	133.0
Net direct investment	48.1	60.5	72.3	88.6
Net portfolio investment[a]	21.7	-6.8	2.5	25.8
Other net investment[b]	3.7	-55.1	-14.9	18.5
Net official flows	4.2	1.9	-14.3	7.0
Total net flows	77.6	0.5	45.6	140.0
Change in reserves	-44.2	-93.1	-238.7	-356.0
Western Asia				
Net private capital flows	12.4	4.6	4.3	-2.3
Net direct investment	5.0	5.2	10.4	8.8
Net portfolio investment[a]	-1.0	-2.4	-1.5	-1.4
Other net investment[b]	8.5	1.9	-4.6	-9.7
Net official flows	4.3	-5.5	-47.6	-54.5
Total net flows	16.7	-0.9	-43.3	-56.8
Change in reserves	-9.0	-1.5	-30.8	-38.2
Latin America and the Caribbean				
Net private capital flows	59.6	36.2	15.2	12.7
Net direct investment	30.8	62.5	34.7	45.4
Net portfolio investment[a]	40.3	0.5	-10.1	-14.2
Other net investment[b]	-11.5	-26.7	-9.5	-18.5
Net official flows	2.7	12.2	8.7	-7.3
Total net flows	62.3	48.5	23.9	5.4
Change in reserves	-19.0	3.9	-35.8	-21.9

Table III.1 (continued)	Average 1993-1997	Average 1998-2002	2003	2004
Economies in transition				
Net private capital flows	8.5	1.0	27.4	13.5
Net direct investment	4.4	7.6	10.0	13.5
Net portfolio investment[a]	-0.2	-3.3	-3.4	-1.4
Other net investment[b]	4.3	-3.4	20.8	1.5
Net official flows	7.2	-0.3	-4.8	0.0
Total net flows	15.8	0.6	22.6	13.5
Change in reserves	-4.9	-9.0	-36.9	-57.1

Source: International Monetary Fund (IMF), World Economic Outlook Database, April 2005.
a Including portfolio debt and equity investment.
b Including short- and long-term bank lending, and possibly including some official flows owing to data limitations.

Table III.2.
Net transfer of financial resources to developing countries and economies in transition, 1993-2004

Billions of dollars												
	1993	1994	1995	1996	1997	1998	1999	2000	2001	2002	2003	2004
Developing countries	69.3	35.8	42.9	19.9	-5.2	-37.9	-127.4	-186.5	-153.7	-205.5	-274.8	-353.8
Africa	1.1	4.0	6.4	-5.8	-4.7	15.6	4.3	-26.2	-14.7	-5.6	-20.2	-32.8
Sub-Saharan (excluding Nigeria and South Africa)	8.6	6.7	7.4	5.3	7.5	12.1	9.1	3.0	7.9	6.4	6.5	3.9
Eastern and Southern Asia	18.7	1.0	22.1	18.5	-31.1	-128.2	-142.7	-121.3	-113.1	-142.1	-147.5	-167.8
Western Asia	33.1	13.2	15.6	5.3	6.2	28.5	-0.9	-39.1	-32.0	-26.7	-47.6	-79.9
Latin America	16.4	17.7	-1.2	1.8	24.5	46.2	11.8	0.1	6.1	-31.1	-59.5	-73.4
Economies in transition	1.8	-3.9	-2.3	-6.2	2.7	3.0	-24.0	-48.8	-30.5	-27.0	-34.4	-57.6
Memorandum item:												
Heavily indebted poor countries (HIPCs)	8.5	7.1	6.3	6.8	7.1	8.6	10.1	8.8	8.8	9.9	10.6	11.3

Sources: UN/DESA, based on International Monetary Fund (IMF), World Economic Outlook Database, April 2005; and IMF, Balance of Payments Statistics Database.

However, reserve accumulation in Asia has now clearly exceeded the need in several countries for self-insurance, raising increasing questions about the balance of costs and benefits of additional accumulation, especially if such reserves are invested in low-yielding assets and particularly in a depreciating currency, the United States dollar.

Divergence in regional trends in private financial flows has also resulted in changes in regional distribution of these flows since the 1990s. The most striking aspect of such developments is the significantly increased concentration of flows to Eastern and Southern Asia, in particular, to China, at the expense of Latin America. Private financial flows to Eastern and Southern Asia recovered at the end of the 1990s and have risen strongly in the last four years. After financial turmoil and crises in the region in the last five years, private financial flows to Latin America, in contrast, have remained far below the 1997 peak (see table III.1).

An important policy issue is whether the new private flows are more stable

As private flows start to recover, an important question for policymakers in developing countries is whether they will be sufficient as well as more stable and less reversible than in the past, leading in turn to less demand for self-insurance through reserve accumulation, and thus eventually reversing the negative net transfer of resources that has characterized the world economy since the Asian crisis.

The dominance of FDI is encouraging, though derivatives may add hidden volatility

In this regard, the dominant role of FDI and the fact that it has been relatively stable in times of crises, are positive. However, as we will see below, not all components of FDI are equally stable. Furthermore, multinational companies, especially those producing for the local market, increasingly hedge their short-term foreign-exchange risks, particularly when devaluations seem likely. This can lead to major temporary outflows of capital and significant pressure on exchange rates (Ffrench-Davis and Griffith-Jones, 2003; Persaud, 2003). More generally, the increasing use of financial engineering and of derivatives (as well as the growing scale and complexity of derivatives discussed below) seems to make the hypothesis of a hierarchy of volatility, whereby some categories of flows are more stable than others, less clear-cut.

Another potentially positive effect is the greater interest shown by institutional investors (such as life insurers) in investing in emerging countries (European Central Bank, 2005). However, the large rise in "carry trade"—that is to say, investment in high-yielding emerging market instruments using debt raised at lower cost in mature markets—makes those flows vulnerable to narrowing of interest rate differentials. Furthermore, the large fall in emerging countries' bond spreads (while naturally positive in itself for borrowing countries) has raised concerns that this may reflect a shift in the investor base towards crossover investors, which can increase the vulnerability of developing countries, especially those with large external financing, to changes in United States interest rates.

Finally, there are two structural trends that may add stability. The first is attested by the greater importance of local currency bond markets in developing countries; the second by the fact that international banks have increasingly "crossed the border", lending from their local branches in local currency, and usually fund themselves via domestic deposits. This makes countries less vulnerable to crises, although it also implies that foreign banks are contributing less—or no—foreign savings.

Policy efforts are essential, in source and recipient countries, to encourage stable flows and discourage reversible ones

There are thus mixed signs in respect of whether the new inflows will be more stable than in the past. Therefore, policy efforts must be made, both in source and in recipient countries, to encourage more stable flows and discourage large flows that are potentially more reversible.

Foreign direct investment

Trends and composition of foreign direct investment

Net FDI flow to developing countries and economies in transition had grown rapidly in the 1990s, peaking in 2001. During the Asian financial crisis and subsequent financial crises in emerging market countries, FDI was the most resilient and became the consistently largest component of net private capital flow to these countries. The different modalities of FDI, greenfield investment and cross-border mergers and acquisitions (M&A) have different effects on the domestic economy, in terms of both net financial contribution and linkages with the host economy.

Liberalization of FDI through legislative and regulatory changes in a growing number of countries since the 1990s has supported high levels of FDI. At the same time, although extensive privatization, particularly in Latin American and Central and Eastern European countries, drove the surge in FDI in the second half of the 1990s, it has largely run its course in many countries. Acquisitions by international investors of distressed financial and non-financial institutions in Asia after the financial crisis also brought direct investment flows through cross-border acquisitions. In turn, the opportunities provided by low production costs and its growing domestic market have been the major sources of attraction towards China, the major recipient of FDI in the developing world.

Exhaustion of State assets available for privatization and mergers and acquisitions, joined by macroeconomic volatility in some developing countries, resulted in a brief decline in FDI in 2002-2003. However, this was followed by a broad-based recovery in FDI flows across developing regions and economies in transition owing to improvement in a combination of cyclical, institutional and structural factors.

Although FDI inflows to developing countries have been more resilient than flows from other sources, they are concentrated in a small number of mainly middle-income countries. The top 10 developing-country recipients of FDI accounted for almost three fourths of total FDI flow to developing countries in 2003. This is true even if estimates are adjusted by the size of the economy. The World Bank estimates that the ratio of FDI to GDP in the top 10 recipient countries was more than twice that in low-income countries in 2003 (World Bank, 2004a, p. 79).

FDI inflows to least developed countries have increased, nevertheless, from the late 1990s, albeit from low levels, raising the least developed countries' share in total FDI in developing countries from approximately 2 per cent in 1995 to 5 per cent in 2003 (World Bank, 2005). In particular, the least developed countries with large natural resource sectors have attracted growing amounts of FDI. There has also been some diversification of investment into the agricultural, brewing and light manufacturing sectors in some African least developed countries (United Nations Conference on Trade and Development, 2004b; Bhinda and others, 1999). In any case, FDI flows to least developed countries are smaller than official development assistance (ODA) in all but a few countries (United Nations Conference on Trade and Development, 2004b).

Growth has been accompanied by significant changes in the composition of FDI. The most important trend has been the rapid growth of investment in services since the 1990s. This process has been associated both with the expansion of transnational corporations into developing countries' service sectors, facilitated in many cases by privatiza-

Net FDI flows to developing countries and economies in transition have been resilient

FDI flows are concentrated in a small number of mainly middle-income countries

FDI flows to least developed countries have increased but remain low

FDI in services has grown rapidly at the expense of FDI in manufacturing

tion and the opening of domestic markets (for example, in financial activities, telecommunications and, to a lesser extent, public utilities) and, more recently, with the rapid growth of offshoring of services by transnational corporations. The share of services in the stock of inward FDI in developing countries increased from 47 per cent in 1990 to 55 per cent in 2002. At the same time, the share of manufacturing in FDI stock declined from 46 to 38 per cent. The small share of the primary sector remained unchanged at 7 per cent. FDI in services has grown at the expense of FDI in manufacturing in all developing regions except Africa. Until the 1990s, FDI in services was primarily in finance and trade, having accounted for over 70 per cent of total inward FDI stock in services by 1990. Since the 1990s, the share of FDI stock in other services, namely, business services, telecommunications and utilities, has increased, while that of finance and trade has declined (United Nations Conference on Trade and Development, 2004b, pp. 29-31 and 99).

The effect of FDI in the service sector on competition in the host country has varied among countries. Agosin and Mayer (2000) suggest that when FDI shifted towards services as the result of privatization in Latin America in the 1990s, there was a crowding out of domestic firms. In general, anti-competitive behaviour by transnational corporations can lead to more negative consequences in cases where domestic competition law is weak. Also, the impact of FDI on competitiveness has varied by country. In the case of large scale FDI in commercial banks in Latin America, the banking sector has not become more competitive (Economic Commission for Latin America and the Caribbean, 2005, p. 113), while the result of FDI liberalization in financial services in Thailand has been more positive (Asian Development Bank, 2004, p. 231). Similarly, in Eastern European countries, after multinational banks acquired a large market share, domestic bank lending to local enterprises increased, complementing multinational bank lending (Weller, 2001).

FDI in offshoring of services, involving relocation of lower value added corporate functions, including computer programming, customer service and chip design, has been increasing in a number of developing countries. This type of FDI has a relatively large spillover effect particularly through improvement of information and communication technologies (ICT) infrastructure and capacity-building in human capital, as in the case of the offshoring of software development in India (United Nations Conference on Trade and Development, 2004b, pp. 169-170). However, because of its relatively high-skill and ICT infrastructure requirements, FDI in offshoring is limited to a small number of countries.

An interesting long-term change in the pattern of FDI has also been the increase in South-South FDI flows. By the end of the 1990s, more than one third of total FDI inflows to developing countries were from other developing countries. This trend has meant the provision of access to more sources of FDI for developing countries, particularly small low-income countries (Akyut and Ratha, 2004). Offsetting this benefit is the possibility that investment flows from developing source countries are more volatile than those from developed source countries, undermining the stability of FDI flows (Levy-Yeyati and others, 2003). Cases in point are the sharp decline in FDI from Asian countries impacted by the 1997 financial crisis and the decline in FDI from Latin American countries in financial crisis in 2000-2002. Any differences in investment and financial strategies between developing-country and developed-country transnational corporations with regard to earnings reinvestment and intercompany loans can also have an impact on the stability of FDI flows.

The effect of FDI in banking on competition has not been positive in Latin America but it has been more positive in some other cases

The increase in South-South FDI flows diversifies sources of FDI but can increase volatility

How stable is FDI?

Total FDI flows to developing countries and economies in transition as a group have been resilient overall during and after economic crises. However, this overall trend masks significant variation in performance by region and country. Since the late 1990s, FDI in non-crisis countries has remained stable, but investment flows to crisis countries have declined (International Monetary Fund, 2004b, pp. 132-133). Further, the different components of FDI flows can differ significantly in their stability in economic crises.

Equity capital flows, which reflect primarily the strategic investment decision by transnational corporations, are the most stable of the three components of FDI. They are also the largest component having constituted more than two thirds of total FDI flows in the period 1990-2002. The size of this component varies by the sector of investment (World Bank, 2004a, pp. 86-87). Initial equity capital flows are extremely large in FDI in many infrastructure industries but smaller in investment in financial institutions and even more so in other service industries such as corporate services. Furthermore, under the conditions of significantly increased risk that existed in 2001-2002 in Latin America, new investment was postponed.

Earnings from foreign operations that are not repatriated and intercompany loans, the other two components of FDI flows, tend to be more volatile. On the one hand, these two categories of investment are sources of recurrent financing for investment in foreign affiliates after the initial equity investment. On the other hand, transnational corporations can adjust the flow of these two components to make short-term changes in their exposure to the financial risks in the host country (Working Group of the Capital Markets Consultative Group, 2003, pp. 25-28).

The share of non-repatriated earnings in total earnings has averaged about 40 per cent since the 1990s but has ranged from 35 to 65 per cent in different industries (World Bank, 2004a, pp. 82-84; United Nations Conference on Trade and Development, 2004b, p. 126). This category of FDI tends to be pro-cyclical with regard to host countries' economic conditions, as transnational corporations increase earnings repatriation and therefore reduce reinvestment to reduce their exposure to deteriorating local economic conditions, potentially exacerbating the situation. During and after the Asian financial crisis and the Argentine crisis, for example, there was a significant increase in repatriation of earnings (World Bank, 2004a, pp. 88 and 90).

Inflows of intercompany loans may be almost as volatile and pro-cyclical as international debt flows. Transnational corporations call loans to foreign affiliates when financial risk in the host country rises, as happened in Brazil during the last crisis. The negative trend in total FDI flows to Indonesia in the aftermath of the Asian crisis was the result of the large repayment of intercompany loans, outweighing steady capital equity inflow (World Bank, 2004a, pp. 87-88). Also, parent companies can reduce intercompany loans as a means of financing for foreign affiliates so as to reduce currency risk in anticipation of the depreciation of the currency of the host country. They may also avoid international capital markets when obtaining extra-corporate financing and turn to the local credit market of the host country, thereby reducing the inflow of capital to the host country at a time when it is most needed. The composition of overall FDI flows can therefore have a significant effect on the stability of net financial flow to developing countries (Kregel, 1996, pp. 59-61).

Total FDI flows have been stable ...

... but non-repatriated earnings and intercompany loans are more volatile

The level of non-repatriated earnings tends to be pro-cyclical

Inflows of intercompany loans may be as volatile and pro-cyclical as debt flows

These two FDI components are also affected by the financial condition of the parent company, which is in turn affected by conditions of the economy of the source country and the global economy. Earnings repatriation and/or intercompany loan repayments are increased when financial resources are needed to improve the overall balance sheet of the parent company (United Nations Conference on Trade and Development, 2004b, p. 127).

Adjustments in earnings repatriation and intercompany loans are less volatile in tradable sectors

In addition to the other features discussed above, adjustments in earnings repatriation and intercompany loans vary among companies in different sectors. Transnational corporations with investment in production of tradables are less quick to make these adjustments, as they are buffered by earnings in foreign exchange. With currency devaluation, the attractiveness of foreign investment in the tradable sectors is also enhanced. This was reflected in the resilience of non-repatriated earnings and intercompany loans flows to Mexico, the Republic of Korea, Thailand and Turkey after currency devaluations following financial crises in the 1990s (World Bank, 2003; Lipsey, 2001). In contrast, investors in non-tradable goods and services lack the foreign-exchange earnings and face a higher currency risk. The decline in FDI in Brazil and Argentina in 2002-2003, for example, illustrated this sensitivity of FDI in infrastructure and financial services. These sectoral differences suggest that a shift in FDI away from infrastructure and financial services and towards tradable services can have a stabilizing effect on FDI flows.

Particular benefits of FDI

Benefits in technology transfer and market access are markedly uneven among host countries ...

In addition to its relatively higher resilience as a source of capital flow to developing countries, FDI is regarded as a potential catalyst for raising productivity in developing host countries through the transfer of technology and managerial know-how, and for facilitating access to international markets. The general conclusion from empirical studies points to net benefits for host countries but the benefits are markedly uneven, both among and within countries (Economic Commission for Latin American and the Caribbean, 2005; Asian Development Bank, 2004, pp. 213-269; United Nations Conference on Trade and Development, 2003a, pp. 142-144; Basu and Srinivason, 2002; Hanson, 2001). Potential negative effects include limited domestic linkages, exacerbating trade deficits, limiting competition and the excessive share of the investment risk assumed by the host country. Additionally, there is strong debate on the magnitude of, and lags in, the materialization of positive effects as well as on the mechanisms by which they are transmitted to the host economy.

There is general agreement that an enabling investment climate in the host country is a necessary condition for encouraging both domestic and foreign investment (see chap. I). In addition, the levels of human resource development and entrepreneurial capacity of the host country are significant factors in the location decisions of investors as well as in the transfer of technology and know-how and the linkages of local firms to international production networks and markets. Besides improving the investment climate and strengthening domestic capacity, developing countries have also put in place fiscal and other incentives to compete for FDI. Evidence suggests, however, that these incentives are relatively minor factors in location decisions of transnational corporations (Asian Development Bank, 2004, p. 260). They thus undermine the fiscal base of developing countries without yielding the desired results.

Developing countries have also historically implemented investment policies to promote the desired benefits and minimize the negative effects of FDI. While there has been a move away from investment policies in the last decade, and the effectiveness of investment policies has been varied, it may be desirable to reinstate the use of investment policies, particularly to promote linkages between foreign firms and the host economy. Moreover, individual countries should have the policy space within which to customize specific interventions that are consistent with their development objectives and concerns with respect to FDI (Asian Development Bank, 2004, p. 262; Economic Commission for Latin America and the Caribbean, 2005).[3] Indeed, according to some analysts, the success of Asian countries was achieved by the Governments' commitment to assessing the results of their FDI policies on an ongoing basis to determine whether they were producing the expected benefits (Economic Commission for Latin America and the Caribbean, 2004a, p. 70).

> Investment policies to promote linkages between foreign firms and the host economy should be reconsidered in developing countries

Transnational corporations can play an important role in providing access to markets, thereby helping to build competitive export capacity in host countries. Intra-firm trade offers access to firm-specific technology and being part of the production network of transnational corporations can provide foreign affiliates with established brand names that have access to international markets. These benefits vary depending, in particular, on the export versus domestic market orientation of transnational corporations in specific countries. Transnational corporations played an important role in building competitive export sectors and expanding exports in China, Mexico and a number of countries in South-East Asia, Central America and Eastern Europe. In other countries, for example, Brazil, Argentina and African countries, these benefits did not materialize. In Brazil, the fact that transnational corporations imported capital goods and focused on selling to the domestic market in the 1990s had a negative effect on the current-account balance; similar results were observed in Argentina (United Nations Conference on Trade and Development, 2003a, p. 143).

> Transnational corporations can provide access to international markets and can build export competitiveness

Transnational corporations have been pursuing in recent decades a strategy of developing integrated international production networks to take advantage of the comparative advantage of different countries. This can result in the derivation of very different benefits from their activities by different recipient countries. While for some this would mean larger export markets for their higher-technology products, for others it might mean specialization in exports with low domestic value added (in the extreme, mere assembly activities). In turn, in the case of transnational corporations servicing the domestic market of the recipient country, it may lead to balance-of-payments pressures. Furthermore, mergers and acquisitions may actually result in the replacement of domestic suppliers by the international outsourcing chain of the new parent firm, thus leading initially to reduced domestic linkages. Over time, transnational corporations will tend to increase local inputs by transferring technologies to local suppliers so as to take advantage of geographical proximity and cost-effectiveness; just-in-time inventory management can provide an additional impetus for this strategy. However, this process is not necessarily rapid or smooth, and active linkage policies, including programmes aimed at accelerating technology transfers from transnational corporations to domestic firms, may thus play a role in speeding it up.

Transnational corporations can transfer not only production technologies but also managerial and organizational practices. Diffusion from foreign affiliates to the host country takes place more generally through competition with local firms, linkage with local suppliers, labour mobility from foreign affiliates to domestic firms, and geographical proximity between foreign and local firms. The transfer of technology and its efficient application depend on both transnational corporations' corporate policies and the level of devel-

> The effective diffusion of technology and managerial practices depends on TNC policies and the host country's level of development

opment in the host country, as manifested in local skills and capabilities and capacities of local affiliates to absorb technology transfer (United Nations Conference on Trade and Development, 2000, p. 175).

There may also be, in this regard, a significant difference between greenfield investment and mergers and acquisitions. Greenfield investment is more likely to involve technology transfer through introduction of imported new capital goods at inception (United Nations Conference on Trade and Development, 2000, p. 176). On the other hand, mergers and acquisitions are more likely to transfer technology and managerial capabilities to already existing local firms, targeting those with the capacity to be integrated into their production network. However, despite the different methods of technology transfer of these two forms of FDI, it is still unclear which exerts the stronger impact on technological upgrading of affiliates over time.

FDI in R&D has a large impact on technology upgrading but only for a limited number of host countries

Research and development (R&D)-related FDI has a relatively large impact on upgrading technology and knowledge capacity in host countries but it has been growing in only a limited number of countries. Since the 1990s, FDI in R&D has shifted from mainly developing products for local markets to reducing the cost of R&D in industrialized countries. This is part of a global trend of offshoring R&D enabled by advanced ICT as well as the emergence of increasing demand for scientific expertise on a global scale (United Nations Conference on Trade and Development, 2005a). A number of primarily middle-income economies place priority on FDI in R&D as a means of moving up the technology ladder and have offered fiscal incentives to encourage it (World Bank, 2005a, p. 173). Asian countries, mainly China and India, have been successful in attracting FDI in R&D because of their abundant supply of engineers and scientists available at relatively low wages, while Latin American countries have been relatively unsuccessful in attracting this form of FDI.

The backward production linkages between foreign affiliates and domestic firms can be a channel for diffusing skills, knowledge and technology from foreign affiliates to local firms. On a large scale, such transfers can in turn lead to spillovers for the rest of the host economy (United Nations Conference on Trade and Development, 2001b, pp. 129-133). However, not all linkages are equally beneficial. For instance, suppliers of relatively simple, standardized low-technology products and services may be highly vulnerable to market fluctuations and their linkages with foreign companies are unlikely to involve much transfer of knowledge. Where there is the requisite level of skill among domestic suppliers, transnational corporations have established supplier development programmes in host countries (Poland, Costa Rica, Brazil, Malaysia, Viet Nam and India) and often provided financing, training, technology transfer and information (United Nations Conference on Trade and Development, 2001b, p. 160).

Policies should target the creation of beneficial linkages

The objective of host countries should therefore be to promote linkages where they are beneficial. As linkage promotion policies are often a function of country circumstances, they need to be adapted accordingly. The focus appears to be on policies designed to address market failures at different levels in the linkage formation process. In this respect, measures to provide information for both buyers and suppliers about linkage opportunities and to bring domestic suppliers and foreign affiliates together in the key areas of information, technology, training and finance are important. Broader measures to strengthen the quality of local entrepreneurship are also vital in inducing foreign affiliates to form beneficial linkages. A few countries (the Republic of Korea, Singapore and Thailand) have introduced financial incentives for firms, including foreign affiliates, to invest in employee training (United Nations Conference on Trade and Development, 2001b, pp. 163-193).

Another way in which FDI can be linked to the domestic economy is via clusters, defined as "geographically proximate groups of interconnected companies, suppliers, service providers, and associated institutions in a particular field, linked by commonalities and complementarities" (World Economic Forum, 2004, p. 23). Examples are the software industry in India and the shoemaking industry in Italy. Such concentrations of resources and capabilities can attract FDI that responds to agglomeration economies. Foreign investors can also add to the strength and dynamism of clusters when they join them by attracting new skills and capital and thereby transmitting benefits to the domestic economy. A virtuous cycle thus builds up and generates the dynamic agglomeration economies, for example, financial services in Singapore and software in Bangalore, India (United Nations Conference on Trade and Development, 2001b, p. xix).

> Clusters constitute a means of linking FDI with the domestic economy ...

The success of clusters depends on an enabling investment climate and especially the competitiveness of domestic enterprises and the available pool of skilled labour. Given these imposing requirements, the development of dynamic clusters that are able to attract and develop a symbiotic relationship with transnational corporations may be more feasible for those developing countries that have the requisite enabling infrastructure and environment.

> ... although their feasibility is limited to countries with the requisite infrastructure and capacity

Financial flows

Bank credit

Trade finance, tied to international trade transactions, has important implications for development. It is provided by banks, goods producers, official export agencies, multilateral development banks, private insurers and specialized firms, and is indirectly supported by insurance, guarantees and lending with accounts receivable as collateral. This type of financing rose sharply in the 1990s up until the Asian crisis. Also, the average spread on trade finance had declined significantly from more than 700 basis points in the mid-1980s to 150 before the Asian crisis and on average was 28 basis points lower than spreads on bank loans over the period 1996-2002 (World Bank, 2004a, pp. 127-130).

Trade finance is particularly important for less creditworthy and poorer countries' access to international loans, as traded goods serve as collateral. Many low-income developing countries, which lack other forms of access to commercial banks, still can borrow for trade finance. In almost every year since 1980, the share of trade finance commitments in total bank lending has been higher for non-investment grade or unrated developing countries than rated ones.

> Trade finance is important for less creditworthy countries as traded goods serve as collateral

Security arrangements linked to traded goods and government policies directed at promoting exports should make trade finance more resilient during crises, and help countries grow out of crises by exporting. However, the opposite pattern has been common during recent crises, as evidenced by the experience of Indonesia, Malaysia and Thailand during the 1997-1998 Asian crisis and by that of Argentina and Brazil in later years. The contraction in trade finance was sharper than justified by fundamentals and risks involved, and ended up exacerbating the crises. After the Asian crisis, more than 80 per cent of domestic firms and 20 per cent of foreign-owned firms showed a drop in trade credit. However, credit from suppliers and customers was more resilient compared with bank credit.

> The contraction in trade finance after financial crises has been sharper than justified by fundamentals and it has exacerbated the difficulties

The multilateral
development banks'
trade finance facilities
and the activities of
export credit agencies
could be used to
mitigate crises

Trade finance recovered following the expansion of developing countries' trade in recent years, but its stability in the future cannot be taken for granted. Governments can facilitate trade finance by providing legal standing for electronic documents and for the assignment of receivables. A more effective approach to alleviating the problem of trade finance collapse during crises could be built around multilateral developing banks' trade finance facilities, complemented by actions by official export credit agencies. The multilateral development banks have indeed used their trade finance facilities to support emerging markets during recent crises, but they could play a more prominent role. For instance, they could act as "insurer of record" on behalf of an emerging market borrower, providing transfer and convertibility risk mitigation through their preferred creditor status, but could reinsure much of the underwritten policy with other insurers.

Trade financing from export credit agencies, including guarantees, insurance and Government-backed loans, has so far declined relative to the private insurance companies, which accounted for nearly half of new commitments by international credit and investment insurers by 2002; the new commitments by private insurers are heavily skewed towards short-term export credit. However, export credit agencies could explore ways in which to play more of a counter-cyclical role, especially in the recovery stage, immediately after crises. This could include rolling over or expanding short-term credit lines and facilitating medium- and long-term financing. Export credit agencies might also give consideration to allowing a special exception to normal credit-risk practices in crisis situations. Formal international rules, such as the World Trade Organization rules on subsidies or the relevant Organization for Economic Cooperation and Development (OECD) guidelines, could be modified to remove the disincentives to counter-cyclical operations of export credit agencies.

Net bank lending to
developing countries
was negative from
1998 to 2002

Other bank lending to developing countries had witnessed a similar large upswing in the 1990s until the Asian crisis. Bank lending was assumed to be more stable than capital market financing; however, recent experience has shown that the dominance of short-term loans makes it easy for banks to rapidly retrench. About one third of international bank lending is short-term and this proportion had risen in the first half of the 1990s. Net international bank lending to developing countries collapsed with the East Asian crisis, and was negative from 1998 to 2002.

The sharp retrenchment following the Asian and Russian crises had occurred in the global context where banks have generally become more risk-sensitive because of banking regulation and greater emphasis on shareholder value. It reflected not only reduced willingness to lend but also a weaker desire for loans by borrowers. However, the improved economic climate of the last two years is supporting the recovery of bank lending to developing countries. Net bank lending turned positive in 2003.

Bank lending to
developing countries
has been recovering
since 2003 and the
maturity of loans
has increased

In addition, maturity of bank loans has increased since the Asian crisis. According to World Bank data, the ratio of short-term to total international bank lending fell from 54 per cent in 1996 to 46.5 per cent in 2000 for all developing countries, with a particularly sharp decline in East Asia and the Pacific. Emerging market banks now have a more balanced external position vis-à-vis banks reporting to the Bank for International Settlements than in 1997-1998 and official reserve coverage of the banking system's net liability positions has increased (International Monetary Fund, 2004a, p. 36).

There has been a general retrenchment of banks from cross-border lending since 1997 and a large scale shift towards lending via domestic subsidiaries, which grew on average by 29.4 per cent annually between 1996 and 2002 (see table III.3). North American and Japanese banks have sharply reduced their cross-border lending to developing countries, while European banks have increased their exposure and now account for nearly two thirds of such lending. Important structural changes also occurred in regional patterns of borrowing. International claims on East Asia and the Pacific declined sharply, although there have been some recent signs of revival. Claims on Latin American countries expanded between 1997 and 2000, but have since stalled. Lending to "emerging Europe" performed better, entirely accounted for by European lenders. In turn, emerging Europe and Latin America have experienced the fastest growth of lending by domestic subsidiaries of foreign banks. Also, as a result of greater lending by European banks, lending to the Middle East, Northern Africa, South Asia and sub-Saharan Africa has edged up compared with that of 1997. In contrast, the presence of banking entities from developing countries in London and New York has substantively contracted since 1996.

International banks have increased their lending through domestic subsidiaries in the local currency, particularly in Eastern Europe and Latin America

Although foreign entry could increase efficiency through competition and modernization, it could also result in the crowding out of domestic banks and vulnerable customers as foreign banks skim the cream off the market. Empirical studies indicate that the competitive pressures exerted by foreign banks vary by country (Clarke and others,

Foreign banks can increase efficiency in the sector ...

Table III.3.
Bank lending in emerging markets, 1993-2002

	Total lending 1996 (billions of dollars)	Average annual growth 1993-1996 (percentage)	Total lending 2002 (billions of dollars)	Average annual growth 1997-2002 (percentage)
East Asia				
Domestic banks	769.5	18.1	876.1	2.4
Local subsidiaries of foreign banks	29.8	15.4	84.9	21.2
Cross-border	282.2	29.0	130.3	-11.6
Latin America				
Domestic banks	563.7	17.3	484.8	-2.7
Local subsidiaries of foreign banks	58.5	28.6	241.7	31.2
Cross-border	199.9	6.2	166.1	-2.8
Eastern Europe				
Domestic banks	242.5	9.4	252.8	0.8
Local subsidiaries of foreign banks	9.6	80.5	96.3	48.5
Cross-border	74.7	1.6	70.4	-0.6
All emerging markets				
Domestic banks	1 575.7	12.7	1 613.7	0.4
Local subsidiaries of foreign banks	97.8	24.4	422.8	29.4
Cross-border	556.7	14.5	366.9	-6.5

Source: International Monetary Fund, *Global Financial Stability Report, September 2004* (Washington, D.C., IMF), p. 128.

2001, p. 17), and that domestic banks displaced by foreign competition might seek new market niches, for example, through providing credit to small and medium-sized enterprises (Bonin and Abel, 2000). One survey in 38 developing and transition countries found that foreign bank penetration improves firms' access to credit, although it benefits large enterprises more than small ones (Clarke and others, 2002, pp. 20-21).

... but there is concern that they might retrench more rapidly during crises

There is legitimate concern in developing countries that foreign banks may curtail their lending more than local banks in times of crisis owing to their risk management system. The sharp drop in lending by foreign banks following recent emerging market crises, confirms this fear. For instance, the real supply of credit had fallen almost continuously in Mexico since the 1994 crisis, dropping from 35 to 10 per cent of GDP by 2001. Although this was basically a reflection of a deep domestic financial crisis, the rapid penetration of foreign banks during those years did not in any way counteract the process. Also, after the Argentine crisis, restrictions on support to ailing subsidiaries severely limited funds supplied by parent companies (Economic Commission for Latin America and the Caribbean, 2003, pp. 140-142).

Foreign banks are also more sensitive to shocks originating in advanced economies. Excessive exposure to banks from a single country increases such risks. There is concern that Latin American banking sectors have become vulnerable to economic fluctuations in Spain owing to the dominance of Spanish banks (Clarke and others, 2001, p. 18).

Portfolio flows

Net portfolio flows tend to be volatile and pro-cyclical

Net portfolio flows tend to be pro-cyclical as well as volatile. Net portfolio investment flows had surged in the early 1990s and at their peak surpassed the level of FDI, but this was followed by a collapse during the series of crises that started in East Asia in 1997. The rapid growth of bond financing was matched during the boom by the increase of foreign purchases of developing-country stocks; both declined thereafter. In the case of stocks, the initial surge had been associated to the privatization processes; later, as foreign investors resorted to direct investment to acquire control of privatized companies, portfolio equity flows declined.

Portfolio debt flows began a downturn in 1997 that lasted until 2003-2004

From 1997, the level of portfolio debt flows, measured by net issuance of debt in the international market had begun a major downturn, reaching a trough in 2001. In 2003-2004, there was a broad-based rebound: net issuance levels reached $82 billion in 2004, far above the $46 billion annual average in 1999-2003 but below the previous peak of $94 billion in 1997 (Bank for International Settlements, 2005, p. 36). In spite of persistent large reversals, net portfolio debt flows became the major source of debt financing for emerging market countries, particularly in Latin America.

While there has been an overall decline in net portfolio debt flows to developing countries since the Asian financial crisis, the pattern differs significantly between crisis and non-crisis countries (International Monetary Fund, 2004b, p. 133). Since 1998, there have been large net portfolio debt outflows from Asian crisis countries. Similarly, in 2000-2002, countries in financial crisis or turmoil, such as Argentina, Brazil and Turkey, experienced sharp declines in net portfolio debt flows. On the contrary, flows to other countries increased.

Countries' sudden loss of access to primary markets for international bonds is measured as a level of very low issuance activity. The across-the-board market closure following the Russian crisis in 1998 was an extreme case of such an episode, while in 2002, loss of access was limited to a small number of countries. The riskiest borrowers were most likely to lose access to financing. Borrowers with lower credit ratings regained access after lower-risk borrowers when markets reopened (World Bank, 2004a, pp. 50-51). When developing countries do not totally lose market access, they are often subject to sharp increases of risk premiums, which are also characterized by significant cross-correlation among issuers (contagion effects). The pro-cyclical downgrades of credit rating agencies often exacerbate both lack of access to the bond market and the spreads at which such bonds can be issued.

Market access can depend on investor reaction not only to events specific to emerging market countries but also to conditions in global financial markets. While the former were dominant in the late 1990s, the latter appear to be exerting an increasing effect on emerging market bond market closure and reopening in recent years (International Monetary Fund, 2004b, p. 66). This was illustrated by the market closure in 2002. In the subsequent rally in emerging bond markets, financial conditions had a positive effect on emerging markets, an experience similar to that of the early 1990s. Low international interest rates and increased investor search for yield was reflected in an increase in the appetite for risk. However, the negative impact of international factors on the emerging market bond market was underscored again when expectations of larger-than-anticipated United States interest rate increases were raised in April 2004 and early 2005, resulting in abrupt and sharp reversals in the tightening of yield spreads of emerging market bonds. Although emerging market countries were able to weather the heightened volatility, these developments raise questions about the sustainability of the favourable external financing environment for developing countries. Currently, there are some signs of increasing risk in emerging bond markets (Institute of International Finance, 2005).

Recent developments in bond markets have also affected the composition of debt flows. The upgrading of credit ratings of a number of developing countries, including the increased number of investment grade emerging market bonds, has broadened the investor base. The increase in "crossover" investors, including institutional investors, who invest in emerging market debt as a supplement to their traditional portfolio of mature market debt, has also made a larger source of funds available. However, crossover investors can generate greater volatility, as their decisions are more sensitive to the returns of other investments in their portfolios. Also, to the extent that international banks have historically had a more diversified portfolio than other investors, increased bond issues by developing countries is not a substitute for the reduction of cross-border bank lending, and may lead to a concentration of capital flows in those countries that are regarded by the market as low-risk borrowers, at the cost of a further marginalization of high-risk borrowers (Bank for International Settlements, 2003, pp. 51-52).

There has also been a rapid development of domestic bond markets in many emerging market economies since the late 1990s aimed at mobilizing domestic saving, reducing dependency on external financing and lowering currency mismatch (see below). These domestic capital markets have attracted increasing financing from domestic as well as foreign investors, but they are not immune to volatility in interest rates. A case in point was the sharp rise in local currency bond spreads in Brazil and Turkey when emerging market bond yield spreads spiked in April and May 2004 (International Monetary Fund, 2004b, p. 23). Also, the stress on Asian local currency bond markets (China, the Republic

A sudden loss of access to international bonds markets results in a loss of financing and increases in risk premiums for developing countries

The recent increase in "crossover" investors in emerging market debt has led to a broadening of the investor base but can also generate greater volatility

Rapidly developing domestic bond markets are not immune to interest rate volatilities

of Korea and Thailand) in 2003 emanated from the sell-off in United States Treasury bonds (Bank for International Settlements, 2004, pp. 74-75). These experiences raise some questions about the effectiveness of local capital markets as a complete buffer against the volatility of external portfolio debt financing.

Net portfolio equity flows declined sharply after 1997 but rebounded in 2003-2004

Net portfolio equity flows have experienced a cycle similar to that of bond financing, but their relative magnitudes differ. They declined sharply between 1997 and 2002 after reaching a peak in the early 1990s but have remained a small source of external financing for emerging market economies, even after the rebound in 2003-2004. The strength of the recovery was concentrated in Asia, with a high level of issuance by China and India.

Volatility in emerging market portfolio equity flows since the late 1990s can be attributed to a sudden loss of access to primary markets, as in the case of portfolio debt flows. In addition, synchronization with mature markets makes emerging market stocks more susceptible to international developments as evidenced by the ramifications of the bursting of the information technology bubble in 2000.

An underlying factor in a long-term decline of portfolio equity flows was the lower risk-adjusted return on emerging market stocks compared with return on portfolio debt investment in the 1990s, making the latter the preferable investment (World Bank, 2003, pp. 100-101). Underdeveloped stock markets, lack of minority shareholder protection, and limited disclosure requirements contribute to the higher risk of emerging market stocks for international investors. Also, higher volatility of returns to emerging market equities relative to bonds in an environment of macroeconomic instability reflects the seniority of debt over equity in bankruptcy proceedings. In addition, as investors seek to exert more control over the operations of enterprises and to protect their own interests, they have shifted from portfolio equity investment to FDI.

Recent liberalization in emerging markets has helped strengthen equity flows

Recent liberalization of ownership and other restrictions in emerging markets has helped strengthen portfolio equity flow. This has been particularly evident in China and India where economic liberalization and prospects for sustained strong economic growth have boosted portfolio equity flow. China has succeeded in raising large amounts of foreign capital for its most successful State-owned enterprises through the listing of shares in the major international stock exchanges, although this limited fund-raising capacity for smaller domestic enterprises (Euromoney, 2004, pp. 92-99).

Impact of derivatives

The 1990s saw an explosion in the volume of global derivatives

The 1990s saw an explosion in the global derivatives market. Financial derivatives became an important factor in the growth of cross-border capital flows, including emerging markets. In Mexico, for example, banks used derivatives to leverage their currency and interest rate exposure. When pressure on the exchange rate began to build, these positions contributed to the Mexican crisis. Bank lending and portfolio flows, especially to Asian developing countries, were increasingly intermediated through structured derivative instruments.

Derivatives can help redistribute risks ...

The growth in derivative products is in large part due to their ability to unbundle and isolate risks. Floating exchange rates gave a major impulse to this growth by generating demand by investors to hedge against changes in exchange rates. Derivatives can redistribute risk away from those who do not want it to those theoretically better able to manage it. Derivatives can also provide a tool for pricing different risks, thus increasing market efficiency. They give investors the ability to hedge specific risks and gain access to others, creating opportunities for portfolio diversification.

At the same time, however, derivative products increase leverage in markets, provide tools for short-term speculation and can increase macroeconomic volatility. Because derivatives are often complex, non-transparent and poorly regulated, they can also be used for tax avoidance, manipulation and fraud. Thus, the use of derivatives has added to systemic risk and macroeconomic volatility, especially for developing countries (see chap. VI regarding systemic risk).

... but they can also foster speculation and increase macroeconomic volatility

Standard derivative contracts used to hedge risk, such as forwards, futures and options, are quite well known. While foreign-currency forwards are traded over the counter (OTC), many basic futures and options contracts are standardized and traded in organized and regulated markets. Futures and forward contracts illustrate how derivatives can transfer risk. The wheat farmer, for example, risks a loss in income from a fall in the price of wheat, while the baker risks a loss from a rise in price. Both risks can be eliminated if, at the beginning of the planting season, they agree to the price at which they will exchange wheat at harvest time. However, in the absence of perfectly offsetting risks, contracts increasingly simply transfer risk from one agent to another. In the absence of a baker, the farmer will transfer his risk to whoever is willing to guarantee the contracted price on the stipulated date. For these agents, contracts are primarily for trading rather than hedging purposes.

Forward contracts in foreign exchange constitute the most liquid derivative instrument traded in emerging markets. In these contracts, counterparties agree to buy one currency and sell the other on a specified date at an agreed upon price. Originally used for hedging purposes, forwards foreign-exchange contracts have increasingly been used for currency speculation. For example, in the early 2000s speculators used forwards as the main tool for betting on an appreciation of the Chinese renminbi. Forward contracts also offer implicit access to the interest rates of the currency being bought, funded by the currency being sold. In what is called the "carry trade", investors use currency forwards to invest in high short-term local interest rates in developing countries, funded by lower United States dollar, yen or euro rates. Forwards also give speculators the ability to short the local currency.

Forward contracts highlight several important characteristics of derivatives and their potentially very problematic impact on developing countries. First, they add leverage to the markets, exacerbating problems of short-term capital flows and hot money. Derivative products that allow investors to leverage currency risk have increased volatility in exchange markets and exacerbated boom-bust cycles in developing countries. For example, open currency and interest rate positions in Asia in the mid-1990s grew to excessive proportions relative to domestic GDP and were a major factor in the Asian crisis (International Monetary Fund, 2002a). This was especially pronounced in Indonesia where, prior to the crisis, otherwise viable companies had been speculating on the exchange rate through foreign-exchange forwards and swaps. These companies were then forced into bankruptcy when the currency devalued. When pressure on the currency built, foreigners sold their local currency positions, and domestic speculators were forced to buy dollars to cover their dollar shorts, causing the currency to fall further.

Derivatives add leverage to markets, exacerbating boom-bust cycles in developing countries

The forwards foreign-exchange market also demonstrates the difficulty of regulating derivatives. As a response to the crisis, Asian central banks attempted to use capital controls to restrict currency speculation through the forwards market. However, the global nature of derivatives, combined with their lack of transparency, made it harder to enforce capital-account regulations. The result has been the growth of offshore or non-deliverable forwards markets designed to circumvent domestic restrictions. For example,

It is difficult to regulate derivatives ...

tightening of controls since the Asian crisis has led to new growth of such markets, so that Asian non-deliverable forwards markets now make up over 70 per cent of all global non-deliverable forwards markets (Ma, Ho and McCauley, 2004).

... partially because offshore markets are hard to control

Because the non-deliverable forwards markets are offshore, it is harder, albeit still possible, for domestic regulators to control them. When Malaysia imposed capital controls during the Asian crisis, it made ringgit deposits abroad illegal, and determined that those held abroad by nationals had to be repatriated. These decisions were aimed at eliminating the offshore market, which had been used by speculators to manipulate the currency (Khor, 2005).

A consideration of the differences between onshore and offshore forward contracts also provides some insight into how derivatives isolate risk. One of the main risks associated with over-the-counter derivatives is local counterparty risk. During the Russian crisis, for example, many foreign investors bought local treasury bills and then hedged the currency risk with Russian local banks through currency forwards. During the crisis, local banks went bankrupt, and refused to honour their contracts. The non-deliverable forwards markets are dominated by foreign banks, and trades outside the developing country (for example, in New York or London); hence, the risk of counterparty default is significantly lower than with onshore forwards. Onshore contracts expose countries to domestic settlement risk and the risk that the central bank will impose currency controls. Non-deliverable forwards markets are not subject to these risks.

Other derivative products unbundle risks even more. For example, contracts can be written that limit exposure to convertibility risk, local settlement risk, etc. The result in respect of these packages is a change in the credit-risk characteristics of the bond whereby risks are shifted to different individuals. Investors can use these products to gain access to their desired emerging market exposure, and borrowers can use them to reduce the cost of funding. However, because of their complexity, they can also be used to hide risks from regulators and, sometimes, even from the investors themselves. In addition, like forwards, they can also increase systemic risk and macroeconomic volatility. In a number of countries where severe restrictions in the cash market prevail, these derivative products allow investors to go around such restrictions (Chew, 1996, p. 49). However, in doing so, they often circumvent the intended limits on short-term hot money.

Complex derivatives hide risks from regulators

The difficulties created by these products can be seen most clearly in the context of the structured credit derivative contracts that expanded rapidly during the late 1990s, one example involving the structured note with an embedded option, often linked to an emerging market currency. These notes carried a higher coupon because they contained an embedded short position in interest rate or foreign-exchange options. In other words, when an investor bought a structured note, she simultaneously sold an interest rate option. Less knowledgeable investors did not realize that by buying these securities, they were selling options or engaging in leveraged bets, because those features were concealed (Chew, 1996, pp. 54-55).

Swaps allow a market that trades without funding

Another structured credit derivative is the total return swap. The objective of this swap is to allow counterparties to exchange risks without actually transferring assets. The borrower receives the total return (coupons plus capital gains or losses) on a reference asset and generally pays the London Interbank Offered Rate (LIBOR) plus a spread. Total return swaps can be tied to almost any asset, index or basket of assets and, like structured notes, can be designed to include the amount of leverage the parties choose to agree on. Swaps allow a global market that trades without any actual funding, and is not affected by any of the limitations of the cash market.

Structured products have also been the basis for the growing market in credit default swaps, which are currently the most popular form of credit derivatives. Credit default swaps are credit swaps embedded in structured notes. Under the terms of the swap, the counterparty buying protection against a credit event makes a periodic payment to the seller. She is paid by the seller if the credit event occurs. Unlike total return swaps, credit default swaps provide protection only against agreed upon credit events, such as bankruptcy, a change in credit ratings, a debt moratorium or a debt restructuring. The most liquid credit default swaps contracts are on sovereign external debt.

While the credit default swaps market provides an efficient tool for pricing credit risk it also opens the way to abuses, and can be particularly difficult to monitor and regulate since, like the non-deliverable forwards market, the credit default swaps market is not domestic. Most trades experience no geographical limitations. Furthermore, credit default swaps can mask the true ownership structure of a country's debt. This becomes an issue if a country goes into default. All bondholders have equal rights to negotiate a settlement; but there can be bondholders who also have a short position through swaps, and might negotiate against other bondholders' interests.

The increasing use of credit derivatives has reduced transparency and increased the difficulty in assessing the final return on funds provided. Many of the contracts used include embedded options and leverage that increase the risk of the position often beyond the investors' knowledge.

Many of these structured products have been expressly designed to hide risk exposure by providing credit enhancements. It is not surprising that bank regulators in emerging economies had difficulty discovering or controlling them. Even in developed countries, regulators have found the monitoring of derivative transactions to be a complicated matter, as was seen in the cases of Long-Term Capital Management (LTCM) and Enron. In developing countries, with weaker institutions and undeveloped markets, poorly regulated derivatives can have an even greater destabilizing effect.

In theory, derivatives can be used to decouple risks, giving investors the opportunity to diversify their portfolios. At the same time, they should lead to additional sources of financing for borrowers, and help develop local capital markets. Furthermore, new instruments can limit risks through diversification.

However, derivatives can also destabilize markets and have contributed to boom-and-bust cycles in emerging markets. The way in which particular swap contracts and credit derivatives combine currency risk and market price risks explains why these markets tend to move in sympathy, creating contagion that can produce unexpected declines and excessive instability in both currency and asset markets during crises. Also, the characteristics of the derivative contracts suggest that they are often motivated by factors not directly related to the allocation of funds to their highest global returns. Rather, they are linked to attempts to circumvent particular prudential regulations and provide banks with fee and commission income, rather than to profit from assessing relative risk-adjusted returns.

Yet, derivatives in developing countries appear set to continue to grow. Recent figures indicate a recovery of cross-border bank lending. In particular, inflows into China have increased substantially, driven by an anticipated appreciation of the Chinese currency. These flows have been encouraged by China's decision to adopt more liberal rules on Derivatives Business of Financial Institutions from March 2004 which allow foreign banks to expand their derivatives activities with Chinese companies. The new rules permit over-the-counter derivatives trades for any commercially reasonable purpose, not just for hedging purposes, as previously required.

Credit default swaps can mask ownership of a country's debt

Even in developed countries, regulators find it difficult to monitor derivatives

Derivatives are often motivated by factors not linked to the best allocation of funds

Derivatives are set to grow in developing countries

One lesson to be derived from the history of derivatives in the 1990s is that short-term instruments linked to currencies and money markets can be particularly destabilizing. The experience of Malaysia, however, shows how well-designed regulations and controls can effectively restrict this market, and can even be used to cut off the development of an offshore market. In the case of China, the new derivatives regulations still require banks to comply with foreign-exchange restrictions. In other words, the new rules do not permit derivatives involving renminbi, so that leveraging or shorting the currency is still apparently restricted. However, the rapid development of derivatives in China may entail new risks that it may be difficult for regulators to monitor.

Well-designed regulations can reduce the risks posed by derivatives

Derivatives tied to longer-term instruments are perhaps less risky, and some risks can be potentially minimized through well-designed regulations (Dodd, 2005). When opening their markets in order to obtain the benefits that derivatives can offer, policymakers need to focus on new regulatory structures so as to minimize not only risk to the investor but above all systemic risk, and undesired potential macroeconomic effects.

Measures to counter pro-cyclicality of private flows

To counter the boom-bust pattern that characterizes private capital flows, several options are available to developing countries. We consider in the present section two alternatives: (a) designing mechanisms to encourage more stable private flows (counter-cyclical guarantees) or that distribute better the risk faced by developing countries throughout the business cycle (indexed bonds and bonds denominated in the currency of developing countries); and (b) introducing prudential regulations on the capital account. We also consider the likely effect of the New Basel Capital Accord (Basel II) on the cyclical patterns of capital flows to developing countries. The use of local currency bond markets to reduce currency mismatches and the design of explicit counter-cyclical prudential regulations were analysed in chapter I. The pro-cyclical pattern of private capital flows gives a compensatory role also to official financing; this issue will be considered in chapters IV and VI, in relation to official development financing and to emergency (balance of payments) financing, respectively.

Counter-cyclical financing instruments

One way of addressing the problems created by the inherent tendency of private flows to be pro-cyclical is for public institutions to issue guarantees that have counter-cyclical elements (Griffith-Jones and Fuzzo de Lima, 2004). In this regard, multilateral development banks and export credit agencies could introduce explicit counter-cyclical elements in the risk evaluations they make for issuing guarantees for lending to developing countries. This would imply that when banks or other lenders lowered their exposure to a country, multilateral development banks or export credit agencies would increase their level of guarantees, if they considered that the country's long-term fundamentals were basically sound. When private banks' willingness to lend increased, multilateral development banks or export credit agencies could reduce their exposure. This implies that the models used to assess risks should utilize measures of risk focused on long-term fundamentals and would therefore be less affected by the short-term fluctuations that tend to influence markets.

To counter boom-bust cycles, measures can be designed to encourage more stable private flows

Alternatively, there could be special stand-alone guarantee mechanisms for long-term private credit that had a strong explicit counter-cyclical element. This could be activated in periods of sharp decline in capital flows and its aim would be to try to catalyse long-term private credit, especially for infrastructure. Multilateral development banks could also play a more active role in issuing guarantees to bonds issued in private capital markets by developing countries during periods of limited risk appetite.

Introducing counter-cyclical elements in public guarantees can help smooth flows

The introduction of counter-cyclical elements in guarantees would become more meaningful if the number of guarantees issued by multilateral and regional development banks expanded to offset the decline in guarantees issued by some export credit agencies. As we will see in chapter IV, existing problems—such as excessive restrictiveness of criteria and approval processes for granting and other related costs—would need to be addressed, and the resources of the international financial institutions should also be better leveraged in providing guarantees.

This would become more meaningful if the volume of multilateral guarantees increased

Commodity-linked bonds can also play a useful role in reducing developing countries' cyclical vulnerabilities. Examples of commodity-indexed bonds include oil-backed bonds, including Petrobonds, which were first issued on behalf of the Government of Mexico (Atta-Mensah, 2004). In such instruments, the coupon or principal payments to the buyer are linked to the price of a referenced commodity. By issuing this type of bond, the developing country can shift some of the risk of a fall in commodity prices to its bond investors. However, commodity-linked bonds can be expensive, owing to the greater complexity of these instruments, in comparison with conventional bonds (Dodd, 2004).

Commodity-linked and GDP-linked bonds can reduce the likelihood of debt crises and of pro-cyclical responses to shocks

There have also been proposals to introduce GDP-indexed bonds. The coupon payments on these bonds would vary in part with the growth rate of the debtor's economy, being higher in years of rapid growth of GDP (measured in an international currency) and lower in years of below-trend growth. It has been argued that such instruments would improve the cushioning of emerging market borrowers against adverse shocks by making debt payments more contingent on the borrower's ability to pay. GDP-indexed bonds would therefore restrict the range of variation of the debt-to-GDP ratio and hence reduce the likelihood of debt crises and defaults. At the same time, they also reduce the likelihood of pro-cyclical fiscal policy responses to adverse shocks.

This instrument would allow countries to insure against a broader set of risks than would commodity-linked bonds, and thus is likely to be more useful for those developing countries that have fairly diversified production and exports and therefore do not have a natural commodity price to link to bond payments (Council of Economic Advisers, 2004; Goldstein, 2005). However, the introduction of GDP-indexed bonds may encounter some obstacles, such as concerns about the quality of GDP data in some developing countries. Their introduction would thus need to be preceded by efforts to improve the quality of macroeconomic information.

It has been suggested that the advanced industrialized countries should issue these instruments first. This would have a demonstration effect and make it easier for developing countries to join in (Shiller, 2005). The precedent of introducing collective action clauses into bonds, undertaken first by developed countries which were later followed by developing countries, would seem to indicate that such demonstration effects can be very effective in introducing innovations in financial instruments.

Industrialized countries should issue such bonds first, to set a precedent

Another alternative for better managing the risks faced by developing countries throughout the business cycle consists in the introduction of local currency-denominated bonds. These bonds offer, in particular, a cure against the currency mismatches that characterize the debt structure of developing countries. At the domestic level, the development

Local currency bonds help countries manage risks

of domestic capital markets, especially bond markets, also creates a more stable source of local funding for both the public and private sectors, thereby mitigating the funding difficulties created by sudden stops in cross-border capital flows (some limitations of these instruments, particularly the relative incapacity to isolate domestic markets from external market shocks, were discussed above). Chapter I has outlined the progress made in developing domestic capital markets in developing countries and the policy options for further encouraging this trend.

Diversified portfolios of local currency debt can make investment in local currency bonds more attractive to foreign investors

In addition to proposals for institutional measures to develop local capital markets, there have also been innovative proposals to make local currency investments more attractive to international investors. Spiegel and Dodd (2004) have suggested raising capital in international markets by forming diversified portfolios of emerging market local currency debt issued by sovereign Governments. These portfolios of local currency government debt securities (LCD portfolios) would employ risk management techniques of diversification to generate a return-to-risk that competed favourably with other major capital market security indices. Based on data starting in 1994, the authors show that a portfolio of emerging market local currency debt can raise rates of return relative to risk that compete with those of major securities indices in international capital markets. The insight offered by portfolio theory is that a portfolio consisting of different securities whose returns are sufficiently independent (especially if they are negatively correlated) can yield risk-adjusted rates of returns superior to those of the individual securities. Thus, the volatility of the whole is less than the sum of its parts. The proposed LCD portfolio would consist of local currency government debt instruments from many different developing countries, so as to have a return and variance that were competitive in international capital markets.

However, the authors admit that there are some challenges that need to be overcome. The first is the disappointing history of local currency funds in the mid- to late 1990s which has led investors to be wary of this asset class. This relates to funds that took large concentrated bets in a few countries, and thus did not maintain a diversified portfolio. As local currency bond markets have continued to develop, there is now a greater possibility of benefiting from portfolio diversification. The second is that Governments may not respond to the interest of foreign investors in local debt by easing regulations and transactions costs involved with investing in these markets. This may be due to the fact that foreign financing may be more attractive, since it is often cheaper than domestic financing. Some countries may also fear the impact that surges and reversals of short-term hot money could have on small domestic capital markets. In this light, regulations can be viewed as a means of restricting capital flows. Given the legitimacy of these concerns, the challenge becomes to construct the portfolio in such a way as to still give policymakers the option to continue to selectively use capital-account regulations to limit short-term inflows. According to Spiegel and Dodd, this can indeed be done and they cite the example of Hungary where foreigners were given permission to buy into long-term closed-end funds even when they were not allowed to access the local bond market directly.

Multilateral development banks can help develop domestic bond markets

As suggested in chapter IV, multilateral development banks could play an active role in the development of domestic bond markets.

Prudential capital account regulations

In the previous section, we suggested a set of financial instruments that could be used in international financial markets to either smooth out private flows to developing countries or manage better the risks they generate. However, there are also important policy measures that can be taken nationally to either smooth private flows or manage such risks, particularly prudential regulations on the capital account and counter-cyclical prudential regulations. The latter were analysed in chapter I; we consider the former in the present section.

The accumulation of risks that developing countries face during capital-account booms depends not only on the magnitude of private and public sector debts but also on maturity and currency mismatches on the balance sheets of financial and non-financial agents. Thus, capital-account regulations potentially have a dual role: as a macro-economic policy tool with which to provide some room for counter-cyclical monetary policies that smooth out debt ratios and spending; and as a "liability policy" designed to improve private sector external debt profiles (Ocampo, 2003e).

Viewed as a macroeconomic policy tool, capital-account regulations aim at the direct source of boom-bust cycles: unstable capital flows. If successful, they provide some room to "lean against the wind" during periods of financial euphoria through the adoption of a contractionary monetary policy and/or reduced appreciation pressures. If effective, they also reduce or eliminate the quasifiscal costs of sterilized foreign-exchange accumulation. During crises, they provide breathing space for expansionary monetary policies. In both cases, capital-account regulations improve the authorities' ability to mix additional degrees of monetary independence with a more active exchange-rate policy.

Capital-account regulations can provide room for counter-cyclical monetary policies and improve external debt profiles

In their role as a liability policy, capital-account regulations recognize the fact that the market rewards sound external debt profiles (Rodrik and Velasco, 1999). This reflects the fact that, during times of uncertainty, the market responds to gross (and not merely net) financing requirements, which means that the rollover of short-term liabilities is not financially neutral. Under these circumstances, a maturity profile that leans towards longer-term obligations will reduce domestic liquidity risks. An essential component of economic policy management during booms should thus be measures to improve the maturity structures of external and domestic liabilities.

Overall, the experiences with capital-account regulations in the 1990s were useful for improving debt profiles, giving Governments more latitude in pursuing stabilizing macroeconomic policies, and insulating countries from some of the vagaries of capital markets. There is much evidence that, if well implemented, the benefits far outweigh the costs (Stiglitz and others, 2005; Epstein and others, 2003; Ocampo and Palma, 2005).

If well implemented, the benefits far outweigh costs

A key question for countries considering capital market interventions is what form the interventions should take. They can be either price-based (unremunerated reserve requirements or taxes) or quantity-based (administrative restrictions on certain forms of borrowing). Aside from price- and quantity-based interventions in capital markets, other domestic prudential regulations can also be used to affect both the ability to borrow abroad and the associated returns. They include limits on banks' short-term foreign borrowing; regulations that force banks to match their foreign currency liabilities and assets; and regulations that restrict them from lending in foreign currencies to firms that do not have equivalent revenues in those currencies, or impose higher capital adequacy requirements or loan-loss provisions for short-term lending in foreign currency and lending that involves a currency mismatch. Authorities can also apply adverse tax or bank-

Interventions can be price- or quantity-based, or both

ruptcy treatment to foreign-denominated borrowing. These interventions are not mutually exclusive, and thus Governments can use a mix of instruments to manage the risks associated to foreign borrowing.

The basic advantages of price-based instruments are their simplicity and their focus on averting the build-up of macroeconomic disequilibria and, ultimately, preventing crises. A highly significant innovation in this sphere during the 1990s was the establishment in Chile and Colombia of an unremunerated reserve requirement for capital inflows. Since the unremunerated reserve requirement could be substituted by a payment to the central bank of its implicit costs, it also operated as a tax on capital inflows. It created a simple, non-discretionary and preventive (prudential) price-based incentive that penalized short-term foreign currency liabilities more heavily.

Unremunerated reserve requirements were an important innovation and were broadly successful

The effectiveness of reserve requirements has been the subject of debate (for review of different positions, see Ocampo, 2003e). It is noteworthy that institutions such as the International Monetary Fund and the Bank for International Settlements have increasingly concluded that these controls were effective in important aspects. There is broad agreement that they were effective in reducing short-term debt flows and thus in improving or maintaining good external debt profiles. There is greater controversy about their effectiveness as a macroeconomic policy tool. Nonetheless, given solid evidence on the sensitivity of capital flows to interest rate spreads in both countries, it can be asserted that reserve requirements influenced the volume of capital flows at given interest rates or (an aspect on which there is broader agreement) helped countries maintain higher domestic interest rates during periods of euphoria in international financial markets. Therefore, in terms of some, and probably most, of their main objectives, the Chilean and Colombian experiences were broadly successful. They clearly helped lengthen maturities and increased space for increasing interest rates, thereby contributing to macroeconomic equilibrium.

On the other hand, traditional foreign-exchange market interventions and quantity-based capital-account regulations might be preferable when the policy objective is to reduce significantly domestic macroeconomic sensitivity to international capital flows. These traditional controls in essence segment the domestic and foreign-exchange markets, basically by limiting the capacity of domestic firms and residents to borrow in foreign currency (except in the cases of some specific transactions such as trade financing and long-term investment) and limiting the capacity of foreign residents to hold some types of domestic financial assets or liabilities.

Simple quantitative restrictions may be easier to administer

Indeed, simple quantitative restrictions of this sort are also preventive in character and can be easier to administer than price-based controls, but an administrative capability must be in place in order for these regulations to work and to prevent the corruption that could be generated by the discretionary decisions that might be involved in their use. Some of them can also be mixed with price-based regulations or with other domestic prudential regulations mentioned in the beginning of this section. Thus, during the 1990s, Chile established a minimum stay period for foreign capital (one year) and was responsible for the direct approval of issuance of American Depository Receipts (ADRs), and Colombia maintained direct regulations on the inflows and composition of the portfolios of foreign investment funds operating in the country.

Quantitative restrictions can be very effective in preventing crises

The experience of the Asian countries that maintained quantity-based restrictions throughout the 1990s suggests that those restrictions might indeed also be particularly effective in preventing crises. China, India, Taiwan Province of China and Viet Nam offer successful examples in this regard. Despite the slow and cautious liberalization that has taken place in several of these economies since the early 1990s, the use of such traditional regulations has helped them prevent contagion from the East Asian crisis (see, for example, in relation to India, Reddy, 2001; Rajaraman, 2001; and in relation to Taiwan Province of China, Agosin 2000).

Malaysia offers one of the most interesting examples of effective use of quantitative regulations during the 1990s. In January 1994, it had introduced outright restrictions on short-term inflows and prohibited non-residents from buying a wide range of short-term securities. These other measures proved highly effective in reversing the booming capital inflows of the previous years (Palma, 2002). In September 1998, Malaysia established quantity-based restrictions on outflows, which basically aimed at guaranteeing that the local currency would be used only in domestic transactions, and thus at eliminating offshore trading of the currency.[4] In February 1999, these regulations were replaced by an exit levy (that is to say, a price-based regulation), which was gradually reduced in later years. Kaplan and Rodrik (2001) show that the Malaysian regulations successfully closed the offshore ringgit market and reversed financial market pressure, and gave the government space within which to enact expansionary monetary and fiscal policies that contributed to the speedy recovery of economic activity.

Although quantity-based restrictions can be effective if authorities wish to limit capital outflows during crises, crisis-driven quantitative controls generate serious credibility issues and may be ineffective in the absence of a strong administrative capacity. This implies that a tradition of regulation may be necessary, and that the tightening or loosening of permanent regulatory regimes through the cycle may be superior to the alternation of different (even opposite) capital-account regimes. In broader terms, this means that it is essential to maintain the autonomy needed to impose capital-account regulations, and thus the freedom to reimpose controls, if necessary (United Nations, 2001a; Reddy, 2001; Ocampo, 2003e). This is indeed a corollary of the incomplete nature of international financial governance, particularly of the absence of a lender-of-last-resort at the global level.

It should be emphasized, in any case, that capital-account regulations should always be seen as an instrument that provides an additional degree of freedom to the authorities with respect to their adopting sensible counter-cyclical macroeconomic policies, but never as a substitute for those policies.

Permanent regulatory regimes that are tightened or loosened through the cycle are superior to ad hoc interventions

Basel II and developing countries

The right regulatory and supervisory regime is essential for maintaining domestic financial stability. In a globalized economy, some common standards of regulation and supervision may be also essential to guarantee global financial stability and to avoid regulatory arbitrage by international banks and other financial agents. This has been the major motivation behind the principles adopted by the Basel Committee on Banking Supervision in recent decades. The second generation of these standards (Basel II), agreed to in June 2004, takes a further step in aligning regulatory capital with the risks in banks lending, and in adapting regulations to the complexities of risk management in the contemporary world. Also, the standardized approach contains several positive features from the perspective of developing countries, such as the reduction of the excessive incentive to short-term lending, which existed in Basel I.

Basel II has a number of positive features

However, there is a risk that it will increase the pro-cyclicality of bank lending ...

However, when judged from the perspective of some of the main market failures that should be addressed by banking regulation, the new regime has a number of problems: it is complex where it should be simple; it is implicitly pro-cyclical when it should be explicitly counter-cyclical; and although it is supposed to more accurately align regulatory capital to the risks that banks face, in the case of lending to developing countries it ignores the proved benefits of diversification.

... reduce such lending to developing countries and increase its cost

There are thus fears that Basel II creates the risk of a sharp reduction in bank lending to developing countries and of an increase in the cost of a significant part of the remaining lending, particularly in the case of low-rated borrowing countries, which also have a limited or costly access to international bond markets. This is contrary to the stated objective of G-10 Governments, which is to encourage private flows to developing countries, and use them as an engine for stimulating and funding growth. An equal cause for concern is the danger that Basel II will accentuate the pro-cyclicality of bank lending, which is damaging for all economies, but particularly so for fragile developing ones, which are more vulnerable to strong cyclical fluctuations of financing.

The internal-ratings based (IRB) approach overestimates risk of lending to developing countries ...

Indeed, the proposed internal ratings-based (IRB) approach of Basel II overestimates the risk of international bank lending to developing countries, primarily because it does not appropriately reflect the clear benefits of international diversification. One consequence of the adoption of this approach by internationally active banks would be that capital requirements for higher-rated borrowers will fall, while those for lower-rated borrowers will rise. This is likely to lead to an excessive increase in regulatory capital requirements and, to the extent that regulatory capital requirements feed through into the pricing of loans, will cause the pricing of loans to lower-rated borrowers—those concentrated in developing countries and particularly the lower-rated borrowing countries—to rise significantly. It has been argued that this is acceptable, since it merely reflects a more accurate assessment of the risks. However, there is a great deal of evidence that by failing to take account of the benefits of international diversification at the portfolio level, capital requirements for loans to developing countries will be significantly higher than is justified on the basis of the actual risks attached to this lending (see, for example, Griffith-Jones, Segoviano and Spratt, 2004a).

... because it ignores the benefits of international diversification

Incorporating the benefits of diversification of lending to developing countries would reduce capital requirements and pro-cyclicality

Therefore, one clear way in which Basle II could be improved so as to reduce the negative and technically incorrect effects on developing countries would be to introduce the benefits of diversification into the internal-ratings based approach. One of the major benefits of investing in developing and emerging economies is their relatively low correlation with mature markets. This hypothesis was tested empirically using a wide variety of financial, market and macro variables (Griffith-Jones, Segoviano and Spratt, 2004a). Every statistical test performed, regardless of variable, time period or frequency, showed that the correlation between developed markets only was higher, in every case, than that between developed and developing markets. Different simulations that compared estimated unexpected losses of portfolios that were diversified across both developed and developing countries with the losses of portfolios in developed countries only, have estimated that the former were from 19 to 23 per cent lower.

The evidence clearly supports the hypothesis that a bank's loan portfolio that was diversified between developed and developing-country borrowers would benefit in terms of lower overall portfolio risk relative to one that focused exclusively on lending to developed countries. Therefore, if risks are measured precisely, this should be reflected in lower capital requirements. Indeed, the Chair of the Basel Committee on Banking Supervision, Jaime Caruana, acknowledged in July 2004, in his speech to the Annual Conference of Latin American Regulators (ASBA), held in Mexico City, that "geographical diversification effects clearly occur. Others have commented on failure of the New Basel Capital Accord (Basel II) to take account of diversification effects as being its major flaw. For example, the Governor of the Mexican Central Bank suggested in July 2004 that "any postponement of incorporating the benefits of diversification runs the risk of discouraging large international banks from maintaining and expanding their loans to emerging markets". He also expressed his serious concern about the negative effects that the new Accord could have on volatility of capital flows to emerging economies (Ortiz, 2004). These concerns have also been expressed by several senior private bankers.

An additional positive effect of taking account of the benefits of diversification is that this makes capital requirements far less pro-cyclical than they otherwise would be. Indeed, if the benefits of diversification are incorporated, simulations show that the variance over time of capital requirements will be significantly smaller than if these benefits are not incorporated. Therefore, introducing the benefits of geographical diversification significantly decreases, though it does not eliminate, the higher pro-cyclicality that the internal-ratings based approach implies. This difference may well be significant enough to prevent a "credit crunch".

This lower pro-cyclicality of capital over time of an internal-ratings based approach that incorporates the benefits of diversification (the Full Credit Risk Model (ICRM)) compared with an internal-ratings based approach that does not incorporate those benefits can be seen in figure III.1. However, even if the benefits of diversification are incorporated, the internal-ratings based approach will still be more pro-cyclical than the standardized approach, which is closer to the principles of the first Basel Capital Accord (Basel I) (see, again figure III.1). Therefore, as well as introducing the benefits of diversification, it seems desirable to introduce counter-cyclical measures (for example, counter-cyclical provisioning against losses) at the same time as Basel II is implemented in 2007.

Counter-cyclical provisioning is also desirable when Basel II is introduced

Figure III.1.
Capital requirements for the United States of America using three regulatory regimes, 1982-2003

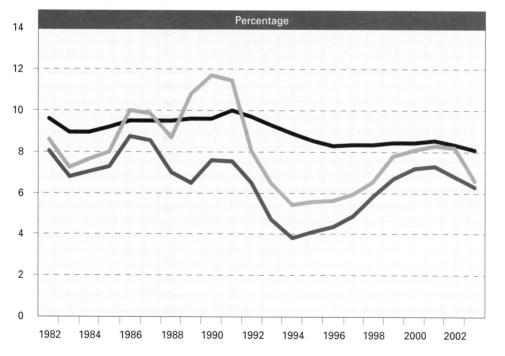

Source:
Simulations based on a data set of Moody's available for United States banks for the period 1982-2003 (Griffith-Jones, Segoviano and Spratt, 2004b).

Introducing the
benefits of diver-
sification would be
technically sound

Introducing the benefits of diversification soon would therefore: (a) clearly lead to a more precise measurement of risk, the main aim of Basel II; (b) appropriately reduce the excessive and inappropriate increase in cost of lending to developing countries, caused by the current lack of precision in measuring risk; and (c) diminish pro-cyclicality in the capital requirement, which will imply incentives for both greater stability in bank lending and greater stability of the whole banking system. It would be technically wrong not to do introduce such changes soon.

Some of the problems in the New Basel Capital Accord may be linked to the fact that developing countries are not at all represented in the Basel Committee on Banking Supervision (see chap. IV for a discussion of the urgent need for developing countries to participate in the Basel Committee).

A greater challenge: encouraging private flows to lower-income developing countries

Most poor countries
are also small
economically ...

One of the pervasive features of poor countries is a low per capita income associated to substandard consumption levels and the vulnerability of a large part of their population. The human asset index, which measures nutrition, education and health status, is significantly below the average of developing countries (United Nations, 2003a). Table III.4 lists 57 low-income developing countries for which information is available. The concentration of countries in the lower left bottom of the table indicates not only that these countries are poor but that their population—and hence their economic size—is generally quite small.[5] In fact, of the 57 countries, 63 per cent have a gross national income (GNI) below US$ 3.25 billion. Most of these countries are in Africa.

... putting them at a
disadvantage
in attracting
financial flows

By and large, the factors that determine private flows—FDI and financial flows—to this group are the same as in middle-income developing countries. Economic size is also an important determinant in FDI and private financial flows. Not only does economic size allow the taking advantage of economies of scale when products go to the domestic market but large markets tend to ease the domestic supply of inputs: available labour with diverse skills and intermediate goods and services, particularly services with large non-tradable components that cannot therefore be imported from abroad.

The economies of
these countries are
also more vulnerable
to shocks

The countries in this group tend to face greater challenges to attracting foreign resources to spur long-term growth. A number of them are post-conflict countries, in many of them the natural resources base is scanty, they are generally more vulnerable to changing climate conditions and fluctuations in primary commodity prices,[6] their skilled labour is scarce and their infrastructure is limited. Very few of them have experienced sustained growth for a significant number of years. Their credit-rating indicators signal a comparatively high risk (World Bank, 2004d). In fact, they receive a very small share of private financial flows going to developing countries and only 5 per cent of FDI, most of which goes to a few oil-exporting countries.[7]

Special national and
international efforts
are needed to increase
private financial flows
to these countries ...

The above suggests that increasing private flows to these countries requires special efforts at the national and the international level, particularly when the type of flows needed help spur long-term development. Policies that enhance the domestic environment, as discussed in chapter I, are necessary. It will take time before substantial flows materialize—unless there is a significant potential in exploitation of natural resources, particularly

Table III.4.
Distribution of least developed countries and other low-income countries by population and economic size, 2002[a]

Population (millions)	Gross national income (billions of dollars)			
	Up to 3.25	Over 3.25 to 7.5	Over 7.5 to 15.0	Over 15.0
Over 40		Ethiopia	Myanmar	Bangladesh Nigeria

Over 20 to 40		Nepal
		Uganda
			Afghanistan
			Democratic People's
			  Republic of Korea
			Kenya
			United Republic of
			  Tanzania	

Over 10 to 20	Burkina Faso Malawi Mali Niger	Cambodia Madagascar Mozambique Zambia	Angola Côte d'Ivoire Sudan Yemen	

Over 5 to 10	Benin
	Burundi
	Chad
	Lao People's
	  Democratic Republic
	Rwanda
	Somalia
	Tajikistan
		Democractic Republic
		  of the Congo
		Guinea
		Haiti
		Senegal		

Over 2.5 to 5	Central African Republic Congo Eritrea Liberia Mauritania Mongolia Sierra Leone Togo			
Up to 2.5	Bhutan Cape Verde Comoros Djibouti Equatorial Guinea Gambia Guinea-Bissau Kiribati Lesotho Maldives Samoa Sao Tome and Principe Solomon Islands Timor-Leste Tuvalu Vanuatu			

Source: UN/DESA.

a Comprising all least developed countries and those countries whose per capita gross national income (GNI) measured in dollars at current exchange rates was below $735 in 2002, whose per capita GNI measured in purchasing power parity was 2.5 times that figure or less, and whose Human Assets Index was 70 or below.

oil. In the meantime, international financial cooperation—official flows and technical assistance—can facilitate the transformations required.

... and determine which flows should be encouraged

In each country, it is the national development strategy that should define the type of external flows to be encouraged as well as the sectors where such flows could be channelled. One key aspect of FDI is the impact on the rest of the economy: diverse types can have very different externalities and their diffusion to the rest of the economy can be large or virtually nil (see above). ODA-financed programmes can be catalytic in encouraging private flows. Renewed, more targeted work of the International Finance Corporation of the World Bank and similar organs of the regional and subregional development banks could lead to the mobilization of additional private resources from sources in developed and developing countries.

Poor countries need risk mitigation instruments suited to their circumstances

Since the Asian crisis, two issues—although not new—have focused the attention of many private players: risk mitigation and improved information flows for potential investors (United Nations, 2004d). In poor countries, market instruments to mitigate risks (for example, future exchange-rate markets) are often unavailable. The various bilateral and multilateral instruments that have been developed to deal with risk mitigation for private investments in developing countries (insurance and guarantee schemes) rarely benefit the countries in the group considered here, since most schemes adhere to rather strict commercially based criteria. It would be useful to undertake an evaluation of existing schemes, in particular their actual impact on different groups of target countries.[8]

Increased donor support for multilateral and bilateral instruments to cover political and other non-commercial risks in these countries should be considered

Donors could also consider providing targeted funding with additional resources to multilateral agencies (such as the Multilateral Investment Guarantee Agency (MIGA) and the political risk insurance facilities being opened up in regional banks) and bilateral agencies to cover political and other non-commercial risk at a lower cost in these countries.[9] Also, a new facility could be set up in the form of a separate fund owned by international financial institutions specifically for these countries to address both the entry cost and post-entry risk barriers for investors. This fund would assist private investments by offering domestic currency loans, and quasi-equity investment capital and guarantees— and by retailing a simplified form of MIGA cover for political risk. Another avenue is to create more effective regional risk cover capacity by an effective decentralization of MIGA operations or by creating regional multilateral political risk insurance agencies affiliated with the regional development banks (United Nations Conference on Trade and Development, 2003b, p. 162).

Further modalities to deal with exchange-rate and regulatory risks in infrastructure are required

In the case of infrastructure projects, which increasingly include operations by the investor once the investment is over, exchange rate and regulatory risks are perceived by foreign investors as some of the most important ones. Several modalities have been developed or proposed to deal with these risks, some of which are applicable to these countries for example, the establishment of credit enhancement arrangements by donors and multilateral development institutions for mobilizing available domestic funding to reduce currency risk. More generally, foreign assistance could help in deepening the domestic financial sector. Its further development would facilitate risk management.

The quality and quantity of information for foreign investors needs to be increased and focused on these poor countries ...

In a rapidly changing world economy and with institutional adaptations in many countries, investment opportunities and risks are not always evident for foreign investors. Often, access to credible and transparent information—including on the intricacies of the foreign investment law and bilateral investment treaties and the progress achieved in macroeconomic management and structural policies—is lacking. Reliable, relevant information on country business environments and opportunities is key to private investments decisions. It might also mitigate risks. The Government has a role to play in providing such information. One avenue that has proved useful is public/private collaboration to increase the quality and quantity of information. Yet, most of the countries in this group need special assistance—multilateral and bilateral, including from other developing countries—in this regard. Open web-based information portals have become a highly cost-effective vehicle for the dissemination of information.

One important source of information for prospective investors comprises the perceptions of within-country domestic and foreign entrepreneurs regarding the investment climate. Work in this area has expanded considerably through private firms, business associations such as the World Economic Forum, and international institutions, particularly the World Bank. Most of this work is focused in middle-income developing countries. Special efforts will be required to expand this kind of information to the countries considered here.

Additionally, as seen in table III.4, the large majority of these countries are small. Thus, special attention should be paid in the national development strategy to the links between investment, in particular foreign investment, and exports. No small-sized economy has been able to grow on a sustained basis without a dynamic export sector. For all small-sized economies, economies of scale are a fundamental consideration if a reasonable degree of efficiency is to be achieved. The minimum size of operations needed for the production of many goods or services with a reasonable degree of efficiency can be large.

Developed countries' preferences for least developed countries have opened important investment opportunities. Regional integration among countries can also spur exports and attract foreign investments. The Southern African Development Community (SADC) has facilitated larger FDI flows from the comparatively larger economies (for example, South Africa) to less developed members. Regional integration can also give impulse to regional stock markets and joint infrastructure projects, which might attract additional private external flows (Economic Commission for Africa, 2004, pp. 141-142).

Remittances

Since most migrant remittances are savings from wage earnings transferred to families in home countries, this flow of funds does not fit the definition of capital flows. However, remittances have become a significant source of foreign exchange for many developing countries and an important source of financial support for recipient families.

Remittance flows have been growing quite rapidly in the last decades, reflecting the increasing flows of migrants around the world; to some extent, it is also a reflection of improvement in the quality of remittance statistics. Global remittances amounted to about US$ 69 billion in 1990, and in 2004, they are over US$ 172 billion. In 1990, developing countries received about US$ 29 billion, in 2004 they received over US$ 116 billion, with an annual rate of growth of over 8 per cent. Regionally, in 2003 Latin America and the Caribbean received 30 per cent of total remittance flows, the highest share of all regions, with absolute numbers well over US$ 42 billion today. Although sub-Saharan Africa has a low share in global remittance flows, just slightly over 5 per cent, it has been growing very rapidly in recent years—22 per cent growth per year (Ratha and Vijayalakshmi, 2004; Solimano, 2005).

For many small countries in various parts of the world, remittances constitute one of the main sources of foreign exchange, reaching in some cases levels of 15 per cent of GDP or more (see table III.5). For example, remittances sent to Middle Eastern countries helped reduce the current-account deficit and improved the region's debt-service abil-

... with special attention given to information on investment climate

National development strategies for these countries should focus on the link between foreign and domestic investment and building a dynamic export sector ...

... which can be promoted by regional integration and developed country trade preferences

Migrant remittances are a significant source of foreign exchange for many developing countries ...

... and have grown rapidly in the past decade

Remittances are an important source of foreign exchange ...

Table III.5.
**Countries or areas with the highest ratio
of remittances to gross domestic product, 2004**

Percentage of GDP	
Country or area	
Lesotho	39.0
Tonga	24.0
Lebanon	23.0
Samoa	20.0
Jordan	18.5
Bosnia and Herzegovina	17.5
Kiribati	17.0
Cape Verde	16.5
Albania	16.0
West Bank & Gaza	15.0

Source:
UN/DESA, based on IMF,
Balance of Payments Statistics
Database; and World Bank,
*World Development Indicators
2004.*

*... particularly for
smaller economies ...*

ity in the 1970s and 1980s (Burney, 1987, p. 756). For Latin American countries such as El Salvador and Nicaragua, the amount of remittances is equivalent to more than 60 per cent of the total foreign currency obtained through exports of goods and services, representing about 14 per cent of their GDP in the late 1990s. Notwithstanding Haiti's acute poverty levels, remittances to this country helped to alleviate the need of foreign exchange in the amount of $720 million, 220 per cent of exports of goods and services (Inter-American Development Bank, 2001).

*... but also for some
larger economies*

Remittances are also becoming quite important for some larger countries. The Central Bank of Mexico reports that remittances, growing at a 20 per cent annual rate during the past three years and expected to continue to grow at equal pace, are becoming the most stable source of foreign exchange for Mexico, similar in magnitude (US$ 16.6 billion) to FDI in 2004 and second only to oil exports, which have been favoured by a recent price hike. Similar patterns are observed in several other mid-size Latin American countries, such as Colombia and Ecuador.

*Aid remains crucial for
many poor countries
where remittances are
not a large source of
foreign exchange*

Even for sub-Saharan countries, where these flows are smaller—owing to a large extent to transmission through informal channels, which are thus officially unrecorded—remittances have had significant effects in some countries. For instance, during the 1980s, remittances financed 80 per cent of the current-account deficit in Botswana; equalled almost three quarters of total commodity export earnings in the Sudan; and formed more than half of Lesotho's foreign-exchange earnings. Similarly, Somalia has received remittances of about $500 million annually, representing "four times the value of livestock, (its) main export" (Sander and Maimbo, 2003, pp. 15-16). Still, the fact that for the majority of the poorest African countries remittances do not represent a large source of foreign exchange provides an incontrovertible additional reason why extra sources of ODA are required for these countries.

*Remittance flows are
more stable than
private and official
financial flows*

The stability of their flows is a widely accepted and distinctive feature of remittances in relation to private capital, particularly financial flows. Indeed, in sharp contrast to financial flows with their high volatility, remittance flows continued to grow steadily during the 1990s and the first half of the current decade (see figure III.2). Since the late 1990s, this may have reflected increased remittance flows because of deterioration of the economies in their countries of origin. Indeed, if remittances are more sensitive to times of

Figure III.2.
World remittance flows, 1980-2003

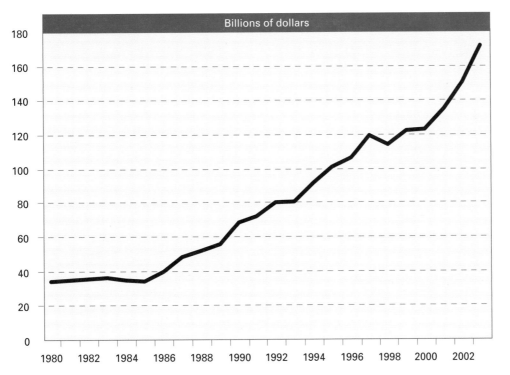

International remittance flows

Source:
World Bank (2004a), based on
IMF (2004b). For data
definitions, see Ratha (2003).

economic hardship in home countries than to downturns (particularly in labour-market conditions) in host countries, as some studies find, these flows would have counter-cyclical characteristics (United Nations, 2004a, pp. 95-126; Adams, 2004). In terms of the "life cycle" duration of individual remittances, theory holds that the longer the duration of migrant status, the lower the probability of large flows of remittances. However, immigrant groups vary in this regard, with some sending still substantial amounts after 5 or 10 years of migrant status.

From the perspective of poor migrant households, remittances may be a vehicle through which to reduce poverty levels by spending on improving nutrition, financing children's schooling or basic health care, or constructing their own home (Adams, 1998, p. 170; Stahl and Habib, 1989, pp. 269-285; Kapur, 2004; Cox and Ureta, 2003). Indeed, a recent survey for Guatemala found that the level, depth and severity of poverty are significantly reduced in households receiving remittances, although the greater impact is on reducing the severity rather than the level of poverty.

The use of formal or informal channels for transmitting remittances may have an effect on the potential uses of remittances. For instance, many remittance senders and receivers use informal channels because, often, they lack access to the financial system in the host country and/or the home country. A combination of the high transaction cost of remittances, and the socio-economic deprivation of migrant families—for example, that of recipients living in rural sectors and/or with low schooling levels—may be the most important factor in the continued use of informal channels. Indeed, the use of remittances for less immediate uses or for more investment-oriented purposes would call for access of remitters and receivers to the financial system. Some financial intermediaries in host and

Remittances reduce
poverty in recipient
households

The high cost of
transmitting
remittances through
formal channels can
limit the amount and
use of remittances

Policy initiatives are
under way to leverage
the development
finance potential of
remittances

home countries have been more active in competing for the remittances market during the last several years by reducing the transmission costs of remittances or offering savings accounts, microcredit and insurance to migrants' families (United Nations, 2004b).

Important policy initiatives have been developed and are currently in process for multiplying the leverage and socio-economic impact that remittances could have in migrants' families and communities and in recipient countries in general. For example, hometown associations have succeeded in sponsoring community investment projects in villages of Mexico and El Salvador, sometimes in partnership with their respective Governments. Similarly, remittances could be a powerful tool with which to finance projects in the tourism industry that could include the construction of large-scale hotels where immigrants participated as shareholders. Remittance-backed housing purchases are a promising engine for transforming remittances flows into better living standards of recipients. Larger access to financial services by immigrants and their families can be linked to the marketing of innovative financial products such as pension funds, and special financial assets for channelling the savings of migrants to the countries of origin may unleash the potential of remittances to serve as an instrument of financing for development. At the global level, mechanisms to reduce the transaction costs of remittances and to use them as a mechanism for "banking" the poor migrants and recipient families have been discussed as part of the initiatives for designing "innovative sources of financing" (see chap. IV).

Notes

1   The literature also indicates that, in the case of developing countries that have been able to issue such liabilities, they are largely used as coverage by foreign investors in those countries. This implies that, even in those countries, there is not net demand by foreign residents for assets denominated in the domestic currency.

2   The net financial transfer of resources statistic adds receipts of foreign investment income and financial inflows from abroad, but subtracts payments of foreign investment income and financial outflows, including increases in foreign reserve holdings. The net financial transfer of a country is thus the financial counterpart of the balance of trade in goods and services. A trade surplus is generated when the total value of domestic production exceeds domestic consumption and investment, with the excess invested abroad instead of being used domestically, and vice versa for a trade deficit.

3   It should be recalled in this regard that domestic contents and export requirements were used widely in the past for this purpose, but were severely limited by the World Trade Organization rules on trade-related investment measures.

4   The use of the ringgit was restricted to domestic transactions by residents. It became illegal to hold ringgit deposits abroad, and all such deposits held by nationals had to be repatriated. Trade transactions had to be settled in foreign currency. Ringgit deposits in the domestic financial system held by non-residents were not convertible into foreign currency for one year.

5   One fourth of these countries have a population below 2.5 million and half of them below 5 million.

6   Their economic vulnerability index is well above the average of developing countries (see United Nations, 2003a).

7   Most of the comparatively small amount of FDI in these 57 countries goes to only 5 oil producers: Angola, Chad, Equatorial Guinea, Nigeria and the Sudan.

8   As of recently, some donor countries (for example, Norway and the United States) have refocused their efforts to reach lower-income countries.

9   Many of these countries are parties to the Cotonou Agreement which offers support for investment and private sector development including a reinsurance scheme to cover FDI. Also, some of these countries can benefit from the activities of the Inter-Arab Investment Guarantee Corporation which offers an intraregional insurance scheme.

Chapter IV
Official development financing

The architects of the post-war international economic system had recognized the need for official financing to counteract the insufficiency of private capital flows and, since the 1960s, there has been an increasing perception of the need to support developing countries, an issue that became embedded in the politics of decolonization and the cold war. The surge of private financing to developing countries beginning in the 1970s and the end of the cold war generated an increasing realization that the era of official development financing had passed. However, the vagaries of private capital flows during the 1980s and, again, since the 1997 Asian crisis, in addition to the increasing marginalization of the poorest countries from the world economy, have led to a renewed focus on the critical role of official development finance. The International Conference on Financing for Development was a landmark in this process. The present chapter explores the issues involved. It looks first at official development assistance (ODA), then at the multilateral development banks and South-South cooperation, and lastly at an array of alternatives that should be grouped under the heading of "innovative sources of financing".

Official development assistance

The transfer of resources from developed to developing countries has been at the centre of policies to promote development in the United Nations since the 1950s. In its resolution 400 (V) of 20 November 1950, the General Assembly had noted that the domestic financial resources of the underdeveloped countries, together with the international flow of capital for investment, had not been sufficient to assure the desired rate of economic development, and that the accelerated economic development of underdeveloped countries required a more effective and sustained mobilization of domestic savings and an expanded and more stable flow of foreign capital investment. Two years later, the Assembly, in its resolution 520 A (VI) of 12 January 1952, called on the Economic and Social Council to draw up plans for a special capital fund to provide grants-in-aid and low-interest long-term loans to underdeveloped countries; and in 1954, the Assembly, in its resolution 823 (IX) of 11 December 1954, requested the International Bank for Reconstruction and Development (IBRD) to proceed with the creation of the International Finance Corporation (IFC).

> ODA is a crucial supplement to mobilization of domestic resources for development

To generate additional aid to that provided within the United Nations system and its specialized agencies, in 1958, the World Council of Churches proposed that developed countries dedicate 1 per cent of their gross domestic product (GDP) as aid for developing countries in the form of grants and concessional loans. This figure was incorporated in the objectives of the First United Nations Development Decade and reconfirmed at the first session of the United Nations Conference on Trade and Development (UNCTAD), held in Geneva in 1964. UNCTAD at its second session, held in New Delhi in 1968, set a target of three quarters of 1 per cent of external flows for ODA. Analysis of the external financial flows required to meet the Second United Nations Development Decade growth

> ODA target of 0.7 per cent of developed-country GNI established by the United Nations in the 1960s

goal of at least 6 per cent per annum by the head of the Committee for Development Planning produced an estimate of 1 per cent of developed-country GDP. Since it was expected that private flows could provide only about 0.3 per cent, it was understood that the remaining sums would have to be met by official flows (Emmerij, Jolly and Weiss, 2001, pp. 55-57).

Already at its eighteenth session in 1963, the General Assembly had noted the slow progress in meeting this objective and by the twenty-first session in 1966 noted with concern the trend towards an increased outflow of capital from developing countries (Assembly resolution 2169 (XXI) of 6 December 1966) and noted with deep concern the fact that, with a few exceptions, the transfer of external resources to the developing countries had not only failed to reach the minimum target of 1 per cent net of individual national income of the developed countries but that the trend since 1961 had been one of continuous decline (Assembly resolution 2170 (XXI) of 6 December 1966). In the mid-term assessment of the Second United Nations Development Decade, the Assembly noted that the performance of countries members of the Development Assistance Committee of the Organization for Economic Cooperation and Development (OECD/DAC) under the ODA target had been even less satisfactory as a whole. The ratio of ODA to their combined gross national product (GNP) had declined from 0.53 per cent during the early 1960s to about 0.39 per cent during the period 1966-1969 and to 0.32 per cent during the period 1970-1973. The poor performance of most of the developed market economy countries with regard to the target of 0.7 per cent of gross national income (GNI) for ODA was due, inter alia, to a lack of political will to reach that target by the middle of the decade (Assembly resolution 3517 (XXX) of 15 December 1975, annex, para. 26).

ODA exceeded 0.5 per cent of GNI in the 1960s but then fell back

Concern that external flows to developing countries would decline further in a system of flexible exchange rates led to a recommendation by the Committee of Twenty on reform of the international monetary and financial system to propose the creation of a Joint Ministerial Committee of the Boards of Governors of the Bank and the Fund on the Transfer of Real Resources to Developing Countries to study and recommend measures on the broad question of the transfer of real resources to developing countries, which the Committee agreed should be given encouragement.[1] The expectation of a decline in aid was confirmed as ODA for 1982-1983 had averaged 0.35 per cent but further fell to a historic low of 0.21 per cent of developed-country GNI at the beginning of the new millennium.

Monterrey Consensus sought to reverse long-term decline in ODA

As a result of this historic declining trend, the Monterrey Consensus of the International Conference on Financing for Development (United Nations, 2002b, annex) sought to restore the central role of ODA, in particular in supporting the poorest countries, and thus reaffirmed the 0.7 per cent target. During and after the Monterrey Conference, many member countries of the OECD/DAC raised their ODA contributions, and many pledged to meet fixed target dates for reaching the 0.7 per cent goal.

Magnitude and composition of ODA

As a result of the Monterrey commitments, the decline in the share of ODA in developed-country GNI was reversed, as it rose to 0.25 per cent in 2003 and 2004. Moreover, if all commitments are met by the target date of 2006, total ODA is projected to reach $88 billion, an increase of almost 50 per cent in nominal terms from the total recorded in 2002. If these pledges, together with additional commitments made by DAC member countries to increase ODA after 2006 are met, ODA is projected to reach $108 billion in 2010

(Organization for Economic Cooperation and Development, Development Assistance Committee, 2005).

Despite the positive trend since 2002, the current and projected levels of ODA for 2006-2010 still fall far short of the various estimates (United Nations, 2001; UN Millennium Project, 2005; Commission for Africa, 2005) of about $150 billion deemed necessary for the developing countries to attain the Millennium Development Goals (World Bank and International Monetary Fund, 2005). Furthermore, as can be seen from figure IV.1, when corrected for price and exchange-rate changes, the recent reversal of the decline in aid flows has barely brought real assistance back to the levels of 1990.

The European Union (EU) and its member States continue to be the largest source of aid, providing more than half of total ODA. Denmark, Luxembourg, the Netherlands, Norway and Sweden already meet or exceed the 0.7 per cent target of their national incomes dedicated to official assistance. In mid-2005, all member States of EU undertook to achieve or maintain the 0.7 per cent ODA/GNI target by 2015. Those member States which joined EU after 2002 will strive to increase or maintain an ODA/GNI ratio of 0.33 per cent. The Secretary-General of the United Nations has urged that other developed countries establish fixed timetables for achieving the 0.7 per cent target of GNI for ODA by 2015 at the latest.

As noted above, the original intention of the United Nations official assistance target was to generate increased external resources in the form of grants and concessional loans to be used to supplement domestic resources so that countries could finance aggregate growth targets in the United Nations Development Decades. Although developing countries succeeded in meeting the modest growth objectives of the First and Second United Nations Development Decades, since the 1980s growth performance in many

> The success of the Monterrey Consensus in reversing the decline in ODA is insufficient to meet the financing requirements of the Millennium Development Goals

> The Millennium Declaration marked a shift in approach compared with that of the United Nations Development Decades

Figure IV.1.
Composition of official development assistance, 1990-2003 (corrected for inflation and exchange rates)

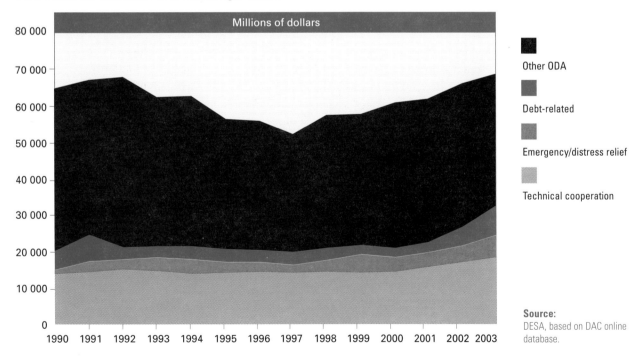

Other ODA

Debt-related

Emergency/distress relief

Technical cooperation

Source:
DESA, based on DAC online database.

developing countries has been disappointing and ODA has declined. The United Nations Millennium Declaration (see General Assembly resolution 55/2) marked a sharp change in approach to the United Nations development goals from those subscribed to in the four United Nations Development Decades. The increasing evidence that the growth and aid targets were not being met, and the continued increase in disparity in the distribution of the benefits of growth in a globalizing international economic system, led to the specification of much more precise targets represented by the Millennium Development Goals. The idea was to set precise, measurable targets that would provide visible improvements in the living conditions of the poorest within a precise time frame.

As the UN Millennium Project report (UN Millennium Project, 2005) makes clear, this will necessitate expenditure lines that require specific amounts of funding over specific time periods. The composition of ODA must thus be changed to finance the specific expenditures needed to achieve the Millennium Development Goals. Figure IV.1 shows that over the 1990s, the shares of debt relief, emergency aid and technical assistance in total aid flows were increasing. While these flows have important objectives, emergency aid is not designed to assist long-term development, and debt relief does not generally provide fresh money to debtor countries. Technical cooperation, in turn, provides a variety of inputs towards development results but its impact in closing financial gaps is hard to gauge.[2] Consequently, despite the recent recovery in recorded donor contributions, ODA has been a declining source of budgetary resources for the developing countries, limiting their efforts to pursue the Millennium Development Goals. The call to increase ODA must thus be qualified to refer to real cash increases to support the Goals.

ODA needs to be targeted to the poorest and least developed countries

Moreover, not only does ODA have to increase substantially in order for the developing countries to have a better chance of achieving the Millennium Development Goals but it is essential that ODA be directed to the poorest and least developed among the developing countries. With the adoption of the Programme of Action for the Least Developed Countries for the 1990s by the Second United Nations Conference on the Least Developed Countries in Paris in September 1990 (United Nations, 1991), developed countries had agreed that, within their 0.7 per cent overall ODA target, they would provide at least 0.15-0.20 per cent of their GNI to assist the least developed countries. A few individual donors met this target but aggregate ODA flows to the least developed countries declined to about half the target during the 1990s. The reversal in trend since Monterrey has been more positive: ODA to least developed countries has increased sharply in recent years. However, a careful look at the composition indicates that the amount of aid for least developed countries in 2003, after exclusion of the emergency, debt relief and reconstruction components, was also only marginally higher than the figure for 1990 (see figure IV.2).

Volatility and conditionality of aid flows

Size is not the only important aspect of ODA—predictability is equally important

There are a number of other factors that must be considered in order to determine the real impact of aid in achieving the Millennium Development Goals. First, predictability of aid flows over time is a precondition for their effective use. However, aid flows tend to rise and fall with economic cycles in donor countries, with policy assessments of the recipient countries, and with a shift in donor policies. This uncertainty has a negative impact on public investment and thus on growth, as well as on the conduct of monetary and fiscal policy. Empirical work suggests that the volatility of aid flows exceeds that of other macroeconomic variables, such as GDP or fiscal revenue. Aid is significantly more volatile than fis-

Figure IV.2.
**Composition of official development
assistance to least developed countries, 1990-2003**

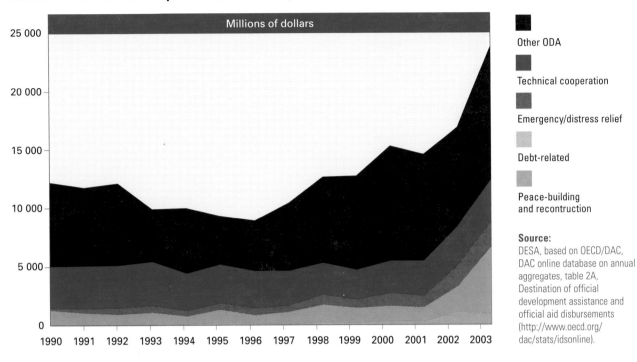

Other ODA

Technical cooperation

Emergency/distress relief

Debt-related

Peace-building
and recontruction

Source:
DESA, based on OECD/DAC,
DAC online database on annual
aggregates, table 2A,
Destination of official
development assistance and
official aid disbursements
(http://www.oecd.org/
dac/stats/idsonline).

cal revenue, and tends to be procyclical on average (Gemmell and McGillivray, 1998). When aid falls, it leads to costly fiscal adjustments in the form of increased taxation and spending cuts that reinforce the cyclical impact of declining aid flows (Pallage and Robe, 2001; Bulír and Hamann, 2003; 2005). In this respect, the volatility in aid flows has a similar impact to volatility in commodity prices in countries that are dependent upon the exports of a single commodity. Indeed, countries receiving aid flows seem to be no better off than emerging market economies receiving private flows for, as shown in table IV.1, the volatility of both types of flows as measured by their standard deviation relative to the mean value is very similar.

Surges in donor flows can also cause macroeconomic problems. In small country recipients, these problems are compounded by low absorptive capacity and the presence of a small and often underdeveloped financial sector. Deeper financial markets in aid-recipient countries have been shown to be associated with more efficient management of aid flows, and to enhance the impact of ODA on growth. They have a positive direct impact on private investment in recipient countries, and diminish negative indirect effects resulting from the impact of ODA on domestic prices, interest rates and the exchange rate (Nkusu and Sayek, 2004). Surges in donor flows may produce exchange-rate appreciation and, if sustained over a length of time, the kind of overvaluation phenomenon known as the "Dutch disease". Attempts to sterilize the monetary effects of foreign exchange inflows can be costly. Increased donor flows may be accompanied by negative private flows or excess reserve accumulation. As a result, the beneficial impact of the aid inflows on growth and poverty reduction may be offset or even reversed.

Surges in donor flows
create special
problems for small
countries

Table IV.1.
Volatility of financial flows and bilateral
DAC ODA, top 10 recipients, 1999-2003

Top 10 emerging market countries (Weighted GDP volume)	Financial flows (Standard deviation/mean)
Brazil	0.35
China	0.77
Hong Kong, SAR[a]	0.34
Korea, Republic of	0.08
Malaysia	0.11
Mexico	0.18
Poland	0.24
Singapore	0.41
Thailand	0.42
Turkey	0.52
Average	0.34
Top 10 net bilateral DAC ODA recipients[b]	Net bilateral ODA (Standard deviation/mean)
Bangladesh	0.12
China	0.35
Egypt	0.22
India	0.32
Indonesia	0.28
Mozambique	0.46
Pakistan	0.43
Serbia and Montenegro	0.55
United Republic of Tanzania	0.11
Viet Nam	0.27
Average	0.31

Sources: DESA calculations on OECD/DAC database; and World Bank, *Global Development Finance 2005* (Washington, D.C., 2005).

a   Special Administrative Region of China.

b   Excluding the Democratic Republic of the Congo.

The gap between aid commitment and aid disbursement also reduces predictability

Volatility of ODA results from more than the year-on-year variability due to donor budget cycles. There is often a large gap between budgeted aid commitments and their actual disbursement in the recipient country. Figure IV.3 shows the divergence between commitments and disbursements for programme and project aid.[3] Further, the actual disbursement of aid, as distinct from its budgetary commitment, tends to be concentrated in periods of high domestic revenue and output. Not only are ODA flows more volatile than either fiscal revenue or GDP, but their relative volatility increases with the degree of aid dependency. It has also been found that countries that suffer from high revenue volatility are also countries that suffer from higher aid volatility, suggesting that aid

Figure IV.3.
Commitments and disbursements of programme and project aid, 1995-2003

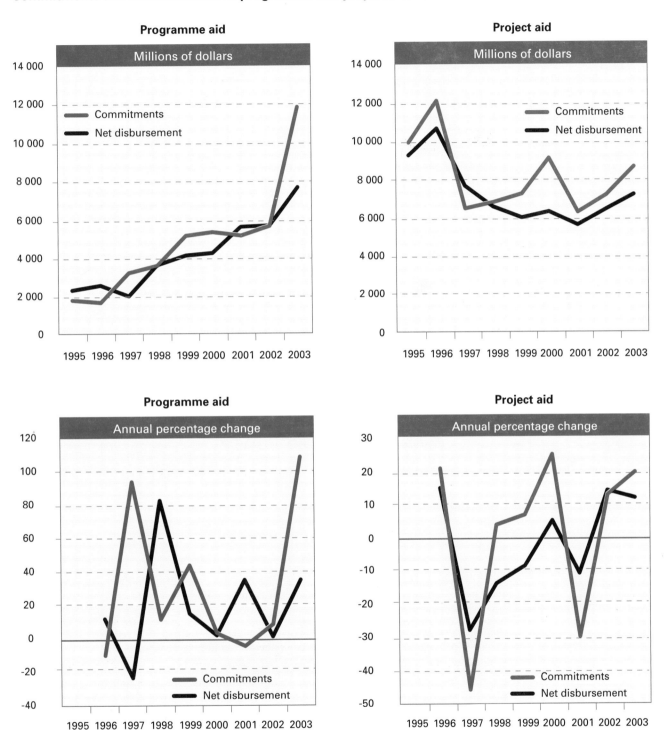

Source: DESA, based on data in World Bank, *Global Development Finance 2005* (Washington, D.C., 2005) and IMF HIPC Initiative-Statistical Update April 11, 2005.

tends to enhance budgetary and overall economic instability (Bulír and Hamann, 2001). Donors have to consider how to reduce these patterns to enable recipient countries to plan their fiscal arrangements in a budget year as well as within the context of a longer-term fiscal policy framework. The erratic behaviour of both budgeted flows and aid disbursement needs to be stabilized if aid is to finance a sustained path of growth and poverty reduction.

Aid conditionality is also a source of volatility in aid flows

Aid conditionality is another source of volatility. This is due not only to the types of specific conditions required by donors, but also to the frequent requirement that aid recipients have the seal of approval of an International Monetary Fund (IMF) programme that is on track. When these programmes go off-track, the negative impact is intensified by the withdrawal of aid flows by donors.

The now conventional view is that conditionality is an ineffective or at least an inefficient means to attain objectives that donors wish to attach to financial support of partner countries. So long as there is no true "ownership" of the policies involved by partner countries—that is to say, so long as they are not backed by strong domestic support—they are unlikely to be sustained. This is strongly associated with the fact that ownership is essential to institution-building, which is generally recognized today as the key to successful development policies. Some authors (Morrissey, 2001) have suggested that donors should support policy processes rather than impose specific policy conditions.

Following this view, some donors have announced radical shifts away from aid conditionality. One of the most significant has been that described in a recent policy announcement by the Government of the United Kingdom. A new policy on conditionality was launched early in March 2005 that will stop making the United Kingdom's aid conditional on specific policies, including in sensitive areas like privatization and trade liberalization. Conditionality is to be limited to fiduciary concerns only and to ensuring that aid is not diverted for purposes other than those intended.

Selectivity of aid flows

Donor selection of recipients reduces predictability of aid

Donor selection of aid recipients has tended to be concentrated in a relatively small number of countries. Figure IV.4 shows that, since the 1980s, the top 20 countries have received more than half of net bilateral aid and that fewer than 50 per cent of aid recipients have received 90 per cent of all aid from DAC donors.[4] This suggests that variations in aid allocations are in large part the result of donors' selection of top aid recipients.

The concentration of aid in a few countries leads to the question whether donors tend to move as a group. Evidence suggests that concentration of aid produces herding behaviour on the part of donors. Thus, donor selectivity compounds the impact of volatility. This similarity in donor behaviour may be the result of the view that aid efficiency is highest in those countries that have made the most positive reform efforts (see below). As a result, aid flows tend to be concentrated in those countries that are viewed by donors as the most successful. Although selectivity of aid has always been present, its impact seems to have increased since the late 1990s. This is partly due to the signalling mechanism set in motion through the processes associated with the Poverty Reduction Strategy Papers (PRSP) and the Heavily Indebted Poor Countries (HIPC) Initiative.

Donor mimetism can be measured

Herding behaviour among donors can also be detected by means of a measure (denoted LSV) devised by Lakonishok, Shleifer and Vishny (1992) and based on the divergence of actual changes in ODA relative to average behaviour. If all donors follow the average behaviour, the difference between actual and average behaviour is zero and there is no

Figure IV.4.
Concentration of official development assistance in recipient countries, 1981-2003

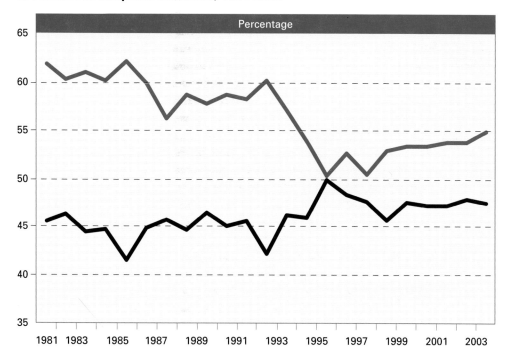

Share of top 20 recipients in bilateral, net aid flows

Proportion of recipient countries accounting for 90 per cent of aid

Source:
DESA calculations based on data from OECD/DAC on geographical distribution of financial flows to Part I countries (excluding the Democratic Republic of the Congo for 2003).

Figure IV.5.
Collective deviation of flows of official development assistance among donors, 1981-2003

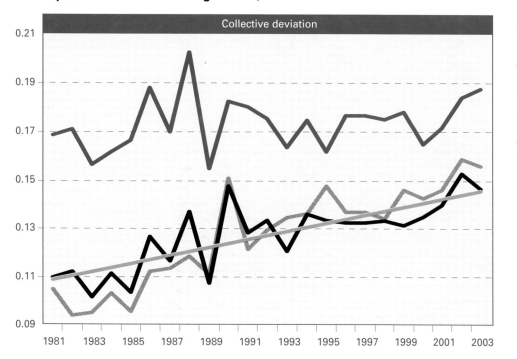

Top donors

Small donors

All donors

Linear (all donors)

Source:
DESA calculations based on data from OECD/DAC on geographical distribution of financial flows to Part I countries (excluding the Democratic Republic of the Congo for 2003).

herding. A value of LSV greater than 0.1 indicates significant herding. Figure IV.5 analyses the behaviour of 10 large and 13 small donors and confirms the existence of herding, especially with respect to the behaviour of small donors, with an average of collective deviation of close to 13 per cent.

Bigger and smaller donors tend to move together both when they increase and when they decrease aid. Overall, historical evidence suggests that a developing country may expect to experience a reduction in net nominal bilateral ODA volumes with a probability of about 25 per cent in any given year (see figure IV.6).

Although the factors that cause co-movement in bilateral selectivity of countries are different compared with the factors that cause herding in private capital markets, the ensuing macroeconomic instability is similar. While many of the discussions on the effectiveness of aid have tended to concentrate on the effects of governance and the domestic policy environment in the recipient countries, the economic costs due to problems in the supply side and limitations to the financial intermediation of donor funds are not insignificant.

Aid selectivity causes volatility similar to that of private capital flows to emerging market economies

Figure IV.6.
Proportion of countries experiencing a decline in bilateral aid volume, by donor grouping, 1981-2003

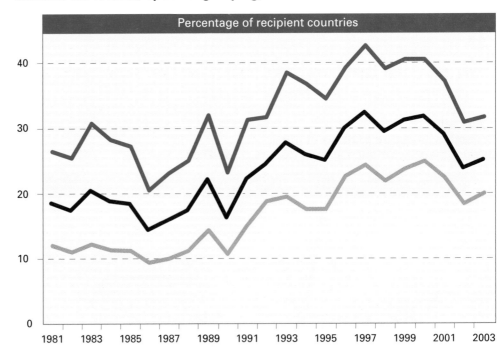

Top 10 donors

Total

Small donors

Source:
DESA calculations based on data from OECD/DAC on geographical distribution of financial flows to Part I countries (excluding the Democratic Republic of the Congo for 2003).

Aid and economic growth in support of the Millennium Development Goals

Aid in support of growth and aid in support of poverty reduction

The specification of official assistance targets to support the International Development Strategies for the United Nations Development Decades assumed that increased aid would contribute to increasing growth in developing countries; since the adoption of the United Nations Millennium Declaration, it has been argued that increased aid would allow countries to achieve the Millennium Development Goals. Nonetheless, sustaining the Millennium

Development Goals will require a sustained increase in growth. However, the experience with official assistance in promoting economic growth in developing countries is, at best, a mixed one. The World Bank (1998) is forthright in recognizing that "if foreign aid has at times been a spectacular success … (it) has also been, at times, an unmitigated failure". This sentence encapsulates the evidence that aid has often had weak effects on growth and poverty reduction.[5] A growing understanding of the factors that constrain the effectiveness of aid has helped identify problems in respect of both the supply of donor funds and the limitations in recipient countries.[6] The challenge for the official donor community, as well as policymakers in developing countries, has thus been to recognize the weaknesses of the earlier approaches in aid delivery and to work towards new frameworks to enhance aid effectiveness.

There are two dominant views on the factors that hinder aid effectiveness in promoting growth and reducing poverty. The first, and more dominant view, is that aid works only when government policies are effective: a more selective allocation of aid to "good policy-high poverty" countries will thus lead to larger poverty reductions at the global level. The second view argues that aid effectiveness is not conditional on domestic policy effectiveness so that more selective allocation may generate other problems, including "aid orphans" and deepening crises in countries regarded by the donor community as "aid pariahs".

Views on the relationships between aid, growth and poverty reduction differ

The first view is based on an influential body of evidence generated by research at the World Bank (1998) indicating that policies matter for aid effectiveness. The implications for aid policy are straightforward: allocate more aid to a country with "good" policies. This message has turned out to be fairly influential and recent empirical work (Collier and Dollar, 1999, 2001; Burnside and Dollar, 1997; 2000) appears to support this view. Using the "Country Policy and Institutional Assessment" (CPIA) as a measure of good policy, these studies estimate that the impact of growth on poverty reduction across countries is higher for countries with better CPIA scores. If aid allocations between countries are directed to countries where the correlation is highest, this will maximize the number of people lifted out of poverty. The studies suggest that a more efficient targeting of aid towards countries with high rates of poverty pursuing good policies could double the number of people lifted out of poverty, this being as much as could be achieved by tripling present aid budgets at the level of their current country allocations. The World Bank research has also revealed that the pattern of the actual aid allocations—particularly bilateral aid—has been highly inefficient, being only weakly targeted to poor countries and even more weakly directed to well-managed countries.

One view is that good policies increase the beneficial impacts of aid on growth and poverty reduction …

Other studies have reached different conclusions. Some of them question the definition and assessment of "good policies" implicit in the CPIA ratings.[7] Some (Beynon, 2003) provide alternative policy interpretations of the World Bank studies,[8] while others (Hansen and Tarp, 2000; and Beynon, 2003) challenge the results on methodological and econometric grounds, in terms, for example, of sensitivity to model specification. They suggest that since aid assists countries in adjusting to external shocks, this may explain why some studies show no significant impact of aid on growth. Another difficulty in measuring the efficiency of aid flows is caused by the fact that aid flows include debt relief and, as suggested above, do not measure the real contribution of cash resources to supporting growth. Furthermore, bilateral flows are often used to clear arrears at the multilateral institutions. An analysis that looks at the composition of aid and focuses on assistance that, plausibly, could stimulate growth, including budget and balance-of-payments support, investments in infrastructure, and aid for productive sectors such as agriculture and industry, finds a positive, causal relationship between this type of aid and economic growth (with diminishing returns) over a four-year period. The impact is large: at least two to three times larger than

… but others argue that appropriate measurement finds a more general benefit of aid

the impact found in studies that consider only aggregate aid. Even at a conservatively high discount rate, a $1 increase in short-impact aid raises output (and income) by $1.64 in present value in a typical country (Clemens, Radelet and Bhavnani, 2004).

Any econometric exercise that measures aid effectiveness should thus be based on data of aid flows that are net of debt relief and aid flows utilized for clearance of arrears. Alternative research suggests that the impact on growth is positive irrespective of the policy environment (Morrissey, 2001) while still other research suggests that a range of other variables are significant such as economic vulnerability (Chauvet and Guillaumont, 2002), external shocks (Collier and Dehn, 2001), recovery from conflict (Collier and Hoeffler, 2002) and geographical factors (Dalgaard and others 2001). Despite these findings, the emphasis on good governance and institutional change continues to dominate the discussion.

Donor efforts to increase effectiveness

The effectiveness of ODA is as important as the amount of ODA

Developed-country donors have been increasingly concerned with the impact of their aid. Initiatives introduced since the late 1990s to strengthen coordination among donors, improve the design of programmes, and improve domestic policy implementation include the Poverty Reduction and Growth Facility (PRGF) and the HIPC Initiative. However, they do not seem to have decreased the erratic nature of the availability of funds (Bulír and Hamann, 2005). The effectiveness of increased use of aid to provide budgetary support for countries that have embarked on the PRSP and entered the HIPC Initiative has also been affected by the volatility of aid disbursements.

Measures to increase effectiveness are receiving increased attention

At the Rome High-level Forum on Harmonization held on 24 and 25 February 2003, a plan of action was elaborated to harmonize aid policies, procedures and practices of donors with those of their developing partner countries. At the second High-level Forum on Joint Progress towards Enhanced Aid Effectiveness, held in Paris from 28 February to 2 March 2005, twice as many countries and new donor countries participated, and for the first time civil society representatives and parliamentarians were also involved. Over 100 countries as well as development institutions committed to a practical blueprint to provide aid in more streamlined ways, and to improve accountability by monitoring the blueprint's implementation. The Paris Declaration on Aid Effectiveness set out five major principles of aid effectiveness: (a) ownership of development strategies by partner countries; (b) alignment of donor support with those strategies; (c) harmonization of donor actions; (d) managing for results; and (e) mutual accountability of donors and partners. The Declaration also contained some 50 commitments to improve aid quality which were to be monitored by 12 indicators. Participants agreed to preliminary quantitative targets for only five of them, and the Declaration is particularly weak on commitments to improve alignment (no target for reliable recipient country systems, for coordinated donor capacity support or for untying of aid) and agreed to set targets for the other indicators by the Summit meeting of the General Assembly in September 2005. The five quantitative targets for 2010 are: (a) at least 75 per cent of partner countries should have operational development strategies; (b) 85 per cent of aid flows should be reported on budgets; (c) at least 75 per cent of aid agreed with time framework should be released on schedule; (d) at least 25 per cent of aid should be provided as "programme-based approaches"; and (e) 75 per cent of partner countries should have results-oriented frameworks. EU announced its own additional set of targets, including reducing the number of uncoordinated missions by 50 per cent, channelling half of government assistance through country assistance, providing all capacity-building through coordinated programmes, resorting more frequently to multi-donor arrangements, and avoiding the establishment of new project implementation units.

In addition to areas covered by the Paris Declaration targets, there are several other areas for improvement in respect of aid effectiveness. First, a follow-up to the commitments made at the World Summit for Social Development (1995), where donors pledged to spend 20 per cent of ODA on basic social services in developing countries, is still needed. Also, despite the evidence on the adverse effects of tied aid which has been available for several decades, this issue remains to be effectively tackled. Although there is an indicator (8) in the Paris Declaration on untying aid, it is the only one on which agreement could not be reached with respect to defining a target by September 2005. While substantial progress has been made in untying aid, it continues to have a high cost: in 2002, it reduced bilateral aid's value by at least $5 billion (Organization for Economic Cooperation and Development, Development Assistance Committee, 2004).

Other aspects of aid effectiveness remain to be tackled

The multilateral development banks

The architects of the post-war international financial system were, in the early years, more concerned with reconstruction than with development finance, but they were clear in their belief that both types of finance should be channelled through multilateral institutions subject to intergovernmental control. The International Bank for Reconstruction and Development (IBRD), established in 1944, was to play this role. (IBRD and the International Finance Corporation (IFC) (established 1956), the International Development Corporation (established 1960), the Multilateral Investment Guarantee Agency (established 1988) and the International Centre for Settlement of Investment Disputes (established 1966) now constitute the World Bank Group.) The World Bank was complemented during the 1950s and 1960s by a number of regional development banks: the Inter-American Development Bank; the Asian Development Bank, the African Development Bank and the European Investment Bank (EIB). The European Bank for Reconstruction and Development (EBRD) was added in 1991. There are also several subregional development banks, particularly in the Latin American and Caribbean region, as well as several Arab institutions, some with a regional reach and others with a broader one.

The multilateral development banks are an important, but unrecognized, source of development assistance

Regional and subregional development banks experienced major shifts and reforms during the 1990s. In general, the financial base of these institutions grew substantially, allowing them to expand their lending activities and to increase their weight, influence and importance. The expanded role of these institutions led to both enhanced cooperation and partnerships with the World Bank, but also to more competition in the provision of services (Sagasti, Bezanson and Prada, 2005). The implementation of a more systemic perspective in the operations of the multilateral development banks and the World Bank, as well as a division of labour between them, will be of fundamental importance for the future of development finance.

Regional development banks are of increasing importance

In this regard, paragraph 45 of the Monterrey Consensus highlighted the vital role that multilateral and regional development banks continue to play "in serving the development needs of developing countries and countries with economies in transition". The paragraph went on to make the following observations:

They should contribute to providing an adequate supply of finance to countries that are challenged by poverty, follow sound economic policies and may lack adequate access to capital markets. They should also mitigate the impact of excessive volatility of financial markets. Strengthened regional development banks and subregional financial institutions add flexible financial support to national and regional development efforts, enhancing ownership and overall efficiency. They also serve as a vital source of knowledge and expertise on economic growth and development for their developing member countries.

Despite this call, and with the exception of the recent recapitalization of IDA and the African Development Bank, only limited commitments have been made to enhancing the role that multilateral development banks play in the international financial system since the International Conference on Financing for Development.

The role of multilateral development banks

Multilateral development banks contribute to development in a variety of ways

Structurally, most multilateral development banks contain a core bank or "hard window" that operates on commercial principles and a "soft-loan" window to support lending to low-income country borrowers. They may also contain private sector financing arms and guarantee agencies (Mistry, 1995). Through these facilities, multilateral development banks fulfil a vast array of financial functions, namely: (a) channelling funds to low-income countries; (b) lending to middle-income countries, and correcting market failures associated with the overpricing of risks, which lead to inadequate access to long-term financing by many middle-income developing countries; (c) acting as a counter-cyclical balance to fluctuations in private capital markets; and (d) facilitating the functioning of private markets by signalling creditworthiness and acting as catalysts for private sector investment. There are also several non-financial functions encompassing (a) the traditional "value added" of multilateral financing, lending related technical assistance, and its capacity-building and institutional development effects; (b) knowledge generation and brokering; and (c) the provision of global and regional public goods, including, in the case of most regional and subregional development banks, their support to regional integration processes.

Regional banks have specific functions determined by regional development needs

Not each and every multilateral development bank is involved in all these functions, but the multilateral development banks as a whole cover all of them. The central role in satisfying the first function is played by IDA, while several regional development banks play a role in concessional lending, particularly the African Development Bank (44 per cent of total lending) and the Asian Development Bank (27 per cent); the Inter-American Development Bank has also a concessional fund for special operations which amounts to 7 per cent of total lending (see World Bank and International Monetary Fund, 2005).

IDA is a special source of aid for the poorest developing countries

In contrast with traditional World Bank lending, IDA lending is mainly funded by donor official development assistance, supplemented by IDA loan repayments and net income from IDA lending and from the operations of the World Bank. In its recently completed fourteenth replenishment (IDA-14), donors contributed $18 billion of new funds to the $34 billion that will be available to the world's poorest developing countries under IDA for the period 1 July 2005-30 June 2008. To improve efficiency, IDA policy will take into account the vulnerability to debt problems of the recipient countries through a forward-looking debt sustainability analysis (see chap. V) while the most heavily debt-distressed countries, mainly in sub-Saharan Africa, will receive all of their IDA assistance on grant terms.

The relative roles of loans and grants in development assistance has long been debated. A number of major donors believe that the discipline of loan repayment sharpens the focus on the costs/benefits of prospective projects, and provides an incentive to ensuring that funds are used effectively. Further, timely servicing of loans for development creates a revolving fund that can form a basis for permanent support, while grants require fresh budget allocations by donors which may depend on political and economic conditions. In this respect, it is important that donor countries agree on measures to cushion the effect of the loss of repayment flows (as grants replace loans) on IDA capacity to support the poor developing countries in the future. Forgone reimbursements will be financed through additional donor contributions on a pay-as-you-go basis. Participants in the fourteenth replenishment of IDA have cautioned, however, against the possibility of grants' leading to excessive new borrowing from other sources by recipient countries, and warned that they could be disqualified from receiving grants if they are found to have engaged in "excessive or unsustainable" borrowing. Millennium Development Goals-based indicators will monitor overall development progress, thereby making possible a better assessment of country performance as well as aid delivery and management. IDA will make financial support contingent on the performance of the recipient country in the areas of economic policy, governance and poverty reduction efforts.

Negotiations on the replenishment of IDA have addressed the respective pros and cons of the roles of loans and grants

It is hoped that these measures will enhance the ability of countries to "graduate" from IDA support. Since 1960, 32 countries have graduated but 10 of the 32 countries subsequently re-entered the list at one time or another (these are known as "reverse graduates") and, after re-entry, some graduated again (see table IV.2).

New approach aims to increase IDA "graduates"

Recently, more attention has been given to the possible benefits of combining concessional IDA flows with other types of assistance so as to gain leverage and provide financing tailored to meet different needs between and within countries. Many developing countries receive IDA resources as well as cheap loans and grants from the concessional facility windows of the various regional development banks and from developed-country aid agencies. Concessional loans and grants can help the poorest (IDA-only) countries to scale up investment and spending to meet the Millennium Development Goals without undermining debt sustainability. As highlighted in the *Global Monitoring Report 2005* (World Bank, 2005e), the poorest countries face the largest gaps in financing needs so as to meet the Millennium Development Goals and must rely on external official financing to a substantial extent in covering those needs. There is broad agreement that the poorest countries should receive highly concessional resources, with amounts adjusted to take performance and absorptive capacity into account. IDA-only countries with per capita incomes below the IDA cut-off have traditionally received grants from bilateral donors and highly concessional loans from multilateral agencies.

The second and third financial functions of multilateral development banks listed above emphasize the role that official development financing continues to play even for middle-income countries. The evolution of multilateral development bank lending in recent years shows that, whereas financing to low-income countries is steadier, lending to middle-income countries is strongly counter-cyclical: it increased substantially during the first half of the 1980s and during the critical years following the Asian crisis (figure IV.7). It is important to emphasize that this counter-cyclical function is distinct from that of IMF, and refers basically to the access of developing countries to long-term borrowing during times of crisis, particularly to maintain critical public sector investment and social spending. The strong contraction in recent years, although consistent with the counter-cyclical function, has been

Multilateral development banks also have important roles in middle-income countries

Table IV.2.
Graduates from IDA assistance

	Country	Fiscal year of last IDA credit	Reverse graduate (year re-entered)
1.	Botswana	1974	-
2.	Cameroon	1981	1994
3.	Chile	1961	-
4.	China	1999	-
5.	Colombia	1962	-
6.	Congo	1982	1994
7.	Costa Rica	1962	-
8.	Côte d'Ivoire	1973	1992
9.	Dominican Republic	1973	-
10.	Ecuador	1974	-
11.	Egypt	1981, 1999	1991
12.	El Salvador	1977	-
13.	Equatorial Guinea	1993	-
14.	Honduras	1980	1991
15.	Indonesia	1980	1999
16.	Jordan	1978	-
17.	Mauritius	1975	-
18.	Morocco	1975	-
19.	Nicaragua	1981	1991
20.	Nigeria	1965	1989
21.	Papua New Guinea	1983	-
22.	Paraguay	1977	-
23.	Philippines	1979, 1993	1991
24.	Republic of Korea	1973	-
25.	Saint Kitts and Nevis	1994	-
26.	Swaziland	1975	-
27.	Syrian Arab Republic	1974	-
28.	Thailand	1979	-
29.	The former Yugoslav Republic of Macedonia	2002	-
30.	Tunisia	1977	-
31.	Turkey	1973	-
32.	Zimbabwe	1983	1992

Source: IDA, "Countries ceasing to borrow from IDA, 1960-2001" (www.worldbank.org/ida).

very strong, leading to negative net flows in 2002 and 2003, and has been accompanied by a significant reduction in net flows to low-income countries.

Excellent access to capital markets associated with high capital/asset ratios, a large ratio of subscribed to paid-in capital, and the capacity to draw on the high risk-ratings of developed-country members allow multilateral development banks to offer excellent credit conditions even to middle-income countries. Even those without developed-country members use risk pooling and good risk management practices to achieve better credit ratings and risk premiums than their individual members (for example, the Andean Development Corporation). The preferential relation of multilateral development banks with borrowers, which has resulted in very low loan losses, represents another advantage

Figure IV.7.
**The counter-cyclical character of the lending
of multilateral development banks, 1970-2003**

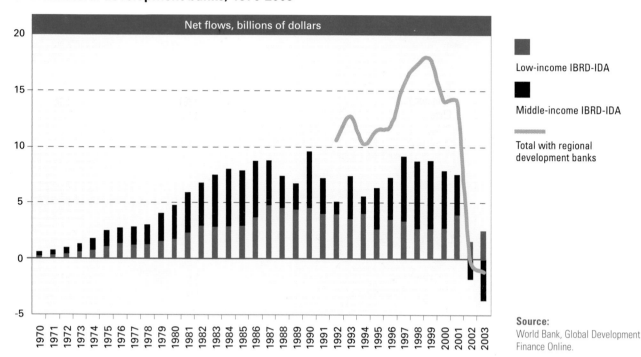

Net flows, billions of dollars

Low-income IBRD-IDA

Middle-income IBRD-IDA

Total with regional
development banks

Source:
World Bank, Global Development
Finance Online.

(The Central American Bank for Economic Integration and the African Development Bank are among the few exceptions in this regard). The fact that borrowing countries are also investors, that credit costs are low relative to market rates, and that those countries have access to borrowing from multilateral development banks even when access to private capital markets is unavailable or available only at high costs, explains this preferred creditor status. In turn, the high quality of the portfolios and the access to capital markets with minimum premiums are reflected in low costs of funding, which is passed on to their borrowers. In terms of both costs and maturities, these institutions are thus able to lend on much better terms than private agents (see table IV.3).

The fourth function, direct financing or co-financing to the private sector (by banks or their associated financial corporations) and provision of guarantee schemes to support public-private partnerships or public infrastructure projects, is of fairly recent origin. However, it has been gaining in importance since the 1990s and should become one of the priorities for multilateral financing in future. It has also been used in recent years in a modest way to support developing countries' efforts to return to markets after crises, but with only limited success in terms of improving the terms of borrowing for developing countries in private capital markets. It could be used to support initial bond issues by developing (particularly poor) countries seeking to position themselves in private capital markets. The full development of these schemes would call for a radical change in the management of guarantees by development banks since their current treatment as being equivalent to lending severely restricts their use.

Multilateral development banks can act as a catalyst for private finance for development

Table IV.3.
Developing countries: average terms of new commitments, 1990-2003

	1990	1991	1992	1993	1994	1995	1996	1997	1998	1999	2000	2001	2002	2003
Average maturity (years)														
Official														
All developing countries	22.4	21	21.3	21.5	22.1	19.2	21.6	19.8	16.2	19.8	20	21	22.7	19.8
Income group														
Low-income	28.1	28.2	29.1	28.7	29.2	28.5	29.6	29.7	31.5	30.9	30.4	31.5	30.4	32.1
Middle-income	19.8	18.8	18.3	19.2	19.6	16.9	18.8	17.1	13.3	17.6	16.8	16.9	18.6	15.8
Private														
All developing countries	11.4	9.7	10.3	9.7	9.1	7.8	8.3	10.6	10.1	8.7	10.5	9.3	25.3	9.9
Income group														
Low-income	13.8	8.2	11.4	9.9	8.8	7.1	7.1	8.1	6.6	8	5.2	7.3	4.8	5.7
Middle-income	11.1	9.8	10.2	9.7	9.1	7.8	8.4	10.7	10.5	8.7	11	9.4	25.9	10
Average interest rate (percentage)														
Official														
All developing countries	5.5	5.5	5.3	4.8	4.8	5.8	4.8	5.2	5.2	4.3	4.9	3.9	3.1	2.9
Income group														
Low-income	3.6	3.7	3.0	2.9	2.8	2.9	3.0	3.0	2.4	2.3	3.0	2.0	2.4	1.3
Middle-income	6.3	6.0	6.1	5.4	5.6	6.5	5.4	5.9	5.7	4.7	5.4	4.7	3.5	3.4
Private														
All developing countries	8.5	7.8	6.7	6.2	6.4	6.6	7.3	7.4	7.6	8.1	8.0	6.8	6.7	5.7
Income group														
Low-income	7.2	8.7	6.8	7.1	6.8	6.3	6.0	6.7	3.7	5.7	4.4	4.9	4.1	3.6
Middle-income	8.7	7.7	6.7	6.2	6.4	6.6	7.4	7.5	8.1	8.1	8.4	6.9	6.8	5.8

Source: World Bank, Global Development Finance Online.

Regional development
banks also provide
regional public goods

The services that are bundled with lending also help to support objectives of the global community: poverty reduction, human development, protection of the environment, financial accountability and better public management standards (Gurría and Volcker, 2001). This indicates that these institutions also play a role in the provision of regional and global public goods. Although regional and subregional institutions are not as important as the World Bank in the provision and financing of such goods, in the 1990s the regional development banks entered into the provision of regional public goods (see below).

Structure and trends

Development banks are
an important source of
long- and medium-
term finance ...

The level of resources provided by multilateral development banks to developing countries is low in comparison with other official flows and (during periods of ample external financing) with private financial flows. The share of different multilateral development banks in total net flows from multilateral sources varies across regions and level of income. Net flows from the World Bank and regional development banks to developing countries represent, respectively, 50 per cent and 41 per cent of total long- and medium-term net flows to developing countries from multilateral sources, with other institutions providing the rest.

However, as table IV.4 indicates, there are crucial regional differences with regard to the role played by different multilateral development banks. The expansion of the regional development banks has focused on middle-income countries where their com-

... but their importance varies across regions

Table IV.4.
Net flows from multilateral development banks by region, 1991-2002

Billions of dollars						
Multilateral financing sources[a]		1991-1994	1995-1998	1999-2002	Total 1991-2002	Relative participation 1991-2002
All developing countries	World Bank	25.42	31.51	23.95	80.87	0.50
	RDBs	20.53	24.65	21.55	66.73	0.41
	Other	6.62	8.55	0.16	15.33	0.09
Income level						
Low-income	World Bank	17.04	12.42	11.46	40.92	0.60
	RDBs	10.74	8.01	5.47	24.23	0.36
	Other	1.30	1.11	0.62	3.02	0.04
Middle-income	World Bank	8.38	19.08	12.49	39.95	0.42
	RDBs	9.79	16.63	16.08	42.50	0.45
	Other	5.33	7.45	-0.47	12.31	0.13
Region						
East Asia and the Pacific	World Bank	7.13	8.12	3.46	18.71	0.61
	RDBs	3.11	5.30	3.15	11.55	0.38
	Other	0.13	0.30	0.08	0.51	0.02
Europe and Central Asia	World Bank	3.17	9.47	7.02	19.66	0.79
	RDBs	0.35	1.94	0.71	2.99	0.12
	Other	3.50	-1.29	0.12	2.33	0.09
Latin America and the Caribbean	World Bank	-1.29	3.46	5.10	7.27	0.17
	RDBs	5.17	10.24	15.93	31.34	0.72
	Other	0.64	6.04	-1.64	5.04	0.12
Middle East and Northern Africa	World Bank	1.15	0.29	-0.37	1.07	0.11
	RDBs	2.27	0.99	-0.26	3.01	0.32
	Other	1.41	2.94	1.03	5.38	0.57
South Asia	World Bank	8.07	3.94	2.14	14.15	0.55
	RDBs	5.09	4.43	1.53	11.05	0.43
	Other	-0.01	0.24	0.28	0.51	0.02
Sub-Saharan Africa	World Bank	7.18	6.23	6.60	20.01	0.71
	RDBs	4.55	1.74	0.49	6.79	0.24
	Other	0.94	0.33	0.28	1.55	0.05

Source: Sagasti and Prada (2005), table 2.

a   Other multilateral sources are export credit and rescheduling operations with the Paris Club.

bined net flows surpass those of the World Bank. This is particularly true in Latin America and the Caribbean, where net flows from the Inter-American Development Bank have steadily and significantly expanded, and surpass by far those of the World Bank. The Middle East and Northern Africa constitute the only region where net flows from "other" institutions, basically the Arab institutions, surpass those of the World Bank and the regional development banks. At the subregional level, the Andean region in South America offers the interesting case in which the net flows from a subregional institution totally owned by member countries, namely, the Andean Development Corporation, surpass those of both the World Bank and the Inter-American Development Bank. More subregional development banks could be created. The lack of this kind of institution in Asia stands in clear contrast with the situation in other regions. Proposals for a development bank for the Middle East and Central Asia and for North-eastern Asia are being discussed.

The emphasis placed on certain operations by regional and subregional institutions reflects the diversity of their constituencies' financial needs. Institutions serving the African region are more focused on concessional loans and grants. Central Asian and European institutions are more focused on private sector activities; this is particularly true of the European Bank for Reconstruction and Development. These differences among regional development banks also apply at the subregional level. For example, the Caribbean Development Bank operates in some of the poorest Caribbean countries and has a larger proportion of concessional lending in comparison with the Central American Bank for Economic Integration, which has a clear mandate to improve intraregional trade (reflected in its higher proportion of trade finance and infrastructure operations). The Andean Development Corporation, operating mainly in middle-income countries, has specialized in other types of operations such as infrastructure projects for regional integration and for improving competitiveness. This supports the general idea behind the creation of regional and subregional institutions: they play specific and localized roles, which are not always covered adequately by global or even by regional institutions (Sagasti, Bezanson and Prada, 2005).

With different regional needs, regional bank portfolios differ

As a result, the loan portfolios of regional and subregional banks also differ. The sectoral evolution of the lending of multilateral development banks has followed two main patterns. The first involves the increasing importance of the social sectors [9] and governance reforms during the 1990s and the current decade, and, to a lesser extent, the environment; and second, the progressive reduction of involvement in the productive sectors through State-owned financial intermediaries which has been partially compensated by the introduction of new financial instruments that directly support private sector investments and private-public partnerships. These include operations with private banks and the development of domestic capital markets that fall under the category of "financial infrastructure", according to the OECD classification.

Along with providing financial sector and capital market support, the regional and subregional banks entered into new areas during the 1990s such as the provision of regional public goods, especially those related to regional transport, energy and communication infrastructure and environmental programmes. ESCAP has proposed the creation of an Asian Investment Bank to finance the region's infrastructure needs (ESCAP, 2005). Initiatives such as the New Partnership for Africa's Development (NEPAD) (document A/57/304, annex), the Initiative for the Integration of South American Regional Infrastructure and the Plan Puebla-Panama (involving Mexico and Central America) will certainly increase the proportion of such undertakings. This is probably a field for the expansion of regional development banks in the future.

The large and ever-growing role of regional and subregional development banks in the international financial system has received limited attention in the literature on international financial reform.[10] Regional and subregional development banks, even those made up entirely of developing countries, are likely to face lower risks than individual members. On the other hand, competition between world and regional organizations in the provision of development bank services and technical services is undoubtedly a desirable arrangement for small and medium-sized countries. The fact that developing countries are better represented in these banks than in the global financial institutions also creates a strong sense of "ownership" and establishes a special relationship between them and member countries that helps to reduce the risks faced by regional and subregional development banks, further encouraging the virtues of risk pooling (Ocampo, 2002a).

The combination of collective action problems and the absence of supranational institutions indicates how important the regional and subregional development banks can be in supporting regional strategies. They can provide member countries with a coordination mechanism through which to plan and finance the provision of regional transborder infrastructure and other regional public goods requiring large initial investments. They also have the ability to provide a regional public good essential for development: the transmission and utilization of region-specific knowledge. That ability positions them to help countries within their respective regions design specific policies most appropriate to their economic needs and political constraints (Birdsall and Rojas-Suarez, 2004).

The regional banks have room to expand their actions to provide development aid …

… particularly in supporting regional strategies

The debate around the multilateral development banks

The multilateral development banks came under criticism after the financial crises of the 1990s. In particular, the Meltzer Commission proposed phasing out multilateral bank lending to developing countries with access to private capital markets, and transforming the World Bank into a world development agency focused on low-income countries, with grants as the essential financing instrument (Meltzer and others, 2000). Other analysts argued, in turn, that the occurrence of capital market failures could not be used to defend the existence of the World Bank but only its role as a "knowledge bank", that is to say, a repository of best practices in development assistance (Gilbert and Vines, 2000).

In contrast, the United States Department of the Treasury (2000) defended the *financial* role of multilateral development banks vis-à-vis not only poor but also middle-income countries, given the fragile access of the latter to private capital markets. It also defended large-scale lending during crises to support fiscal expenditure in critical social services and financial sector restructuring. It argued, however, that multilateral development banks should improve coordination among themselves, and should focus their activities on areas of high development priority, be more selective in their lending to emerging economies and encourage eventual graduation of these countries from development assistance. Finally it defended the role of multilateral development banks lending as a catalyst for private lending.

Two independent reports have also underscored the essential role that multilateral development banks will continue to play in the international financial system. The report by the Institute of Development Studies of the University of Sussex (2000) emphasized three essential roles of these institutions: financial resource mobilization; capacity-building, institutional development and knowledge-brokering; and provision of global and

The role of development banks was criticized in the 1990s …

… but also defended

Multilateral development banks play a key role in the international financial system

regional public goods. It also underscored the need for multilateral development banks to embrace intellectual diversity in their role as knowledge brokers, an issue that has also been emphasized by Stiglitz (1999).

In turn, the report of the Commission on the Role of the Multilateral Development Banks in Emerging Markets (Gurría and Volcker, 2001) emphasized, in terms similar to those of the United States Treasury, that volatility of financial markets implied that the access of emerging markets to private capital markets could be "unreliable, limited and costly". As crises hurt the poor, the counter-cyclical character of multilateral development bank financing is consistent with the role in poverty reduction of the multilateral development banks. The Commission nonetheless suggested that pricing of loans by multilateral development banks should be set in a differential way so as to encourage graduation and correct the pro-cyclical effects of credit ratings. It also emphasized the need to strengthen the relationship between multilateral development banks and the private sector, particularly to encourage private infrastructure financing in developing countries. The catalytic role that multilateral development banks can play in this regard should be based on guarantee schemes, through which multilateral development banks help to cover the government and regulatory risks that private investors are likely to face.

Multilateral development banks need to improve efficiency and reduce costs of providing development finance

Among other issues that have been the subject of concern to developing countries are the high costs of doing business with many multilateral development banks caused by long negotiation processes and conditionalities attached to lending. Indeed, some developing countries have decided to prepay loans from multilateral development banks with funds borrowed in private capital markets when such financing is available (a mechanism that is equivalent to an automatic "graduation"). This may explain the negative net transfers from several of these institutions in recent years (see figure IV.7). Mohammed (2004) has recommended reviewing the pricing of loans, the conditions attached to them and the complex body of safeguard/fiduciary policies that have accumulated over the years for "ring-fencing" the World Bank from risk, as well as the restraints applied to the purposes for which the World Bank lends, in order to reverse the erosion of the competitiveness of the Bank as a development lender.

World Bank has unused loan capacity as repayments exceed new lending

The Intergovernmental Group of Twenty-Four on International Monetary Affairs and Development, in its communiqué on its April 2005 Ministerial meeting, noted with concern "the sharp increase in recent years in net negative transfers to developing countries from the multilateral development banks, particularly the World Bank" (para. 17). Furthermore, it urged the Bank "to take effective action to reduce the financial and non-financial costs of doing business with the Bank, including by clarifying policies, simplifying procedures, streamlining internal processes, and reducing conditionality in lending operations" (para. 18). The fact that operations of multilateral development banks are financed by net income generated mainly from lending operations conducted with middle-income countries has also been a subject of concern. Retained earnings have also increased their share in the capital of many multilateral development banks, including IBRD, as the share of paid-in capital has declined over the years.

The most controversial issue since the 1980s has been, however, the role of lending-associated conditionalities, particularly structural conditionalities, and the most recent governance conditionalities. A World Bank study recognized in 1998 that conditionality had not influenced the success or failure of its programmes.[11] Nonetheless, and following the debate on aid effectiveness, the report argued that such success or failure was not independent of the economic policies that countries followed.

Of particular interest in this regard are the conclusions of the World Bank Operations Evaluation Department (World Bank, Operations Evaluation Department, 2004e) about the World Bank's role in poverty reduction strategies. This report indicated that this initiative had enhanced the focus on poverty reduction of national strategies and the Bank's country programmes, bolstered the role of already robust Governments in aid coordination, and involved new actors in the development dialogue. At the same time, it underscored the fact that there was "an inherent tension in the design of a BWI-driven initiative involving conditionality that is simultaneously meant to foster a country-driven process", and made the following point: "The Bank management's process for presenting a PRSP to the Board undermines ownership. Stakeholders perceive this practice as Washington signing off on a supposedly country-owned strategy." It thus recommended "that management develop a review procedure that is more transparently supportive of ownership and more effectively linked to decisions about the Bank's programme". The Development Committee, in its 17 April 2005 communiqué, recognized once again the significance of these issues, underlining the importance of "aligning assistance better with medium-term country strategies, streamlining conditionality, building institutional capacity and strengthening the focus on development results (para. 12)."

The World Bank's approach to poverty reduction has highlighted the tensions between ownership and conditionality

The way forward

The recognition by the Monterrey Consensus of the need to strengthen the role of multilateral development banks in the service of developing countries should lead to concrete actions. They may be associated to past practices, particularly the strong support to low-income countries, but they should also be linked to emerging issues. In respect of the latter, as noted in chapter III, the trade financing facilities of multilateral development banks can play a role, for example, in counteracting the collapse of trade finance during crises. Operations in this area include guarantees of trade instruments issued by local banks and on-lending facilities through commercial banks that have been used in recent crises in Asia, the Russian Federation and Brazil.

This issue is closely associated to the counter-cyclical role of multilateral development banks in financing. However, expanding this role vis-à-vis emerging economies would require a significant increase in resources or a more active use of co-financing and credit guarantees by these institutions. These facilities could be activated in periods of sharp decline in capital flows and could aim to catalyse long-term private financing and investment. Existing guarantee mechanisms may need to be improved or enhanced and/or new mechanisms may need to be created. Existing problems—such as excessive restrictiveness of criteria and approval processes for granting guarantees and other related costs— would need to be addressed. Most importantly, the resources of the multilateral development banks should also be better leveraged in providing guarantees, eliminating the practice of equating guarantees with loans in terms of the accounting of the associated programmes. Guarantees should also be better targeted, for example, by focusing on later stages of long-term projects. Counter-cyclical lending facilities could also be devised, inter alia, by explicitly managing counterpart funds in a counter-cyclical way, or by allowing developing countries to "save" those counterpart funds in the multilateral development banks (for example, for social protection programmes) and use them when they were required during crises.

The Multilateral development banks could play a greater role in creating economic and financial stability

The role of multilateral development banks as "market makers" has grown in recent years as reflected in the support to public-private partnerships in infrastructure, and in the issuance of long-term bonds in the domestic markets of some developing countries and the subsequent lending to those countries in their own currencies. The Asian Development Bank is already providing extensive support to the ASEAN+3 Asian Bond Markets Initiative. A more active role could be taken in lending in domestic currencies of developing countries, and in extending the benchmark "yield curve" in their domestic bond markets. These market-making activities could be extended to commodity- or GDP-linked bonds; the associated lending could be securitized to be sold in international private capital markets. However, since these institutions are assumed to be "risk-free", it should be emphasized that this innovation, as well as the more active use of guarantees, would involve a major change in the underlying principles involved in the management of multilateral development banks.[12] The expertise developed by the World Bank as market maker for the sale of carbon credits under the provisions of the Kyoto Protocol could provide a basis for these activities. Although the strong portfolio is clearly one of the strengths of multilateral development banks, they also have an essential function in correcting market failures that may involve some risks.

The revealed success of several regional and subregional development banks clearly indicates that this is a promising area of cooperation among developing countries. There are successful financial institutions that have operated with a good credit rating without capital from industrialized countries. Furthermore, more appropriate conditionality makes these institutions attractive to borrowing countries (Sagasti, Bezanson and Prada, 2005). This should thus become a priority for South-South cooperation.

South-South cooperation

South-South cooperation is mainly technical cooperation ...

Development banking is one form of cooperation among developing countries that has made some progress but has still an untapped potential. The association of the activities of these institutions with trade and other integration processes is particularly promising. The same is true of monetary and macroeconomic cooperation, where initiatives are more limited (see chap. VI). These are thus areas where South-South cooperation can make major strides in the future.

The major form of South-South development cooperation is technical cooperation. A recent multinational initiative in this regard is the India-Brazil-South Africa (IBSA) Dialogue Forum. The IBSA Dialogue Forum serves as a mechanism for political consultation and coordination, as well as for strengthening cooperation in particular economic and sectoral areas, and for improving economic relations among the three participating countries.[13]

China is one of the leading proponents among developing countries of South-South cooperation and was the first developing country donor to the Voluntary Trust Fund for the Promotion of South-South Cooperation. With its Technical Cooperation and Development network comprising of 26 centres of excellence, China has begun to establish the appropriate national policy and institutions to advance South-South cooperation. China launched its first South-South Cooperation Demonstration base in Fuzhou with the support of the United Nations Development Programme (UNDP) Special Unit for Technical Cooperation among Developing Countries. China's development cooperation policy with developing countries also focuses on human resource development. As at December 2003, it had trained some 7,000 African personnel in a wide range of professions in a variety of training programmes.[14]

India has spent over $2 billion over the years in wide-ranging programmes in the area of South-South cooperation. Under the India Development Initiative, founded in March 2003, India plans to provide financial and technical support to other developing countries through the sharing of development experiences and institutional capacity. Grants and loans from India to other developing countries have grown markedly, from $83 million to $140 million since 2000 (World Bank, 2005d, p. 100).

... but financial cooperation is playing an increasing role

Brazil and Morocco underwrite scholarships to various universities and support technical and professional training for students of developing countries. Singapore offers a wide array of training programmes, and Sri Lanka offers training on indigenously developed technology (crab breeding, use of banana fibre, etc.). Cuba has provided medical training as well as experts and support for health-care systems in and outside of Latin America and the Caribbean.

Nigeria, since 1976, has promoted South-South cooperation through the Nigeria Trust Fund, under the administration of the African Development Fund. The South-South development cooperation policy of the Republic of Korea centres on promoting sustainable economic development, through, inter alia, the transfer of technology and information related to its development experiences in human resource and communications. Over the past few years, Turkey has allotted, on average, 80 per cent of its development cooperation budget to South-South initiatives.[15]

Some technical cooperation agreements have been concluded with the support of developed countries. For instance, Japan, through the Japan International Cooperation Agency (JICA), has been an active supporter of the Third Country Training Programme (TCTP) since its introduction in 1975. TCTP activities are located mainly in Central and South America and the countries members of the Association of Southeast Asian Nations (ASEAN).

South-South cooperation can also take the form of providing debt relief to debt-distressed developing countries. For instance, Mexico and Costa Rica have offered major debt relief to the HIPC countries in Central America. In 2000, China provided debt relief of RMB 10.5 billion ($1.27 billion) to 31 African countries and pledged to continue in the future to offer assistance to other developing countries.[16] India and many other developing countries have made significant contributions to the HIPC Initiative. In early 2005, developing countries pledged about $200 million in emergency assistance to the victims of the Asian tsunami.

There is also some financial support in the form of debt relief ...

To a limited extent, some developing countries have also been donors of ODA to other developing countries. Among the developing countries in Western Asia, Saudi Arabia has been, for many years, the largest ODA donor, followed by the United Arab Emirates and Kuwait. Total ODA contributions (almost all bilateral ODA) from this group has risen threefold since 1999. The ODA of the Republic of Korea has risen by almost one third since 2002, owing to contributions to the regional development banks and the replenishment of IDA. One third of bilateral ODA went to regions outside of Asia.

... and ODA

Innovative sources of financing

As noted at the beginning of this chapter, the weak political will to meet the official assistance target of 0.7 per cent of GNI as ODA to developing countries was already noticeable in the mid-term review of the Second Development Decade. In recent years, a focus of attention has been the decreasing efficiency of official aid flows in providing real cash financing for meeting the Millennium Development Goals. This has led to a search for other sources of financing. In the context of the five-year review of the implementation of the outcome of the World Summit for Social Development, the General Assembly, in its resolution S-24/2 of 1 July 2000, called for a rigorous analysis of the advantages, disadvantages and other implications of proposals for developing new and innovative sources of funding, both public and private (para. 142(g)). Paragraph 44 of the Monterrey Consensus further called upon member States to pursue the consideration of innovative sources of financing.

Recent initiatives to increase aid flows have involved innovative approaches

Significant steps have been taken in response. At the request of the General Assembly, the Department of Economic and Social Affairs of the United Nations Secretariat commissioned the World Institute for Development Economics Research (WIDER) of the United Nations University (UNU) to consider existing proposals, which led to the publication of a study (Atkinson, 2004). At the Summit of World Leaders for Action against Hunger and Poverty held at United Nations Headquarters in September 2004, a report by the Technical Group on Innovative Financing Mechanisms[17] was presented and is being actively followed up by its members. Other important analyses had been carried out for the Development Committee[18] and were discussed at its 2004 fall and 2005 spring meetings. A report was also presented to French President Jacques Chirac by the Working Group on New International Contributions to Finance Development,[19] on the possible bases, allocation and management of new development resources.

The proposals vary in the participation and time required for their implementation and in their potential revenue

The economic and social impact of the proposals for additional flows, and for aid in general, would be enhanced if they were designed so as to be stable and predictable, with a view to enabling recipient countries to focus on human and physical capital investment needs. Such proposals may be distinguished according to their feasibility and potential revenue. The vertical axis in figure IV.8 measures whether a specific initiative can be

Figure IV.8.
Map of main proposals on innovative sources of financing

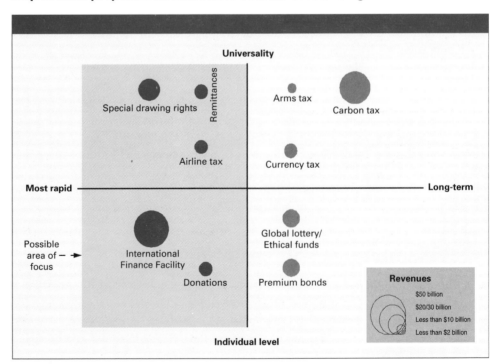

Source:
DESA calculations.

implemented by an individual country or requires broader participation for success including, at the extreme, universal participation. The horizontal axis measures the time frame required for adoption and implementation, running from most rapid to long-term. The mix of these two dimensions indicates what could be areas of focus so as to allow some proposals to be adopted rapidly without requiring universal acceptance. The size of the circle estimates, in turn, the magnitude of the potential revenue from a given financial source.

Major mechanisms in the short run

Taxing air transport makes economic sense, as underscored by the World Bank and International Monetary Fund (2005). In fact, the level of taxation on air transport is lower than on other means of transport, since aviation fuel is tax-exempt. Aircraft play a major role in global warming; however, they are not covered by the Kyoto Protocol[20] to the United Nations Framework Convention on Climate Change.[21] Several options seem to be technically feasible. Taxing aviation fuel would have a major positive environmental impact. As for a tax on airline tickets, it could easily be instituted and would present no legal obstacles, as the World Bank points out. However, considering the still fragile situation of the airline industry, some suggest instead that a small contribution be levied on ticket prices, with the airlines' support. The favourable perception by passengers of such a contribution, for which there are reasonable prospects of feasibility in the short term, could be achieved through its being allocated to a precise fund. In view of the small size of this levy, it is expected that there would be minimal impact on the activity of airlines. A 5 per cent rate applied to first-class and business class tickets would yield $8 billion per annum, while a $1 contribution on each ticket issued would yield about $3 billion per annum. Another alternative would involve the indirect taxation of air flight corridors: revenues could reach $10 billion per annum. An indirect tax on passenger transportation could reach $20 billion per annum. Germany and France have recently proposed creating a pilot project for an international solidarity levy based on air transport.

> A levy on air transport could be a pilot project

The International Finance Facility (IFF) was initially proposed by the United Kingdom of Great Britain and Northern Ireland in 2003. The Secretary-General has called upon the international community to launch it in 2005.[22] It builds on commitments to reach the 0.7 per cent of GNI for ODA target no later than 2015. Its particular feature is that it enables front-loading aid flows through a bond mechanism guaranteed by participating Governments, allowing aid commitments to be spent before they are budgeted. The British proposal shows that with an initial $16 billion payment and regular increases through triennial pledging rounds over a 15-year period, donors can reach a $50 billion financing objective. If disbursements were to begin in 2006 ($10 billion), they would reach $50 billion by 2010, decrease after 2015 and end by 2020, with IFF drawing down donor pledges to pay off its bonds until 2032.

> Short-term measures include the International Finance Facility

As the IFF mechanism seems to show great potential, it should now be examined experimentally before larger-scale implementation is undertaken. In this regard, the pilot project that will be launched in 2005, joining a small-scale facility ("IFFIm") of $4 billion over 10 years to the public-private partnership of the Global Alliance for Vaccines and Immunization (GAVI), should be scrutinized. The analysis of its financial architecture is likely to show a straightforward absorption by financial markets and a low-cost financing, as issuances of government-backed bonds will certainly obtain the highest ratings (AAA). To insure additionality, longer-term support should be considered to supplement the Facility through refinancing mechanisms.

The response to the
2004 tsunami crisis
shows the growing
importance of
voluntary giving

Donations may also be fostered in the short run, as they account for a small but growing share of funds geared towards development. Voluntary contributions by individuals channelled through non-governmental organizations have doubled since 1990 in nominal terms, from $5 billion to $10 billion. The will of private citizens to participate in global poverty reduction initiatives is strong too, as was recently observed after the Asian tsunami of 2004, which led to the perception of a "globalization of solidarity". Gifts may not, however, be mixed with ODA in as much as they are a complement to, rather than a substitute for, the latter.

Donations can be encouraged through tax deductions: the usefulness of this procedure rests on the assumption that reduction in tax revenues will be more than compensated by the donations they encourage. Mechanisms suggested in this perspective generally include voluntary contributions that are paid together with the income tax slip, either through an opt-in system in which taxpayers choose to pay the tax, or an opt-out in which taxpayers can refuse the tax. Donations on acts of consumption have also been suggested, either through credit card payments or through utility bills. Within EU, the yield of credit card gifts equivalent to 1 per cent of Visa debits would reach $10 billion per annum. It is important to note in this regard that mechanisms linked to voluntary contributions benefit from but do not require international coordination.

Remittances have been
growing and can be
better utilized to
support development

Facilitating transfers of remittances offers a significant means of gearing new resources towards development financing. Although remittances can hardly be considered an innovative source of finance with which to complement ODA, they do possess a number of crucial features for recipient countries in the developing world. First, they amount to vast sums: $93 billion for developing countries in 2003 according to current estimates. Second, they reach the population and, even though they are geared towards consumption, they may serve as tools to foster some forms of investment. It has been suggested in this regard that the cost of transfers through regulated financial institutions can be reduced. This could be achieved on the sending side by facilitating the access to banking institutions of foreign workers—including by "formalizing" their status—and by creating banks and products designed for their needs. On the recipient side, this could be achieved with the support of local financial institutions to the launching of joint procedures with institutions in sending countries in order to reduce transfer costs. At both ends of the transfer, remittances could also be used to "bank" the poor. Another approach to increasing the gains of remittances for development would consist in diffusing the flows more adequately, by fostering investments in housing, in micro enterprises and small enterprises, or in financial instruments in the recipient countries. Such measures might require international coordination which could be obtained within the United Nations framework.

Using special drawing rights (SDRs) for development purposes (Soros, 2002) would involve the allocation by developed countries of SDRs to a dedicated trust fund, either by gift or through a redistribution of quotas, which would require amending the IMF Articles of Agreement. An amendment was approved in 1997 by the IMF Board of Governors for a special and unique allocation to double cumulated allocations to SDR 43 billion ($65 billion); however, the consensus for a modification has yet to be achieved. Other major innovative financing proposals include a global lottery and global premium bonds, and various taxes that could be earmarked for development objectives.

Major mechanisms in the longer run

Global taxation in support of development has a long history (Jenks, 1942; Stoessinger, 1964) and it is often criticized on grounds of feasibility. Thus, to avert their being perceived as encroachments on participating countries' fiscal sovereignty or as mechanisms triggering new international bureaucracies—which would undermine the possibility of a large consensus among stakeholders—these taxes need to be designed as financing tools that are nationally applied and internationally coordinated, and that entail limited management and process costs. While universal participation is not indispensable, it would serve the interest of development, as more resources would be raised. This should be the ultimate goal, but in the short term, progress can be made with the participation of a smaller group of countries.

One type of tax that has been commonly suggested is the currency transaction tax, for which estimated revenues would range from $30.6 billion to $35.4 billion per annum if it was equivalent to two basis points of market currency transactions, and from $16.8 billion to $19.2 billion if it was equivalent to one basis point (Nissanke, 2003). Other estimates, considering that the negative impact of the tax on volumes would be minimal or nil, yield even higher revenues, namely, $60 billion per annum (Clunies-Ross, 2004). However attractive the tax might be in terms of revenue potential its implementation is constrained by a number of obstacles. The tax base will have to be defined so as to exclude transactions by market-makers and special treatment for derivatives to avoid duplicate taxation (Spahn, 2002). It will also have to be protected from erosion, for even if all major financial centers participate, there is a risk that smaller centres will attract an increasing volume of activity from those wishing to evade the tax. Finally, strong opposition by a number of stakeholders must be overcome.

Taxes applied to domestic financial transactions in many countries could be applied to international financial transactions

Another suggested tax, which can be defended on environmental efficiency grounds, would be applied to carbon emissions. It would build on the dynamic launched by the United Nations Framework Convention on Climate Change, adopted on 9 May 1992 by the Intergovernmental Negotiating Committee for a Framework Convention on Climate Change, inviting partner States to decrease greenhouse gas emissions. Carbon dioxide is the main gas at stake and its emissions might be moderated through a tax that would thus have the advantage of correcting negative externalities in addition to being a significant source of development financing. On the basis of a figure of $21 per ton (5 cents per gallon of gasoline), revenues would reach $130 billion per annum and $61 billion per annum in the case where the tax was restricted to rich countries. Governments would levy the tax and dispense it to an international agency, according to a procedure that remains to be defined. However, several challenges would need to be addressed including: the need to consider "free-riding" risks presented by countries not applying the tax and of tax evasion at the company or the country level; the need to coordinate the tax with the current practice involving negotiable emissions permits established by the Kyoto Protocol, adopted by the Conference of the Parties to the Framework Convention at its third session in 1997; and redistributive effects which might require an international agreement on compensations.

Carbon emissions taxation has also been considered

A tax on the arms trade could yield between $2.5 billion and $8 billion per annum. This tax is advocated as a means to secure resources to finance development while discouraging military expenditures (Clunies-Ross, 2000). However, if its full potential is to be realized, it is important to ensure that the tax is passed through from the seller to the buyer so that the cost of acquiring arms is effectively increased. Also, if the mechanism is to be efficient, it would be crucial to obtain a large coalition of participants, including all major arms producers and exporters.

A United Nations development fund?

Given that the previously described proposals do not entail investing the United Nations with the authority to impose taxes, it is legitimate to consider a development fund that could encourage a significant stepping up of voluntary contributions. One option would be to establish a new fund, like the "special fund to combat hunger and poverty", called for by the World Leaders for Action against Hunger and Poverty in January 2004. This would also fit with new SDR allocations-related proposals for a development trust fund, as mentioned earlier.

Another option would be to use an existing fund such as the World Solidarity Fund. The General Assembly at its fifty seventh session (in resolution 57/265 of 20 December 2002) endorsed the decision of the World Summit on Sustainable Development to establish the Fund. The Fund is currently subject to the financial rules and regulations of the Executive Board of UNDP and the United Nations Population Fund (UNFPA). Making the Fund fully operational would require, inter alia, adapting those financial rules and regulations.

Notes

1   The Development Committee, as it has come to be called, was established by parallel resolutions of the Boards of Governors of the World Bank and the International Monetary Fund at their annual meetings in October 1974.

2   Statement by Richard Manning, Chairman, OECD Development Assistance Committee (DAC), to Development Committee Spring Meeting, Washington, 17 April 2005, para. 5.

3   The problem can be traced to donors' own budgetary procedures. It is linked to the way donors' budgets are approved and administered. In many of the donor countries, there is a disconnect between donor development agencies and those that approve and disburse budgets.

4   Data excludes the Democratic Republic of the Congo for 2003, as important debt relief operations made this country an outlier for that year. (Including the Democratic Republic of the Congo, the share of the top 20 recipients would have been 59 per cent, and 46 per cent of countries would have accounted for 90 per cent of net bilateral aid in 2003.)

5   In this regard, Boone (1996) provides evidence that, on average, aid does not foster economic growth. On the other hand, Burnside and Dollar (2000) and Collier and Dollar (2002) qualify the Boone-type results to indicate that aid promotes growth in good policy environments. Hansen and Tarp (2001) disagree with this view and provide a contrary perspective.

6   At times aid allocations are not guided by development objectives and, in such cases, it would be very difficult to establish the links among aid, growth and poverty reduction. The discussion in the present section does not focus on such cases. Nor does it focus on some extreme cases of leakages through outright corruption and rent-seeking.

7   Critics of this approach question the definition and assessment of good policy implicit in the CPIA ratings (see, for example, European Network on Debt and Development (Eurodad, 2002). In the view of these critics, performance-based allocation puts too much emphasis on old Washington consensus types of policies. The approach ignores bad performance due to structural factors such as the inability to withstand commodity price shocks.

8   Among these alternative interpretations, we should include the following points: (a) Collier and Dollar's model confirms that the impact of reallocating aid on the basis of poverty criteria is greater than that of reallocating aid on the basis of policy; (b) World Bank evidence that aid is fungible and

that ex ante conditionality is ineffective can also be questioned; (c) growth is not the only route to poverty reduction nor is growth the only benefit of aid: other benefits include, inter alia, health, educational and distributional effects, environmental development, empowerment and security and; (d) adopting the poverty reduction strategy at the level of each country as opposed to having a single global target could significantly alter the pattern of poverty-efficient aid allocations.

9   From its creation through the 1960s, the World Bank financed mainly infrastructure projects (representing 75 per cent of its total portfolio). The creation of the first regional development bank, the Inter-American Development Bank, in 1959, could be seen partly as a reaction by Latin American countries to World Bank lending policies which had given little attention to the social and agriculture sectors (which represented only 3 per cent of the World Bank's portfolio). In the first 10 years of Inter-American Development Bank operations, those sectors received almost 50 per cent of total Inter-American Development Bank disbursements (Kapur, Lewis and Webb, 1997).

10 Some exceptions are United Nations (2001a), Ocampo (2002a), Ocampo and Griffith-Jones (2003) and Birdsall and Rojas-Suarez (2004).

11 See World Bank (1998), chap. 2 and appendix 2; and also Gilbert, Powell and Vines (1999), Stiglitz (1999) and Gilbert and Vines (2000).

12 Kapur (2003a) has argued that the increasingly stringent safeguards that have the objective of protecting the World Bank from risk are imposing high financial and opportunity costs on the Bank's borrowers, pointing out that "(it) is trivially easy for the major shareholders to insist on standards whose costs they do not bear".

13 See "Cape Town Ministerial Communiqué, India-Brazil-South Africa (IBSA) Dialogue Forum", press release, 13 March 2005, Republic of South Africa Department of Foreign Affairs, available from www.dfa.gov.za/docs/2005/ibsa0311.htm.

14 See "Let us build on our past achievements and promote China-Africa friendly relations", address by Wen Jiabao, Premier of the State Council of the People's Republic of China, at the opening ceremony of the Second Ministerial Conference of the China-Africa Cooperation Forum, Addis Ababa, 15 December 2003, available from http://chinaembassy.ru/eng/wjdt/zyjh/t56252.htm.

15 See report of the Secretary-General (A/58/319) entitled "State of South-South cooperation", para. 42.

16 See statement by Minister Xiang Huaicheng, Head of the Delegation of the People's Republic of China at the International Conference on Financing for Development, 21 March 2002, Monterrey, Mexico, available from http://www.un.org/ffd/statements/chinaE.htm.

17 The September 2004 report, entitled "Action against Hunger and Poverty", was derived from the January 2004 Geneva Declaration signed by the leaders of Brazil, Chile and France, backed by the Secretary-General and endorsed later by Spain, Germany and Algeria.

18 See Development Committee, 25 April 2004 communiqué, para. 7.; 2 October 2004 communiqué, para. 9., and background paper DC2004-0012/Add.1 of 29 September 2004 entitled "Aid effectiveness and financing modalities"; and the paper prepared by the Staff of the World Bank and the International Monetary Fund for the 17 April 2005 Spring Meeting, entitled "Moving forward: financing modalities toward the Millennium Development Goals" (SM/05/104, 3/17/05).

19 Report of the Working Group on New International Contributions to Finance Development (Paris, La documentation française, September 2004).

20 United Nations, Treaty Series, vol. 1771, No. 3 08 22.

21 FCCC/CP/1997/7/Add.1, decision 1/CP.3, annex.

22 Report of the Secretary-General entitled "In larger freedom: towards development, security and human rights for all" (A/59/2005) of 21 March 2005, para. 51.

Chapter V
External debt

External finance is meant to supplement and support developing countries' domestic resource mobilization. However, since the nineteenth century, developing countries have experienced repeated episodes of rapidly increasing external indebtedness and debt-service burdens that have brought slower growth or recession and eventually produced renegotiation and restructuring. For this reason, the Monterrey Consensus of the International Conference on Financing for Development (United Nations, 2002b, annex) emphasized the importance of sustainable debt levels in mobilizing resources for development.

The present chapter analyses the current debate on debt and development in historical perspective. It starts with a brief review of the evolution of developing-country debt and rescheduling in the post-war period. The second section surveys measures to deal with the problem of excessive indebtedness, such as the Heavily Indebted Poor Countries (HIPC) Initiative, as well as more recent proposals for additional relief for low-income countries and new Paris Club arrangements for middle-income countries. Efficient use of external resources requires an adequate understanding, and an operative specification, of debt sustainability. The third section presents and critically assesses recent proposals for sustainability to be applied to low-income countries under the fourteenth replenishment of the International Development Association (IDA-14). In the last analysis, when failure to attain sustainability produces default, renegotiation is necessary. The final section reviews recent experience in this area that suggests the need for urgent action for new approaches to the problem, and provides an assessment of various proposals on the table for discussion by the international community.

Debt and development

The post-war approach to lending to developing countries

In the early post-war period, it had been assumed that development finance would take place in the form of grants or concessional borrowing from multilateral development banks. The potential for private flows was considered limited, given the volatility of such flows in the interwar period and their virtual disappearance (except for trade credits) following the Great Depression. Official flows were to be multilateral, administered by institutions such as the United Nations Capital Development Fund or through the International Bank for Reconstruction and Development (IBRD). In the event, private and bilateral official flows dominated international finance for development. Multilateral lending tended to be restricted to large project financing of infrastructure, evaluated according to efficient use of capital resources, and based on a notional social rate of return. As a consequence, it did not take into account the ability of the country to generate the foreign-exchange resources required to service the debt. Bilateral lending was carried out on an ad hoc, country-by-country basis with little coordination within different agencies in donor countries and with even less cooperation among lenders, with outcomes dominated

From grants and concessional loans to private lending and official bilateral aid by political or domestic concerns through tied aid, and also with little concern for the impact on the country's ability to service the loans.

Similar problems arose–and, if anything, became more acute—when private markets became the dominant source of financial inflows to developing countries in the 1970s. Foreign currency loans with adjustable interest rates were extended to private sector borrowers or public sector enterprises on the basis of domestic performance and creditworthiness, or were driven by competitive pressures on lending banks to retain market shares, without reference to the borrowing country's ability to service the debt. There had been little coordination among private lenders concerning overall foreign currency exposure at the country level or with respect to assessing the implications of possible changes in dollar exchange rates and interest rates before they sharply increased at the end of the decade. Thus, even when external finance had a positive impact on development, it could be frustrated by the lack of capacity to service the loans, irrespective of whether it was official aid or private market financing. Financing for development could be counterproductive if debt service diverted resources from development purposes.

Capacity to service debt was not a major consideration in lending for development

Rapid external borrowing and debt rescheduling in the 1960s and 1970s

Debt-servicing difficulties were already visible in the 1960s...

Evidence of rapidly increasing indebtedness producing a negative impact on development had already been present during the First United Nations Development Decade. Although developing countries easily achieved the minimum target of an annual rate of growth of gross domestic product (GDP) of 5 per cent by 1970 about half of official foreign-exchange receipts were committed to repayment of debt to official lenders.[1] The decline in official flows during this period, noted in chapter IV, made debt servicing even more difficult and required debt rescheduling. The first Paris Club rescheduling was conducted in 1956 and during the 1960s and early 1970s countries accounting for more than half of outstanding developing-country debt were involved in official refunding or rescheduling negotiations.

...leading to frequent debt rescheduling and calls for debt forgiveness

The continuing decline in official assistance and increasing concentration of multilateral assistance in the poorer developing countries, particularly in sub-Saharan Africa, along with a rapid increase in private sector liquidity due to the expansion of the Eurodollar market in the early 1970s, brought an increase in private market borrowing by a number of fast growing developing countries. Borrowing by non-oil-exporting developing countries in Eurocurrency from private banks jumped from $300 million in 1970 to $4.5 billion in 1973, bringing their share of Eurobanks' loans to over 20 per cent. However, the collapse of the commodity price boom that had preceded the 1973 oil crisis quickly created servicing difficulties and by 1974 the Group of 77 were calling for debt cancellation in addition to rescheduling.[2]

In the 1970s, private lending becomes the principal source of external resources for development

The period after the oil crisis and the breakdown of the Bretton Woods system of fixed exchange rates had brought an increase in outstanding non-oil-exporting developing-country debt from $78.5 billion at the end of 1973 to $180 billion in 1976 with about 60 per cent borrowed from private banks through syndicated loans. The result was another round of debt renegotiations (Wellons, 1977) before a final surge of lending at the end of the decade brought the outstanding international indebtedness of developing countries to over $600 billion at the end of 1981. There were to be 50 official or private negotiations leading to restructuring agreements between 1978 and 1982, the year of the Mexican default.

The International Monetary Fund (IMF) became increasingly involved in official debt negotiations by providing both estimates of the debtor's ability to pay and a stand-by programme to countries in debt renegotiation.[3] This usually entailed an estimate of the debtor's external financing gap and the provision of short-term standby credit to finance it, subject to the introduction of an external adjustment programme to ensure that the gap would be eliminated and to permit the country to return to debt servicing.[4]

As a result of the increase in debt problems in the 1970s, both private creditors and IMF formulated statistical techniques to identify factors that would signal an imminent need for debt restructuring. Among the best indicators of rescheduling identified in a survey of 13 of the studies published between 1971 and 1987 were: the ratio of debt service or debt service due to exports, to GDP, and to reserves; the ratio of amortization to debt; and the ratio of debt to exports, and to GDP (Lee, 1993).

Private and official lenders sought indicators of borrowers' impending debt difficulties

Debt resolution in the 1980s

The numerous defaults by Latin American countries in the 1980s changed the nature of the response to debt renegotiations. Initially, debtors had been encouraged to introduce external adjustment policies in the belief that a return to high growth with external surpluses would provide the resources to repay arrears. These policies produced substantial current-account surpluses but only at the cost of prolonged domestic stagnation and import compression in what came to be called the "lost decade".

Major defaults in the 1980s changed the approach to resolution of debt servicing difficulties

The Brady Plan, introduced at the end of the decade, recognized that the debt could not be repaid through current-account surpluses at acceptable levels of growth and sought to induce creditors to accept write-downs, by offering new credit-enhanced assets in exchange for old debts, and to induce debtors to create domestic conditions that would restore their access to international debt markets, by offering structural adjustment lending. Creditors accepted write-offs, while the issue of Brady bonds allowed Latin American debtors to return to international capital markets, and effectively created a secondary market for debt issued by emerging economies which facilitated this process. The search for yield generated by low interest rates in the United States of America also contributed on the supply side, while decisions to liberalize financial markets and privatize State-owned enterprises contributed on the demand side. As a result, debt reduction was followed by a new phase of international indebtedness.

Brady Plan combined forgiveness and new lending supported by credit enhancement

While private flows were increasing to middle-income countries, there was an increase in the share of official assistance going to the poorest developing countries, in particular in sub-Saharan Africa. The major proportion was in the form of loans that produced an increase in debt stocks from about $6 billion in 1980 to about $11 billion in the late 1990s. Debt-service growth was less pronounced owing to repeated debt restructuring, increasing debt-service relief and an increasing use of grants. Because multilateral financial institutions did not in general provide debt relief, or provide aid in the form of grants, while bilateral official aid increasingly took this form, the relative share of multilateral institutions in debt service and debt stocks continued to rise from about one seventh to almost one third, while the share of debt service increased from about one tenth to one third.

The poorest developing countries remained dependent on official assistance

In addition, as a result of the increasing amounts of official aid, net transfers to these recipients—the poorest developing countries—were positive throughout the 1980s and 1990s, and in most countries constituted as much as ten per cent of national income. Since net official aid flows exceeded debt service, the rise in debt stocks did not cause the difficulties that the rise in private debt stocks caused in middle-income Latin American

Both official and private flows can create excessive debt service

countries, although it did create problems for bilateral donors. Since an increasing share of bilateral aid was being used to meet the rising share of debt service due to multilateral institutions, increasing amounts of bilateral aid or relief was required to prevent the debt overhang from having a negative impact on economic performance. Thus, while middle-income countries faced negative net resources transfers in the 1980s, low-income borrowers were faced with an increase in the share of aid used to pay debt service and thus with a decline in real resources for domestic development.[5] Since solutions similar to the Brady initiative were not possible for these borrowers, a more direct approach was required to reduce debt stocks, which eventually took the form of the HIPC Initiative (see below).

Debt burdens continued to increase through the 1990s

Despite substantial differences in their conditions, both low- and medium-income countries reached the 1990s with expanding levels of official and private debt. Figure V.1 shows the sharp increase in the ratio of total debt to gross national income (GNI) that occurred in the last half of the 1970s and its continuation through the mid-1990s when the ratio stabilized, largely owing to the impact of the Brady and HIPC initiatives.

Another measure of the impact of debt is the use of export revenues to meet debt service, since this precludes their use to finance the imports needed for development purposes and implies either increasing indebtedness or slowing of the development process. The severe pressure placed on developing countries by the debt crisis of the 1980s can be seen in figure V.2, with the substantial improvements in the 1990s largely due to the decline in global interest rates during the decade.

The Monterrey Consensus, noting the negative impact of debt service on development expenditures, recognized that the elimination of excessive debt burdens would make available a major source of additional finance for development and therefore called on debtors and creditors to share responsibility for preventing and resolving unsustainable debt situations.

Figure V.1.
Ratio of total debt to gross national income, 1970-2003

Least developed countries

HIPC countries

All developing countries

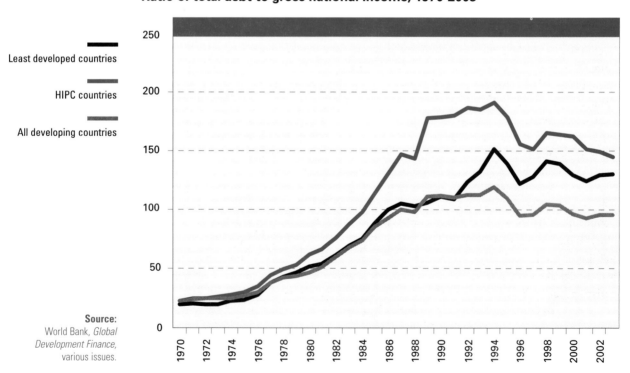

Source:
World Bank, *Global Development Finance,* various issues.

Figure V.2.
Ratio of total debt service to exports, 1970-2003

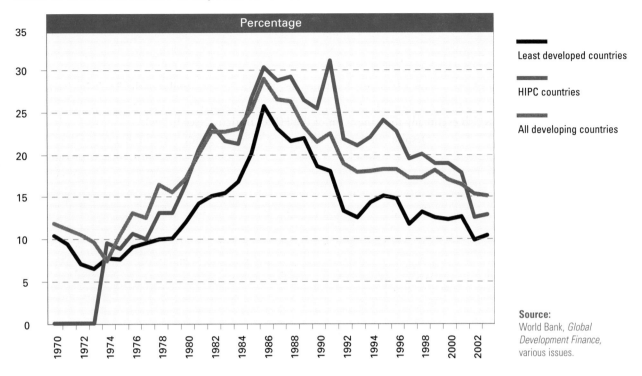

Least developed countries

HIPC countries

All developing countries

Source:
World Bank, *Global
Development Finance*,
various issues.

Debt relief

The Heavily Indebted Poor
Countries (HIPC) Initiative

In contrast to the debt burdens of developing countries in general, those of the poorest developing countries continued to increase through the first half of the 1990s (see figure V.1). Recognition of the negative impact of this debt overhang on investment, growth and development in the poorest, heavily indebted countries led to the creation of the Heavily Indebted Poor Countries (HIPC) Initiative in 1996 to reduce the debt of the poorest countries to a level that would make it sustainable and provide an exit from serial rescheduling at the Paris Club. It was intended that any resources freed from debt service should be additional to existing support and available to support growth and poverty reduction.

The HIPC Initiative sought to alleviate debt burden for poorest developing countries

As the original framework was considered to be insufficient for the attainment of debt sustainability by many poor countries, an "enhanced" HIPC initiative was introduced in 1999 to provide deeper, broader and quicker debt relief. According to the criterion for eligibility in the enhanced HIPC Initiative, a country should face unsustainable debt even after the full use of traditional relief mechanisms.[6] In an extension of the work noted above that had been undertaken in the 1970s by private banks and IMF on predicting the need for debt renegotiation, the HIPC Initiative used similar variables to determine debt sustainability.[7]

Original approach enhanced in 1999 to provide more rapid relief

By mid-April 2005, 27 countries had received debt relief, with 18 countries having reached completion point and 9 countries at decision point.[8] Together with other debt-relief initiatives, HIPC has provided a reduction in debt stocks of the 27 countries of about two thirds. As a proportion of exports, debt service declined from 17 per cent in 1998 to 10

Twenty-seven countries currently receiving relief under the Initiative

per cent in 2003. Savings from lower debt-service payments provide the potential to increase expenditures targeted to poverty reduction. Among complementary measures of particular importance are those of the Paris Club whose members have granted debt relief beyond HIPC terms. Overall, for these 27 countries, reductions have been funded in roughly equal parts by Paris Club and other bilateral and commercial creditors, on the one hand, and multilateral creditors, on the other. The former group contains three HIPC countries which are themselves creditors: the United Republic of Tanzania and Cameroon, which have agreed to provide HIPC relief on all their claims, and Rwanda, which has provided relief to Uganda. Although the Initiative had been scheduled to expire at the end of 2004, it was extended for a further two years to allow those countries that were eligible to benefit from debt relief.

An additional nine countries could qualify ...

The total cost of providing debt relief to all of the 38 countries potentially eligible for assistance under the HIPC Initiative has been estimated at $58 billion in 2004 net present value (NPV) terms. A little more than 50 per cent will come from debt forgiveness by bilateral creditors, while the rest will be provided by multilateral lenders, such as IMF, World Bank and the regional development banks. The share of debt relieved by IMF will be financed from income from the investment of the net proceeds from off-market gold sales in 1999 deposited in the Poverty Reduction and Growth Facility (PRGF)-HIPC Trust Fund, plus contributions from member countries. The World Bank has created the IDA HIPC Trust Fund, financed by contribution, to provide funds to reimburse IDA for HIPC debt relief, and to support debt relief provided by eligible regional and subregional creditors. In addition, Paris Club creditors have provided relief to qualifying countries and most have pledged to provide assistance over that required under the HIPC Initiative.

... but the Initiative is still lacking its full funding

However, the Initiative is still not fully funded. IDA has a financing gap of about $12.3 billion of which about $1.7 billion will materialize during the IDA-14 period. Ensuring participation from non-Paris Club bilateral and private creditors has been particularly difficult. Of the 51 non-Paris Club countries participating in the HIPC programme, 28 have committed to deliver some or all of their pledged amounts. Securing the participation of non-Paris Club official bilateral (and private) creditors has been a challenge since the creation of the Initiative and recently there have been setbacks. The Libyan Arab Jamahiriya, has withdrawn its commitment to participate, citing its failure to obtain ratification of the commitment from appropriate authorities. Other creditors complained about obstacles complicating delivery of debt relief, including Algeria, where the majority of debt is in kind, thereby making the valuation of repayment obligations problematic. The costs associated with the Sudan, Somalia and Liberia will need to be met by the IMF HIPC Trust Fund when these countries are ready to benefit from HIPC relief, at a total increased cost of $2.1 billion. Within IMF, low interest rates over the period from 2000 have opened a potential gap in the resources available from the Special Disbursement Account (SDA) to meet IMF costs for HIPC relief.

Paris Club plays a crucial role in the success of HIPC

Paris Club negotiations require a country to seek comparability of treatment from other creditors. However, most commercial creditors have not provided their share of traditional and HIPC debt relief. In the case of at least nine HIPCs, commercial creditors and other bilateral creditors have refused to match Paris Club decisions and have instead pursued full recovery via litigation. In a survey of HIPC countries conducted by IMF in August 2003, nine countries responded that they were facing litigation initiated by commercial creditors and two non-Paris club creditors. Non-delivery of debt relief and resources lost in litigation can substantially affect the debt outlook of HIPCs. Moreover, pending and ongoing litigation can seriously jeopardize the relationship of HIPCs with the international financial community and their access to finance in the future.

It is now generally recognized that most of the debt reduction that was achieved in the HIPC countries took the form of writing off bilateral debts already in arrears, thus freeing up a smaller amount of real resources for poverty reduction spending than had been originally foreseen. Table V.1 shows the nominal debt-service relief for countries that have reached completion point and the arrears at decision point. Nearly 22 per cent of the debt relief classified as aid flows took the form of a write-off of arrears.

Although there are many countries where debt-service ratios and debt management practices have improved, there are others where these debt ratios have deteriorated. Figure V.3 traces debt service before countries had achieved decision point and debt service in 2004 for those of them that had reached completion point. Countries located above the 45-degree line had an increase in debt service and those below had a decrease. Countries located below the -25 per cent and -50 per cent trajectories experienced reduction in debt service of more than 25 and 50 per cent, respectively. Debt service for three of the completion point countries, Mali, Mozambique and Bolivia, was higher than it had been before decision point. If the interest burden of the domestic treasury bills issued to sterilize the impact of aid flows on domestic liquidity had been taken into account, Uganda would have

Reducing debt-service burdens does not necessarily free resources for poverty reduction programmes

Table V.1.

Debt relief and reduction in arrears for selected HIPC completion point countries

	Enhanced HIPC debt relief		Arrears (principal and interests on long-term debt to official creditors)			
	Completion point	Nominal debt service relief[a]	Year before decision point[a]	Year before completion point or last available (2003)[a]	Year after completion point or last available (2003)[a]	Change since decision point (percentage)
Benin	Mar-03	460	77	20	0	-100
Bolivia	Jun-01	2 060	21	21	0	-100
Burkina Faso	Apr-02	930	39	42	41	4
Ethiopia	Apr-04	3 275	668	593	b	b
Ghana	Jul-04	3 500	13	33	b	b
Guyana	Dec-03	1 353	129	147	122	-6
Madagascar	Oct-04	1 900	725	699	b	b
Mali	Mar-03	895	589	34	115	-80
Mauritania	Jun-02	1 100	535	349	333	-38
Mozambique	Sep-01	4 300	375	898	431	15
Nicaragua	Jan-04	4 500	1 759	1 014	b	b
Niger	Apr-04	1 190	104	60	b	b
Senegal	Apr-04	850	5	17	b	b
Uganda	May-00	1 950	147	147	241	64
United Republic of Tanzania	Nov-01	3 000	1 748	888	1 050	-40
Total		31 263	6 934	4 961		
			22%	16%		

Source: International Monetary Fund and International Development Association (2005b).

a   In millions of dollars.

b   Completion point after 2003.

Figure V.3.
Evolution of debt service for countries that had reached completion point

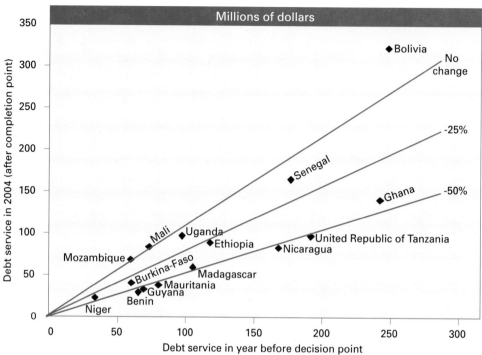

Sources:
DESA, based on data in World
Bank, *Global Development
Finance 2005* (Washington,
D.C., 2005); and IMF, HIPC
Initiative—Statistical Update,
11 April 2005.

also been located above the 45-degree line. In Senegal, the reduction in debt service was less than 25 per cent, while a third of the countries had reductions in the ranging from 25 to 50 per cent and a third had reductions of just above 50 per cent.

In some cases, debt reduction was insufficient because forecasts of future conditions were over-optimistic

The success of the Initiative in providing sustainable debt relief has been hampered by the overly optimistic growth and debt-service projections made in assessing country performance. External shocks (commodity price shocks in particular) have not only led to the inability of some countries to meet those projections but also added additional difficulties. In the case of Uganda, the debt-to-exports ratio was 50 per cent higher in June 2003 than before relief had been obtained under the HIPC Initiative. Furthermore, although the Poverty Reduction Strategy Papers (PRSPs) that accompany the HIPC Initiative have been successful in increasing social spending, for some countries the commitments on social spending have exceeded the savings on debt service, leading to accumulation of additional indebtedness. On the other hand, since such programmes are not currently embedded in the country's overall development strategy, the higher priority given to their application has led to neglect of other national priorities. In addition, in many cases, the relief provided has been too slow, especially in the interim period between decision and completion points. As a result of all of these factors, there is an emerging consensus that, despite the Initiative, many poor developing countries may continue to suffer from a debt overhang.

Further, since the introduction of the original HIPC scheme in 1996, there has been a sharp decline in total net official development assistance (ODA) compared with previous trends, and levels have not recovered despite a rise in bilateral aid flows after 2001. Indeed, bilateral ODA flows to HIPCs, after deduction of debt forgiveness, have been stagnant since 1997, and food aid and emergency aid have increased at the expense of project-related grants, which have the largest potential impact for stimulating long-term growth (see chap. IV).

Additional HIPC debt-relief proposals

The deficiencies identified in the HIPC Initiative have spawned a wide range of proposals for augmented debt relief. In line with its objective to front-load the aid resources needed to finance the Millennium Development Goals (see chap. IV), the United Kingdom of Great Britain and Northern Ireland has proposed 100 per cent reduction of debt service for loans from international financial institutions contracted before 2004; such debt-service reductions would apply for the period 2005-2015 in post-completion point HIPC countries and non-HIPC IDA-only countries with transparent and solid public expenditure management as supported by a Poverty Reduction Support Credit with the World Bank. According to this proposal, donors would contribute in line with their global share of IDA. The cost for IMF would be covered by use of IMF gold reserves. Canada has made a similar proposal, but with bilateral donors financing the debt relief. The United States of America has made an alternative proposal for full relief for HIPC countries' outstanding debt to IMF, IDA and the African Development Bank African Development Fund with funding for IMF debt forgiveness coming from the reserve account of the PRGF-HIPC Trust Fund and the Special Disbursement Account. IDA and African Development Fund debt would be cancelled without replenishment and funded by reducing the IDA and African Development Fund allocations for each beneficiary country.

Proposals are under consideration for further debt relief for the poorest countries

Other proposals would enhance existing relief mechanisms. France would reinforce the HIPC approach by providing liquidity grants, funded by additional bilateral IDA and African Development Fund contributions, for countries facing debt-service problems owing to external factors. Japan has proposed lowering the debt-to-export threshold from 150 to 120 per cent (including private and bilateral debt) for pre-completion point HIPC countries, while post-completion point countries would be granted additional relief if they had a high debt overhang after HIPC debt cancellation.

Concerns have been expressed about full cancellation of multilateral claims

Recently, Norway has proposed a Millennium Development Goal debt sustainability mechanism[9] based on principles drawn from the existing proposals. The approach stresses that any new initiatives must confirm and fully finance earlier commitments and cover all present and future HIPC costs to IDA and regional and subregional creditors as well as preserve the ability of international financial institutions to provide high levels of concessional loans in future. Such initiatives should ensure equitable treatment and base multilateral debt relief beyond HIPC on debt sustainability analyses as proposed in IDA-14. It also notes that multilateral debt-service reduction seems preferable to debt stock reduction.

Norway has proposed a compromise approach

In early June 2005, G-8 Finance Ministers agreed on a proposal for additional debt reduction under HIPC to be submitted for approval by Heads of State and Government at the G-8 Summit in July and by the shareholders of the participating lending institutions at their respective annual meetings in September. Donors agreed to provide additional development resources to provide full debt relief on outstanding obligations to IMF, the World Bank and the African Development Bank, and to IDA and the African Development Fund for HIPC countries that have reached the completion point and to extend similar relief to qualifying countries when they reach the completion point. Donors also agreed to a formula to ensure meeting the full costs of the measures so that they would not reduce the resources available to the lending institutions for support of other developing countries and to ensure the long-term financial viability of international financial institutions. The agreement did not make proposals for dealing with low and middle-income countries that face similar debt burdens but are not eligible for the HIPC process.

G-8 Finance Ministers adopt a compromise proposal on full debt relief for some HIPC countries in June 2005

New measures for official debt relief for middle-income countries (Evian approach)

Middle-income
countries also face
debt-servicing
difficulties

In October 2003, the G-7 finance ministers agreed to adopt a new initiative, termed the "Evian approach", providing more flexible debt restructuring through the Paris Club for non-HIPC and middle-income countries. The novelty of the approach was the introduction of a debt sustainability framework to provide an orderly, timely and predictable debt workout so as to reduce the occurrence and severity of financial crises. The negotiations are thus carried out on the basis of long-term debt sustainability analysis provided by IMF with specific attention being paid to evolution of debt ratios over time and the debtor's economic potential. The decision on sustainability rests ultimately with the creditors.

Paris Club is offering a
new approach...

It is expected that the analysis will distinguish between liquidity problems and medium- and long-term debt problems. The former will be dealt with under existing arrangements with reductions in debt payments tailored to the debtors' financing requirements. When debtors have medium- and long-term problems that create questions of debt sustainability, a more comprehensive, country-specific treatment that encompasses coordination with private creditors and puts particular emphasis on comparability of treatment with private creditors will be applied. The treatment thus combines flow treatment and debt stock re-profiling or debt stock reduction. It is expected that the treatment will allow exit from the Paris Club and that comparability will be applied by private creditors. Where necessary, the cut-off date, which for many countries may be traced back to the early 1980s, will be moved forward to determine the debts eligible for restructuring. The approach retains the traditional links to IMF conditionality.

...involving a
comprehensive three-
stage process

The comprehensive treatment of debt will consist of a three-stage negotiation procedure. In the first stage, a flow rescheduling will be provided under a Fund arrangement that could range from one to three years determined by the past performance of the debtor. The second stage will provide exit treatment, with exact terms and approach dependent upon the results of the debt sustainability analysis of the Fund. In the final stage, exit treatment could be provided in a phased manner over the span of a second Fund programme. The debtors progress and record of payment to the Paris Club would determine the final outcomes of these negotiations.

There are still some technical challenges that need to be worked out so as to make the approach fully operational, such as that posed by the definition of sustainability, in regard to which a transparent framework is required to allow applicant countries to make their own assessments of sustainable debt levels as a basis for negotiation (see the discussion on debt sustainability below). As the Paris Club emphasizes a case-by-case approach to debt restructuring, lack of sufficient transparency in this process could lead to debt-relief outcomes being guided by political considerations. A framework is also needed to enable creditors to distinguish liquidity problems from insolvency. A clear criterion is also needed to determine the new cut-off dates. Finally, clear, transparent principles by which to determine comparability of treatment with private creditors need to be agreed.

Experience with the
new Evian approach is
limited...

The experience with the Evian approach is still limited. Kenya, which applied to the Paris Club for financing for a PRGF programme with IMF, was the first country treated. Assessed as experiencing a liquidity problem, Kenya was therefore granted flow rescheduling under Houston terms.

...but Iraq has received
relief under its terms

Iraq was the first country to receive comprehensive treatment under the Evian approach. Iraq's emergence from the conflict that had followed an economic blockade resulted in high demand for investment in critical social areas and an unsustainable debt

Figure V.4.
Composition of Iraq's debt[a]

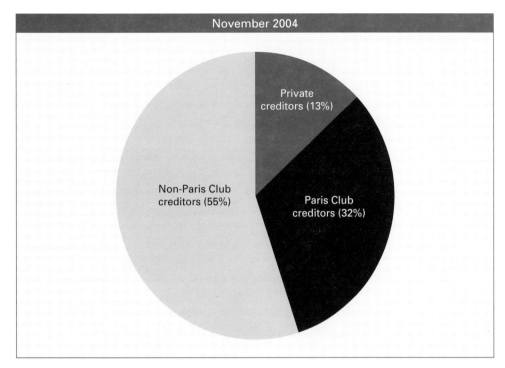

November 2004

Private creditors (13%)

Non-Paris Club creditors (55%)

Paris Club creditors (32%)

Source:
Paris Club presentation at the
UN Multi-stakeholder Meeting.

a   Excluding reparations but
    not including late interest.

burden. This produced an agreement with IMF for Emergency Post-Conflict Assistance to Iraq in September 2004 and Paris Club relief in November 2004 on an estimated indebtedness of $120.2 billion, conditional on a promise by Iraq's then interim Government to seek comparable treatment from other creditors, who accounted for more than two thirds of the outstanding debt (see figure V.4).

The negotiations were based on a debt sustainability analysis that had considered Iraq's particular situation regarding reconstruction needs and combined short-term and medium-term needs. Based on assumptions about oil production and exports associated with discounted oil prices, the debt sustainability analysis concluded that an 80 per cent debt stock reduction would be required to produce sustainability. This implied that Iraq would have, in 2015, debt ratios in line with commonly accepted international standards: external debt at 86 per cent of GDP; external debt at 162 per cent of exports; and debt service at 36 per cent of exports.

This would reduce the total debt stock due to the Paris Club from US$ 38.9 billion to US$ 7.8 billion. If there is comparable treatment by non-Paris Club creditors, the ratio of total debt to GDP would fall from 500 per cent in 2004 to 80 per cent in 2008 and the ratio of total debt to exports would fall from 700 per cent in 2004 to 150 per cent in 2008. The treatment is tied to the conditionality and performance criteria included in the Fund's programme.

Debt sustainability

Debt sustainability analysis for low-income countries

Measuring debt sustainability is a crucial component of decisions on debt relief

Identifying sustainable levels of debt and debt service is crucial in determining when external finance supports or hinders domestic resource mobilization. During the 1980s and 1990s, despite access to low-cost financing, many low-income countries accumulated high levels of debt that imposed a heavy burden on their economies, a problem whose resolution ultimately required costly debt relief. The fact that many "graduated" HIPCs are experiencing rising debt burdens, and that debt ratios in some other low-income countries are at elevated levels, suggests a need for better understanding of sustainable debt levels. A new approach is particularly important in assessing the appropriate financing of the sizeable social expenditures that will be required to achieve the Millennium Development Goals. Further, as noted in chapter IV, one of the major changes introduced in IDA-14 is the use of debt sustainability analysis to determine eligibility for access to grants.[10] The Evian approach, discussed in the previous section, is also centred on debt sustainability analysis.

Debt sustainability in the HIPC Initiative was based on historical experience

As noted above, debt sustainability under the HIPC programme had been based on threshold values of standard debt indicators calculated on historical experience, with an ad hoc adjustment in the enhanced Initiative designed to provide a cushion for external shocks. The new approach[11] evolved an analytical country-specific framework grounded in indicative policy-dependent thresholds and a forward-looking analysis of debt dynamics. The basic novelty was to quantify debt sustainability thresholds on the basis of the quality of policies and institutions, reflecting the idea that countries with stronger policies and institutions could support a higher level of debt on a sustainable basis. In contrast with the HIPC approach, which deals with existing debt overhang, the new approach is intended to provide guidance on new borrowing.

A new, forward-looking approach is currently being studied ...

The approach proposed threshold values for traditional debt ratios based on the World Bank Country Policy and Institutional Assessments (CPIAs) that could be used to classify countries in "poor", "medium" and "strong" policy performance categories. In assessing policy, governance was given a higher relative weight. As an example, a country classified as a strong policy performer, with a value of the CPIA index above 3.9, would be regarded as having a sustainable debt burden if its ratio of NPV of debt to GDP was below 60, its ratio of NPV of debt to exports below 300, its ratio of NPV of debt to revenue (excluding grants) below 350, its ratio of debt service to exports below 35, and its ratio of debt service to revenue (excluding grants) below 40 (see table V.2, entries for sub-item entitled "Strong policy" under first subheading entitled "Original proposal").

... based on a number of different measures of debt sustainability

In response to a request for lower threshold ratios, particularly for strong performers, in March 2005, IMF and IDA set out revisions based on a series of options (see also table V.2). Option 1 maintains the original threshold for NPV of debt to exports at 100 per cent for a weak policy performer, but lowers the ratio to 150 per cent for medium performers and to 200 per cent for strong performers. This option would reduce the new lending permitted to strong and medium performers and require an increase in grant resources for the latter to substitute for their lower share of loans in normal assistance flows. Option 2 is even more conservative, setting the thresholds for the ratio of NPV of debt to exports at 50/100/150 per cent, respectively, for weak/medium/strong. This option would need additional debt relief beyond the HIPC Initiative, as both weak and medium-risk countries would be graduated from the HIPC Initiative with higher debt ratios than these country-specific

Table V.2.
Debt-burden thresholds under alternative options[a]

Percentage					
	NPV of debt as share of			Debt service as share of	
	Exports	GDP	Revenue[b]	Exports	Revenue[b]
Original proposal					
Weak policy (CPIA $\leq$ 3)	100	30	200	15	20
Medium policy (3 < CPIA < 3.9)	200	45	275	25	30
Strong policy (CPIA $\geq$ 3.9)	300	60	350	35	40
Option 1: Narrower band with same lower bound[c]					
Weak policy (CPIA $\leq$ 3.25)	100	30	200	15	25
Medium policy (3.25 < CPIA < 3.75)	150	40	250	20	30
Strong policy (CPIA $\geq$ 3.75)	200	50	300	25	35
Option 2: Narrower band with upper bound equivalent to HIPC Initiative threshold[d]					
Weak policy (CPIA $\leq$ 3.25)	50	20	150	10	20
Medium policy (3.25 < CPIA < 3.75)	100	30	200	15	25
Strong policy (CPIA $\geq$ 3.75)	150	40	250	20	30
Option 3: Asymmetric threshold adjustment					
Weak policy (CPIA $\leq$ 3.25)	100	30	200	15	25
Medium policy (3.25 < CPIA < 3.75)	150	40	250	20	30
Strong policy (CPIA $\geq$ 3.75)	150	40	250	20	30

Source: International Monetary Fund and International Development Association (2005).

a   All ratios are rounded, in line with the original presentation.

b   Defined exclusive of grants.

c   Implying a probability of distress of about 18-22 per cent.

d   Implying a probability of distress of about 16-19 per cent.

thresholds. Option 3 proposes a combination of options 1 and 2 by keeping the lower bound of the original threshold range for weak performing countries, while applying the enhanced HIPC threshold to others. The Fund staff has expressed a preference for option 1.

The new approach also proposes the use of contemporaneous values for debt burden denominators to avoid the criticism directed at the backward-looking three-year averages used under the original HIPC framework. Another departure is the choice of discount rates for calculation of NPVs in the African Development Fund. Instead of six-month averages of the currency-specific reference long-term commercial interest rates, the new framework relies on aggregate debt-service projections in United States dollars using the corresponding United States dollar discount rate to derive NPVs.

Since the new approach is based on the view that good policy environments enhance the ability to sustain debt and inasmuch as these policy assessments are based on the summary CPIA indicator that includes subjective evaluations of the policy and institutional environment, the approach is not wholly transparent. The World Bank has indicated that it will publish the CPIA indicators. A further improvement would be greater transparency in particular with respect to the information that enters as inputs into the calculation of these indicators. It might be more appropriate if the Bank had discussions on the appropriate inputs and findings with the country concerned.

The new approach is based on the idea that domestic policies influence sustainability

As noted above, the new approach is designed to serve as a guide to lending and policy advice within IDA and for other donors. This creates the possibility that both multilateral and bilateral creditors will base their lending decisions on the same CPIA-based indicator and thus reinforce the already existing tendency to herding.

An assessment of debt sustainability analyses

All debt sustainability analyses rely on identifying critical threshold values of debt ratios ...

As we have seen, the key determinants of this and similar debt sustainability analyses are the existing stock of debt, the development of fiscal and external repayment capacity that is closely linked to economic growth, and the availability of new external financing, both concessional and non-concessional. The accepted methodology is to identify "critical" threshold levels for the ratio indicators, most of which were already identified in the earlier studies mentioned above. In the HIPC process, these threshold levels had been arrived at using historical averages of debt indicators prevailing when the countries experienced debt crises. Later analysis established critical values for debt indicators that caused sharp increases in the incidence of default or market-based indicators of risk (such as the premium over benchmark interest rates on debt securities traded in the secondary market). In recent years, the World Bank and IMF have moved away from the latter approach owing to the wide dispersion of the levels of these indicators in countries experiencing debt crises. While IMF continues to monitor these traditional debt sustainability indicators, the multilateral institutions have recognized the limitations of the indicator approach and the necessity of formulating an alternative approach (IMF, 2003f).

... and define sustainability as the ability to continue to service debt without large changes in income and expenditure ...

However, in line with the approach to the work in the 1970s taken by private sector lenders and the Fund in their attempt to forecast the probability of rescheduling,[12] debt *sustainability* is still defined "as a situation in which a borrower is expected to be able to continue servicing its debts without an unrealistically large future correction to the balance of income and expenditure".[13] This calculation of *debt dynamics* concentrates on the evolution of the values of the various indicators under alternative assumptions about the behaviour of key internal and external variables and the probabilities of their occurrence.[14] These calculations have been improved by a focus on the components of both historical and projected debt dynamics that attempt to identify whether the stability of debt ratios arises from the behaviour of interest rates, growth rates, inflation or real exchange-rate changes.

... despite elaboration and refinement in their calculation

The Fund has also made efforts to further elaborate the variables affecting solvency in both the external and public sectors by "unpacking" the endogenous debt dynamics. Much of this research, spurred by emerging market currency crises in the 1990s, attempted to identify significant variables that predict debt crises, such as shares of short-term debt, reserve levels, public sector contingent liabilities, appropriate exchange-rate regimes, market responses such as credit ratings and spreads, and the degree of serial and cross-correlation of major variables during crises. It has also led to increasing scrutiny of existing practice. For example, the use of NPV as the measure of outstanding debt has been questioned owing to lack of a clear criterion for the choice of discount rates that are based on fluctuating interest rates of Organization for Economic Cooperation and Development (OECD) countries. This has led to suggestions that a fixed discount rate would be more appropriate.

Further, recent IMF debt sustainability analyses have included "stress testing" where debt dynamics are evaluated under an increasingly wide variety of conditions. These tests include: (a) *baseline projections* of external debt/exports and public debt/revenue with macro assumptions at central forecasts; (b) *sensitivity tests* using both two-standard-deviation shocks and historical averages; and (c) an *assessment of the external risks* surrounding the scenario and the particular vulnerability of the country in question.

Given the difficulties in forecasting both the movements of macroeconomic variables and the vulnerability of a given country to cross-correlations between variables in the case of an external shock, the major challenge has been to establish, given simple probabilities, what shocks and scenarios can be considered "reasonable". This has been made more arduous by the fact that recent capital-account crises produced values of debt indicators that exceeded the upper bounds of the stress-test ranges (IMF, 2003f).

An associated difficulty in this respect is how to distinguish a *liquidity* crisis from *insolvency* or, in terms of the objectives of the 1970s forecasting models, how to determine when a restructuring is appropriate, since only insolvency would require debt relief.[15] Based on these earlier models, the evolving approach still regards the inability of a debtor to access finance as the cause of the inability to service debt, without determining whether this is due to a shortage of liquidity or insolvency.[16] However, such a distinction has serious implications for debt restructuring. The debt sustainability analysis results are based on probabilities of certain outcomes, one of them being that of the country's access to finance in the future which is in itself volatile and subject to error components in predictions. Thus, given the difficulties of forecasting the time-path of crucial variables, there are obstacles in making a country-by-country distinction between chronic and transitory resource gaps, and determining the appropriate perspective (short-, medium- or long-term) to apply in a situation of imminent default.[17] As a result, IMF debt sustainability analyses cannot determine the level of debt that may be considered sustainable for individual countries, and thus the point at which a liquidity problem becomes a solvency problem. A liquidity crisis could turn into insolvency if it is not rapidly contained, through decisive action either by domestic authorities or by multilateral lenders.[18]

This lacuna has increased significance, since the proposed Evian approach explicitly relies on debt sustainability analysis to assess the amount of debt relief. The negotiations to return countries to sustainable debt paths will be complicated by the fact that the value of an indicative ratio that is good for one country may be a signal of distress for another, or the same value of a ratio may have a different significance at different points of the economic cycle. The solvency-liquidity distinction forms an important basis for considering debt stock treatments rather than debt flow treatments (for example, a deferral or rescheduling of payments). The lack of a strong and consistent analytical tool to separate liquidity from solvency crises remains a fundamental gap in the evaluation of debt sustainability. In addition, an analysis of the link between debt restructuring and debt sustainability based on past debt negotiations is required. Since the interest rates charged on non-ODA debt in the bilateral agreements after a Paris Club negotiation are often higher and at times vary from those stipulated in the original contract, developing countries frequently complain that they more than repay their obligations in terms of the original contract.

Furthermore, the distinction between liquidity and solvency has other policy implications. The policy advice for an insolvent debtor should generally be for it to pursue a debt-reducing strategy, but advice to an illiquid debtor should be for it to borrow so as to make timely interest payments and prevent the loss of creditworthiness that would lead to insolvency. While the new approach has succeeded in giving a broader range to debt dynamics by taking into account variables that have emerged from a study of recent crises, the analysis still falls short of providing an analytical base for defining threshold levels at which debt is to be considered sustainable.

Forward-looking measures depend on the reliability of forecasting critical variables ...

... and have difficulty distinguishing between liquidity and insolvency crises

The new approach still has difficulty determining a general approach to sustainability

Distinguising between illiquidity and insolvency is important in framing debt-relief policy

The recent advent of financial crises driven by the build-up of debt underscores the need for analysis and the development of debt sustainability frameworks that are flexible enough to take into account differences across regions and countries. IMF generally regards stable debt ratios as sustainable and rising debt ratios as problematic. Goldstein (2003) points to the difficulties of associating stable debt ratios with debt sustainability. For a middle-income country, the ability to pay depends on the degree of trade openness. Threshold levels for debt-to-export ratios cannot be uniformly applied to all countries. In all of the recent work on debt sustainability, GDP is used as a denominator for threshold levels to reflect the size of the economy. However, the relation between national output and debt sustainability will depend on the ability of the country to divert resources from the non-tradable sector to the tradable sector so as to generate foreign exchange.

A precise measure of public debt is also important in measuring sustainability

Especially since the Asian financial crisis, an additional problem has been the definition of "public debt".[19] Earlier, this was seen as debt contracted by the sovereign, but it now includes implicit liabilities of the public sector as well. This inclusion was largely driven by the lessons learned form the Asian crisis where large contingent liabilities due to exorbitant bank recapitalization costs in many cases dwarfed the contractual obligations of the sovereign to its external debtors.[20] Recent research on the strong links between debt and banking crises and the lack of a comprehensive bankruptcy framework in many emerging markets has led to a recognition of the need to consider contingent sovereign obligations under the umbrella of public debt.

In recent years, developing countries have been advised to develop domestic markets for bonds denominated in local currency. This measure is seen as a means not only to deepen domestic financial markets but also to shield debtors from external exchange-rate and interest rate shocks (see chap. I). As a result, domestic debt levels have risen dramatically since the Asian crisis, especially in East Asia. The emergence of liquid domestic debt markets and the increasing domestic debt burdens of sovereign borrowers have added a new dimension to debt sustainability, reflected in the explicit consideration of domestic debt in recent debt sustainability analyses conducted by IMF. There is concern that the rise of domestic indebtedness may lead to a new emerging market debt crisis in the medium term.[21]

Emphasis on access to external finance in measuring sustainability may have unintended consequences

Paradoxically, since access to finance appears as an important element of the Fund's approach, the concentration on *debt dynamics* may unintentionally lead to more borrowing. It inadvertently encourages the practice of engaging in new borrowing to meet claims of existing creditors and thus creates the risk of a country's being caught in an endless spiral of increased borrowing to service rising debt levels. Moreover, capital flows are volatile and thus making judgements on a sustainable level of debt based on the access to external financial flows is bound to produce errors.

A better approach to sustainability would place development objectives at the centre of the analysis

As noted, both the approach to prediction of rescheduling in the 1970s and the recent efforts at redefining debt sustainability deal with the ability to meet debt service, with an increasing focus on the currency and term structure of the debt. However, this does not in effect deal with the sustainability of debt in terms of the ability of the country to generate the resources necessary to meet debt service without sacrificing its domestic development. A truly viable alternative approach to the problem would place development objectives at the centre of sustainability.[22] The essence of such an approach was reflected in the call by the Secretary-General (document A/59/2005) for debt sustainability to be defined as the level of debt that allowed a country to achieve the Millennium Development Goals and still service its obligations. In addition to debt dynamics, this would mean that work on debt sustainability should take into account the sources of the capacity to service debt. Thus, more work is needed on defining debt sustainability in terms of:

- The ability to pay.

- The capacity to repay debt taking domestic priorities of human development and poverty reduction into account.

- A level of debt that is growth enhancing, not one that hinders growth.

- Criteria that take the cyclicality of capital flows into account.

Debt resolution and debt relief involving private creditors

New approaches and initiatives

The 1990s saw a series of increasingly large financial crises that required access by members to balance-of-payments support well beyond their normal quota drawings on Fund resources. On the one hand, this raised questions concerning the adequacy of existing credit lines to manage crises that had their origin in the capital account rather than the current account, and the level of Fund resources necessary to preserve global financial stability (see chap. VI). On the other hand, it gave credence to arguments that Fund support of capital-account crises had created a risk of moral hazard among private creditors who had come to depend on large Fund support programmes to protect them from loss.

Frequent debt crises in the 1990s led to a search for a new approach to debt relief …

For this reason, critics as diverse as the International Financial Institutions Advisory Commission (2000) and the United Nations Conference on Trade and Development (2001a) argued in favour of strict limits on access to IMF resources. In order to counter the belief that IMF crisis support was simply being used to "bail out" private creditors, leaving the costs of adjustment to domestic residents, many argued in favour of measures to "bail in" the private sector through a new approach to debt crisis and restructuring. This approach reversed normal practice, in which an IMF agreement was considered a precondition for opening negotiations for restructuring in the case of default by requiring the involvement of the private sector in sharing the burden of restructuring in order for it to receive IMF support. However, the experience of debt restructuring following financial crises also led to a number of proposals to provide a more orderly resolution of financial crises caused by excessive external indebtedness.

… and brought the appropriate role of IMF in debt crises under discussion

In 2001, IMF reformulated proposals made since the 1970s[23] for a debt work-out mechanism based on private sector bankruptcy legislation and introduced its own proposal for a sovereign debt restructuring mechanism (SDRM).[24] The proposal sought to provide a legal framework within which to deal with restructuring of debt in an orderly manner. It met with opposition from private and Paris Club creditors, as well as from some developing countries that preferred voluntary arrangements. The private sector was concerned about the problem of moral hazard and the Paris Club creditors resisted the proposal to place the ad hoc arrangements of the Paris Club within a new legal structure. IMF was also not regarded by some as a neutral arbitrator because of the presence of a conflict of interest arising from the role of IMF as arbitrator and its preferred creditor status.[25] Some emerging market economies feared that the initiation of the procedure would result in an increase in their borrowing costs or even in a loss of access to international capital markets. In addition, the proposed new insolvency procedure required an amendment to the IMF Articles of Agreement which would then have to feed into national legislations. In the absence of strong support for the measure, attention shifted to the broader use of col-

In 2001, IMF formally proposed a statutory debt workout mechanism

lective action clauses (CACs) in bond issues, as well as to the drafting of a voluntary framework in the form of a code of conduct for debt resolution that could be agreed on by debtors and creditors.

Collective action
clauses in bonded debt
indentures have also
been introduced

The increasing use of bonded debt to finance developing countries has been accompanied by an increase in the number of individual creditors, increasing the difficulty in reaching an agreement on resolution in the case of default. CACs provide a solution to this dilemma of collective action and representation by enabling a qualified majority of bondholders to make decisions that become binding on all bondholders and specify voting rules.[26] This allows Governments facing difficulty in servicing their bonded debt to declare a standstill without exposing themselves to disruptive legal actions. While a CAC, in principle, does not preclude legal action taken against the debtor by the courts, the inclusion of this provision generally prevents a small group of investors or individual investors from taking disruptive legal action, as has been seen in the recent debt workouts for Ecuador and Argentina.

During the latter part of 2003 and early 2004, some emerging market borrowers, representing more than 75 per cent of the total value of bonds issued in that period, have taken steps to include such clauses in their international sovereign bonds issued under New York law. While Italy had adopted CACs in 2003, as of 2004, German and Swiss legislation still did not include CACs.

It is difficult to
introduce these
clauses into
existing bonds ...

Inclusion of a CAC does not necessarily imply that it will be invoked at the time of a debt restructuring. For example, Pakistan in 1999 restructured its international bonds without invoking the CACs included in these bonds, preferring an offer for a voluntary bond exchange. By contrast, Ukraine made use of the CACs included in four of its outstanding international bonds in April 2000, thereby obtaining the agreement of 95 per cent of its bondholders even though the holders of bonds were widely spread out. Debt restructuring can also take place using mechanisms different from CACs. In mid-1999, Ecuador carried out a restructuring of its bond debt by inviting eight of the larger institutional holders of its bonds to join a consultative group, with the aim of providing a formal communications mechanism.

Concerns that the inclusion of CACs in bond issues might lead to an increase in the cost of borrowing for the issuer do not appear to be warranted in light of the experiences of Mexico, Brazil, South Africa, Venezuela and Belize. Moreover, a recent study comparing the yield on bonds issued in the Euromarket with CACs, and bonds issued in the United States market and Euromarket without CACs, shows that the inclusion of CACs in bond issues in the Euromarket did not impact secondary market yields as of early 2003 (Gugiatti and Richards, 2003).[27]

... so the proposal will
be fully effective only
when all outstanding
bonds are retired

One difficulty with CACs as a substitute for a more formal mechanism is that only newly issued bonds would contain CACs, so that the collective action problems could be resolved only once all outstanding bonds were retired. Conversion plans to effect the retroactive coverage by CACs of bonds issued without CACs are considered problematic (Krueger, 2003). In addition, there are perceived risks in the use of the clause, inasmuch as debtors, in alliance with a majority of the creditors, may be able to discriminate against a minority. Another difficulty is that a debtor may be in a position to manipulate the voting process by putting real or fictitious claims in the hands of the creditors that are under the influence of the sovereign. Experience with aggregation thus far has been limited to countries that have issued bonded debt on a relatively small scale, such as Ecuador, Pakistan, the Republic of Moldova, Ukraine and Uruguay, and it remains to be seen if the problems of aggregation can be resolved for larger sovereign debtors.

The SDRM proposal aimed at a comprehensive framework within which to deal with sovereign debt problems and relied on various statutory instruments to achieve this objective, such as aggregation of claims, targeted stay on litigation, and a dispute resolution forum; and CACs constitute an instrument that is targeted at facilitating the restructuring of bonds. In conclusion, the objective of codes of conduct for private creditors and sovereign debtors is to develop a comprehensive voluntary framework within which to address potential debt-servicing problems while preserving to the maximum extent possible contractual arrangements. In its communiqué of 24 April 2004 issued on the occasion of its spring 2004 meeting, the International Monetary and Financial Committee of the Board of Governors of IMF encouraged sovereign debtors and private creditors to continue their work on a voluntary code of conduct, and looked forward to reviewing further work on issues of general relevance to the orderly resolution of financial crises. The finance ministers of the Group of Seven (G-7) have also welcomed efforts at the Group of Twenty (G-20) to develop a code of conduct. The idea is to initiate a voluntary dialogue between debtors and creditors so as to promote corrective policy action to reduce the frequency and severity of a crisis and codes that would lead to an orderly debt workout.

The voluntary code of conduct is perceived by debtors as a framework within which they can formally engage creditors and provide information to them. Creditors, on the other hand, see the code as a framework within which debtors would make stronger commitments to engagement and the provision of information. It is expected that a code of conduct will clarify the roles of the sovereign debtor and creditor, help to avoid disruption in the process of crisis resolution and effect a more balanced distribution of the financial burden.

Recently, a voluntary code of conduct has been proposed ...

The Institute of International Finance has drafted four key pillars: information sharing and transparency; close debtor-creditor dialogue and cooperation; good faith during a restructuring process; and fair treatment. It is expected that an early dialogue between issuers and investors will lead to a quick rehabilitation of debtors and restore market access. A technical group consisting of Brazil, the Republic of Korea and Mexico has been established to work closely with the private sector representatives and work out a draft code for discussions at the G-20. Creditors do not consider the code as more robust than current market practices. The increased emphasis on sharing information between investors and debtors and investor-creditor relations, which is being given support under the code of conduct is asymmetric, with debtors providing more information but creditors doing nothing about improving the flow of information from their side.

... and a draft issued for discussion by the G-20

Whether voluntary efforts, such as those reflected in these principles, can provide a sufficiently strong basis for an effective crisis resolution mechanism has yet to be tested. In the long run, it may have to be combined with internationally sanctioned standstills to be used when needed. It is thus essential that the explorations of debt workout mechanisms, including voluntary codes and international mediation or arbitration mechanisms, continue with full support of all stakeholders. Since it will take time for this to be implemented, a transitional framework may also be needed. Overall, there has been less progress in providing institutional mechanisms for the debt problems facing middle-income countries. The experiences of some of these countries are analysed in the next section.

None of the current proposals have yet been made fully effective

Experiences of alternative debt restructuring mechanisms[28]

Debt restructuring has thus proceeded on an ad hoc basis

In the absence of the implementation of a multilateral framework for debt restructuring like those outlined above, debt crises in the 1990s relied increasingly on voluntary country-by-country negotiations between debtors and creditors. At the same time, resolution moved farther away from the pattern of the Brady Plan. As noted above, the initial response to the Mexican default of 1982 had been voluntary rescheduling and domestic adjustment policies, complemented in the Baker plan by additional IMF and private financing. It was only when the Brady Plan added substantial debt write-downs backed by credit enhancements in the form of collateral for the new Brady bonds that debtors managed to meet their debt service through a return to international credit markets. During the 1990s, the fear that large IMF lending, such as that provided to Mexico in 1994, would create moral hazard led to the view that the market mechanism should be allowed to determine restructuring, as IMF assistance was cut back. This was evident first in the withdrawal of the debt enhancements as part of IMF support in the Russian default.

The Russian Federation provides an example of a restructuring that allowed a rapid return to international markets

Under an IMF facility arrangement, the Russian Federation had implemented a domestic stabilization through control of the money supply that required its fiscal deficit to be financed through market sales of treasury securities (known by the acronyms GKO and OFZ) at interest rates substantially above international levels. This led to a rapid increase in debt service that reached about one third of federal spending in the first quarter of 1998. The major buyers were Russian banks which borrowed dollars through repurchase agreements using the bonds as collateral, earning substantial profits from the large interest rate differential. Given IMF support for a stable exchange rate, the risk of devaluation was considered to be low. Non-residents accounted for about a quarter of the subsequently defaulted debt, financing their purchases with rubles received from repurchase agreements with Russian banks. These investors hedged their currency risks with forward contracts from Russian as well as from Western banks. Falling export revenues due to the collapse of commodity prices after the Asian crisis reduced government revenues and external earnings. Attempts to offset the decline with higher interest rates failed to attract sufficient external inflows to finance government deficits and caused rising debt service that the Government could no longer meet. In August 1998, the Russian Federation suspended payment of debt service and payments on forward contracts. This meant that the collateral behind the repurchase agreements was worthless and banks and foreign investors faced losses of 100 per cent of their investments. The situation was aggravated by the suspension of payment on forwards by Western banks. Russian banks' attempts to repay borrowed dollars increased downward pressure on the exchange rate and international reserves, led to the collapse of the currency and brought technical insolvency for the banks.

In March 1999, a novation scheme accepted by over 99 per cent of creditors (by value) offered 10 per cent of par value in cash, 20 per cent in 3- and 6-month debt securities and 70 per cent in 4-to-5-year securities. The proceeds received by non-residents were deposited into special ruble-denominated accounts that were not freely convertible into foreign exchange or cash rubles. Owing to the complexity of the scheme, there is no reliable estimate of the loss incurred by investors. In a strategy that would later be followed by Ecuador, the Russian Federation suspended service on former Soviet Union foreign debt and began accumulating arrears, but stayed current on all its Eurobond issues and other external debt denominated in foreign currencies contracted by the Russian Federation.

A new agreement with IMF in 1999 contained even more stringent conditionality, but it seems that the major purpose of the new loan was to allow the Russian Federation to stay current on its payments to IMF and to reach agreements with other creditors. In August 1999, a rescheduling was agreed with the Paris Club and in August 2000 with the London Club, exchanging obligations of the Bank for Foreign Economic Affairs for Eurobonds issued by the Russian Federation.

A new IMF agreement was part of the restructuring

This multistage process of write-offs and renegotiation, accompanied by a recovery in commodity prices, in particular petroleum, rising fiscal receipts, and external budget surpluses along with growth rates in excess of 5 per cent, led international credit rating agencies to classify Russian sovereign debt as investment grade by the end of 2004.

In Ecuador, debt enhancement was not offered and the support of IMF remained questionable in the early stages of its debt renegotiation process. Following a series of climatic, external earnings and political shocks that had led to a banking crisis in August of 1999, Ecuador missed payment of interest on the Brady bond portion of its $13.6 billion external debt. A month later it announced that it would default only on the Discount Brady bonds, since these bonds had credit-enhanced interest collateral that could be invoked on a 25 per cent vote by holders. When this decision was taken, it activated cross-default clauses in other bonds and made automatic default on the principal of the $6 billion in Brady bonds, as well as the $500 million in Eurobonds.

Restructuring in Ecuador progressed only after an IMF agreement

Unable to agree a support programme with IMF, Ecuador initially attempted a domestic stabilization programme based on dollarization. By April 2000, the Government had been granted a one-year IMF standby loan for about $306 million accompanied by nearly $2 billion in additional multilateral support. In July, about 97 per cent of Brady investors accepted an offer to exchange the defaulted bonds for about $4 billion in new 30-year bonds and about $1 billion in cash to cover accrued interest and amortization. Since the Brady bonds did not contain CACs, any change in terms required the unanimous decision of all the creditors. In order to induce creditors to participate in the restructuring, Ecuador used carefully crafted exit consents that required only a supermajority, plus upfront cash disbursements and principal reinstatement clauses to encourage participation. The haircut of approximately 40 cents on the dollar was marginally worse than the 36 per cent estimated for the Russian default. The restructuring resulted in a reduction of Ecuador's Brady bond and Eurobond stock by 40 per cent and a reduction in service of $1.5 million over the first five years of the exchange. It also opened the way for a Paris Club agreement restructuring 100 per cent of its $887 million official debt.[29]

Ecuador's restructuring provides an example of a successful voluntary restructuring of securities held by a heterogeneous group of bondholders with competing interests in the absence of CACs. However, it is not clear that this market-based approach dependent on the relative bargaining strengths of debtors and creditors has provided long-term debt sustainability, given that Ecuador's current ratios of debt to exports of above 25 per cent and debt to GDP of over 50 per cent place it in the high-risk category according to the new approach to debt sustainability.

Ecuador is an example of a successful voluntary restructuring without a return to sustainability

In contrast to both the Russian Federation and Ecuador, Argentina was not even provided with additional multilateral financial support after its default in 2001. Argentina had already received exceptional access to IMF resources of 800 percent of quota when IMF suspended a review of an existing arrangement, halting disbursement and effectively declaring to financial markets that it no longer considered Argentina's external debt sustainable. The government default declaration less than a month later made rollover of maturing Fund borrowing the equivalent of "lending into arrears",[30] and thus subject to

Argentina provides an example of an alternative voluntary approach in the absence of an institutional workout mechanism "good faith" negotiations with creditors. This meant that Argentina was subject to IMF conditionality on its recovery programme and debt renegotiations without receiving any additional resources to support them. This was a clear application of the new approach of refusing to use Fund resources to bail out external creditors,[31] and to leave restructuring to voluntary market processes.

The decision to suspend current programmes, along with the Fund's position as a preferred creditor, meant that Argentina faced its creditors in very different conditions from those of previous debt renegotiations and thus that debt sustainability required a substantially larger debt reduction. Further, Argentina was denied new support to avoid moral hazard problems but at the same time, under lending-into-arrears principles, was required to provide a settlement with creditors to avoid having to repay maturing programmes. Under these conditions, it was difficult or outright impossible to follow a market solution.

On the grounds that about 50 per cent of the population was below the poverty line as the result of the crisis that it had been undergoing, Argentina argued that it had made sufficient contribution and that the only equitable debt renegotiation was one that allowed a rate of growth that provided for a recovery of the living conditions of the population and offered the assurance that the solution was sustainable on a long-term basis. Rather than view the negotiation as providing the means by which it could borrow what was required to meet post-restructuring debt service, Argentina argued that the solution would have to make it possible to meet debt service without additional borrowing. Thus, the break with the Brady solution of providing additional funding, write-offs and debt enhancement to ensure a return to capital markets was met in Argentina with a refusal to consider the return to international borrowing as a solution to its debt sustainability. After a series of adjustments to unilateral proposals to creditors, Argentina made an exchange offer at the end of 2004 that implied about a 75 per cent haircut which was accepted by over 75 per cent of creditors.

Although it is still unclear if major creditor countries consider this result to have met the good-faith conditions that would allow rollover of existing credits, and although some outstanding creditors have attempted to achieve full consideration through challenges in the courts, the Argentine experience may herald a new post-Brady era in debt renegotiations that highlights the difficulties of the market-based approach and reinforces the need for a new multilateral approach to default resolution.

Without additional IMF support, Argentina faced novel conditions compared with previous debt restructuring experience

What constitutes fair burden-sharing between debtors and creditors?

Argentina highlights and reinforces the need for a new multilateral approach to default resolution

Notes

1   Concessional bilateral credits accounted for about 60 per cent of funds loaned to developing countries, with 6 per cent multilateral credits and a third in direct investment and trade credits in the period. See D'Arista (1979, pp. 57-58).

2   An assessment of the pre- and post-debt rescheduling experience of seven developing countries notes that a majority experienced slower growth, investment and net resources transfers after rescheduling, suggesting the need for more susbstantial relief measures. See United Nations Conference on Trade and Development (1974).

3   See United Nations Conference on Trade and Development (1975), where the tendency for creditors to require an IMF standby arrrangement as a prior condition for renegotiation is noted.

4   United Nations Conference on Trade and Development (1975) notes that the main focus of IMF assessments was on short-run economic problems.

5   See Birdsall, Claessens and Diwan (2004, pp. 59-62). These authors show that the result has been for countries with higher debt stocks to receive higher aid flows, irrespective of the policies they follow, thus limiting the policy selectivity that is supported by official donors.

6   Regarding the eligibility criteria, it has been argued by some authors that eligibility ratios are not based on a comprehensive measure of either poverty or indebtedness, and that as a result some poor and some heavily indebted countries are not HIPC-eligible. The scope of country selection is also regarded by some analysts as too narrow, as the "IDA-only" criterion disqualifies some otherwise debt-strapped non-IDA countries. It has also been asserted that political and cost factors excluded countries that met eligibility criteria (see Gunter, 2001; G-24 Secretariat, 2003; United Nations Conference on Trade and Development, 2004e).

7   These threshold levels were largely based on empirical work undertaken by Underwood (1990) and Cohen (1996). A critique of HIPC using market-based indicators can be found in Cohen (2001).

8   In April 2005, Honduras, Zambia and Rwanda reached completion point.

9   See Ministry of Foreign Affairs, Kingdom of Norway (2005).

10   This reassessment process was initiated in the International Monetary Fund (2002b).

11   In a series of papers by IMF and International Development Association (2004 and 2005).

12   The Fund's analysis of how outstanding stocks of liabilities evolve over time includes projections of the flows of revenue, expenditure and debt servicing, current account and exchange-rate changes. Assessments of fiscal sustainability are an import element of the debt sustainability exercise and include indicators of public debt and deficits and medium-term fiscal projections. The projected debt *dynamics* in turn depends upon macroeconomic and financial market developments. A key variable is the availability of financing.

13   IMF (May 2002b), p. 4.

14   The distinction between an analysis of debt dynamics and a broader view of debt sustainability is elaborated in Schneider (2005b).

15   Debt relief here refers to a write-off of debt leading to a reduction in the stock of debt. Much confusion arises from the fact that the term is commonly used for both debt write-off and debt rescheduling which allows the debtor grace periods before repaying the amount treated in the rescheduling.

16   "Sustainability thus incorporates the concepts of solvency and liquidity, without making a sharp demarcation between them" (International Monetary Fund, 2002b, p. 4).

17   This distinction is examined in detail in Roubini (2001).

18   As has been stressed by Kenen (2001), and explored further using a more theoretical formulation by Haldane and Kruger (2004).

19   See Goldstein (2003) for a discussion within the Brazilian context.

20   See figure 3.1 on "Public debt in emerging market economies" in International Monetary Fund (2003a).

21   See International Monetary Fund (2003a).

22   See Schneider (2005). This issue was consistently addressed in the Multi-stakeholder consultations on sovereign debt for sustained development, held in New York in March 2005 and in Maputo, Mozambique, also in March 2005, and undertaken by the Department of Economic and Social Affairs of the United Nations Secretariat as part of the financing for development process.

23   In 1978, the United Nations Conference on Trade and Development raised the question of debt relief, proposing a mechanism of debt reorganization that would be "carried out within an institutional framework that would ensure the application of the principles of international financial cooperation and protect the interests of debtors and creditors equitably" (see UNCTAD, 1978, annex II, p. 2). A more detailed proposal was made in 1980 to create "a multinational forum agreed upon by the debtor and the creditors" see the annex to section B of Trade and Development Board resolution 222 (XXI) of 27 September 1980 which endorsed a set of features to guide members in future operations relating to the debt problems of interested developing countries. The United Nations Conference on Trade and Development subsequently proposed a mechanism based on the 1978 reform of United States bankruptcy law; see annex to chapter VI of *Trade and Development Report, 1986* (United Nations Conference on Trade and Development, 1986) which contains a proposal based on the analysis provided by a New York law firm. Similar proposals have also been made in the 1998 and 2001 editions of the *Trade and Development Report* (United Nations Conference on Trade and Development, 1998 and 2001a).

24   For a survey of the various prior proposals in this area, see Rogoff and Zettelmeyer (2002) who curiously do not refer to the prior proposals by UNCTAD.

25   A recent proposal seeks to remedy this by using the G-20 to create an independent entity to oversee the mechanism. See Berensmann and Schroeder (2005).

26   The use of CACs in bond issues governed by English, Japanese and Luxembourg law has been an established practice. Historically, such bonds issued under United States, German, Italian or Swiss law did not include such clauses. The largest market for sovereign bonds is in New York; however, bonds issued under New York law have traditionally included only majority enforcement provisions, not majority restructuring provisions.

27   There is as yet no evidence how CACs may perform if a major sovereign defaults on its bonds that include CACs. The Emerging Market Credits Association has largely remained silent on the type of CAC that should be included.

28   For a more complete discussion, see United Nations (2001a), sect. 3.

29   Ecuador's default was not well received by private creditors who objected that Ecuador's Brady Plan had already involved a 45 per cent write-down and was supposed to have provided permanent resolution. In addition, some accused IMF of having precipitated the default in order to test its new approach to "bailing in" private sector creditors. See BradyNet Forum (http://www.bradynet.com/bbs/bradybonds/100090-0.html).

30   Conceived in the late 1980s as a means of resolving the debt crisis, the scope of the Fund's policy concerning lending into sovereign external payments arrears to private creditors required the debtor to pursue appropriate policies and make a good faith effort to reach a collaborative agreement with its creditors. See IMF (2002c).

31   Although some suggested that the exceptional access granted in 2001 allowed foreign creditors to bail out before the crisis (see Cafiero and Llorens, 2002). This is confirmed by the large increase in capital outflows reported in November of 2001 (see Comisión Especial de la Cámera de Diputadas, República Argentina, 2005).

Chapter VI
Systemic issues

The systemic agenda addressed by the Monterrey Consensus of the International Conference on Financing for Development (United Nations, 2002, annex) covers two broad groups of issues. The first relates to the structural features of the international monetary system, and the possible vulnerabilities that they pose for the world economy or for specific groups of countries. The second relates to the institutional design of the current international financial system.

With respect to the first set of issues, the analysis undertaken in the present chapter starts with the major macroeconomic imbalances that characterize the world economy today, which many observers fear may become unsustainable. This issue relates, at least in part, to the design of the international reserve system, particularly to the role of the United States dollar as the major international currency. The following section looks at the evolving structure of private international financial markets and its potential vulnerability to systemic risk. A particular source of concern is the potential interaction between the macroeconomic risks associated with the current global imbalances and the potential vulnerabilities generated by the financial innovations and consolidation that are taking place. A third issue relates to the asymmetries that characterize the international financial system which not only subject developing countries to pro-cyclical private capital flows but also limit their room for manoeuvre in adopting counter-cyclical macroeconomic policies. The major implications of this problem were dealt with in chapter III; this chapter considers its implications for the role of the international financial institutions in crisis prevention and resolution.

The analysis of these problems includes some issues relating to institutional design, such as the role of multilateral surveillance, the possible role of the International Monetary Fund (IMF) in the coordination of macroeconomic policies among major industrialized nations, the surveillance of domestic policies and emergency financing during crises. The last three sections deal with a selected set of additional institutional issues: the role of special drawing rights (SDRs), the only genuinely international reserve currency in the current system; the role of regional reserve funds and other regional monetary arrangements; and the voice and representation of developing countries in decision-making in the international financial system.

The Monterrey Consensus addresses two broad systemic issues

The first comprises the international monetary system's vulnerabilities, one current example of which are the global macroeconomic imbalances

The second is institutional design, including different aspects of the role of the International Monetary Fund

Global macroeconomic imbalances and the international reserve system

The global economy has large and widening imbalances across regions, reflected in a large current-account deficit in the United States of America which is matched by an aggregate of surpluses in a number of other countries, mainly in Asia and Europe, and including a group of oil-exporting countries. These imbalances are continuing to widen and policymakers worldwide are increasingly concerned about their sustainability, about the risks associated with various adjustment processes and, ultimately, about their implications for global financial stability and the growth of the world economy. Even if the imbalances are

Policymakers are increasingly concerned about the sustainability of current-account imbalances

sustainable or if there is a smooth adjustment, questions remain whether such large and skewed imbalances constitute an efficient and equitable allocation of global resources across countries.

The United States
current-account deficit
has risen rapidly
since 2000

The current-account deficits of the United States have been the rule for most of the past three decades, with only a brief period of balance (see figure VI.1), and have risen rapidly since 2000 to a record high of more than $600 billion. As a result, the United States, the world's largest economy, has accumulated net international debts of about $3 trillion, making it the world's largest debtor. These changes in national holdings of international assets are both a counterpart to the current-account imbalances and their mirror image, as reflected in national differences between savings and investment. The external deficit of the United States corresponds to a shortfall of its savings in relation to its investment and surpluses of savings over investment elsewhere, with the United States absorbing at least 80 per cent of the savings that other countries do not invest domestically. The solution to the problem of the global imbalances can therefore be seen either from the trade perspective or from the point of view of rebalancing savings and investment across countries.

Chronic United States
deficits are related to
the use of the dollar as
the major reserve
currency

These chronic large United States imbalances are closely related to the nature of the current international reserve system and international monetary arrangements. A central feature of the international reserve system is the use of the national currency of the United States as the major reserve money and instrument for international payments. Other major currencies, the euro and the yen, play a supplementary and slightly larger role than in the past, with the exchange rates among the three major currencies being subject to supply and demand, or "floating".

Figure VI.1.
United States current-account deficit, 1970-2004

CAB GDP[a]

Dollar index

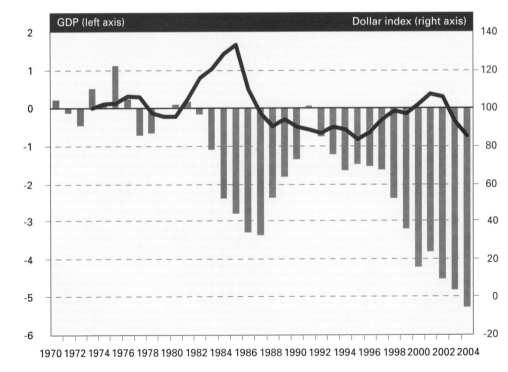

Sources:
United States Department of
Commerce, Bureau of Economic
Analysis, and United
States Fed.

a   The ratio of
current-account
balance of GDP.

As early as the 1960s, Robert Triffin (1960) focused on a dilemma facing the international reserve system. He pointed out that the rest of the world needed the United States to run balance-of-payment deficits in order to provide the additional liquidity necessary to fuel continued world economic growth. However, when the deficit of the United States rose, the excess supply of dollars eroded confidence in the value of the dollar, weakening its foundation as the world's reserve currency. This inconsistency would lead to a perpetual cycle of expansion and contraction in the external deficit of the United States, along with instability in exchange rates and in the growth of the world economy.

Although the dilemma posed by Triffin was set in the context of the Bretton Woods system and presaged its collapse, it remains broadly relevant to the current international monetary arrangements. One important difference is that the origin of the external imbalances of the United States has changed. In the 1960s, they were the counterpart of the global investment activities of large United States firms, whereas now they are the consequence of low domestic savings within the United States.

As the issuer of international reserve money, the United States is able to have persistent external deficits and to finance them in its own currency, with virtually no need for foreign-exchange reserves. Facing external constraints that are more limited than those of other countries, the United States can, if it deems necessary, adopt policies that are more stimulatory than those of other countries. In contrast, most other, particularly developing, countries have to use the dollar and other international currencies, rather than their own national currencies, in their international transactions and as a medium for accumulating foreign-exchange reserves; their capacity to run external deficits is constrained by their supply of foreign exchange and their access to global credit markets, both of which are limited.

The United States also profits more concretely from its role as the world's banker. A large part of its liabilities are the foreign-exchange reserves accumulated by other countries, usually held in a combination of cash, and short-term and liquid longer-term securities paying a relatively low interest rate, while its assets consist mostly of its long-term loans and equity investment in foreign countries, which yield higher returns. Thus, and despite its position as a net international debtor, the United States continues to have a positive net inflow of investment income from abroad.

Historically, adjustments to the large external deficits of the United States have involved considerable volatility in foreign exchange and world financial markets and a contractionary effect on both the United States and the global economy. In the early 1970s, adjustment led to the collapse of the Bretton Woods system and the transition to a floating exchange-rate system among major currencies, including a major downward correction of the dollar (see figure VI.1). It was also one of the factors that contributed to the end of the "golden age" of post-war economic growth in the developed countries.

During the 1980s, when the United States faced "twin" fiscal and external deficits, the adjustment had involved, in 1985, a sharp fall in the value of the dollar. Until the current account was rebalanced in 1991, the dollar declined by about 40 per cent against a basket of other major currencies, despite many efforts at international policy coordination among the major developed countries, such as the Plaza Accord of 1985 and the Louvre Accord of 1987.[1] Meanwhile, the equity market in the United States had tumbled in 1987 and, in addition to the correction of the deficit, there was a slowdown

Historically, adjustments to the large external deficits of the United States have had contractionary effects on both the United States and the global economy in growth of gross domestic product (GDP) in the United States, culminating in a recession in 1990. The United States recession led, in turn, to a global economic slowdown in 1989-1991.

The rebalancing of the deficit in the United States during the late 1980s was matched by a rebalancing of surpluses in Germany and a few other developed countries, a number of developing countries in Asia and some oil-exporting developing countries. In contrast, Japan's large external surplus declined only marginally and rebounded in the following years, even though the yen had appreciated significantly against the dollar since the mid-1980s. The experience of Japan during the 1980s and the 1990s shows that currency revaluation in a surplus country may not necessarily result in the necessary adjustment in the external imbalance; this is contrary to the conventional wisdom, which relies exclusively on exchange rates to adjust current-account imbalances and still underpins some analyses.

The global imbalances today have become larger and lasted longer than in the 1980s

Today's global imbalances have become larger and lasted longer than in the 1980s. Some analysts argue that increasing global economic integration, particularly deepening global financial integration, have made current imbalances different from those of the 1970s and 1980s in terms of their sustainability and their implications for the world economy. The difference, however, can be only in quantity, not in quality. As the imbalances continue to increase, the risks of an abrupt and disorderly reversal also rise, suggesting risks of larger adjustment costs for the world economy in the future.

As the imbalances continue to rise, the risk of an abrupt adjustment increases

Other analysts have argued that current imbalances could be sustained for a long time (see Dooley, Folkerts-Landau and Garber, 2003; 2004a; 2004b). This school of thought contends that the intervention required to prevent Asian currencies from appreciating will continue to provide an important part of the financing needed by the United States to continue its current-account deficits. According to this point of view, for many developing countries, the economic benefits of stable and weak exchange rates exceed the costs of reserve accumulation.[2] In turn, continued reserve accumulation by some Asian and other central banks allows the United States to rely on domestic demand to drive its growth and to run the resulting large current-account deficits. After a decline from 70 per cent in the 1960s to almost 50 per cent in the early 1990s, the share of United States dollar assets in total world official holdings of foreign exchange has since rebounded, to about 64 per cent (see table VI.1); the share of the euro remains less than 20 per cent and that of the Japanese yen less than 5 per cent.[3]

Many observers fear that the United States current-account deficit is unsustainable because it finances mainly consumption, because United States investment is shifting towards non-tradables and because the deficit is increasingly funded by short-term flows, including by central banks

However, an increasing number of observers fear that three features may cause the rising United States current-account deficit to become unsustainable in the next few years First, the deficit is financing consumption rather than investment; second, United States investment is shifting towards non-tradable sectors; and third, the deficit is increasingly being funded by short-term flows (Summers, 2004). It is such factors that have made current-account deficits less likely to be sustainable than in the past, in both developed and developing countries. In addition, the financing needed by the United States to sustain its deficits has been provided by the world's central banks, not by private investors, during certain recent periods (Higgins and Klitgaard, 2004).

For these reasons, many argue that the value of the dollar could fall significantly: the financing required to sustain United States current-account deficits may be increasing faster than the dollar reserves of the world's central banks inasmuch as their willingness to continue to build up those reserves is affected by the many potential sources of instability built into the system (see, for instance, Williamson, 2004; International

Table VI.1.

Share of national currencies in identified official holdings of foreign exchange, end of year,[a] 1994-2003

	Percentage									
Currency	1994	1995	1996	1997	1998	1999	2000	2001	2002	2003
All countries										
United States dollar	53.1	53.4	56.8	59.1	62.6	64.9	66.6	66.9	63.5	63.8
Japanese yen	7.8	6.7	6	5.1	5.4	5.4	6.2	5.5	5.2	4.8
Pound sterling	2.8	2.8	3	3.3	3.5	3.6	3.8	4	4.4	4.4
Swiss franc	0.6	0.5	0.5	0.5	0.5	0.4	0.5	0.5	0.6	0.4
Euro[b]	..	..	..	..	13.5	16.3	16.7	19.3	19.7	
Deutsche mark	15.3	14.7	14	13.7	13.1	..	..	..	..	..
French franc	2.5	2.4	1.9	1.5	1.7	..	..	..	..	..
Netherlands guilder	0.7	0.5	0.4	0.5	0.5	..	..	..	..	..
European currency units (ECU)[c]	6.8	5.9	5	0.8	..	..	..	..	..	..
Unspecified[d]	9.5	12.1	11.5	11.3	12	12.1	6.6	6.4	7.1	6.8

Source: International Monetary Fund, Annual Report of the Executive Board for the financial year ended 30 April 2004.

a   Including only IMF member countries that report their official holdings of foreign exchange.

b   Not comparable with the combined share of euro legacy currencies in previous years because amounts exclude the euros received by euro area members when their previous holdings of other euro area members' legacy currencies were converted into euros on 1 January 1999.

c   In the calculation of currency shares, the ECU is treated as a separate currency. ECU reserves held by the monetary authorities existed in the form of claims on both the private sector and the European Monetary Institute (EMI), which issued official ECUs to European Union central banks through revolving swaps against the contribution of 20 per cent of their gross gold holdings and United States dollar reserves. On 31 December 1998, the official ECUs were unwound into gold and United States dollars; hence, the share of ECUs at the end of 1998 was sharply lower than a year earlier. The remaining ECU holdings reported for 1998 consisted of ECUs issued by the private sector, usually in the form of ECU deposits and bonds. On 1 January 1999, these bonds were automatically converted into euros.

d   Difference between total foreign exchange reserves of IMF member countries and the sum of the reserves held in the currencies listed in the table.

Monetary Fund, 2005a; Roubini and Setser, 2005). One of these sources of instability is the tension between the growing need of the United States for financing to cover its current-account and fiscal deficits and the losses that those lending to the United States in dollars are almost certain to incur. There are also concerns that rising trade deficits will lead to protectionist pressures, especially against Chinese products; signs of a new burst of protectionism are already apparent. These growing signs that the system is under stress raise doubts that the present massive rate of reserve accumulation will continue for an extended period.

Globally, owing to the particular role that the dollar plays in the world economy, the income and wealth effects that the devaluation of the dollar generates tend to run counter to the relative price effects, resulting in limited overall adjustment. Dollar depreciation may therefore counteract the more fundamental rebalancing of growth rates among major economies which is required to correct the global imbalances (United Nations, 2005). In particular, appreciation of their currencies is likely to lead to reduced investment demand and growth in Europe and the economies of Asia, thus increasing, rather than reducing, the savings surplus of these regions. The fact that the wealth effects of dollar

There are tensions between the growing need to fund the United States current account and the losses that those lending in dollars are likely to incur

depreciation are also adverse for those holding dollar assets is likely to reduce their spending, particularly where those assets are held by private agents (as is the case in Europe). Appreciation of the yen may also slow the effort of Japan to overcome price deflation and a large-scale appreciation of other currencies could eventually generate deflation in the economies concerned.

So far, concerns about the deficit of the United States have been reflected mainly in foreign exchange markets but not in bond and equity markets. The decline of the dollar in the foreign-exchange market in the past few years has not been accompanied by major sales of the foreign holdings of United States government bonds or stocks during the same period (as indicated, respectively, by the flat yield curve and narrow spreads in the market for United States government securities and the relatively stable equity market). The risk is that this dichotomy between the foreign-exchange market and the capital market may be a short-run anomaly and that there will eventually be a large movement away from dollar-denominated securities by foreign holders. This could increase interest rates in the United States, as well as in the global capital market; this, in turn, could have negative effects on the United States economy and on the rest of the world, particularly on the developing countries.

This highlights the need to mitigate the risks of an abrupt adjustment of the global economy. In this regard, there is a large degree of agreement that measures should be taken simultaneously in two broad areas (see, for example, International Monetary Fund, 2005a, 2005b; United Nations, 2005). First, the United States should reduce its fiscal deficit; and second, the surplus countries in Europe and Asia should adopt more expansionary policies to stimulate their aggregate demand. Despite the growing consensus on these priorities, implementation has been very limited. Further delay could cut short the present period of improved widespread global growth.

Smooth global rebalancing requires more international policy cooperation and coordination. Given the systemic risks associated with global imbalances, purely national approaches to the macroeconomic policies of major economies are inadequate. In choosing their policy stance, national policymakers should take into account the interdependence and spillover effects of their policies on others. Consequently, their domestic policies should at least be based on mutually consistent assumptions and preferably be designed in a cooperative manner that recognizes global interdependence.

The establishment of the roles of IMF in surveillance of major economies and in surveillance of developments in the international financial system—one of the most important innovations introduced during the Asian crisis—are as important as ever. These roles could be complemented by its more prominent role as an honest broker in policy coordination among major economies (Ocampo, 2001). Despite the problems of representation addressed below, IMF is the only institution where developing countries have a voice on macroeconomic imbalances of major economies and could eventually have a voice on global macroeconomic policy consistency.

It has thus been suggested that there is a need to rethink the role of the Fund in the management of the international monetary system (King, 2005). With the advent of financial globalization, surveillance should focus not only on crisis-prone countries but, increasingly, on the stability of the system as a whole and on major economic challenges that require a global cooperative approach (de Rato, 2004). Consequently, rather than be confined to occasional lending to middle-income countries hit by financial crises and balance-of-payments financing for low-income countries, the Fund should play a more active role in supporting the management of the world economy.

The problem could be accentuated if declines in the value of the dollar were accompanied by falls in the prices of bonds and stocks

There is agreement on the measures to be taken, both by major deficit and by major surplus countries, but implementation has been limited

IMF could have a larger role in policy coordination among major economies ...

... and thereby play a more active role in supporting the management of the world economy

Compared with the Bretton Woods system, the current international reserve system has the merit of flexibility. However, such a system can hardly be considered efficient if it consistently fails to correct large balance-of-payments disequilibria across countries. Nor can the arrangement be deemed equitable when adjustment of the global imbalances often places heavy burdens asymmetrically on many developing countries. The international community should begin to address the long-term and ultimate goal of the reform of the international reserve and international monetary system so as to overcome these systemic weaknesses. More urgent and decisive cooperative action is required to ensure that the imbalances do not result in the derailment of global growth in the short term, an occurrence that itself would have substantial adverse long-term effects.

Urgent and decisive action is required to ensure that the imbalances do not derail global growth

Changes in the structure of global financial markets

Risk implications of changes in global financial markets

The global financial system has undergone a profound transformation over the past decades. Many of the impediments to the free flow of capital across borders have been dismantled and domestic financial markets deregulated. The collapse of the Bretton Woods system of fixed parities among major currencies has brought increased volatility to exchange rates. This, together with interest-rate fluctuations, has generated a rapid expansion of new financial instruments aimed at managing the risks to specific financial institutions or investors dealing in these instruments. This has resulted in greater risk diversification but it has also led to the transfer of risk across segments of the financial system. Advances in data processing and telecommunications technologies have radically reduced costs of financial transactions. As a result of all of these factors, financial activity now represents a much larger share of aggregate economic activity than it did 20 or 30 years ago.

Technological innovation and deregulation have led to a profound transformation of the global financial system

The increase in securitization—brought about, in part, by efforts to introduce risk-based capital requirements—has moved many financial assets off the balance sheets of regulated financial institutions, reducing the monitoring functions of these institutions and increasing the monitoring of the performance of debt relationships by the capital market. This process has led to the growing role of non-bank institutional investors as well as to an increase in trading activities of all financial institutions. It has also made the debt relationships more anonymous, and increased the sensitivity of all market agents to short-term variations in the valuation of assets.

The increase in securitization has resulted in a growing role of non-bank financial institutions and in a rise in trading activities

Another important change has been the consolidation of the financial industry. In the United States, this has resulted from a liberalization of financial regulation that has encouraged branch banking and eliminated the segmentation of commercial and investment banking. For instance, the top five United States domestic bank holding companies now hold about 45 per cent of banking assets, almost twice the share that they held 20 years ago. At the same time, as a result of increased securitization, and despite their increased size and scale, depository institutions now hold only about one fifth of all assets held by United States financial institutions, or less than half the share that they held in 1984. The reduction in their traditional deposit business, along with the reduced restric-

The consolidation in the financial industry and its globalization have resulted in the formation of a small group of global financial conglomerates

tions on their activities, has led to expansion in other areas such as derivatives. The notional value of outstanding derivatives held by the five largest United States banks is more than half of the global total and 95 per cent of the total held by all United States banks. The degree of concentration in the market for credit derivatives—the newest and fastest growing segment—is even greater, with one bank holding more than half of total United States holdings. As a result, there has been a sharp increase in the share of assets that are intermediated by institutions that are not subject to consolidated risk-based capital frameworks (Geithner, 2004).

Increasing concentration has been observed in all regions, including emerging market countries. At the same time, the diminishing obstacles to capital flows and foreign establishment, as well as improved communication and information, have facilitated the expansion of these financial conglomerates across borders. Given the size and reach of such institutions into national markets and financial systems around the globe, the phrase "too big to fail" has acquired a stronger and more urgent connotation than in the past decade.

Alongside these changes, there has also been substantial convergence in the type of financial transactions performed by bank-centred and non-bank affiliated financial intermediaries. With the growing marketability of assets produced by increased securitization and the development of secondary markets, portfolio investors, such as insurance companies and pension funds, have diversified into areas that used to be the exclusive domain of banks. For their part, commercial banks have increased their involvement in the securities business.

The trends towards consolidation and a broadening of the range of activities performed by any given player have culminated in the formation of a rather small group of dominant global financial institutions. In addition to being engaged in different forms of intermediation in many countries, these firms are the main trading partners of, and most important providers of leverage to, so-called highly leveraged institutions (HLIs). These institutions have been largely unregulated in the past but are coming within the purview of regulatory authorities.[4]

These structural trends have manifested themselves in greater convergence and growing linkages among different segments of the global financial system—between financial institutions and markets, among different types of financial institutions, and among different countries. They have important implications for the transformation of financial risk. The fact that a much larger, more complex and interlinked financial sphere has emerged, in which the market has replaced government regulators, means that problems in the financial system can have larger consequences for the real economy than in the past.

With growing concentration, a failure of one financial institution could have a broader impact than in the past

The growing size of large financial institutions and the diversity of their activities probably make them less vulnerable to shocks. However, the combining by financial firms of commercial and investment banking operations, and insurance and brokerage services raises potential concentration risks. In these large, internationally active financial institutions, a common capital base underpins an increasing number of activities such as on-balance sheet intermediation, capital market services and market-making functions. Losses in one activity could put pressure on other activities of the firm, and a failure of one of them could have a broader impact than in the past and be considerably more difficult to resolve. In sum, the systemically significant financial institutions are larger and stronger than in the past, but they are not invulnerable and the impact of a failure would be greater.

Also, numerous new financial instruments, including derivatives, tailored to a broader set of investors, have permitted the independent pricing of risk factors that were previously bundled together in the same instrument (see chap. III). As a result, risk transfer mechanisms have become more efficient at the microeconomic level. To the extent that new financial instruments have improved the technology of risk management, they improve the climate for real and financial investment.

However, the unbundling process does not necessarily eliminate or reduce risk, and may simply transform and redistribute it among different holders. The development of risk transfer markets has strengthened the links between different types of risk. For the same reasons, the similarities of underlying risks are becoming more apparent, regardless of the type of financial firm incurring them. Owing to the layering of direct and indirect links through the markets, assessment of true underlying risks becomes difficult (Knight, 2004b). Besides, the increased opportunities for risk transfer mean that more risk may end up in parts of the financial system where supervision and disclosure are weaker, or in parts of the economy less able to manage it. Despite the positive effects of financial innovations, it is necessary to ask whether they could have the same destabilizing impact in the present cycle that deregulation had in earlier ones (*Financial Times*, 2005).

Recent macroeconomic events have also introduced specific implications for financial risk. While the extent of leverage is now lower than in 1998, when its perils became obvious amid the collapse of a large United States hedge fund, increases in liquidity in response to the recent recession have provided more funds to borrow. Indeed, the search for yield in the low interest rate environment characteristic of recent years resembles the period after the recession of the early 1990s and has prompted a yield famine that has led financial institutions and their customers to take positions in swaps and options in derivatives markets for the purpose of making bets on changes in interest and exchange rates. As the spread between short- and long-term interest rates narrowed, institutions borrowed more in order to take the larger positions needed to bolster shrinking profit margins.

In their 2004 reports, both the Bank for International Settlements (BIS) and IMF pointed out that increased speculation had made the financial sector more vulnerable to unexpected shifts in economic activity or interest rates. IMF also noted that hedge fund assets had grown by 20 per cent globally in 2004 as large banks and brokers, as well as institutional investors increased their presence in the hedge fund business (International Monetary Fund, 2005h, pp. 50-51). This movement of regulated entities into less regulated hedge fund activities suggests that leveraged risk-taking has expanded and may continue to expand over time.

Implications for prudential regulation and supervision

The evolution of the financial system and the changing nature of financial risk have had profound implications for prudential regulation and supervision. The major trend in this area has been towards improving risk sensitivity of regulatory arrangements at both the national and the international level. Risk-focused supervision implies that supervisors are expected to concentrate their efforts on ensuring that financial institutions use the processes necessary to identify, measure, monitor and control risk exposures. The first Basel Capital Accord (Basel I) and the New Basel Capital Accord (Basel II) are considered to constitute a major step in that direction. It is still unclear, however, whether improvements in

New financial instruments have resulted in more efficient risk transfer mechanisms ...

... but assessment of true underlying risks becomes very complicated

More risk may end up in parts of the financial system where supervision is weaker

The regulatory response to the changing nature of financial risk has been a move to risk-based supervision ...

risk management practices can more than compensate for the dangers implicit in the changes in the financial structure. Furthermore, most regulation applies to financial institutions, but not to the markets in which they trade. This is especially true of over-the-counter derivatives.

... to an indirect approach to financial regulation ...

Another important development has been the move towards an indirect approach to financial regulation, which is considered to be more consistent with the evolving financial environment. This involves the establishment of a framework of rules and guidelines intended to set minimum standards of prudent conduct within which financial institutions should be freer to take commercial decisions. In other words, there has been a move away from codified regulation and towards supervision, that is to say, towards an assessment of the overall management of a financial firm's business and the multiple sources of risk that it is likely to confront (Crockett, 2001a).

Within this approach, special attention is being paid to large, systemically important financial firms. It has been argued that large financial firms should maintain capital cushions over and above those stipulated by regulatory standards. Also, the internal risk management regime needs to meet a more exacting standard (Geithner, 2004). However, it is hard to know what constitutes an adequate cushion when so much financial activity that could pose a systemic threat is outside the banking system, and the degree of leverage in finance is so hard to gauge.

... and to greater convergence in prudential frameworks across financial lines and national jurisdictions

Another notable development is the convergence in prudential frameworks across functional lines. The growing similarities of underlying risks call for greater consistency in the supervisory treatment of financial risk across functional segments of the industry. For instance, by now, capital adequacy, supervisory review of risk management processes, and enhanced public disclosure are all emerging as common elements of regulation in both the banking and insurance industries (Knight, 2004a). Also, the United States Securities and Exchange Commission (SEC) has outlined a framework that provides a form of consolidated supervision of the major investment banks with a risk-based capital framework based on Basel II. The proposed new regime will add a consolidated approach to risk-based capital and an intensified focus on the risk management regime to the traditional SEC focus on enforcement for investor protection and market integrity. This will be similar to the European Union (EU) implementation of Basel II, which will be applied to all financial institutions.

The trend towards convergence has also manifested itself in the consolidation of financial sector supervision into a single agency in over 30 countries. Internationally, this trend has led to the creation of the Joint Forum, which brings together representatives of regulatory authorities in banking, securities and insurance. With globalization of financial activity, the pressure to adopt similar regulatory and financial reporting arrangements across countries has also intensified (Knight, 2004a).

The liberalization of the financial sector has resulted in greater pro-cyclicality ...

It is also worth noting that, with the advent of liberalization, the financial sector, at both the national and the international level, has tended to become much more pro-cyclical. Having realized this, supervisors are searching for techniques that can help make financial systems more resilient to the financial cycle.

... and this has increased the likelihood of boom-bust cycles, with the "endogenous" component of risk becoming more prominent

The transformation of the financial system has increased the likelihood of boom-bust cycles. Those cycles have common features. Credit and debt levels rise in the upturn, with lenders and investors becoming increasingly vulnerable to the same shocks owing to common risk exposures. As a result, the "endogenous" component of risk, which reflects the impact of the collective actions of market participants on prices and liquidity of financial assets, and on system-wide leverage, becomes more prominent. In the downswing, this process goes into reverse with significant and long-lasting costs to the economy.

In this regard, it has been argued that, at least in part, the financial problems of the past 15 years or so are the result of the sustained period of credit expansion and increasing asset prices in the industrialized countries in the 1990s (White, 2003). An important development in this respect is that, while inflation in the prices of goods and services has become less of a problem in the developed countries, increases in liquidity tend to be reflected in increases in asset prices. These excesses, combined with overvalued exchange rates and currency mismatches in many emerging market economies, have contributed to the financial crises both in developed and in developing economies.

Consequently, policymakers in developed countries should pay more attention to preventing harmful feedback effects of financial excesses. The existing tools, however, are not very useful for that purpose. Indeed, regulators rarely consider the probability of shocks generated endogenously in the system. The risk assessments of rating agencies are highly pro-cyclical (Reisen, 2003) and tend to react to the materialization of risks rather than to their build-up, in relation to both sovereign and corporate risk. Most risk models rely heavily on market-determined variables like equity prices and credit spreads that may be biased towards excessive optimism when imbalances are emerging. Furthermore, the use of similar market-sensitive risk models, together with other features of financial markets (for example, benchmarking and evaluation of managers against competitors), may increase herding behaviour (Persaud, 2000).

Most risk models rely heavily on market-determined variables, which may increase herding

Improving the safeguards against instability for a financial system that is larger and more interconnected, and whose endogenous component of risk is more prominent, calls for a modified approach to prudential regulation with a system-wide perspective and a focus on endogenous components of risk. This systemic or macro orientation of prudential regulation requires a shift away from the notion that the stability of the financial system is simply a consequence of the soundness of its individual components.

The rising importance of the endogenous component of risk calls for the strengthening of macroprudential regulation

The importance of this macroprudential perspective as a complement to the more traditional microprudential focus is widely recognized (see, for instance, Crockett, 2000, 2001a; Knight, 2004b; Ocampo, 2003). Its objective is to limit the risk of episodes of financial distress with significant losses in terms of real output for the economy as a whole. Consequently, it stresses the need to establish cushions as financial imbalances build up during the upswing in order to both restrain excesses and give more scope to supporting losses in the downturn. This implies introducing some counter-cyclicality into financial regulation, which would compensate for the tendency of financial markets to behave in a pro-cyclical manner (see chap. I).

An important impediment to implementing macroprudential policies in practice is uncertainty about the significance of potential systemic problems. Relevant analyses are now carried out in various forums, including IMF, the World Bank, the Financial Stability Forum (FSF) and the Bank for International Settlements. The process of convergence within the global financial system across markets, institutions and national jurisdictions makes it very important to have appropriate institutions for this purpose.

Among existing institutions, the Financial Stability Forum stands out in its capacity to ensure macroprudential monitoring and appropriate policy response. However, the Forum has no power to propose or to sanction, and insights gained from its deliberations may not necessarily be turned into policy actions. The need for stronger international governance in the area of financial regulation has been suggested by several analysts (see, for instance, Eatwell and Taylor, 2000), but these proposals face constraints associated to the desire of major countries to retain sovereignty over national financial regulations and supervisory systems.

There are concerns that Basel II may increase the pro-cyclicality of lending

The regulatory approach will be seriously tested for the first time during and after the implementation of the New Basel Capital Accord (Basel II), which, according to many observers, may increase pro-cyclicality of bank lending especially for developing countries, because of its increased risk-sensitivity (see chap. III). To alleviate these concerns, the architects of Basel II have noted that supervisory oversight and market discipline should reinforce the incentive for banks to maintain a cushion of capital above the minimum so as to have a margin of protection in downturns. They are also urging financial institutions to adopt risk management practices that take better account of the evolution of risk over time (thus taking better account of the full business cycle) and that are not excessively vulnerable to short-term revisions. It has also been argued that because of greater disclosure built into Pillar 3 of Basel II, markets may become less tolerant and more suspicious of risk assessments that are too volatile and lead to substantial upgrades in good times (Borio, 2003). However, as noted above, rating agencies and other market actors themselves often have strong pro-cyclical biases. More broadly, the regulators' success in dealing with the problem of the pro-cyclicality of the New Accord remains an issue of serious concern.

Crisis prevention and resolution

Avoiding financial crises is crucial to ensuring that the benefits of capital inflows create permanent increases in national welfare. Since the Asian crisis, increased attention has been given to the design of measures at the national and international levels aimed at better managing external shocks and preventing financial crises.

Domestic macroeconomic policies

Many developing countries have better control overinflation and are pursuing more prudent fiscal policies

Developing countries have the primary responsibility for their own macroeconomic policies and thus for crisis prevention. In this regard, important progress has been made since the Asian crisis. Inflation rates have tended to fall and stabilize at historically low levels in all developing-country regions. Also, despite setbacks and variations across countries, fiscal policy has become more prudent in its general thrust. Strong external accounts have led to a reduction in external debt ratios and the accumulation of foreign-exchange reserves. Greater global liquidity and reduced risk aversion have contributed to declining spreads between emerging market sovereign borrowing rates and developed-country benchmark interest rates. All these factors, together with strong growth in world trade and high commodity prices, have led to rapid economic growth in all developing-country regions in 2004 and 2005, for the first time in three decades (United Nations, 2005).

Nevertheless, their budgets are more vulnerable to shocks than those of developed countries

However, owing to higher and more volatile interest rates paid by emerging market Governments, their budgets are more vulnerable to interest rate shocks than those of developed countries. Also, many developing countries depend heavily on commodity exports and thus are much more vulnerable to risks of sharp external price swings. Indeed, improved terms of trade due to high commodity and energy prices of recent years might have made underlying fiscal and external positions in some countries look healthier than they actually are.

There has also been a gradual shift of developing countries towards more flexible exchange rates. Greater exchange-rate flexibility is considered by some observers to have contributed the most to the reduction of the risk of future crises (Fischer, 2002) but it also carries the risk of exchange-rate instability in the face of volatile capital flows.

In this regard, there is now strong evidence that capital-account liberalization has increased growth volatility, without clear benefits in terms of more rapid growth (Prasad and others, 2003). Vulnerability to capital-account shocks is compounded by the tendency to adopt pro-cyclical macroeconomic policies that reinforce rather than mitigate the effects of external financial cycles (Kaminsky and others, 2004). Despite some advances (for example, the introduction of structural benchmarks for fiscal policy and the design of fiscal stabilization funds by some countries), limited progress has been made in introducing explicit objectives of counter-cyclical management of macroeconomic (that is to say, fiscal, monetary and exchange rate) policies, or in designing instruments that cushion developing borrowers against adverse economic developments by linking debt payments more directly to the borrower's ability to pay (see chap. III).

Given the evidence that capital-account liberalization increases macroeconomic volatility, many developing countries have continued to use capital controls. The evidence shows that there has been a slowdown in the removal of capital controls in developing countries since 1998 (International Monetary Fund, 2003a). To reduce currency mismatches, which have been a prominent feature of every major emerging market financial crisis of the past decade, local currency bond markets have expanded in developing countries. At the same time, lending by foreign banks has shifted from largely dollar-denominated cross-border loans to local currency loans through local affiliates. As a result, in many emerging economies, currency mismatches were reduced (see also chap. III).

There has also been progress in strengthening financial regulation and supervision. Supervisory and regulatory regimes of many developing countries have been brought in line with international practices as codified in the Basel Core Principles for Effective Banking Supervision. Also, in spite of the fact that there is no implementation timetable for non-Group of Ten (G10) members, many developing and emerging market countries have already begun to deal with implementation of the new capital adequacy framework (Basel II). It is expected that, by 2010, almost 75 per cent of banking assets in the developing world will be covered by Basel II arrangements (Bank for International Settlements, 2004).

Irrespective of the exchange-rate regime adopted, to ensure themselves against sudden shifts in market sentiment, most emerging economies have kept increasingly high stocks of international reserves. This "self-insurance" option entails significant costs and could constrain global growth as it reduces global aggregate demand. Nevertheless, in the absence of efficient market-based private alternatives or appropriate international official facilities, and given the enormous costs of financial crises, reserve accumulation remains a reliable, although costly, option for coping with volatility.

To reduce external vulnerabilities, many developing countries have moved towards more flexible exchange rates ...

... have taken a more cautious stance on capital-account liberalization, have reduced currency mismatches ...

... and have strengthened financial regulation and supervision

In the absence of satisfactory alternatives, most emerging economies have had to increase their holdings of reserves, as "self-insurance"

Multilateral surveillance

Surveillance of national macroeconomic and, since the Asian crisis, financial policies remains at the centre of IMF crisis prevention efforts. It has been argued, however, that increasing complexity of financial markets may have rendered the existing instruments of surveillance such as the Article IV consultations, the Financial Sector Stability Assessments and programmes, and the reviews of the observance of international codes and standards, less effective than assumed so far in identifying and preventing crises (Commonwealth Secretariat, 2004).

In July 2004, the IMF Executive Board concluded the latest biennial review of the surveillance activities. The review identified key priorities for further strengthening surveillance. It has been agreed that surveillance activities should be focused on improving analytical tools for early identification of vulnerabilities, including more rigorous assessments of balance-sheet weaknesses and stress-testing in regard to possible macroeconomic shocks.

More effective surveillance requires increased focus on a country-specific approach ...

To raise the effectiveness of surveillance, increased focus on country-specific areas of vulnerability is considered necessary. This requires surveillance that is tailor-made for addressing mainly those macroeconomic issues that are relevant in each member country. In addition, there is a need to better understand the constraints on a country's ability to take certain actions. It is therefore necessary to consider institutional, social and political realities in order to offer realistic policy advice.

... and on ways to enhance the room for economic policy manoeuvre

As in the case of national efforts, more attention should be given to increasing the room for manoeuvre to enable countries to adopt counter-cyclical macroeconomic policies in the face of trade and, particularly, capital-account shocks. Greater attention within IMF surveillance on ways to enhance such room for manoeuvre would improve the effectiveness of crisis prevention efforts and financial support.

To increase the transparency of surveillance, IMF moved from voluntary to presumed publication of Article IV surveillance reports and programme documents. Increased transparency is thought to help improve both countries' policies and the quality of the Fund's work. However, there could be a potential tension between greater transparency and the Fund's role as a provider of candid and frank advice. Hence, in the handling of sensitive topics during surveillance exercises, there is a need for an appropriate balance between candour and confidentiality.

The Fund's ability to influence policies is most limited with regard to large non-borrowing countries

The Fund's ability to influence policies through surveillance is most limited with regard to large non-borrowing, mostly developed countries. At the same time, some of those countries have the greatest global impact. As was emphasized in the first section of this chapter, the role of IMF in macroeconomic surveillance of major economies and as an honest broker in policy coordination among these countries thus deserves special attention.

The role of emergency financing and precautionary financial arrangements

International emergency financing is essential to reducing the burden of adjustment

At the country level, central banks have acted for many decades as lenders of last resort, to prevent systematic banking or other financial crises, and to prevent their deepening when they do occur. Equivalent international mechanisms are still at an embryonic stage, with the current IMF arrangements operating more under the principle of the "emergency financier", which is a function different from that of the lender of last resort as performed at the national level, since there is no automaticity in the availability of financing during crises (Ocampo, 2002a). Enhanced provision of emergency financing at the international level in response to external shocks is essential to lowering unnecessary burdens of adjustment. Appropriate facilities should include a liquidity provision to cover volatility in export earnings—particularly that caused by fluctuations in commodity prices—sudden stops in external financing and, as recently emphasized, natural disasters.

The evidence of the adverse effects of terms-of-trade shocks on economic growth is strong. Particularly important is the finding that their negative effects on growth and poverty reduction can be very large (Collier and Dehn, 2001). However, the major IMF facility designed to compensate for terms-of-trade shocks, the Compensatory Financing Facility (CFF), has become increasingly ineffective. Since its modification in early 2000, which basically tightened conditionality for access, the CFF has not been used, in spite of the additional shocks affecting developing countries (International Monetary Fund, 2003a).

During the 1990s, capital-account liberalization and large capital-account volatility greatly increased the need for official liquidity to deal with sudden and large reversals of flows. There is an increasing consensus that many of the recent crises in emerging markets have been triggered by self-fulfilling liquidity runs, rather than by fundamental disequilibria or incorrect policies (see, for instance, Hausmann and Velasco, 2004). Indeed, capital outflows could be provoked by many factors not related to countries' policies. Among those factors are changes in financial conditions in industrialized countries and the pro-cyclical behaviour of capital markets, as well as contagion effects.

Greater volatility of liberalized capital accounts has increased the need for official liquidity

The enhanced provision of emergency financing in the face of capital-account crises is important not only to manage crises when they occur, but to prevent such crises and to avert contagion (Cordella and Yeyati, 2005; Griffith-Jones and Ocampo, 2003). Indeed, lending of last resort at the national level is basically conceived as a tool for crisis *prevention*, particularly prevention of systemic crises.

Enhanced provision of emergency financing is important not only to manage crises better, but to prevent them and their contagion

To address this obvious need, IMF has made efforts in recent years to improve its lending policy during capital-account crises. In 1997, the Supplemental Reserve Facility (SRF) was established. The SRF provides larger and more front-loaded financing to countries hit by a capital-account crisis, at a higher interest rate than that of other Fund facilities. Also, in some cases, the Fund softened its requirements and accelerated the approval process in the renewal of credits extended under this Facility, as was the case for Brazil in 2003 and 2004.

However, large-scale access by certain emerging economies led to criticism by some IMF members who considered that such large-scale lending should be more strictly limited. To a large measure, these debates have been provoked by cases of exceptional access to Fund resources not accompanied by an agreement on the conditions that should determine eligibility for such special treatment. In February 2003, the IMF Executive Board approved a new framework for exceptional access in capital-account crises, which included the following criteria for eligibility: exceptionally large need; a debt burden that would be sustainable under reasonably conservative assumptions; good prospects of regaining access to private capital markets during the period of the IMF loan; and indications that the country's policies had a strong chance of succeeding.

A major problem of many recent Fund-supported programmes, especially in cases of capital-account crisis, has been the lower-than-expected levels of private financing, resulting in sharper and more abrupt current-account adjustment and steep output declines (International Monetary Fund, 2004a). Past experience has shown that the catalytic effects of

In many recent Fund-supported programmes, private financing has been lower than expected

IMF financing on private capital flows may work only in rather rare situations when there is no doubt about debt and exchange-rate sustainability. This means that a further analysis of the optimal mix between financing and adjustment, as well as of the catalytic effects of Fund-supported programmes, is required (International Monetary Fund, 2005c).

The evidence that even countries with good macroeconomic fundamentals might be subject to sudden stops of external financing also gave broad support to the idea that a precautionary financial arrangement, closer to the lender-of-last-resort functions of central banks, had to be added to existing IMF facilities. The goal was to create a mechanism to prevent self-fulfilling liquidity crises.

The introduction of the CCL was not successful

In response to these demands, in 1999 the IMF had introduced the Contingent Credit Line (CCL). The facility was never used, however, and was discontinued in November 2003. Among the factors that may have contributed to the fact that countries failed to avail themselves of the CCL, observers have emphasized the "entry" and "exit" problems (Buira, 2005). Contrary to what was desired, access to the CCL was seen as an announcement of vulnerability that could harm confidence. Another problem was that, even with a CCL, the country had to go back to the IMF Executive Board to secure a loan. There was also a lack of clarity regarding the amount of support that would be available and its timing.

The exploration of precautionary financial mechanisms continues

Since the expiration of the CCL, IMF has been exploring other ways to achieve its basic objectives. Opponents note that precautionary arrangements with exceptional access could potentially increase the risk of moral hazard (Fischer, 2002). The alternative view is that the case made for moral hazard issues associated with IMF lending—particularly moral hazard on the side of IMF borrowers—is exaggerated and lacks adequate empirical evidence. Furthermore, if a country was insured ex ante against self-fulfilling runs, such a scheme could prevent the massive real and financial costs associated with crises.

A recent proposal suggests automatic access, with eligibility linked to Maastricht rules

A recent proposal suggests the creation of a country insurance facility (CIF) to help stop and reverse liquidity runs (Cordella and Yeyati, 2005). Through this facility, eligible countries would have automatic access to a line of credit at a predetermined interest rate to cover short-term financing needs. Automaticity, which is essential for pre-empting liquidity runs, would distinguish the CIF (or any similar facility) from the late CCL, which required a pre-qualification process. The eligibility suggested would focus primarily on Maastricht-type rules, with a debt-to-GDP ratio not higher than 60 per cent and a fiscal deficit of 3 per cent or less being natural candidates for eligibility criteria. This has many merits, although the level of reserves should also be included, so that net indebtedness may be considered. Following lender-of-last-resort principles, the proposal envisages short-term lending (up to one year) at a penalty rate relative to pre-crisis levels.

It is assumed that, by replacing the standard ex post conditionality with voluntary ex ante conditionality, more countries would have the incentive to adopt sustainable policies conducive to solvency and eligibility. Furthermore, a well-designed CIF, or a similar facility designed to prevent liquidity runs, would be used very infrequently or, possibly, never. However, its impact should be visible in an increasing number of eligible countries and lower emerging market risk premiums. Indeed, the essential advantages of such a facility is that, by offering instant liquidity, it "would place a ceiling on rollover costs—thus avoiding debt crises triggered by unsustainable refinancing rates, much in the same way as central banks operate in their role of lenders of last resort" (International Monetary Fund, 2005d).

The additional demand for IMF lending facilities that was evident during the succession of the Asian, Russian and Latin American crises in the late 1990s also made evident the fact that a significant strengthening of the resource base of IMF might be needed, and that the potential loss to the global economy of failing to act was much higher than the opportunity costs of a larger Fund size (Kelkar, Chaudhry and Vanduzer-Snow, 2005). Existing mechanisms, which allow the Fund to borrow from major economies when such exceptional demands arise, may be suboptimal relative to the option of strengthening the resource base of the Fund, via SDRs. This issue is explored below.

A strengthening of the IMF resource base is needed

Strengthening IMF financing of poor countries

In September 1999, the IMF transformed the previously existing Enhanced Structural Adjustment Facility (ESAF) into the Poverty Reduction and Growth Facility (PRGF) for lending operations in its poorest member countries. PRGF-supported programmes are framed around Poverty Reduction Strategy Papers (PRSPs), the major policy instrument of concessional lending from both IMF and the World Bank, as well as of debt relief under the Heavily Indebted Poor Countries (HIPC) Initiative. In the case of IMF, PRGF-supported programmes are designed to cover mainly areas that constitute the primary responsibility of the Fund, such as exchange-rate and tax policy, fiscal management, budget execution, fiscal transparency, and tax and customs administration.

Concessional lending under the PRGF is administered by IMF through the PRGF and PRGF-HIPC Trusts. The PRGF Trust borrows resources from official institutions at market-related interest rates. The difference between the market-related interest rate paid to PRGF Trust lenders and the rate of interest of 0.5 per cent per year paid by the eligible borrowing members is financed by contributions from bilateral donors and the International Monetary Fund's own resources. As of March 2005, 78 low-income countries were eligible for PRGF assistance. At end-February 2005, total loan resources provided by PRGF creditors amounted to SDR 15.8 billion, of which SDR 13.3 billion have already been committed and SDR 11.7 billion disbursed.

A major issue under debate is how to improve existing arrangements so as to assist low-income countries in dealing with shocks. One of the most appropriate mechanisms could be to increase significantly access under the PRGF arrangements (called PRGF augmentation in recent IMF analysis) and diminish conditionality, as well as make the conditionality more supportive of growth and poverty reduction. This could be done, for example, by allowing—where feasible, that is to say, in post-stabilization countries with low levels of inflation—higher levels of government spending and particularly that implying positive impacts on growth (see Oxfam, 2003).

Access under the PRGF arrangements should be increased

Given that about half the eligible low-income members have PRGF arrangements, this would be an important channel, which would provide such liquidity support at subsidized rates. Augmentation of the PRGF has in fact been the main vehicle the Fund has used to provide financing for low-income countries hit by shocks. However, as IMF (2003a) itself recognizes clearly, the "small size and infrequency of PRGF arrangements suggests that there may be room for a more systematic response". Indeed, in PRGF programmes where the Fund staff has estimated the direct impact of the shock (on average, 70 per cent of quota), PRGF augmentation has been very small in relation to the impact (only

12 per cent of quota, that is to say, less than a fifth of the IMF impact of the quota). These augmentations have also been very infrequent. It is therefore desirable that there be a genuine liberalization of the PRGF. An important source of concern would then be whether the resources available for the PRGF are sufficient to meet the liquidity needs of low-income countries facing external shocks.

For low-income countries without PRGF arrangements, other options should be available, such as a subsidized CFF

For low-income countries that do not have PRGF arrangements, but are eligible for assistance from this Facility (about half), there are a number of options available for financing shocks outside their control ("silent crises"). One option, which seems very appropriate, would be to liberalize access to the CFF, liberalize its conditionality and introduce a subsidy element into it for low-income countries. Another option would be for PRGF-eligible countries that do not have such a programme to be granted subsidized loans from the Fund via a standby-like window, within the PRGF Trust.

Low-income countries are also vulnerable to natural disasters. In early 2005, IMF agreed to subsidize emergency assistance for natural disasters to PRGF-eligible members. However, the total amount allocated has been very limited, and was to an important extent, used up in the first few months.

Conditionality of IMF lending

The increase in the number of structural conditions in IMF programmes ...

As important as the lending facilities of IMF is the conditionality attached to them. Conditionality in IMF-supported programmes had been introduced in the 1950s and incorporated as a requirement into the Articles of Agreement in 1969. Until the 1980s, conditionality mainly focused on monetary, fiscal and exchange-rate policies. However, in the late 1980s, and especially in the 1990s, in addition to traditional quantitative targets for macroeconomic variables, IMF financing was increasingly made conditional on structural changes, involving changes in policy processes, legislation and institutional reforms. This resulted in a significant increase in the average number of structural conditions in Fund-supported programmes. These climbed from 2-3 per year per programme in the mid-1980s to 12 or more per year per programme by the second half of the 1990s, and to as high as 117 in the case of Indonesia after its financial crisis in 1997 (International Monetary Fund, 2003b). This change was also reflected in increasing numbers of performance criteria, structural benchmarks and prior actions.

... has raised concerns about programme effectiveness ...

The increase in the number of structural conditions raised concerns that IMF was exceeding its mandate and expertise. It has also been argued that the number and detail of structural policy conditions attached to IMF loans were too extensive to be fully effective (United Nations, 2001b). In this regard, it has been observed that the rate of member countries' compliance with Fund-supported programmes fell from over 50 per cent in the late 1970s and early 1980s to about 16 per cent in the 1990s, if compliance is defined as that which permitted the full disbursement of the loan (Buira, 2003).

... and about their national ownership, credibility and catalytic role

There were also concerns that excessive conditionality might have undermined the national ownership of programmes thereby impeding their implementation. Indeed, following closely the arguments related to external assistance in general (see chap. IV), it has become clear that lack of real domestic ownership is the most important obstacle to effective programme implementation, and that conditionality is not a substitute for government commitment. In this regard, it has also been argued that "ownership" can be promoted only by an effective plural discussion of the virtues of alternative types of "structural reforms" (Griffith-Jones and Ocampo, 2003).

In response to these concerns, in September 2002, the IMF Executive Board approved new conditionality guidelines, the first revision since 1979. A review of the new guidelines is scheduled for early 2005. The basic objective of the 2002 guidelines is to streamline conditionality and enhance programme ownership. Accordingly, conditionality is to be focused on policies essential to restoring and maintaining macroeconomic stability and growth, and better tailored to the country's circumstances. Structural issues are to be covered only if critical for these objectives. In this regard, the new guidelines stress a test of "criticality" for any variable selected for conditionality. The guidelines also stress the need to seek national ownership of programmes but they do not provide any formal guidance on how to identify and foster domestic ownership of sound policies.

New conditionality guidelines stress the test of "criticality" and the need to seek national ownership

The progress in implementing new guidelines is rather difficult to assess. There may still be a temptation to use IMF financial leverage when the country is in a difficult situation, and this temptation needs to be resisted (Allen, 2004). Also, it has been noted that since 2000-2001, the first phase of the "streamlining" initiative, the number of conditions in programmes has not declined but stayed fairly constant, with about 15 conditions per year per programme (IMF, 2004b; Allen, 2004), which is similar to the average of the 1990s.

Thus far, conditionality streamlining has been slow and indecisive

A key challenge is to determine which actions are critical to the success of programmes. There appears to be no consensus among IMF Executive Directors regarding the extent to which structural conditionality should be streamlined (IMF, Independent Evaluation Office, 2005). IMF staff may have different views on the new policy (Killick, 2004). This can explain, at least partly, why conditionality streamlining has been so slow.

Another concern is that the reduction of the number of structural conditions in Fund-supported programmes may lead to an expansion of conditionality by the World Bank with the aggregate conditionality burden remaining unchanged or even increasing. There are differences between the two organizations in terms of mandates, cultures and structures (Commonwealth Secretariat, 2004). Finding the appropriate collaborative framework is an issue of great priority.

The role of SDRs in the international financial system

The creation of SDRs in 1969, as a result of international financial debates in the 1960s, was a major advance in the design of the international financial system. It gave birth to a true world money, with the potential to generate a more balanced distribution of powers of seigniorage. In a world characterized by the use of the national currencies of major industrialized countries as international monies, the accumulation of reserves and their cost generate, in fact, a redistribution of income from developing economies to the major industrialized countries, a large flow of so-called reverse aid (see Zedillo report (United Nations, 2001a)).

The creation of the SDR was a major advance in the design of the international financial system ...

Unfortunately, no allocations of SDRs to IMF member countries have been made since 1981. The IMF Board of Governors did approve in 1997 a special one-time allocation of SDRs that would have doubled cumulative SDR allocations to SDR 42.9 billion and would have corrected the fact that new IMF members (since 1981) had never received an SDR allocation. However, this decision has not become yet effective.

... but no allocations of SDRs have been made since 1981 ...

... with negative effects
for developing
countries

The cessation of SDR allocations had negative effects for developing countries, as it coincided with a growing demand for international reserves. In recent years, in particular, many developing countries (especially, but not only, in Asia) accumulated substantial foreign-exchange reserves, partly to protect themselves against the risk of future financial crises due to reversible capital flows. However, holding such high levels of reserves with the aim of "self-insurance" implies high costs which are particularly onerous for low-income countries. Polak and Clark (2005) estimate the significant cost of the holding by low-income countries of about SDR 90 billion of reserves at about US$ 10 billion per year; this is about one sixth of total annual net official development assistance (ODA).

Such high demand for reserves also reduces aggregate world demand and therefore has a deflationary effect at the global level. There are therefore clear benefits to be derived from internationally issued reserves which, together with emergency financing during crises, would provide developing countries with a "collective insurance" that was cheaper and therefore more efficient than "self-insurance" via foreign-exchange reserve accumulation.

Proposals to renew
SDR allocations have
increased in recent
years, with one model
suggesting temporary,
counter-cyclical
issuances of SDRs that
would not increase
total liquidity

Proposals to renew SDR allocations have been increasing in recent years. They follow two different models. The first calls for SDRs to be issued in a temporary way during episodes of financial stress and destroyed once financial conditions normalize (United Nations, 1999; Camdessus, 2000; Cooper, 2002; Ocampo, 2002a). This would develop a counter-cyclical element in world liquidity management, as sudden drops in private lending would be partly compensated by increased official liquidity; furthermore, total long-term liquidity would not increase, since normalization of private lending would imply a cancellation of those SDRs issued during the preceding crisis. Output in developing countries currently lowered by temporary shocks would be higher than otherwise, and the risk of additional world inflation would be minimal.

This proposal would solve the problems of adequately financing needs for extraordinary and temporary official liquidity but not the distributive issues associated with uneven distribution of seigniorage powers. The solution to this problem requires permanent allocations. Such allocations could go (directly or indirectly) to developing countries only or to the entire Fund membership. The advantage of the former is that it would focus SDR issues on the countries that need them the most. Furthermore, it would avoid the risk of creating more SDRs than the membership would collectively want to have. Alternatively, allocations of SDRs to industrialized countries could be used to finance important international objectives, particularly increased international development cooperation (see chap. IV).

For developing countries, holding additional SDR reserves would have a zero net cost or even a net benefit, as payment by the country for its reserves would be equal to or lower than the interest earned if they did hold them (Polak and Clark, 2005). There would also be no fiscal cost to industrialized countries if IMF issued SDRs, and they held them. Indeed, if an industrialized country is allocated SDRs, it will also have either zero net costs, or even a small positive net benefit (see UK Treasury, 2003).

Currently, greater SDR liquidity could allow other countries, including developing countries, to relax their efforts directed at increasing current-account surpluses (Williamson, 2004). Furthermore, it would help somewhat to reduce the massive dependence of the United States on the foreign central banks financing its deficit, a dependence that may be or could become problematic for the United States authorities.

One of the main reasons for traditional opposition of some industrialized countries to SDR issues is that those issues could increase inflation globally. This concern seems exaggerated, as the amount of SDRs that were issued would constitute an extremely small proportion of the world's total money supply. For example, in the most recent allocation of SDRs approved in 1997, but not yet ratified, an issue was proposed of SDR 21 billion, or approximately US$ 30 billion. If we compare this with the total money supply (M2) of the United States, of over US$ 6,000 billion, the amount of possible SDR issue is less than 0.5 per cent, and therefore represents an even smaller proportion of the world's total money supply (Griffith-Jones and Gottshalk, 2004). Furthermore, if SDRs were issued in a counter-cyclical way, the risk of inflationary impact would be even smaller, as they would be compensating for a decline in private liquidity.

The risk of an increase in inflation would be minimal

The role of regional financial arrangements

A strong case can also be made for the creation and development of regional reserve funds, which can provide a valuable complement to multilateral and national mechanisms in the case of capital-account crises. The large currency crises of the last decade have been regional in nature. Therefore, neighbouring countries have a strong incentive to extend financial assistance to each other in the face of potentially contagious threats to stability "to help put out a fire (a financial crisis) before it spreads to them" (Ito, Ogawa and Sasaki, 1999). Also, despite contagion, critical demands for funds do not coincide exactly in time, a fact that generates the possibility of a useful role for regional reserve funds as a first line of defence during crises. Besides, regional institutions can and should play a stronger role in relation to small and medium-sized countries, which will usually receive less attention and have a weaker bargaining position than larger countries with multilateral institutions. Indeed, a case could even be made that they could provide full support to the small and medium-sized countries within some regions, as well as part of the financing for larger countries. Furthermore, greater attention—especially in East Asia—to the formation of regional financial arrangements reflects frustration with the slow reform of the international financial system, and particularly the limitations of multilateral official emergency lending (Ocampo, 2002a).

There are several important reasons for creating regional reserve funds

Looking into the future, an organizational structure for crisis prevention and regulation could be conceived entailing the establishment of a dense network of multilateral, regional and subregional financial institutions to provide official financing, basically on a complementary basis. This model could be extended to macroeconomic surveillance, again with regional institutions complementing multilateral ones, whereas regional arrangements might be especially suitable for macroeconomic policy coordination. Such a network of institutions would in the future be similar in some ways to federal arrangements, like those of the United States Federal Reserve Board, or to a form of slightly looser integration, like that provided by the European Central Bank. Indeed, the post-war European experience of building financial cooperation, combined with growing macroeconomic surveillance, may offer some interesting lessons at the global level.

In the future, multilateral, regional and subregional institutions could provide complementary financing

Despite these potentialities, existing regional financial arrangements among developing countries are only in an embryonic stage. The valuable role that regional reserve funds can play is illustrated by the Andean Reserve Fund, which became the Latin American

Existing regional arrangements are embryonic ...

Reserve Fund (FLAR). Its main function is the provision of short-term liquidity support to countries in crises. Though the total of its loans has been relatively small (between 1979 and 2004, it disbursed loans of US$ 4.9 billion), it provided 60 per cent of the exceptional financing lent by IMF to the Andean countries in that period. In some cases, this institution was the only one to disburse loans, as was the case for Peru in 1988. Furthermore, disbursements of loans have always been rapid (Titelman and Uthoff, 2004).

The Latin American Reserve Fund is financed by the capital of member countries. These countries have always paid back their loans promptly, even when some of them had moratoriums with other creditors. This zero default and preferential creditor status contributes to the very high credit ratings of the Reserve Fund, well above the rating of the countries that constitute it.

After the East Asian crisis, Japan had proposed the creation of an Asian monetary fund. Though the proposal was well received throughout the region, the idea was shelved owing to objections from outside the region (Park, 2004). However, a more modest version was created in 2000, when the Association of Southeast Asian Nations (ASEAN), China, Japan and the Republic of Korea created a system of bilateral currency swap arrangements known as the Chiang Mai Initiative (CMI). They also institutionalized meetings of finance ministers for policy dialogue and coordination, and are working on a plan to establish a surveillance system. In May 2005, the Initiative was increased significantly from its $39 billion level. It is based on 16 bilateral swap arrangements, and thus any country in need of short-term liquidity must discuss activation with all swap-providing countries individually.

Disbursement of 20 per cent of the maximum drawing would be automatic; a country drawing more than 20 per cent is placed under an IMF programme. In this sense, the Initiative is of somewhat limited size and clearly complementary to IMF lending facilities. Its efficacy in firefighting crises has not yet been tested. In the meantime, efforts are being undertaken to overcome potential problems, such as the bilateral nature of swap arrangements, which could reduce the speed of response of the mechanism, so essential in times of speculative attacks. There is an understanding that the multilateralization of the bilateral swap arrangements would require a more formalized and rigorous surveillance system. However, there are some doubts concerning the ability of the member countries to develop appropriate surveillance mechanism acceptable to all (Park, 2004).

... but some, like FLAR in Latin America, have been successful

The Chiang Mai Initiative was created after the Asian crisis and its bilateral swap arrangements have recently been increased

Enhancing the voice and participation of developing countries in international financial decision-making

The Monterrey Consensus stressed the need to enhance participation of developing countries in the Bretton Woods institutions and in other policymaking bodies

The Monterrey Consensus of the International Conference on Financing for Development stressed the need to broaden and strengthen the participation of developing countries and countries with economies in transition in international economic decision-making and norm-setting. It encouraged the Bretton Woods institutions to continue to enhance the participation of all developing and transition economies in their decision-making. However, the Monterrey Consensus goes beyond the Bretton Woods institutions and highlights the need to extend the discussion of voice and participation to other policymaking bodies, including informal and ad hoc groups. Although the discussion below will focus on two of those institutions, the Basel Committee on Banking Supervision and the Financial Stability Forum, the principle is applicable to similar organizations.[5]

There were two main reasons behind the position adopted at Monterrey. It seemed necessary to review the governance of these institutions in the light of the vast changes that had taken place since their creation, in particular the increasing importance of emerging economies. Also, these institutions would be more effective and efficient if their agenda and decisions better reflected the needs and issues of the majority of the countries affected by them.

The Bretton Woods institutions have taken some limited action to make more effective the participation of developing countries, leading, inter alia, to strengthening the offices of African Directors in IMF and establishing an Analytical Trust Fund to support the African Chairs at the World Bank. Modalities for consultations in the Basel Committee and the International Stability Forum have also widened; yet, in respect of the crucial issue of participation of developing countries in decision-making, there has been no progress.

The limited actions to date have not included any progress on participation in decision-making

In the Basel Committee and the Financial Stability Forum, developing countries are not represented at all. The Basel Committee defines regulations—including the capital adequacy regulations discussed in chapter III and the Core Principles for Effective Banking Supervision— that strongly influence, in turn, the cost and distribution of bank lending, as well as banking stability, in developed and developing countries. Lack of any representation by developing countries makes their analysis incomplete in crucial aspects, as shown by the new Capital Accord (Basel II) (see chap. III).

In bodies like the Basel Banking Committee, developing countries are not represented ...

All members of the Basel Committee are developed countries: 10 Western European countries, Canada, Japan and the United States. There is no representation of developing countries in this Committee. Notwithstanding, the Basel Committee does liaise with developing and transition economies. However, consultations are no substitute for having a seat at the decision-making table. A Basel Committee with a more appropriate representation from the world economy could result not only in a fairer system, but also in better regulation leading to a more stable financial system with welfare-enhancing effects for all.

... although the Committee does liaise with developing economies

The question of strengthening representation of developing countries is now clearly in the agenda of the Bretton Woods institutions. The voting structure and composition of the Executive Board of IMF determine to a large extent the policies of the Fund, in particular those that affect the use of IMF resources. Yet, policy discussions and policy formulation in the Board and the International Monetary and Financial Committee often involve areas in which IMF resources are not directly involved. Such discussions and the policy orientations that they provide deal mostly with international economic and financial cooperation, but they also touch upon policy orientations of individual countries or groups of countries. In fact, such policy orientations exert a significant influence on the scope for autonomous policy formulation. This illustration relates to IMF, but the same arguments are applicable to the World Bank.

The question of strengthening the representation of developing countries is receiving more attention

The report of the IMF Executive Board to the International Monetary and Financial Committee on quotas, voice and representation of 24 September 2004 (IMF, 2004c) lays out the elements that would need to be considered to make additional progress on these questions: a general quota increase with a relatively large selective element allocated by means of a new quota formula; ad hoc quota increases with the objective of addressing the clearest cases where the relation between quota and economic size is significantly out of line; and an increase in basic votes to correct the erosion of voting power of countries with small-sized economies, such as many in Africa.

The way in which quotas are calculated is central to the relative voting power of individual countries and country groupings. Also, the individual country quota determines the amount of financing the country can obtain from the Fund. A central consideration in determining the quota is the capacity to contribute. Thus, the economic size of a country largely determines its quota level. From the perspective of a potential user of IMF resources, the eventual need to finance its balance of payments is a key factor to be considered. Currently, the formula to calculate the quota includes GDP or gross national income (GNI), current-account transactions, official reserves and a measure of variability of receipts in foreign currency (for example, exports of goods and services plus income revenues).

Even without a change in the IMF Articles of Agreement,[6] there are several changes in the method of calculating the quota that would lead to a comparatively larger quota for developing countries as a whole. Those widely mentioned in current discussions include: using the GNI measured in purchasing power parity (PPP) instead of GNI at average exchange rates as a measure of economic size in the quota formula; excluding the amount of trade among EU members that adopted the euro, as it does not generate potential balance-of-payments difficulties; and increasing the coefficient assigned in the quota formula to the indicator of variability of receipts.

Using GNI measured in terms of purchasing power parity could offer the most potential for redefining IMF quotas ...

The first of the aforementioned factors could be the most critical in redefining quotas. Purchasing power parities (PPPs) represent an effort to apply a common set of prices to the same activities in all countries so that measures of aggregate output and similar variables are comparable. For a variety of reasons, market exchange rates do not necessarily achieve this comparability. Particularly for developing countries, they do not necessarily reflect market conditions, as they sometimes experience long periods of misalignment and are often volatile. PPP exchange rates provide a more accurate reflection of the relevant weight of individual countries in the world economy and, correspondingly, are more stable (since economic weight does not itself change much in the short term). For these reasons, several international organizations prefer to use GNI/PPP directly when making cross-country comparisons or to use them indirectly as weights when aggregating certain country data. For example, the Organization for Economic Cooperation and Development (OECD) incorporates GNI/PPP in much of its statistical and analytical work. GNI/PPP is also used to determine budget allocations for the structural funds used to reduce economic disparities among the members of EU (McLenaghan, 2005). Of particular relevance to the matter of voice in the Bank and the Fund is the fact that IMF utilizes the GNI/PPP to estimate rates of growth at regional and world levels in its *World Economic Outlook*. Even more pertinently, because of the shortcomings of official exchange rates for these purposes, a PPP conversion factor was adopted by IMF in the 1980s and 1990s when the economies in transition joined IMF and their quota levels had to be decided. This suggests that there is a strong case for using PPPs for quota calculations in IMF. If they were used, developing countries' share of IMF quotas would be 40 per cent, compared with 31 per cent at present (see table VI.2).

... and would substantially increase the quota of developing countries, especially those in Asia

As table VI.2 indicates, the use of purchasing power measures of GNI would increase substantially the quota of developing countries. Most of the increases in the quota share would go to developing Asian countries, particularly China, India and the Republic of Korea. Indeed, the quota share of developing Asia is barely 17 per cent while its share of GNI/PPP is 28 per cent. This would require, as the table also suggests, a significant adjustment of the share of the European countries whose quota share as a whole is 1½ times its GNI/PPP share.[7]

Enhanced representation of small countries could be achieved by restoring basic votes to their original weight

On the other hand, enhanced representation of countries with small size economies can be increased only by restoring basic votes to close to their original weight. There are also strong arguments to do so. Basic votes initially constituted about 11 per cent of total voting power in the Fund; with the increases in quota since the creation of the Fund and no adjustment in basic votes, the latter represent only 2 per cent of total voting

Table VI.2.

Shares in world total of IMF quotas and GNI/PPP, 2002

Country or region	IMF quota share (percentage of total IMF quotas)	GNI/PPP share (percentage of world GNI/PPP)
United States	17.4	21.5
Japan	6.2	7.1
EU-25	32.2	22.5
Other European	8.5	5.9
Australia, Canada, New Zealand	4.9	3.3
Subtotal	69.2	60.3
Developing countries	30.8	39.8
Memorandum items:		
Brazil	1.4	2.8
China	3.0	12.2
India	2.0	5.8
Republic of Korea	0.8	1.7

Sources:
IMF, International Financial Statistics; World Bank, World Development Indicators, 2004; and DESA estimates.

power. This figure of 2 per cent becomes even more insignificant when the size of the IMF membership—which grew—is taken into account.

In any event, a sizeable quota increase with a large selective component would be necessary to move in the desired direction. The adjustment in relative positions can be implemented only by measurable increases in countries whose calculated quota is higher than actual quota, unless those countries with calculated quota lower than actual quota accept a lower absolute quota.

In the end, the way the variables are defined and the magnitude of the coefficients used for each variable in the quota formula will depend on their acceptability to the members of the IMF Executive Board—and, by extension, the Executive Board of the World Bank. This would require an essentially political decision. Representation in other international financial institutions, particularly those setting international norms, requires additional political determination. Because democracy has become such an important aim of nations and of the international community, it is to be hoped that such political agreement can be reached.

Notes

1   According to some analysts, the Plaza Accord might have exacerbated the downturn of the dollar, contrary to its initial objective of achieving an orderly devaluation of the United States currency. The purpose of the Louvre Accord was to stabilize the dollar. For a detailed account of policy coordination during the late 1980s, see Frankel (1994).

2   This view, that maintaining weak exchange rates to fuel export growth should be the goal of exchange-rate interventions in Asia, ignores certain facts behind recent foreign-exchange pressures in Asia, particularly the fact that the largest accumulation has taken place in Japan, a country that has already experienced a sizeable appreciation of its currency, that some countries have also allowed their exchange rates to strengthen and, particularly, that the pressure on others (including China) come more from the capital account than from current-account surpluses. See, in this regard, Genberg and others (2005).

3   Japan's holdings of foreign exchange reserves, approaching $1 trillion, are much larger than foreign holdings of Japanese yen as foreign-exchange reserves, suggesting that the "net" role of Japanese yen as an international reserve money is limited.

4   In the United States, the Securities and Exchange Commission (17 CFR Parts 275 and 279 [Release No. IA-2333: File No. S7-30-04] RIN 3235-AJ25), "Registration Under the Advisers Act of Certain Hedge Fund Advisers"), now requires certain advisers to hedge funds to register with the Commission under the Investment Advisers Act of 1940. While registration and compliance with the Advisers Act require maintenance of business records for perusal by the Commission, provision of disclosure statements to clients and a legal fiduciary obligation to clients, they do not entail the imposition of a detailed regulatory regime.

5   Examples include the Bank for International Settlements, the International Association of Insurance Supervisors, the International Accounting Standards Board, the International Organization for Standardization and the International Federation of Stock Exchanges.

6   A decision to increase the number of basic votes would also lead to an increase in the share of the voting power of developing countries, in particular the countries of small economic size (see below). However, such a decision would require an amendment to the Articles of Agreement.

7   Several observers have suggested this should be seen in the context of EU policies and the possibility of one chair representing the Union.

Bibliography

Acharya, Robin, and Michael Daly (2004). Selected issues concerning the multilateral trading system. *World Trade Organization Discussion Paper*, No.7. Geneva.

Adam, Christopher, Benno Ndulu and Nii Kwaku Sowa (1996). Liberalisation and seigniorage revenue in Kenya, Ghana and Tanzania. *Journal of Development Studies*, vol. 32, No. 4, pp. 531-553.

Adams, Richard H., Jr. (1998). Remittances, investment, and rural asset accumulation in Pakistan. *Economic Development and Cultural Change*, vol. 47, No. 1, pp. 155-174. Chicago, Illinois: The University of Chicago Press.

_____ (2004). Remittances and poverty in Guatemala. *World Bank Policy Research Working Paper*, No. 3418. Washington, D.C.: World Bank. September.

Agosin, Manuel (2000). Corea y Taiwan en la crisis financiera asiática. In *Crisis financieras en economías 'exitosas'*, Ricardo Ffrench-Davis ed. Santiago: ECLAC/McGraw-Hill.

_____, and Ricardo Mayer (2000). Foreign investment in developing countries: does it crowd in domestic investment? *UNCTAD Discussion Papers*, No. 146. Geneva: United Nations Conference on Trade and Development. February.

Alexandraki, K., and H. P. Lankes (2004). The impact of preference erosion on middle-income developing countries. *IMF Working Paper*, No. WP/04/169. Washington D.C.: IMF Policy Development and Review Department. September.

Allen, Mark (2004). IMF conditionality and ownership. Remarks prepared for the Development Policy Forum on "Conditionality Revisited" organized by the World Bank, Paris, 5 July.

Anderson, K., and others (2001). The cost of rich (and poor) country protection to developing countries. Discussion Paper, No. 0136. Adelaide, Australia: Centre for International Economic Studies, Adelaide University. September.

Andriamananjara, Soamiely (1999). On the size and number of regional integration arrangements: a political economy model. Department of Economics, University of Maryland at College Park, Maryland.

Aoki, Masahiko (2001). *Toward a Comparative Institutional Analysis*. Cambridge, Massachusetts: The MIT Press.

Asian Development Bank (2004). *Asian Development Outlook 2004*. Manila.

Atkinson, Anthony (2005). *New Sources of Development Finance*. Oxford, United Kingdom: Oxford University Press.

_____, and Joseph Stiglitz (1980). *Lectures on Public Economics*. New York: McGraw-Hill.

Atta-Mensah, Joseph (2004). Commodity-linked bonds: a potential means for less-developed countries to raise foreign capital. *Bank of Canada Working Paper*, No. 2004-20. Ottawa.

Attanasio, Orazio, Lucio Picci and Antonello Scorcu (1997). Saving, growth and investment: a macroeconomic analysis using a panel of countries. Washington, D.C.: World Bank.

Aykut, Dick, and Dilip Ratha (2004). South-South FDI flows: how big are they? *Transnational Corporations,* vol. 13, No. 1 (April), pp.149-176. Geneva: United Nations Conference on Trade and Development.

Azam, Jean-Paul (1998). Politiques macro-économiques et réduction de la pauvreté. Communication à l'atelier «Pauvreté, répartition des revenus, et questions relatives au marché du travail» du Centre de recherche en économie appliquée (CREA), Algiers.

_____, Augustin Fosu and Njuguna S. Ndung'u (2002). Explaining slow growth in Africa. *African Development Review,* vol. 14, No. 4 (December), pp. 177-220.

Bacchetta, Marc, and B. Bora (2004). Industrial tariffs, LDCs and the Doha Development Agenda. In *The WTO, Developing Countries and the Doha Development Agenda: Prospects and Challenges for Trade-Led Growth,* B. Guha-Khasnobis, ed. Basingstoke, United Kingdom: Palgrave Macmillan.

Baldwin, Robert (2003). Openness and growth: what's the empirical relationship?, *NBER Working Paper,* No. 9578. Cambridge, Massachusetts: National Bureau of Economic Research. March.

Bank for International Settlements (2003). *Quarterly Review* (September), Basel, Switzerland.

_____ (2004). *Quarterly Review* (June), pp. 67-79. Basel, Switzerland.

_____ (2005). *Quarterly Review* (March), pp. 31-39. Basel, Switzerland.

_____ (2004a). Implementation of the new capital adequacy framework in non-Basel Committee member countries. Financial Stability Institute Occasional Paper, No. 4.

Basu, Anupam, and Krishna Srinivasan (2002). Foreign direct investment in Africa?some case studies, *IMF Working Paper,* No. WP/02/61. Washington, D.C.: IMF. March.

Berensmann, Kathrin, and Frank Schroeder (2005). A proposal for a new international debt framework (IDF) for the prevention and resolution of debt crisis in middle-income countries. Paper for the Multistakeholder Consultation on Systemic Issues in Lima, 17 and 18 February 2005. Available from http://www.new-rules.org/docs/ffdconsultdocs/berensmanna-shroeder.pdf.

Berensztein, Eduardo, and Paulo Mauro (2004). The case for GDP-indexed bonds. *Economic Policy,* vol. 19, pp. 165-216.

Beynon, J. (2003). Poverty efficient aid allocations: Collier/Dollar revisited. *ESAU Working Paper,* No. 2. London: Economics and Statistics Analysis Unit, Overseas Development Institute.

Bhinda, Nils, and others (1999). *Private Capital Flows to Africa: Perception and Reality.* The Hague: Forum on Debt and Development (FONDAD).

Bies, Susan (2002). Banking supervision and its application in developing countries. Speech delivered at the World Bank Group Finance Forum, Chantilly, Virginia, 20 June. Available from www.bis.org.

Bigsten, Arne, Jorgen Levin and Hakan Persson (2001). Debt relief on growth: a study of Zambia and Tanzania. Paper prepared for the WIDER Development Conference on Debt Relief, Helsinki.

Birdsall, Nancy (2004). Seven deadly sins: reflections on donor failings. *Center for Global Development Working Paper*, No. 50. Washington, D.C.: Center for Global Development. December. Also available from http://www.cgdev.org/docs/Working%20Paper%2050,pdf.

_____, and A. Hamoudi (2002). Commodity dependence, trade, and growth: when "openness" is not enough. *Center for Global Development Working Paper*, No. 7. Washington D.C.

_____, and Liliana Rojas-Suarez, eds. (2004). *Financing Development: The Power of Regionalism*. Washington, D.C.: Center for Global Development.

_____, Stijn Claessens and Ishac Diwan (2004). Policy selectivity forgone: debt and donor behaviour in Africa. In *Debt Relief for Poor Countries*, Tony Addison, Henrik Hansen, and Finn Tarp, eds. New York: Palgrave Macmillan, in association with the United Nations University.

Bonin, J. P. and István Ábel (2000). Retail banking in Hungary: a foreign affair?. Background paper for *World Development Report, 2002* (New York, Oxford University Press, 2002). Middletown, Connecticut: Wesleyan University.

Boone, Peter (1996). Politics and the effectiveness of foreign aid. *European Economic Review*, vol. 40, No.2, pp. 289–329.

Borio, Claudio (2003). Towards a macroprudential framework for financial supervision and regulation? *BIS Working Papers*, No. 128. Basel, Switzerland: Bank for International Settlements.

Bosworth, Barry, and Susan M. Collins (2003). The empirics of growth: an update. *Brookings Papers on Economic Activity*, No. 2, pp. 113-206. Washington, D.C.: The Brookings Institution.

Boughton, James M. (2001). *Silent Evolution: The International Monetary Fund 1979-1989*. Washington, D.C.: IMF.

BradyNet Forum. Http://www.bradynet.com/bbs/bradybonds/100090-0.html.

Brown, D.K., A.V. Deardorff and R.M. Stern (2002). Multilateral, regional, and bilateral trade-policy options for the United States and Japan. Research Seminar in International Economics Discussion Paper, No. 490. School of Public Policy, University of Michigan, Ann Arbor, Michigan. 16 December.

Buira, Ariel (2003). An analysis of IMF conditionality. G-24 Discussion Paper, No.22, p. 19. August. UNCTAD/GDS/MDPB/G24/2003/3.

_____ (2005). Financial crises and international cooperation. Briefing note prepared for "the Orderly Resolution of Financial Crises: A G20-led Initiative", 29 and 30 January 2005, Mexico City. 30 January. Available from www.globalcentres.org.

Bulír, Aleš, and A. Javier Hamann (2001). *How Volatile and Unpredictable are Aid Flows, and What are the Policy Implications?* WIDER Discussion Paper, No. 2001/143. Helsinki: United Nations University World Institute for Development Economics Research.

_____ (2003). Aid volatility: an empirical assessment. *IMF Staff Papers*, vol. 50, No. 1, pp. 64-89. Also available from http://www.imf.org/External/Pubs/FT/staffp/2003/01/bulir.htm.

_____ (2005). Volatility of development aid: from the frying pan into the fire? International Monetary Fund paper presented at the Seminar on Foreign Aid and Macroeconomic Management, Maputo, 14 and 15 March.

Burney, Nadeem (1987). Workers' remittances from the Middle East and their effect on Pakistan's economy. *The Pakistan Development Review*, vol. 26, No. 4 (winter). Islamabad: Pakistan Institute of Development Economics, Ouaid-i-Azam University.

Burnside, Craig, and David Dollar (1997). Aid, policies and growth. *Policy Research Working Paper*, No. 1777. Washington, D.C.: Development Research Group, World Bank. June.

_____ (2000). Aid, policies and growth. *American Economic Review*, vol. 90, No. 4 (September), pp. 847-868.

Cafiero, Mario, and Javier Llorens (2002). *La Argentina Robada*. Buenos Aires: Ediciones Macchi.

Camdessus, Michel (2000). An agenda for the IMF at the start of the 21st Century. Remarks at the Council on Foreign Relations, New York. February.

Caprio, Gerard, Jr., and Aslï Demirgüç-Kunt (1997). The role of long term finance: theory and evidence. Policy Research Department, World Bank. February.

Carrol, Christopher, and David Weil (1993). Saving and growth: a reinterpretation. *NBER Discussion Paper*, No. 4470. Cambridge, Massachusetts: National Bureau of Economic Research.

Chauvet, L., and P. Guillaumont (2002). Aid and growth revisited: policy, economic vulnerability and political instability. 7 July 2002 version of paper presented at the Annual Bank Conference on Development Economics, ABCDE-Europe, Oslo, 24-26 June.

Chenery, Hollis, Sherman Robinson and Moshe Syrquin (1986). *Industrialization and Growth: A Comparative Study*. New York: Oxford University Press.

Chew, Lillian (1996). *Managing Derivative Risks: The Use and Abuse of Leverage*. New York: John Wiley.

Claessens, S., S Djankov and L. Lang (1999). Who controls East Asian Corporations? *World Bank Policy Research Working Paper*, No. 2054. Washington, D.C.: World Bank. February.

Clarke, George, and others (2001). Foreign bank entry: experience, implications for developing countries and agenda for further research. *Policy Research Working Paper*, No. 2698. Washington, D.C.: World Bank.

_____, Robert Cull and Maria Soledad Martinez Peria (2001). Does foreign bank penetration reduce access to credit in developing countries? evidence from asking borrowers. World Bank Development Research Group. *Policy Research Working Paper*, No. 2716. Washington, D.C.: World Bank. November.

Clemens, Michael, Steven Radelet and Rikhil Bhavnani (2004). Counting chickens when they hatch: the short-term effect of aid on growth. Working Paper, No. 44. Washington, D.C.: Center for Global Development.

Clunies-Ross, Anthony (2000). A tax on foreign-exchange transactions: report of a
            consultation held by Coopération Internationale pour le Développement et la
            Solidarité (CIDSE) in collaboration with the University of Antwerp (UFSIA),
            22 October 1999. February.

_____ (2004). *Imminent Prospects for Additional Finance: What Might Be Done Now or
            Soon and Under What Conditions.* Research Paper, No. 2004/45. Helsinki: United
            Nations University World Institute for Development Economics Research. July.

Cohen, Daniel (1996). The sustainability of African debt. *World Bank Policy Research Working
            Paper*, No. 1621 (July). International Finance Division, International Economics
            Department, World Bank.

_____ (2001). The HIPC initiative: true or false promises. *International Finance,* vol. 4,
            No. 3, pp. 363-380.

Collier, Paul, and Jan Dehn (2001). Aid, shocks and growth. *Policy Research Working Paper*,
            No. 2688. Washington, D.C.: Development Research Group, World Bank.

Collier, Paul and David Dollar (1999). Aid allocation and poverty reduction. *Policy Research
            Working Paper*, No. 2041. Washington, D.C.: Development Research Group,
            World Bank. January.

_____ (2001). Can the world cut poverty in half? How policy reform and effective aid
            can meet the international development goals. *World Development*, vol. 29, No.
            11, pp. 1787-1802.

_____ (2002). Aid allocation and poverty reduction. *European Economic Review*, vol 46,
            No. 8, pp. 1475-1500.

Collier, Paul, and Anke Hoeffler (2002). Aid, policy and growth in post-conflict countries.
            Policy Research Working Paper, No. 2902. Washington, D.C.: Development
            Research Group, World Bank. October.

Comisión Especial de la Cámara de Diputados, 2005, República Argentina (2005). *Fuga de
            Divisas en la Argentina: Informe Final.* Buenos Aires: Comisión Latinoamérica de
            Ciencias Sociales (Flacso) Siglo XXI.

Commission for Africa (2005). *Our Common Interest: Report of the Commission for Africa.*
            Available from
            http://www.commissionforafrica.org/english/report/thereport/cfafullreport_/.pdf
            (accessed 13 June 2005).

Commonwealth Secretariat (2004). Review of IMF/World Bank issues. Paper prepared by the
            Commonwealth Secretariat, London, pp. 4 and 8. August.

Cooper, Richard (2002). Chapter 11 for countries? *Foreign Affairs*, vol. 81, No.4.

Cordella, Tito, and Eduardo Levy Yeyati (2004). Country insurance. IMF *Working Paper*, No.
            WP/04/148.

_____ (2005). A (new) country insurance facility. *IMF Working Paper*, No. WP/05/23.
            January.

Council of Economic Advisers (2004). Growth-indexed bonds: a primer. 22 November.
            Mimeo.

Cox, Alejandra, and Manuelita Ureta (2003). International migration, remittances and schooling: evidence from El Salvador. *NBER Working Paper*, No. 9766. Cambridge, Massachusetts: National Bureau of Economic Research.

Crawford, Jo-Ann, and Roberto V. Fiorentino (2005). The changing landscape of regional trade agreements. *WTO Discussion Paper*, No. 8, p. 3. Geneva: World Trade Organization.

Crockett, Andrew (2000). Marrying the micro- and macro-prudential dimensions of financial stability. 21 September. Available from www.bis.org.

_____ (2001a). Banking supervision and regulation: international trends. Remarks at the 64th Banking Convention of the Mexican Bankers' Association, 30 March. Available from www.bis.org.

_____ (2001b). Monetary policy and financial stability. 13 February. Available from www.bis.org.

Dalgaard, Carl-Johan, and Henrik Hansen (2001). On aid, growth and good policies. *Journal of Development Studies*, vol 37, No. 6, pp. 17-41.

_____ and Finn Tarp (2002). On the empirics of foreign aid and growth. *CREDIT Research Paper*, No. 02/08. Nottingham, United Kingdom: University of Nottingham Centre for Research in Economic Development and International Trade.

D'Arista, Jane (1979). Private overseas lending: too far, too fast? In *Debt and the Less Developed Countries*, Jonathan David Aronson, ed. Boulder, Colorado: Westview Press, pp. 57-58.

de Aghion, Beatriz Armendáriz (1999). Development banking. *Journal of Development Economics*, vol. 58, No. 1 (February), pp. 83–100.

Demirgüç-Kunt, Aslï, and Vojislav Maksimovic (1996). Institutions, financial markets and firm debt maturity. *Policy Research Working Paper*, No. 1686. World Bank. September.

Department for International Development (DFID) (2004). Rethinking tropical agricultural commodities. Available from http://dfid-agriculture-consultation.nri.org/summaries/wp10.pdf (accessed 13 June 2005). London.

Dimaranan, B., T. Hertel and R. Keeney (2004). OECD domestic support and developing countries. In *The WTO, Developing Countries and the Doha Development Agenda: Prospects and Challenges for Trade-Led Growth*, B. Guha-Khasnobis, ed. Basingstoke, United Kingdom, and New York: Palgrave Macmillan and UNU/WIDER.

Dobson, Wendy, and Gary Hufbauer, assisted by Hyon Koo Cho (2001). *World Capital Markets: Challenge to the G-10*. Washington, D.C.: Institute for International Economics. May.

Dodd, Randall (2004). Protecting developing economies from price shocks. *Special Policy Brief* 18. Washington, D.C.: Financial Policy Forum. 21 September.

_____ (2005). The consequences of liberalizing derivative markets. *Initiative for Policy Dialogue: Capital Market Liberalization Companion Volume*. New York: Oxford University Press. Forthcoming.

Dollar, David, and Aart Kraay (2001). Trade, growth, and poverty. *Policy Research Working Paper*, No. WPS 2615. Development Research Group, World Bank. June.

Dooley, Michael P., David Folkerts-Landau and Peter Garber (2003). An essay on the revived Bretton Woods system. *NBER Working Paper*, No. 9971. Cambridge, Massachusetts: National Bureau of Economic Research. September.

_____ (2004a). The revived Bretton Woods system: the effects of periphery intervention and reserve management on interest rates and exchange rates in center countries. *NBER Working Paper*, No. 10332. Cambridge, Massachusetts: National Bureau of Economic Research. March.

_____ (2004b). The US current account deficit and economic development: collateral for a total return swap. *NBER Working Paper*, No. 10727. Cambridge, Massachusetts: National Bureau of Economic Research. August.

Easterly, William (2001). *The Elusive Quest for Growth: Economists' Adventures and Misadventures in the Tropics*. Cambridge, Massachusetts, and London: The MIT Press.

_____ and Ross Levine (2001). It's not factor accumulation: stylized facts and growth models. *The World Bank Economic Review*, vol. 15, No.2, pp. 177–291.

Eatwell, John, and Lance Taylor (2000). *Global Finance at Risk: The Case for International Regulation*. New York: The New Press.

Economic and Social Commission for Asia and the Pacific (2005). Implementing the Monterrey Consensus in the Asian and Pacific Region: Achieving Coherence and Consistency. Sales No. E.05.II.F.8. New York: United Nations.

Economic Commission for Africa (2004). *Economic Report on Africa 2004: Unlocking Africa's Trade Potential on the Global Economy*. Sales No. E.04.II.K.12. United Nations: Addis Ababa.

Economic Commission for Latin America and the Caribbean (1994). *Open Regionalism in Latin America and the Caribbean: Economic Integration as a Contribution to Changing Production Patterns with Social Equity*. LC/G.1801/Rev.1-P/I. Sales No. E.94.II.G.3. Santiago: ECLAC.

_____ (2002). *Growth with Stability: Financing for Development in the New International Context*. Sales No. E.02.II.G.20. Santiago: Economic Commission for Latin America and the Caribbean. March.

_____ (2003). *Foreign Direct Investment in Latin America and the Carribean 2002*. Santiago: ECLAC.

_____ (2004a). *Foreign Investment in Latin America and the Caribbean 2003*. Sales No. E.04.II.G.54. Santiago: ECLAC.

_____ (2004b). Desarrollo Productivo en Economías Abiertas. LC/G.2234(SES.30/3). Santiago: Economic Commission for Latin America and the Caribbean. 11 June.

_____ (2005). *Foreign Investment in Latin America and the Caribbean* 2004. Sales No. E.05.II.G.32. Santiago: ECLAC.

Eichengreen, Barry (2004). Financial instability. In *Global Crises, Global Solutions*, Bjorn Lomborg, ed. Cambridge, United Kingdom, and New York: Cambridge University Press.

Eichengreen, Barry (2004). Global imbalances and the lessons of Bretton Woods. *NBER Working Paper*, No. 10497. Cambridge, Massachusetts: National Bureau of Economic Research. May.

_____ (2005). Preparing for the next financial crisis. Briefing note prepared for "The Orderly Resolution of Financial Crises. A G-20 led Initiative", 29 and 30 January 2005, Mexico City. Available from www.globalcentres.org.

_____, Ricardo Hausman and Ugo Panizza (2003). Currency mismatches, debt intolerance, and original sin: why they are not the same and why it matters. *NBER Working Paper*, No. 10036. Cambridge, Massachusetts: National Bureau of Economic Research.

Emmerij, Louis, Richard Jolly and T.G. Weiss (2001). *Ahead of the Curve? UN Ideas and Global Challenges*. Bloomington, Indiana: Indiana University Press.

Epstein, Gerald, Ilene Grabel and Jomo Kwame Sundaram (2003). Capital management techniques in developing countries: an assessment of experiences from the 1990s and lessons for the future. Paper presented at the XVIth Technical Group Meeting of the G-24 in Port of Spain, Trinidad and Tobago, 13 and 14 February 2003.

Escaith, Hubert (2004). El crecimiento económico en América Latina y sus perspectivas más allá del sexenio perdido. *Problemas del Desarrollo* (Mexico), vol. 35, No.139 (October- December).

Euromoney (2004). December, pp. 92-99. London.

European Central Bank (2005). Financial flows to emerging market economies: changing patterns and recent developments. *Monthly Bulletin* (January 2005), pp. 59-73. Frankfurt am Main, Germany.

European Network on Debt and Development (Eurodad) (2002). Moving beyond good and bad performance. Brussels, 26 June.

Ffrench-Davis, Ricardo, and Stephany Griffith-Jones (2003). *From Capital Surges to Drought: Seeking Stability for Emergency Economies*. UNU-WIDER Studies in Development Economics and Policy Series. Basingstoke, United Kingdom: Palgrave Macmillan.

Financial Times (2005). Shock of the new: a changed financial landscape may be eroding resistance to systemic risk. Comment and analysis. 16 February.

Fischer, Stanley (2002). Financial crises and reform of the international financial system. *NBER Working Paper*, No. 9297. Cambridge, Massachusetts: National Bureau of Economic Research. October.

Fraga, Arminio, Ilan Goldfain and Andre Minella (2003). Inflation targeting in emerging market economies. *NBER Working Paper*, No. 10019. Cambridge, Massachusetts: National Bureau of Economic Research. October.

François, Joseph, Hans van Meijl and Frank van Tongeren (2003). Economic implications of trade liberalization under the Doha Round. Centre d'Etudes Prospectives et d'Informations Internationales Working Paper, No. 2003-20. Ministry of the Economy, Finance and Industry, Paris. 30 April.

Frankel, Jeffrey (1994). Exchange rate policy. In *American Economic Policy in the 1980s*, Martin Feldstein, ed. Chicago, Illinois, and London: The University of Chicago Press, pp. 293-341.

García, A. Bonilla, and J.V. Gruat (2003). *Social Protection: A Life Cycle Continuum Investment for Social Justice, Poverty Reduction and Sustainable Development.* Geneva: International Labour Office.

Gavin, Michael, Ricardo Hausman and Ernesto Talvi (1997). Saving behavior in Latin America: overview and policy issues. Working Paper, No. 346. Inter-American Development Bank, Office of the Chief Economist, Washington, D.C. May.

Geithner, Timothy (2004). Changes in the structure of the U.S. financial system and implications for systemic risk. Remarks before the Conference on Systemic Financial Crises at the Federal Reserve Bank of Chicago, Illinois, 1 October.

_____ (2005). Further investments to strengthen the financial system. Remarks before the Economic Club of Washington, Washington, D.C., 9 February. Available from www.bis.org.

Gemmell, N, and M. McGillivray (1998). Aid and tax instability and the government budget constraint in developing countries. *CREDIT Research Paper*, No. 98/1. Nottingham, United Kingdom: University of Nottingham Centre for Research in Economic Development and International Trade.

Ghosh, Sucharita, and Steven Yamarik (2004). Does trade creation measure up? a reexamination of the effects of regional trading arrangements. *Economic Letters*, vol. 82, No. 2, pp. 213-219.

Gilbert, Christopher L. (1987). International commodity agreements: design and performance. *World Development*, vol 15, No. 5, pp. 591-616.

_____, A. Powell and D. Vines (1999). Positioning the World Bank. *Economic Journal*, vol. 109 (November).

_____, and D. Vines (2000). *The World Bank: Structure and Policies.* Cambridge, United Kingdom: Cambridge University Press.

Gilbert, John, Robert Scollay and Bijit Bora (2001). *Assessing Regional Trading Arrangements in the Asia-Pacific Region.* United Nations Conference on Trade and Development, Policy Issues in International Trade and Commodities Study Series, No. 15. UNCTAD/ITCD/TAB/16. Sales No. E.01.II.D.21.

Goldstein, Morris (2003). Debt sustainability, Brazil and the IMF. Washington, D.C.: Institute for International Economics, February. wp 03-1.

_____ (2005). A note on improving the international financial architecture. Briefing note prepared for "The Orderly Resolution of Financial Crises. A G-20 led Initiative", 29 and 30 January 2005, Mexico City. 30 January. Available from www. globalcentres.org.

Goodhart. C., and J. Danielsson (2001). The inter-temporal nature of risk. Presented at the 23rd European Money and Finance Forum (SUERF) Colloquium on "Technology and finance: challenges for financial markets, business strategies and policy makers", Brussels, October. Available from www.bis.org.

Gorton, Gary B., and K. Geert Rouwenhorst (2005). Facts and fantasies about commodity futures. *Yale International Center for Finance Working Paper*, No. 04-20. 28 February. Available from the Social Science Research Network Electronic Paper Collection website http://ssrn.com/abstract=560042 (accessed 13 June 2005).

Griffith-Jones, Stephany (1998). *Global Capital Flows: Should They be Regulated?* Basingstoke, United Kingdom, and New York: Macmillan and St. Martin's Press.

_____, and José Antonio Ocampo (2003). *What progress on international financial reform? why so limited?* Prepared for the Expert Group on Development Issues. Sweden.

_____, Miguel Angel Segoviano and Stephen Spratt (2003). Submission to the Basel Committee on Banking Supervision: CP3 and the developing world. Institute of Development Studies, University of Sussex, Brighton, United Kingdom. Available from www.stephanygj.com.

_____ (2004a). Basilea II: los países en desarrollo y la diversificación de la cartera. In *Revista de la CEPAL: Agosto 2004,* pp.153-169. Santiago: ECLAC.

_____ (2004b). CAD3 and developing countries: the potential impact of diversification effects on international lending patterns and pro-cyclicality. Institute of Development Studies, University of Sussex. August. Available from www.stephanygj.com.

_____, and Ana Fuzzo de Lima (2004). Alternative loan guarantee mechanisms and project finance for infrastructure in developing countries. In *The New Public Finance, Responding to Global Challenges*, Inge Kaul and others, eds. New York: Oxford University Press. Forthcoming.

_____, and Ricardo Gottschalk (2006). Costs of currency crises and benefits of international financial reform. Currently available from www.stephanygj.com.

Groupe de travail présidé par Jean-Pierre Landau (2004). *Les nouvelles contributions financièrs internationales.* Paris: La documentation française.

Gugiatti, Mark, and Anthony Richards (2003). Do collective action clauses influence bond yields? new evidence from emerging markets. Research Discussion Paper, RDP 2003-02. Reserve Bank of Australia, Sydney. March.

Guillaumont, P., and L. Chauvet (2001). Aid and performance: a reassessment. *Journal of Development Studies*, vol. 37, No. 6, pp. 66-92.

Gunter, Bernhard G. (2001). Does the HIPC Initiative achieve its goal of debt sustainability? United Nations University/World Institute for Development Economics Research (UNU/WIDER) Discussion Paper, No. 2001/100. September. Available from www.wider.unu.edu/publications/dps/dp2001-100.pdf.

_____ (2003). Achieving long-term debt sustainability in all heavily indebted poor countries (HIPCs). Discussion paper prepared for the Intergovernmental Group of 24 (G-24) XVI Technical Group Meeting in Trinidad and Tobago, 13 and 14 February.

Gurría, José Angel, and Paul Volcker (2001). *The Role of the Multilateral Development Banks in Emerging Market Economies.* Washington, D.C.: Carnegie Endowment for International Peace, EMP Financial Advisors, LLC, and the Inter-American Dialogue.

G-24 Secretariat (2003). Heavily Indebted Poor Country (HIPC) Initiative. Briefing paper, No. 2. March.

Haldane, Andrew G., and Mark Kruger (2004). The resolution of international financial crises: an alternative framework. In *The IMF and its Critics: Reform of Global Financial Architecture*, David Vines and Christopher L. Gilbert, eds. New York: Cambridge University Press.

Hansen, H., and F. Tarp (2001). Aid effectiveness disputed. *Journal of International Development*, vol. 12, pp. 375-398.

Hanson, Gordon H. (2001). Should countries promote foreign direct investment? *G-24 Discussion Paper Series*, No. 9 (February 2001). United Nations Conference on Trade and Development and Center for International Development, Harvard University. United Nations: Geneva and New York.

Harrison, Glenn, Thomas Rutherford and David Tarr (2001). Chile's regional arrangements and the Free Trade Agreement of the Americas: the importance of market access. *World Bank, Policy Research Working Paper*, No. 2634. Washington, D.C. July.

_____, and others (2003). Regional, multilateral and unilateral trade policies of MERCOSUR for growth and poverty reduction in Brazil. *World Bank Policy Research Working Paper*, No. 3051. Washington, D.C. May.

Hausman, Ricardo, and Ugo Panizza (2003). The mystery of original sin. Kennedy School of Government, Harvard University, and Inter-American Development Bank, Washington, D.C.

_____, and Andres Velasco (2004). The causes of financial crises: moral failure versus market failure. December. Available from http://ksghome.harvard.edu.

Herman, Barry (2004). How well do measurements of an enabling domestic environment for development stand up. Paper prepared for the XVIII Technical Group Meeting of the Group of 24, Geneva, 8 and 9 March 2004.

Hindustan Times (2003). Developing muscles. 13 November.

Hoekman, Bernard., F. Ng and M. Olarreaga (2003). Reducing agriculture tariffs versus domestic support: what is more important for developing countries? *World Bank Policy Research Paper*, No. 2918, revised. Washington D.C. March.

_____, and L. Alan Winters (2005). Trade and employment: stylized facts and research findings. World Bank. March.

Imboden, Kathryn (2005). Building inclusive financial sectors: widening access, enhancing growth, alleviating poverty. 10 March. United Nations Capital Development Fund.

Institute of Development Studies, University of Sussex (2000). *A Foresight and Policy Study of the Multilateral Development Banks*. Sussex, United Kingdom.

Institute of International Finance (2005). Statement by the Managing Director at the Annual Meeting of the Asian Development Bank, 4 May. Available from www.iif.com.

Inter-American Development Bank (2001). Remittances to Latin America and the Caribbean: comparative statistics. Paper prepared by the Inter-American Development Bank/ Multilateral Investment Fund for the Regional Conference: Remittances as a Development Tool, Washington, D.C., May 2001.

Inter-American Development Bank/Multilateral Investment Fund (2004). Remittances and the Dominican Republic: survey of recipients in the Dominican Republic and senders in the United States. Power Point presentation at IDB/MIF New York Conference, Columbia University, New York City, 23 November 2004. Available from http://www.iadb.org/mif/v2/files/bendixen_NYNov04.pdf.

Inter-American Development Bank/Multilateral Investment Fund/Pew Hispanic Center (2003). Receptores de remesas en México: encuesta de opinión pública, septiembre–octubre 2003. Power Point presentation at IDB/MIF Conference in Mexico City. Available from http://www.iadb.org/mif/v2/spanish/files/BendixenME2003spa.pdf.

International Centre for Trade and Sustainable Development (ICTSD) (2003). Special and differential treatment. *Doha Round Briefing Series*, vol. 1, No. 13 (February). Geneva: ICTSD.

_____ (various years). *BRIDGES Weekly Trade News Digest*. Geneva.

International Development Association (2005). Countries ceasing to borrow from IDA, 1960-2001. Available from www.worldbank.org/ida (assessed on 8 June 2005).

International Financial Institutions Advisory Commission (IFIAC) (2000). *Report of the International Financial Institutions Advisory Commission*. Washington, D.C. March.

International Labour Organization (2005). *World Employment Report, 2004-05*. Geneva: International Labour Office.

International Monetary Fund (2000). Debt and reserve-related indicators of external vulnerability. Paper prepared by the Policy Development and Review Department in consultation with other Departments. Washington, D.C. 23 March.

_____ (2001). The challenge of maintaining long-term external debt sustainability. Paper prepared by the Staffs of the World Bank and the International Monetary Fund. Washington, D.C. 20 April.

_____ (2002a). *Global Financial Stability Report, December 2002*. Washington, D.C.

_____ (2002b). Assessing sustainability. Paper prepared by the Policy Development and Review Department. Washington, D.C. 28 May.

_____ (2002c). Fund policy on lending into arrears to private creditors: further consideration of the good faith criterion. Paper prepared by the International Capital Markets, Policy Development and Review and Legal Departments. Washington D.C. 30 July.

_____ (2003a). *World Economic Outlook September 2003: Public Debt in Emerging Markets*. Washington, D.C.: IMF.

_____ (2003b). *Global Financial Stability Report: Market Developments and Issues: March 2003*. Washington, D.C.: IMF.

_____ (2003c). *Global Financial Stability Report: Market Development and Issues: September 2003*. Washington, D.C.: IMF.

_____ (2003d). *IMF Survey*, vol. 32 (Supplement 2003).

_____ (2003e). Debt sustainability in low-income countries: towards a forward-looking strategy. Paper prepared by the Staff of the Policy Development and Review Department. Washington, D.C. 23 May.

_____ (2003f). Sustainability assessments: review of application and methodological refinements. Paper prepared by the Policy Development and Review Department in collaboration with the Monetary and Financial Systems Department and in consultation with other Departments. Washington, D.C. 10 June.

_____ (2003g). The restructuring of sovereign debt: assessing the benefits, risks, and feasibility of aggregating claims. Paper prepared by the Legal Department. Washington, D.C. September.

_____ (2004a). *Global Financial Stability Report, April 2004*. Washington, D.C.

_____ (2004b). *Global Financial Stability Report, September 2004*. Washington, D.C.

_____ (2004c). Communiqué of the International Monetary and Financial Committee of the Board of Governors of the International Monetary Fund. Press release No. 04/84. 24 April.

_____ (2004d). Report of the Executive Board to the International Monetary and Financial Committee (IMFC) on quotas, voice and representation. Prepared by the Finance and Secretary's Departments. 24 September. Available from www.imf.org.

_____ (2004e). Progress report to the International Monetary and Financial Committee on crisis resolution. Washington, D.C. 20 April.

_____ (2004f). Fund conditionality: a provisional update. *IMF Staff Paper* (June). Available from www.imf.org.

_____ (2004g). IMF Executive Board discusses financial sector regulation: issues and gaps. *Public Information Notice (PIN)*, No. 04/131. 22 November. Available from www.imf.org.

_____ (2004h). IMF Executive Board discusses "Fixed to float: operational aspects of moving toward exchange rate flexibility". *Public Information Notice (PIN)*, No. 04/141. 30 December. Available from www.imf.org.

_____ (2004i). The design of Fund-supported programs: overview. Policy Development and Review Department, p. 24. 24 November.

_____ (2004j). Debt sustainability in low-income countries: proposal for an operational framework and policy implications. Prepared by the Staffs of the IMF and the World Bank. Washington, D.C. 3 February.

_____ (2004k). Financial sector regulation: issues and gaps. Background paper, Monetary and Financial Systems Department. 17 August. Available from www.imf.org.

_____ (2004l). Sovereign debt structure for crisis prevention. Discussion paper prepared by the Research Department, pp. 59-60. 2 July.

_____ (2005a). Heavily Indebted Poor Countries (HIPC) Initiative: Statistical Update. 11 April.

_____ (2005b). IMF Executive Board approves proposal to subsidize emergency assistance for natural disasters for PRGF-eligible members. *Public Information Notice (PIN)*, No. 05/8. 27 January. Available from www.imf.org.

_____ (2005c). IMF Executive Board discusses balance sheet approach to analysis of debt-related vulnerabilities in emerging markets. *Public Information Notice (PIN)*, No. 05/36. 22 March. Availabe from www.imf.org.

_____ (2005d). IMF Executive Board discusses program design. *Public Information Notice (PIN)*, No. 05/16. 8 February. Available from www.imf.org.

_____ (2005e). *IMF Survey*, vol. 34. No. 5 (21 March).

_____ (2005f). Subsidization of IMF emergency assistance for natural disasters. Press release, No. 05/90. 22 April.

_____ (2005h). *Global Financial Stability Report, April 2005*. Washington, D.C.: IMF.

_____, Independent Evaluation Office (2003). Evaluation of fiscal adjustment in IMF-supported programs. Washington, D.C. 9 September.

_____, Independent Evaluation Office (2005). Draft issues paper for an evaluation on structural conditionality in IMF-supported programs. 18 March. Available from www.imf.org.

_____, and International Development Association (2004). Debt sustainability in low-income countries: further considerations on an operational framework and policy implications. Prepared by the Staffs of the IMF and the World Bank. Washington, D.C. 10 September.

_____ (2005). Operational framework for debt sustainability assessments in low-income countries: further considerations. Prepared by the Staffs of the IMF and the World Bank, Washington, D.C. 28 March.

International Task Force on Commodity Risk Management in Developing Countries (ITF) (1999). Dealing with commodity price volatility in developing countries: a proposal for a market-based approach. Discussion Paper for the Roundtable on Commodity Risk Management in Developing Countries. Washington, D. C.

Ito, Takatoshi, Eiji Ogawa and Yuri Sasaki (1999). Establishment of the East Asian Fund. In *Stabilization of Currencies and Financial Systems in East Asia and International Financial Cooperation*. Tokyo: Institute for International Monetary Affairs, chap. 3.

Jansen, Marion (2004). Income volatility in small and developing economies: export concentration matters. Geneva:World Trade Organization.

Jenks, C. Wilfred (1942). Some legal aspects of the financing of international institutions. *Transactions of the Grotius Society*, vol. 28, pp. 87-132.

Johnson, S., and A. Subramanian (2005). Aid, governance, and the political economy: growth and institutions. International Monetary Fund paper presented at the Seminar on Foreign Aid and Macroeconomic Management, Maputo, 14 and 15 March.

Kaldor, Nicholas (1978). *Further Essays on Economic Theory*. London: Duckworth.

Kaminsky, Graciela L., Carmen M. Reinhart and Carlos A. Végh (2004). When it rains, it pours: procyclical capital flows and macroeconomic policies. *NBER Working Paper*, No. 10780. Cambridge, Massachusetts: National Bureau of Economic Research.

Kaplan, Ethan, and Dani Rodrik (2001). Did the Malaysian capital controls work? John F. Kennedy School of Government, Harvard University, Cambridge, Massachusetts.

Kapur, Devesh (2003a). Do as I say not as I do: a critique of G-7 proposals on reforming the Multilateral Development Banks. *G-24 Discussion Paper Series*, No. 20. United Nations: New York and Geneva. February.

_____ (2003b). Remittances: the new development mantra? Paper prepared for the G-24 Technical Group Meeting. Harvard University, Cambridge, Massachusetts, and Centre for Global Development, Washington, D.C. 25 August.

_____, John Lewis and Richard Webb (1997). *The World Bank: Its First Half Century*, vol. 1., *History*. Washington, D.C.: The Brookings Institution.

Karacaovali, Baybars, and Nuno Limão (2005). The clash of liberalizations: preferential versus multilateral trade liberalization in the European Union. *World Bank Policy Research Working Paper Series*, No. 3493.

Keck, A., and P. Low (2004). Special and differential treatment in the WTO: Why, when and how? *WTO Staff Working Paper*, No. ERSD-2004-03. Geneva: Economic Research and Statistics Division, World Trade Organization. May.

Kelkar, Vijay, Praveen Chaudhry and Marta Vanduzer-Snow (2005). Time for change at the IMF. *Finance & Development*. (March).

Kenen, Peter (2001). *The International Financial Architecture: What's New? What's Missing?* Washington, D.C.: Institute for International Economics.

_____ (2005). Stabilizing the international monetary system. Contribution presented at the Annual Meeting of the American Economic Association, Philadelphia, Pennsylvania. 8 January.

Kessler, Tim, and Nancy Alexander (2004). Assessing the risks in the private provision of essential services. G-24 Discussion Paper Series, No. 31. UNCTAD/GDS/MDPB/G24/2004/7. Geneva and New York: United Nations.

Keynes, John Maynard (1936). *General Theory of Employment, Interest and Money*. Collected Writings of John Maynard Keynes, vol. 7: The General Theory, Donald Moggridge, ed. London: Macmillan, for the Royal Economic Society, 1973.

Khor, Martin (2005). The Malaysian Experience in Financial-Economic Crisis Management: An Alternative and Challenge to the IMF-Style Approach. In *Initiative for Policy Dialogue: Macroeconomic Companion Volume*. New York: Oxford University Press. Forthcoming.

Kikeri, Sunita, and John Nellis (2004). An assessment of privatization. *The World Bank Research Observer*, vol. 19, No. 1 (spring).

Killick, Tony (2004). Did conditionality streamlining succeed? Remarks prepared for the Development Policy Forum "Conditionality Revisited", organized by the World Bank, Paris, 5 July.

Kindleberger, Charles P. (1978). *Manias, Panics, and Crashes: A History of Financial Crises*. New York: Basic Books.

King, Mervin (2005). The international monetary system. Speech at the "Advancing Enterprise 2005" Conference, London, 4 February. Available from www.bis.org.

Kingdom of Norway, Ministry of Foreign Affairs (2005). Pursuing the MDGs: the contribution of multilateral debt relief. Oslo. 14 April.

Knight, Malcolm (2004a). Regulation and supervision in insurance and banking: greater convergence, shared challenges. Speech at the International Association of Insurance Supervisors (IAIS) 11th Annual Conference, Amman, 6 October. Available from www.bis.org.

_____ (2004b). Markets and institutions: managing the evolving financial risk. Speech delivered at the 25th European Money and Finance Forum (SUERF) Colloquium, in Madrid, 14 October.

Kose, M. Ayhan, Guy Meredith and Christopher Towe (2004). How Has NAFTA affected the Mexican economy? review and evidence. *IMF Working Paper*, No. WP/04/59. April.

Kregel, Jan (1996). Some risks and implications of financial globalization for national policy autonomy. *UNCTAD Review,* 1996, pp. 55-62. Geneva.

_____ (2004). External financing for development and international financial instability. *G-24 Discussion Paper Series*, No. 32 (October 2004). United Nations Conference on Trade and Development and Intergovernmental Group of Twenty-four. New York and Geneva: United Nations.

Krueger, Anne (2003). The need to improve the resolution of financial crisis: an emerging consensus. Address to the Harvard Business School's Finance Club, Boston, Massachusetts. 27 March.

Krugman, Paul (1994). The myth of the Asian economic miracle. *Foreign Affairs,* vol 73, No. 6 (November-December).

Laird, S., L. Cernat and A. Turrini (2003). Back to basics: market access issues in the Doha Agenda. UNCTAD/DITC/TAB/Misc.9. New York and Geneva: United Nations.

_____, S. Fernandez de Cordoba and D. Vanzetti (2003). Market access proposals for non-agricultural products. CREDIT Research Paper, No. 03/08. July.

Lakonishok, J., A. Shleifer and R. V. Vishny (1992). The impact of institutional trading on stock prices. *Journal of Financial Economics*, vol. 32 (August), pp. 23-43.

Lall, Sanjaya (2001). Competitiveness indices and developing countries: an economic evaluation of the global competitiveness report. *World Development*, vol. 29, No. 9, pp. 1501-1525.

La Porta, R., F. Lopez-de-Silanes and R.W. Vishney (1996). Law and finance. NBER Working Paper, No. 5661. Cambridge, Massachusetts: National Bureau of Economic Research.

Lee, Boon-Chye (1993). *The Economics of International Debt Renegotiation: The Role of Bargaining and Information.* Boulder, Colorado: Westview Press.

Lee, Eddy (2005). Trade liberalization and employment. Paper prepared for the United Nations DESA Development Forum on "Integrating Economic and Social Policies to Achieve the United Nations Development Agenda", 14 and 15 March 2005, New York.

Lensink, Robert, and Oliver Morrisey (2000). Aid instability as a measure of uncertainty and the positive impact of aid on growth. *Journal of Development Studies*, vol. 36 (February), pp. 31-49.

_____ (2003). On the welfare cost of economic fluctuations in developing countries. *International Economic Review*, vol. 44 (May), pp. 677-698.

Levy-Yeyati, Eduardo, Ugo Panizza and Ernesto Stein (2003). The cyclical nature of North-South FDI flows. *Inter-American Development Bank Research Department Working Paper*, No. 479. Washington, D.C.: IADB. January.

Levy Yeyati, Eduardo, Alejandro Micco and Ugo Panizza (2005). State-owned banks: do they promote or depress financial development and economic growth? Background paper prepared for the conference on Public Banks in Latin America: Myth and Reality, organized by the Inter-American Development Bank, 25 February, Washington, D.C.

Lewis, W. Arthur (1954). Economic development with unlimited supplies of labour. *The Manchester School,* vol. 22, No. 2, pp. 139-191.

Limão, N. (2003). *Preferential trade agreements as stumbling blocks for multilateral trade liberalization: evidence for the U.S.* University of Maryland, College Park, Maryland. Mimeo. December.

_____, and A. Venables (1999). Infrastructure, geographical disadvantage and transport costs. *World Bank Policy Research Working Paper*, No. 2257. Washington, D.C. December.

Liou, F. M., and C. G. Ding (2002). Subgrouping small States based on socioeconomic characteristics. *World Development*, vol. 30, No. 7, pp. 1289-1306.

Lipsey, Robert E. (2001). Foreign direct investors in three financial crises. *NBER Working Paper*, No. 8084. Cambridge, Massachusetts: National Bureau of Economic Research.

Loayza, Norman, and others (1998). Saving in the world: stylized facts. Washington, D.C.: World Bank. November.

Ma, Guonan, Corrinne Ho and Robert N. McCauley (2004). The markets for non-deliverable forwards in Asian currencies. *BIS Quarterly Review* (June). Basel, Switzerland.

Maizels, Alfred (1994). *Commodity Market Trends and Market Instabilities: Policy Options for Developing Countries.* Sales No. E.94.II.D.19. Geneva: United Nations.

Mandelson, P. (2004). Trade at the service of development. Speech delivered at the London School of Economics. SPEECH/05/77. 4 February.

Manduna, A. (2004). The WTO services negotiations: an analysis of the GATS and issues of interest for least developed countries. *Trade-Related Agenda, Development and Equity (T.R.A.D.E.) Working Paper*, No. 23. South Centre. December.

Manning, Richard (2005). OECD/DAC statement to the Development Committee Spring Meeting, Washington, D.C., 17 April.

Martin, W., and F. Ng (2005). Sources of tariff reductions. Background paper for World Bank, *Global Economic Prospects, 2005.*

Mattoo, Aaditya, and Arvind Subramanian (2005). Why prospects for trade talks are not bright. *Finance and Development*, March 2005.

McGillivray, M (2003). *Aid Effectiveness and Selectivity.* WIDER Discussion Paper, No. 2003/71. Helsinki: United Nations University World Institute for Development Economics Research.

McLenaghan, John B. (2005). Purchasing power parities and comparisons of GDP in IMF quota calculations. Paper presented to the G24 Technical Group Meeting, Manila, 17 and 18 March.

Mead, Russell Walter, and Sherle R. Schwenninger (2000). A financial architecture for middle-class-oriented development: a report of the Project on Development, Trade, and International Finance. A Council on Foreign Relations Paper. New York: Council on Foreign Relations.

Mehmet, Ozay, and M. Tahiroglu (2003). Globalization and Sustainability of Small States. *Humanomics*, vol. 19, No. 1/2, pp. 45-59.

Meltzer, A. H. (Chair) and others (2000). Report to the United States Congress of the International Financial Institutions Advisory Commission. Washington, D.C. March.

Micco, Alejandro, and Ugo Panizza (2005). Public banks in Latin America. Background paper prepared for the conference on Public Banks in Latin America: Myth and Reality, organized by the Inter-American Development Bank, 25 February, Washington, D.C.

Michaely, Michael (1977). Exports and growth: an empirical investigation. *Journal of Development Economics*, vol. 4, No. 1, pp. 49-53.

Minsky, Hyman P. (1982). *Inflation, Recession and Economic Policy*. Sussex, United Kingdom: Wheatsheaf Books.

Mistry, Percy S. (1995). *Multilateral Development Banks: An Assessment of their Financial Structures, Policies and Practices*. The Hague: Forum on Debt and Development (FONDAD).

Modigliani, Franco, and Shi Larry Cao (2004). The Chinese saving puzzle and the life-cycle hypothesis. *Journal of Economic Literature*, vol. XLII, pp. 145-170.

Mohammed, Aziz Ali (2004). Who pays for the World Bank? Working paper presented to the G-24 Technical Group Meeting, Geneva, February 2004.

Morrissey, O. (2001). Does aid increase growth? *Progress in Development Studies,* vol. 1, No. 1, pp. 37-50.

Nissanke, M. (2003). Revenue potential of the Tobin tax for development finance: a critical appraisal. Paper presented at the WIDER Conference on Sharing Global Prosperity, Helsinki, 6 and 7 September 2003. Available from http://www.wider.unu.edu/conference/conference-2003-3/conference2003-3.htm (accessed 23 June 2005).

Nkusu, Mwanza, and Selin Sayek (2004). Local financial development and the aid-growth relationship. *IMF Working Paper*, No. WP/04/238. Washington, D.C. International Monetary Fund. December.

Nye, Howard, Sanjay Reddy and Kevin Watkins (2002). Dollar and Kraay on 'Trade, Growth, and Poverty': a critique. Columbia University, New York. 24 August.

Ocampo, José Antonio (1992). Developing countries and the GATT Uruguay Round: a (preliminary) balance. In *International Monetary and Financial Issues for the 1990s: Research Papers for the Group of Twenty-Four*, vol. 1. UNCTAD/GID/G24/1. New York: United Nations.

_____ (2001). *International Asymmetries and the Design of the International Financial System*. Serie Temas de Coyuntura, No. 15. Sales No. E.01.II.G.70. Santiago: Economic and Social Commission for Latin America and the Caribbean, p. 23.

_____ (2002a). Recasting the international financial agenda. In *International Capital Markets in Transition*, John Eatwell and Lance Taylor, eds. New York: Oxford University Press.

_____ (2002b). Small economies in the face of globalization. Third William G. Demas Memorial Lecture at the Caribbean Development Bank, 14 May.

_____ (2003). Capital account and counter-cyclical prudential regulations in developing countries. In *From Capital Surges to Drought: Seeking Stability for Emergency Economies*, Robert Ffrench-Davis and Stephany Griffith-Jones, eds. UNU-WIDER Studies in Development Economics and Policy Series. Basingstoke, United Kingdom: Palgrave Macmillan.

_____ (2005). The quest for dynamic efficiency: structural dynamics and economic growth in developing countries. In *Beyond Reforms: Structural Dynamics and Macroeconomic Vulnerability*, José Antonio Ocampo, ed. Palo Alto, California: Stanford University Press and ECLAC.

_____, and Lance Taylor (1998). Trade liberalization in developing economies: modest benefits but problems with productivity growth, macro prices, and income distribution. *Economic Journal*, vol. 108, No. 450, (September), pp. 1523-1546.

_____, and Juan Martin eds. (2003). *Globalization and Development: A Latin American and Caribbean Perspective*. Palo Alto, California: Stanford University Press and World Bank.

_____, and María Ángela Parra (2003). The terms of trade for commodities in the twentieth century. *Cepal Review*, No. 79 (April).

_____ and José Gabriel Palma (2005). Dealing with volatile external finances at source: the role of preventive capital account regulations. Initiative for Policy Dialogue. Columbia University, New York.

Organization for Economic Cooperation and Development (1988 and 1992). *Agricultural Policies, Markets and Trade: Monitoring and Outlook*. Paris: OECD.

_____ (2004). *Agricultural Policies in OECD Countries at a Glance*. Paris: OECD.

Organization for Economic Cooperation and Development/Development Assistance Committee (2004). *The DAC Journal: Development Co-operation Report 2004*. Paris: OECD, chap. I.

_____ (2005). OECD calls for more aid, used more effectively, to bring safer, healthier lives. 18 January. OECD press release. Available from www.oecd.org/dac. See inset entitled "Final ODA data for 2003".

Ortiz, Guillermo (2004). Basel II and Latin American economics. Speech given at the Annual Meeting of the Association of Latin American Regulators (ASBA), Mexico City, July 2004.

Oxfam (2003). The IMF and the Millennium Goals: failing to deliver for low income countries. *Oxfam Briefing Paper*, No 54. September.

Page, Sheila, and Adrian Hewitt (2001). *World Commodity Prices: Still a Problem for Developing Countries?* London: Overseas Development Institute.

_____, and T. Conway (2004). *Assessing the Poverty Impact of the Doha Development Agenda*. London: Overseas Development Institute. February.

Pallage, S., and M. A. Robe (2001). Foreign aid and the business cycle. *Review of International Economics*, vol. 9, No. 4, pp. 641–672.

Palma, Gabriel (2002). The three routes to financial crises: the need for capital controls. In *International Capital Markets: Systems in Transition*, John Eatwell and Lance Taylor, eds. New York: Oxford University Press.

Park, Yung Chul (2004). Regional financial integration in East Asia: challenges and prospects. Paper prepared for presentation at the Conference on Regional Financial Arrangements, United Nations, New York, 14 and 15 July.

Peachey, Stephen, and Alan Roe (2004). Access to finance: a study for the WSBI (World Savings Banks Institute). Oxford Policy Management, Oxford, United Kingdom, October.

Persaud, Avinash (2000). Sending the herd off the cliff edge: the disturbing interaction between herding and market-sensitive risk management practices. Institute of International Finance Competition in Honour of Jacques de Larosiere. First Prize Essay on Global Finance for 2000. Washington. D.C.

_____ (2003). Liquidity black holes: why modern financial regulation in developed countries is making short-term capital flows to developing countries even more volatile. In *From Capital Surges to Drought: Seeking Stability for Emergency Economies*, Robert Ffrench-Davis and Stephany Griffith-Jones, eds. UNU-WIDER Studies in Development Economics and Policy Series. Basingstoke, United Kingdom: Palgrave Macmillan.

Pitigala, Nihal (2005). What does regional trade in South Asia reveal about future trade integration. *World Bank Policy Research Working Paper*, No. 3497. Washington, D.C. February.

Polak, Jacques J., and Peter B. Clark (2005). A new perspective on SDR allocations, new rules for global finance. Available from http://www.new-rules.org/docs/polak.pdf (accessed 23 June 2005).

Prasad, Eswar, and others (2003). Effects of financial globalization on developing countries: some empirical evidence. Washington D.C.: International Monetary Fund.

Prasad, Naren (2003). Small islands' quest for economic development. *Asia-Pacific Development Journal*, vol. 10, No. 1 (June).

Rajaraman, Indira (2001). Capital account regimes in India and Malaysia. National Institute of Public Finance and Policy, New Delhi. Mimeo.

Ratha, Dilip (2003). Workers' remittances: an important and stable source of external development finance. In *Global Development Finance 2003*. Washington, D.C.: World Bank.

_____, and K.M. Vijayalakshmi (2004). Recent trends in international remittance flows. Note presented at the Technology of Remittances Workshop convened by the Inter-American Development Bank and World Resources Institute, San Francisco, California, 11 December.

Rato, Rodrigo de (2004). The IMF at 60: evolving challenges, evolving role. Opening remarks at the conference on "Dollars, Debts and Deficits: 60 Years After Bretton Woods", Madrid, 14 June. Available at www.imf.org.

_____ (2005). Is the IMF's mandate still relevant?. *Global Agenda* (January).

Reddy, Y.V. (2001). Operationalizing capital account liberalization: the Indian experience. *Development Policy Review* (London), vol 19, No. 1.

Reisen, H. (2003). Ratings since the Asian crisis. *From Capital Surges to Drought: Seeking Stability from Emerging Economies*, Ricardo Ffrench-Davis and Stephany Griffith-Jones, eds. Hampshire, United Kingdom: Palgrave.

Republic of South Africa Department of Foreign Affairs (2005). Cape Town Ministerial Communique, India-Brazil-South Africa (IBSA) Dialogue Forum. Press release. 13 March. Also available from http://www.dfa.gov.za/docs/2005/ibsa0311.htm.

Rodríguez, Francisco, and Dani Rodrik (1999). Trade policy and economic growth: a sceptic's guide to the cross-national evidence. *NBER Working Paper*, No. 7081. Cambridge, Massachusetts: National Bureau of Economic Research. April.

Rodrik, Dani (2000). Comments on 'Trade, Growth, and Poverty' by D. Dollar and A. Kraay. Harvard University, Cambridge, Massachusetts. October.

_____ (2000a). Saving transitions. *The World Bank Economic Review*, vol. 14, No. 3 (September).

_____ (2001). The global governance of trade: as if development really mattered. Paper prepared for the United Nations Development Programme.

_____ (2004). Getting institutions right. Cambridge, Massachusetts: Harvard University. Unpublished.

_____, and Andrés Velasco (1999). Short-term capital flows. *NBER Working Paper*, No. 7364. Cambridge, Massachusetts: National Bureau of Economic Research.

Rogoff, Kenneth, and Jeromin Zettelmeyer (2002). Bankruptcy procedures for sovereigns: a history of ideas, 1976–2001. *IMF Staff Papers*, vol 49, No. 3, pp. 470-507.

Romer, Paul (1987). Growth based on increasing returns due to specialization. *American Economic Review*, vol. 77, No. 2, pp. 56-62.

Roubini, Nouriel (2001). Debt sustainability: how to assess whether a country is insolvent. New York: New York University, Stern School of Business. 20 December. Available from http://pages.stern.nyu.edu/~nroubini/papers/debtsustainability.pdf.

Roubini, Nouriel, and Brad Setser (2005) Will the Bretton Woods 2 regime unravel soon? the risk of a hard landing in 2005-2006. Paper prepared for the Symposium on "The Revived Bretton Woods System: A New Paradigm for Asian Development?", organized by the Federal Reserve Bank of San Francisco and the University of California, Berkeley, San Francisco, 4 February.

Sachs, Jeffrey D., and Andrew Warner (1995). Economic reform and the process of global integration. *Brookings Papers on Economic Activity*, No. 1. Washington, D.C.

Sagasti, Francisco, and Fernando Prada (2005). Regional Development Banks: a Comparative Perspective. Forthcoming.

_____, Keith Bezanson and Fernando Prada (2005). *The Future of Development Financing: Challenges, Scenarios and Strategic Choices*. Hampshire, United Kingdom: Palgrave Macmillan. Forthcoming.

Samuelson, Paul A. (2004). Where Ricardo and Mill rebut and confirm arguments of mainstream economists supporting globalization. *Journal of Economic Perspectives*, vol. 18, No. 3 (summer), pp. 135-146.

Sander, Cerstin, and Samuel Munzele Maimbo (2003). Migrant labour remittances in Africa: reducing obstacles to development contributions, *African Region Working Paper Series*, No. 64. Washington, D.C.: World Bank.

Schiff, Maurice, and Yanling Wang (2003). Regional integration and technology diffusion: the case of the North American Free Trade Agreement. *World Bank Policy Research Working Paper*, No. 3132. Washington, D.C. September.

Schmidt-Hebbel, Klaus, Luis Servén and Andrés Solimano (1996). Saving and investment; paradigms, puzzles, policies. *The World Bank Research Observer*, vol. 11, No. 1.

Schneider, Benu (2005a). Do global standards and codes prevent financial crisis? some proposals on modifying the standards-based approach. *United Nations Conference on Trade and Development Discussion Papers*, No. 177. UNCTAD/OSG/DP/2005/1. April.

_____ (2005b). Clubbing in Paris: is debt sustainability and illusion. In *Sovereign Debt Workouts*, Joseph Stiglitz and José Antonio Ocampo, eds. Initiative for Policy Dialogue, Columbia University, New York.

Sharma, Krishnan (2001). The underlying constraints on corporate bond market development in Southeast Asia. *World Development*, vol. 29, No. 8, pp. 1405-1419.

Shiller, Robert (2005). In favor of growth-linked bonds. *The Indian Express* (10 March).

Solimano, Andrés (2005). Remittances by emigrants: issues and evidence. In *New Sources of Development Finance*, A.B. Atkinson, ed. UNU-WIDER Studies in Development Economics. New York: Oxford University Press.

Soloaga, Isidro, and L. Alan Winters (1999). Regionalism in the nineties: what effect on trade? *C.E.P.R. Discussion Paper Series*, No. 2183. London: Centre for Economic Policy Research. June.

Soros, George (2002). Special drawing rights for the provision of public goods on a global scale. Remarks delivered at the Roundtable on "New Proposals on Financing for Development.", Institute for International Economics, Washington, D.C., 20 February.

Spahn, B. (2002). On the feasibility of a tax on foreign exchange transactions. Report to the Federal Ministry for Economic Cooperation and Development, Bonn. February. Available from http://www.wiwi.uni-frankfurt.de/professoren/spahn/tobintax/ (accessed 23 June 2005).

Spiegel, Shari, and Randall Dodd (2004). Up from sin: a portfolio approach to salvation. A study for presentation to the XVIII G24 Technical Group Meeting, Palais des Nations, Geneva, 8 and 9 March 2004.

Stahl, Charles W., and Ahsanul Habib (1989). The impact of overseas workers' remittances on indigenous industries: evidence from Bangladesh. *The Developing Economies*, vol. 27, No. 3, pp. 269-285. Tokyo: Institute of Developing Economies, Japan External Trade Organization (IDE-JETRO).

Stallings, Barbara, and Wilson Peres (2000). *Growth, Employment and Equity: The Impact of the Economic Reforms in Latin America and the Caribbean*. Washington, D.C.: Brookings Institution Press and ECLAC.

_____, and Rogerio Studart (2002). Financial regulation and supervision in emerging markets: the experience of Latin America since the Tequila crisis. Discussion Paper, No. 2002/45. Helsinki: UNU/WIDER. April.

Stiglitz, Joseph E. (1994). The role of the State in financial markets. In *Proceedings of the World Bank Conference on Development Economics, 1993*. Washington D.C.: World Bank.

_____ (1999). The World Bank at the Millennium. *Economic Journal*, vol. 109 (459), pp. F577-F597.

_____ (2000). Lessons from the global financial crisis. In *Global Financial Crises: Lessons from Recent Events*, J. R. Bisignano, William C. Hunter and George G. Kaufman, eds., pp. 89–107. Boston, Massachusetts, Dordrecht, Netherlands, and London: Kluwer Academic.

_____, and others (2005). *Stability with Growth: Macroeconomics for Development*. New York: Oxford University Press. Forthcoming.

_____, and A. Charlton (2004). *The development round of trade negotiations in the aftermath of Cancún*. Report prepared for the Commonwealth Secretariat with the Initiative for Policy Dialogue.

Stoessinger, John, and associates (1964). *Financing the United Nations system*. Washington, D.C.: The Brookings Institution.

Subramanian, A. (2003). Financing of losses from preference erosion: note on issues raised by developing countries in the Doha Round. WT/TF/COH/14. 14 February. Geneva.

Summers, Lawerence H. (2004). The U.S. current account deficit and the global economy. Per Jacobson Lecture, Washington, D.C.

Taylor, John (2004). New directions for the international financial institutions. Keynote address at the Conference "Global Economic Challenges for the IMF's New Chief", American Enterprise Institute, Washington, D.C. Available from www.treas.gov.

Technical Group on Innovative Financing Mechanisms Report (2004). Report of the Technical Group on Innovative Financial Mechanisms: Actions against Hunger and Poverty. September.

Thomas, Vinod and others (1991). *Best Practices in Trade Policy Reform*. Oxford, United Kingdom: Oxford University Press.

Titelman, Daniel, and Andras Uthoff (1998). The relationship between foreign and national savings under financial liberalization. In *Capital Inflows and Investment Performance: Lessons from Latin America*, Ricardo Ffrench-Davis and Helmut Reisen, eds. Paris and Santiago: OECD Development Centre and Economic Commission for Latin America and the Caribbean.

_____ (2004). Sub-regional financial institutions in Latin America and the Caribbean. Paper prepared for presentation at the Conference on Regional Financial Arrangements. United Nations, New York, 14 and 15 July.

Triffin, Robert (1960). *Gold and the Dollar Crisis: The Future of Convertibility*. New York: Garland.

Underwood, John (1990). The sustainability of international debt. International Finance Division, World Bank, Washington, D.C. Mimeo.

United Kingdom Treasury and the International Monetary Fund (2003). Strengthening the international financial system. In *Stability, Growth, and Poverty Reduction*. Chap. 3). London.

United Nations (1949). *National and International Measures for Full Employment*. Report by a Group of Experts appointed by the Secretary-General, United Nations, Department of Economic Affairs. Lake Success, New York. December 1949. E/1584. Sales No. 1949.II.A.3.

_____ (1991). *Report of the Second United Nations Conference on the Least Developed Countries, Paris, 3-14 September 1990.* A/CONF.147/18, part one.

_____ (1992). *Report of the United Nations Conference on Environment and Development, Rio de Janeiro, 3-14 June 1992*, vol. I, *Resolutions Adopted by the Conference.* Sales No. E.93.I.8 and corrigendum.

_____ (1999). *World Economic and Social Survey, 1999.* Sales No. E.99.II.C.1.

_____ (2001a). Towards a new international financial architecture: report of the Task Force of the Executive Committee on Economic and Social Affairs of the United Nations. Available from http://www.un.org/esa/coordination/ecesa/ecesa-1.pdf.

_____ (2001b). Finding solutions to the debt problems of developing countries: report of the Executive Committee on Economic and Social Affairs of the United Nations, Sect. 3. Available from http://www.un.org/esa/coordination/ecesa/ecesa-2.pdf.

_____ (2001c). International financial architecture and development, including net transfer of resources between developing and developed countries: report of the Secretary-General. A/56/173, Sect. III.D.

_____ (2001d). Letter dated 25 June 2001 from the Secretary-General to the President of the General Assembly, transmitting the report of the High-Level Panel on Financing for Development (Zedillo report). 26 June.

_____ (2002a). *World Economic and Social Survey, 2002*, Sales No. E.02.II.C.1.

_____ (2002b). *Report of the International Conference on Financing for Development, Monterrey, Mexico, 18-22 March 2002.* Sales No. E.02.II.A.7.

_____ (2002c). International financial system and development: report of the Secretary-General. A/57/151, Sect. III.E. 2 July.

_____ (2003a). Report of the Committee for Development Policy on the fifth session (7-11 April 2003). *Official Records of the Economic and Social Council, 2003, Supplement No. 13* (E/2003/33).

_____ (2003b). *Report of the International Ministerial Conference of Landlocked and Transit Developing Countries and Donor Countries and International Financial and Development Institutions on Transit Transport Cooperation, Almaty, Kazakhstan, 28 and 29 August 2003.* A/CONF.202/3.

_____ (2003c). State of South-South Cooperation: report of the Secretary-General. A/58/319.

_____ (2004a). *World Economic and Social Survey 2004: International Migration*, Sales No. E.04.II.C.3.

_____ (2004b). *World Economic Situation and Prospects 2004.* Sales No. E.04.II.C.2.

_____ (2004c). A review of progress in the implementation of the Programme of Action for the Sustainable Development of Small Island Developing states: report of the Secretary-General. E/CN.17/2004/8.

_____ (2004d). Summary by the President of the Economic and Social Council of the special high-level meeting of the Council with the Bretton Woods institutions and the World Trade Organization (New York, 26 April 2004): addendum 2: summary of informal hearings of the business sector on financing for development (New York, 24 March 2004). A/59/92/Add.2–E/2004/73/Add.2. 1 June.

_____ (2005). *World Economic Situation and Prospects 2005*. Sales No. E.05.II.C.2.

United Nations Conference on Trade and Development (1974). External debt experience of developing countries: economic development following multilateral debt renegotiations in selected developing countries. TD/B/C.3/AC.8/9. 19 November.

_____ (1975). Present institutional arrangements for debt renegotiation: note by the UNCTAD secretariat. TD/B/C.3/AC.8/13. 13 February.

_____ (1978). Report of the Intergovernmental Group of Experts on the External Indebtedness of Developing Countries. TD/B/670 TD/AC.2/7. 28 July.

_____ (1986). *Trade and Development Report, 1986*. Sales No. E.86.II.D.5.

_____ (1992a). *Trade and Development Report, 1992*. Sales No. E.92.II.D.7, pp. 103-104.

_____ (1992b). *UNCTAD VIII: Analytical Report by the UNCTAD Secretariat to the Conference*. Sales No. E.92.II.D.3. Geneva: United Nations.

_____ (1994). A Survey of commodity risk management instruments. UNCTAD/COM/15/Rev.1. Geneva. December.

_____ (1995). Legal and regulatory aspects of financing commodity exporters and the provision of bank hedging line credit in developing countries. Study by Nicholas Budd. UNCTAD/COM/56. Geneva, 3 February.

_____ (1998a). Government policies affecting the use of commodity price risk management and access to commodity finance in developing countries. UNCTAD/ITCD/COM/7. Geneva. November.

_____ (1998b). *Trade and Development Report, 1998*. Sales No. E.98.II.D.6.

_____ (2000). *World Investment Report, 2000: Cross-border Mergers and Acquisitions and Development*. Sales No. E.00.II.D.20. New York and Geneva: United Nations.

_____ (2001a). *Trade and Development Report, 2001*. Sales No. E.01.II.D.10. pp. 136 ff.

_____ (2001b). *World Investment Report, 2001: Promoting Linkages*. Sales No. E.01.II.D.12. New York and Geneva: United Nations.

_____ (2002). *Trade and Development Report, 2002*. Sales No. E.02.II.D.2.

_____ (2003a). *Trade and Development Report, 2003: Capital Accumulation, Growth and Structural Change*. Sales No. E.03.II.D.7. New York and Geneva: United Nations.

_____ (2003b). *World Investment Report, 2003: FDI Policies for Development: National and International Perspectives*. Sales No. E.03.II.D.8. New York and Geneva: United Nations.

_____ (2003c). *Economic Development in Africa: Trade Performance and Commodity Dependence*. Sales No. E.03.II.D.34. Geneva.

_____ (2003d). A primer on new techniques used by the sophisticated financial fraudster, with special reference to commodity market instruments: report prepared by the UNCTAD secretariat. UNCTAD/DITC/COM/39. Geneva. 7 March.

_____ (2003e). Improving trade and development prospects of landlocked and transit developing countries: report by the UNCTAD secretariat. UNCTAD/DITC/TNCD/2003/7. 8 August.

_____ (2003f). Report of the meeting of eminent persons on commodity issues. TD/B/50/11. Geneva. 30 September. Also A/58/401 of 2 October 2003.

_____ (2003g). Trade preferences for LDCs: An early assessment of benefits and possible improvements. UNCTAD/ITCD/TSB/2003/8. New York and Geneva: United Nations.

_____ (2004a). *The Least Developed Countries Report 2004: Linking International Trade with Poverty Reduction.* Sales No. E.04.II.D.27. New York and Geneva: United Nations.

_____ (2004b). *World Investment Report, 2004: The Shift Towards Services.* Sales No. E.04.II.D.33. New York and Geneva: United Nations.

_____ (2004c). *Economic Development In Africa: Debt Sustainability, Oasis or Mirage?,* Sales No. E.04.II.D.37. UNCTAD/GDS/AFRICA/2004/1.

_____ (2004d). Is a special treatment of small island developing States possible? UNCTAD/LDC/2004/1.

_____ (2004e). Review of developments and issues in the post-Doha work programme of particular concern to developing countries: a post-UNCTAD-XI perspective: note by the UNCTAD secretariat. TD/B/51/4. 31 August.

_____ (2004f). São Paulo Consensus. TD/412, part II.

_____ (2004g). Strengthening participation of developing countries in dynamic and new sectors of world trade: trends, issues and policies: background note by the UNCTAD secretariat. TD/B/COM/1/EM. 26/2 and tables 1-3. 15 December.

_____ (2004h). Development and globalization: Facts and Figures. UNCTAD/GDS/CSIR/2004/1 (Sales No. E.04.II.D.16).

_____ (2005a). Report of the Expert Meeting on the Impact of FDI on Development, Trade and Development Board, Commission on Investment, Technology and Related Financial Issues, 24–26 January 2005 TD/B/COM.2/EM.16/3. Geneva. 16 February.

_____ (2005b). Trade in services and development implications: note by the UNCTAD secretariat. TD/B/COM.1/71. 20 January.

UN Millennium Project (2005). *Investing in Development A Practical Plan to Achieve the Millennium Development Goals.* London: Earthscan. 25 August.

UN Millennium Project, Task Force on Trade (2005). *Trade for Development.* London: EARTHSCAN for United Nations Development Programme.

United States Department of the Treasury (2000). Response to the Report of the International Financial Institutions Advisory Commission. June 8.

Venables, Anthony (1999). Regional integration agreements: a force for convergence or divergence? Paper prepared for the Annual Bank Conference on Development Economics, Paris, June 1999.

Viner, Jacob (1950). *The Customs Union Issue.* New York: Carnegie Endowment for International Peace.

Virmani, A. (2004a). India's economic growth: from socialist rate of growth to Bharatiya rate of growth. Indian Council for Research on International Economic Relations, Working Paper, No. 122. New Delhi.

_____ (2004b). Sources of India's economic growth: trends in total factor productivity. Indian Council for Research on International Economic Relations, Working Paper, No. 131. New Delhi.

Wachtel, Paul (1999). Discussion. In *Global Financial Turmoil and Reform: A United Nations Perspective,* Barry Herman ed. Tokyo: United Nations University Press.

Wacziarg, Romain (2001). Measuring the dynamic gains from trade. *The World Bank Economic Review,* vol. 15, No. 3, pp. 393-429.

Weller, Christian (2001). The supply of credit by multinational banks in developing and transition economies: determinants and effects. *DESA Discussion Paper,* No. 16. ST/ESA/2001/DP.16. New York: United Nations.

Wellons, Philip A. (1977). *Borrowing by Developing Countries on the Euro-Currency Market.* Paris: Organization for Economic Cooperation and Development.

Wen, Jiabao (2003). Let's build on our past achievements and promote China-Africa friendly relations. Address at the opening ceremony of the Second Ministerial Conference of the China-Africa Cooperation Forum, Addis Ababa, 15 December. Available from http://chinaembassy.ru/eng/wjdt/zyjh/t56252.htm.

White, William (2003). International financial crises: prevention, management and resolution. Speech at the conference on "Economic governance: the role of markets and the State", Berne, 20 March. Available from www.bis.org.

_____ (2004). Making macroprudential concerns operational. Speech presented at the Financial Stability Symposium organized by the Netherlands Bank, Amsterdam, 25 and 26 October 2004. Available from www.bis.org/speeches.

Williamson, John (2003). Proposals for curbing the boom-bust cycle in the supply of capital to emerging markets. In *From Capital Surges to Drought: Seeking Stability for Emergency Economies,* Robert Ffrench-Davis and Stephany Griffith-Jones, eds. UNU-WIDER Studies in Development Economics and Policy Series. Basingstoke, United Kingdom: Palgrave Macmillan.

_____ (2004). The future of the global financial system. *Journal of Post-Keynesian Economics,* vol. 26, No. 4 (summer).

Winters, L. Alan (2000). Trade and poverty: is there a connection? Geneva: World Trade Organization.

_____ (2002). The economic implications of liberalizing Mode 4 trade. Paper prepared for the Joint World Trade Organization-World Bank Symposium on "The Movement of Natural Persons (Mode 4) Under the GATS, World Trade Organization, Geneva, 11 and 12 April.

Woo, Wing Thye (2004). Serious inadequacies of the Washington Consensus: misunderstanding the poor by the brightest. In *Diversity in Development,* Jan Teunissen and Age Akkerman, eds. The Hague: Forum on Debt and Development (FONDAD).

Working Group of the Capital Markets Consultative Group (2003). Foreign direct investment in emerging market countries: report of the Working Group of the Capital Markets Consultative Group. Washington, D.C.: IMF. September.

World Bank (1987). *World Development Report 1987.* New York: Oxford University Press.

_____ (1998). *Assessing Aid: What Works, What Doesn't and Why.* New York: Oxford University Press.

_____ (2001). Measuring IDA's effectiveness. Development Research Group, World Bank, Washington, D.C. Mimeo. 4}

_____ (2002a). *Global Economic Prospects and the Developing Countries 2002: Making Trade Work for the World's Poor.* Washington, D.C.: World Bank. 2}

_____ (2002b). *The Role and Effectiveness of Development Assistance: Lessons from World Bank Experience.* Washington, D.C.: World Bank.

_____ (2003). *Global Development Finance, 2003.* Washington, D.C.

_____ (2004a). *Global Development Finance, 2004.* Washington, D.C.

_____ (2004b). *Global Economic Prospects and the Developing Countries 2004: Realizing the Development Promise of the Doha Agenda.* Washington, D.C.: World Bank.

_____ (2004c). *Global Economic Prospects 2005.* Washington, D.C.: World Bank, pp. 29-30 and 42.

_____ (2004d). *World Development Indicators, 2004.* Washington, D.C.

_____ (2004e). *The Poverty Reduction Strategy Initiative: An Independent Evaluation of the World Bank Support Through 2003.* Washington, D.C.: World Bank. Also available from http://worldbank.org/oed. {4}

_____ (2004f). Strengthening the foundations for growth and private sector development: investment climate and infrastructure development. Paper prepared by the staff of the World Bank for the 2 October 2004 Development Committee Meeting. DC2004-0011. 17 September.

_____ (2005a). *World Development Report, 2005: A Better Investment Climate for Everyone.* New York and Washington, D.C.: Oxford University Press and World Bank.

_____ (2005b). *Global Development Finance, 2005.* Washington, D.C.

_____ (2005c). *Global Development Finance* Heavily Indebted Poor Countries (HIPC) Initiative Statistical Update, April.

_____ (2005d). *Global Development Finance 2005: Mobilizing Finance and Managing Vulnerability: vol. I, Analysis and Statistical Appendix.* Washington: D.C.: World Bank, p. 100.

_____ (2005e). *Global Monitoring Report 2005: Millennium Development Goals: From Consensus to Momentum.* Washington, D.C.: World Bank.

_____, Operations Evaluation Department (2001). *Annual Review of Development Effectiveness: From Strategy to Results.* Washington D.C.: World Bank.

_____ and International Monetary Fund (2005). Aid effectiveness and financing modalities and moving forward: financing modalities toward the Millennium Development Goals. Development Committee papers. April.

World Economic Forum (2004). *The Global Competitiveness Report, 2004-2005.* Geneva: World Economic Forum.

World Trade Organization (2001a). World Trade Organization Conference, fourth session, Doha, 9-14 November 2001: Ministerial Declaration adopted on 14 November 2001. WT/MIN(01)/DEC/1. 20 November.

كيفيـة الحصـول على منشـورات الأمـم المتحـدة

يمكن الحصول على منشـورات الأمم المتحـدة من المكتبات ودور التوزيع في جميع أنحـاء العالم . استعلم عنها من المكتبة
التي تتعامل معها أو اكتب إلى : الأمـم المتحدة ، قسم البيـع في نيويورك أو في جنيـف .

如何购取联合国出版物

联合国出版物在全世界各地的书店和经售处均有发售。请向书店询问或写信到纽约或日内瓦的
联合国销售组。

HOW TO OBTAIN UNITED NATIONS PUBLICATIONS

United Nations publications may be obtained from bookstores and distributors throughout the
world. Consult your bookstore or write to: United Nations, Sales Section, New York or Geneva.

COMMENT SE PROCURER LES PUBLICATIONS DES NATIONS UNIES

Les publications des Nations Unies sont en vente dans les librairies et les agences dépositaires
du monde entier. Informez-vous auprès de votre libraire ou adressez-vous à : Nations Unies,
Section des ventes, New York ou Genève.

КАК ПОЛУЧИТЬ ИЗДАНИЯ ОРГАНИЗАЦИИ ОБЪЕДИНЕННЫХ НАЦИЙ

Издания Организации Объединенных Наций можно купить в книжных магазинах
и агентствах во всех районах мира. Наводите справки об изданиях в вашем книжном
магазине или пишите по адресу: Организация Объединенных Наций, Секция по
продаже изданий, Нью-Йорк или Женева.

COMO CONSEGUIR PUBLICACIONES DE LAS NACIONES UNIDAS

Las publicaciones de las Naciones Unidas están en venta en librerías y casas distribuidoras en
todas partes del mundo. Consulte a su librero o diríjase a: Naciones Unidas, Sección de Ventas,
Nueva York o Ginebra.

Litho in United Nations, New York
32269—June 2005—4,770
ISBN 92-1-109149-7

United Nations publication
Sales No. E.05.II.C.1
E/2005/51/Rev.1
ST/ESA/298

_____ (2001b). Guidelines and procedures for the negotiations on trade in services: adopted by the special session of the Council for Trade in Services on 28 March 2001. S/L/93. 29 March.

_____ (2001c). Implementation-related issues and concerns: decision of 14 November 2001. WT/MIN(01)/17. 20 November.

_____ (2003). Implementation of paragraph 6 of the Doha Declaration on the TRIPS Agreement and public health: decision of 30 August 2003. WT/L/540. 2 September.

_____ (2004a). *World Trade Report 2004*. Geneva: World Trade Organization.

_____ (2004b). Doha Work Programme: decision adopted by the General Council on 1 August 2004.WT/L/579. 2 August.

Xiang Huaicheng (2002). Statement at the International Conference on Financing for Development, Monterrey, Mexico. 21 March.